2002

D1568236

CHAUCER STUDIES XXV

MASCULINITIES IN CHAUCER

Approaches to Maleness in the
Canterbury Tales and *Troilus and Criseyde*

How does Chaucer portray the various male pilgrims in the *Canterbury Tales*? How manly is Troilus? To what extent can the spirit and terminology of recent feminist criticism inform the study of Chaucer's men? Is there such a thing as a distinct 'Chaucerian masculinity', or does it appear in a multitude of different forms? These are some of the questions that the contributors to this ground-breaking and provocative volume attempt to answer, using a diversity of critical methods and theories. Some look at the behaviour of noble or knightly men; some at clerics, or businessmen, or churls; others examine the so-called 'masculine' qualities of female characters, and the 'feminine' qualities of male characters. Topics includes the Host's bourgeois masculinity; the erotic triangles operating in the *Miller's Tale*; why Chaucer 'diminished' the sexuality of Sir Thopas; and whether Troilus is effeminate, impotent or an example of true manhood.

PETER G. BEIDLER is the Lucy G. Moses Distinguished Professor of English at Lehigh University.

CHAUCER STUDIES

ISSN 0261-9822

MASCULINITIES IN CHAUCER
Approaches to Maleness in the
Canterbury Tales and *Troilus and Criseyde*

Edited by
PETER G. BEIDLER

D. S. BREWER

First published 1998
D. S. Brewer, Cambridge

ISBN 0 85991 434 8

D. S. Brewer is an imprint of Boydell & Brewer Ltd.
PO Box 9, Woodbridge, Suffolk IP12 3DF, UK
and of Boydell & Brewer Inc.
PO Box 41026, Rochester, NY 14604–4126, USA

A catalogue record for this book is available
from the British Library

Library of Congress Cataloguing-in-Publication Data
Masculinities in Chaucer : approaches to maleness in the "Canterbury
tales" and "Troilus and Criseyde" / edited by Peter G. Beidler.
   p.   cm. – (Chaucer studies, ISSN 0261–9822 ; 25)
Includes bibliographical references.
ISBN 0–85991–434–8 (hardback : alk. paper)
   1. Chaucer, Geoffrey, d. 1400 – Characters – Men.   2. Chaucer,
Geoffrey, d. 1400. Canterbury tales.   3. Chaucer, Geoffrey, d. 1400 –
Knowledge – Psychology.   4. Chaucer, Geoffrey, d. 1400. Troilus
and Criseyde.   5. Masculinity (Psychology) in literature.   6. Man–
woman relationships in literature.   7. Ethics, Medieval, in literature.
8. Sex role in literature.   9. Men in literature.   I. Beidler, Peter G.
II. Series.
PR1928.M45M37   1998
821'.1 – dc21   97–28793

This publication is printed on acid-free paper

Printed in Great Britain by
St Edmundsbury Press Ltd, Bury St Edmunds, Suffolk

Contents

DEDICATED TO

Derek Brewer, a "gentil" man

List of Contributors

MARK ALLEN is associate professor in the Division of English, Classics, Philosophy, and Communication at the University of Texas at San Antonio. He is co-author (with John H. Fisher) of *The Essential Chaucer* (1987), bibliographer of the New Chaucer Society, and moderator of the Online Chaucer Bibliography.

PETER G. BEIDLER is the Lucy G. Moses Distinguished Professor of English at Lehigh University in Bethlehem, PA. He teaches and publishes in both medieval British and contemporary Native American literature. Recent books in medieval studies are *The Wife of Bath* and (with Elizabeth M. Biebel) *Chaucer's Wife of Bath's Prologue and Tale: An Annotated Bibliography 1900–1996*.

ELIZABETH M. BIEBEL has recently completed her dissertation on the Wife of Bath at Lehigh University. She has published on Chaucer and medieval drama in the *Chaucer Yearbook*. She has recently published (with Peter G. Beidler) *Chaucer's Wife of Bath's Prologue and Tale: An Annotated Bibliography 1900–1996*.

MARTIN BLUM has recently completed his dissertation on representations of otherness in Middle English literature at the University of British Columbia in Vancouver, Canada. He has published on fabliaux as normative texts which regulate human sexuality. He teaches at Douglas College, New Westminster, British Columbia.

DEREK BREWER is emeritus professor at Emmanuel College, Cambridge, England. He has written too many books on medieval literature to list here and is responsible for publishing many more through the D. S. Brewer imprint at Boydell and Brewer Ltd. He has spent his life enriching the study of medieval literature and culture.

GLENN BURGER is associate professor, associate chair for graduate studies of the Department of English, and a director of the Medieval and Early Modern Institute at the University of Alberta, Edmonton, Canada. He teaches courses in Chaucer, medieval British literature, and gay literature. His most recent publications have dealt with the intersection between Chaucer and queer studies.

JEFFREY JEROME COHEN is assistant professor of English and Human Sciences at George Washington University in Washington, DC, where he teaches medieval studies, cultural studies, and critical theory. He has recently edited two collections of essays: *Monster Theory* and (with Bonnie Wheeler) *Becoming Male in the Middle Ages*.

STEPHANIE S. DIETRICH is working toward her Ph.D. in English at the University of Houston, where she concentrates on medieval literature. She teaches writing and literature courses there and at Houston Community College.

CAROL A. EVEREST is associate professor of English at the King's University College, Edmonton, Alberta, Canada. She has published several papers on medieval medicine and Chaucer. She is also editor-in-chief of the *Speculum naturale* translation project, which aims to produce a hypertext translation of Vincent of Beauvais' encyclopedia.

PATRICIA CLARE INGHAM is assistant professor of English at Lehigh University, in Bethlehem, PA, where she teaches Old and Middle English language and literature. She is currently at work on a book-length analysis of the political, cultural, and sexual reverberations of Middle English Arthurian Romance in the changing cultural identities of late-medieval Britain.

JEAN E. JOST is associate professor of English at Bradley University in Peoria, IL, where she specializes in medieval literature. She is co-editor of the *Chaucer Yearbook* and has published widely. She has published *Ten Middle English Romances, Chaucer's Humor*, and many articles. She is currently editing the Southern Recension of the *Pricke of Conscience*.

MAUD BURNETT MCINERNEY is visiting assistant professor of English at Haverford College in Haverford, PA. She has published on *Pearl* and Julian of Norwich, and is working on a book on the medieval construction of virginity.

DANIEL F. PIGG is associate professor of English at the University of Tennessee at Martin, where he teaches medieval and Renaissance British literature. He has published on several Old and Middle English texts. He is currently working on identity politics in *The Dream of the Rood* and on a book about *Piers Plowman* and medieval sign theory.

ANDREA ROSSI-REDER is assistant professor of English at Baylor University in Waco, TX, where she teaches courses in Old and Middle English literature and women's studies. Her interests include women's writing in the Middle Ages and Anglo-Saxon bestiaries. She is currently working on a book-length study of race in the Middle Ages.

DANIEL RUBEY is professor and chief librarian at Lehman College (The City University of New York), and director of the comparative literature program. He teaches world literature, Japanese and Chinese film, and popular culture. He has published articles on medieval, Renaissance, and American literature, on literary theory, and on contemporary film and art.

MICHAEL D. SHARP is a doctoral candidate in English at the University of Michigan, Ann Arbor. He has written on sexuality and history in film and is currently completing his dissertation on forms of male community in Middle English literature.

PAUL R. THOMAS is associate professor of English at Brigham Young University in Provo, UT, where he teaches and publishes on medieval and Renaissance literature. He has recently published *Plays for Corpus Christi Day*. He co-directs the Chaucer Studio and is collating all of the MSS of Fragment VII for the Canterbury Tales Project.

Acknowledgments

I happened to sit next to Derek Brewer at one of the sessions on Chaucer at the 31st International Congress on Medieval Studies in May, 1996, at Western Michigan University in Kalamazoo, Michigan. I had been encircling some of the titles of papers that seemed to reflect an emerging focus on masculinity in the many Chaucer papers that were being read at the four-day conference.

After the first paper in the session I showed some of my encirclings to Derek and whispered, "Why don't you get some of these papers together and do a book on *Masculinities in Chaucer* in the Chaucer Studies series at Boydell and Brewer?" He shook his head, and we both listened to the next paper.

After that paper Derek had weakened slightly and whispered to me, "Would YOU edit it?" I shook my head, and we both listened to the third paper.

By the end of the third paper, I had weakened slightly and asked him whether, if I did edit it, he would submit the paper he was presenting on whether Troilus is "a man or a mouse." He said he might rework the paper for publication, but really I should talk to Richard Barber, of Boydell and Brewer, about the volume. Two nights later Derek and Richard and I had dinner together at the Blue Dolphin, and the upshot of that conversation is in your hand.

I express my gratitude to Derek both in the dedication of the volume and by giving him the last word in the volume. He is the beginning and ending of this work. I thank Richard Barber for agreeing to publish the volume and for helping work toward the many decisions we had to reach. I thank Aaron Ensminger, my research assistant at Lehigh, who did almost all of the computer work connected with the volume by formatting the seventeen disks submitted from all sorts of wordprocessors. I am most grateful to Caroline Palmer and Pru Harrison for their work in the Boydell and Brewer trenches in bringing this book into being. I also, of course, thank the many contributors who so graciously put up with my heavy editorial hand.

P.G.B.

Abbreviations

Introduction

PETER G. BEIDLER

All seventeen essays in this collection are published here for the first time, though many of them were in some earlier form presented as conference papers. By design they have little in common except that they all have some connection to the shifting and complex notion of "masculinity" and what that term means to readers of Chaucer's works. This volume of essays is in no way designed to be a "masculinist revolt" against feminist readings. Indeed, virtually all of the contributors would agree that feminist readings have so enriched our understanding of Chaucer and medieval culture that the approaches and terminology of feminists must be more widely applied.

Here are some of the questions that these seventeen essays attempt to answer. How does the Host demonstrate bourgeois masculinity? In what sense are Palamon and Arcite homosocial rivals? How do the various erotic triangles work in the *Miller's Tale*? How does the Reeve symbolically rape the Miller? Why is the Wife of Bath sometimes referred to as "masculine"? What kinds of rivalries and attractions inform the relationship of the Summoner and the Friar? Why does January really go blind? How does Dorigen's immobility define her response to her husband's mobility? How does identity politics work in the *Physician's Tale*? Why is the merchant of Saint Denis not so bad a man as his wife says he is? Why did Chaucer "diminish" the sexuality of Sir Thopas? What message does Chaucer speak to the boy-king Richard II in the *Tale of Melibee*? How does the Monk offer a sustained exploration of secular masculinity in his prologue and tale? How does the Nun's Priest send up traditional masculinity in his portrayal of the cock-of-the-walk? Is Troilus effeminate, impotent, or manly?

Previous scholars have, of course, talked about masculinity. The term itself has been around a long time, but it has been inconsistently applied to Chaucer studies. When my research assistant, Aaron Ensminger, searched for the terms "masculine," "male," and "man" in the on-line annotated bibliography that Mark Allen puts together for *Studies in the Age of Chaucer*, he came up with a strange list of articles and books that told us little of value. There was no consistency in the 40-odd items that turned up and, curiously, almost half involved the Wife of Bath and her tale. "Masculinity" – and related variations on the concept, like "manhood," "maleness," and even "malehood" – did not become a serious subject for Chaucerians until the 1990s. In this decade it suddenly became prominent on the programs of most medieval conferences and in the tables of contents of books and journals in medieval studies.

A glance through the footnotes to this volume will help readers who seek to discover more about masculinity as a cultural phenomenon. Three recent books stand out, however, as foundational in the study of masculinity in medieval literature. The first, a collection of essays edited by Clare A. Lees, *Medieval Masculinities*,[1] unfortunately makes no mention of Chaucer. The second, Susan Crane's *Gender and Romance in Chaucer's Canterbury Tales*,[2] takes up only the five romances in the *Canterbury Tales*. The third, Anne Laskaya's *Chaucer's Approach to Gender in the Canterbury Tales*,[3] is of broader interest to Chaucerians. Laskaya's book has the triple virtues of being entirely about Chaucer's *Canterbury Tales*, of discussing more than the romances, and of presenting a single-author consistency of approach and point of view. The present volume shares the second of those virtues with Laskaya's volume. It goes beyond her book by discussing in some detail the Host and fourteen of the Canterbury stories and by presenting three essays on Troilus in *Troilus and Criseyde*. Our book does not, by its very design, present a single-author consistency of

---

1   The full title of Lees' book is *Medieval Masculinities: Regarding Men in the Middle Ages* (Minneapolis: University of Minnesota Press, 1994). Readers should also be aware that an earlier electronic discussion of "Medieval Masculinities: Heroism, Sanctity, and Gender" occurred in 1992 and was published via the World Wide Web in 1993 (Jeffrey Jerome Cohen and the members of Interscripta, *Interscripta* [November–December 1993, revised October 1995], http://www.georgetown.edu/labyrinth/e-center/interscripta/mm.html). It was also published as a journal article edited by Jeffrey Cohen, "The Amour of an Alienating Identity," in *Arthuriana* 6.4 (1994): 1–24. There is some mention of Chaucer, and the discussion involved several of the contributors to the present volume. A fourth book recently appeared that may be of interest to some of our readers: *Becoming Male in the Middle Ages*, ed. Jeffrey Jerome Cohen and Bonnie Wheeler (New York: Garland, 1997). Two of the essays deal with Chaucer, Glenn Burger's on the *Miller's Tale* and Robert S. Sturges's on the Pardoner.
2   Susan Crane, *Gender and Romance in Chaucer's Canterbury Tales* (Princeton: Princeton University Press, 1994). The first chapter is entitled "Masculinity in Romance." The five romances she discusses are those of the Knight, the Man of Law, the Wife of Bath, the Clerk, and the Franklin.
3   Anne Laskaya, *Chaucer's Approach to Gender in the Canterbury Tales* (Cambridge: D. S. Brewer, 1995). Only six of the tales are discussed in any detail, those of the Knight, the Miller, the Man of Law, the Wife of Bath, the Merchant, and the Second Nun. Laskaya devotes a few pages each to the tales of the Friar, the Summoner, the Clerk, the Franklin, the Physician, the Pardoner, and the Prioress.

approach or point of view, but it has an alternative virtue: the sometimes discordant tones of a variety of voices. The point of this volume is to bring between two covers the views of a number of recent scholars who are all thinking about the notion of masculinity as it is revealed in Chaucer's works.

As editor of these essays, I have encouraged contributors to define masculinity in their own words or to imply through their own approaches what they mean by the masculine. The definitions that we find in these pages emerge in all the richness of diversity that this book was designed to encourage. Indeed, in inviting contributions I have purposefully selected the kinds of scholars who would give the widest possible view of Chaucerian masculinities. The plural form of the term is one this book insists on. Represented in the following pages are both men and women scholars, both straight and gay scholars, and both graduate students still at work on their academic requirements and retired professors. My scheme was to bring together the broadest array of approaches that I could.

The various contributors have not read and so do not refer to each other's essays, but it goes without saying that we will not necessarily agree with each other. The range of views – most obviously on the masculinity of Troilus – is so great that no agreement is possible. Nor is it desirable. The purpose of this collection is not to attempt the final word on Chaucerian masculinities, but to stimulate scholarly thinking about them. Our book reflects only the most general theses:

– For Chaucer, masculinity is a continuum that involves heterosexual and homosexual, military and domestic, noble and ignoble, mercantile and agrarian, ecclesiastical and lay, married and unmarried, and both the sexual and nonsexual relations of both men and women.

– Chaucerian masculinity is more a matter of gender than of sex. That is, masculinity has little to do with one's biology but much with one's reaction to and relations with others, one's reaction to and relation with the culture of medieval Europe.

– Although the adjective "patriarchal" is now almost always used to suggest the oppression of women, the patriarchy has through the years also done much damage to men by limiting the roles men can acceptably play in a society that tends rather to essentialize than to individualize, to assume or impose sameness rather than encourage diversity, to encourage action rather than the expression of feeling.

It goes without saying – but let me say it anyhow – that it is not part of our project to "erase" women by spending all these pages on masculinities. We share the concerns of Anne Laskaya when she writes:

Frequently the point of discussing concepts like "masculinity" and "femininity" seems to be to dismiss or avoid them and to aim for "gender" as a preferable term. Indeed, collapsing sex role differences into one word, "gender," may indicate the discomfort we seem to be experiencing with difference. But any dream of escaping differences or of combining differences into "androgyny," "polysexuality," or "performance" often suggests an erasure of women and can be a way for a patriarchal society to disguise its on-going powerful preference for the masculine.[4]

We also share the concerns of Thelma Fenster, who decries the fact that in the past the "historical discourse," although written largely by men, about men, and for men, too often limited the notion of what men were:

> As that reductive narrative obscured the many, flattening diversity and failing to record difference, obliterating *men as men*, it projected the local, the gendered, and the temporally bounded onto a universal, genderless, and atemporal screen, willingly ignoring the power imbalances thus served. In that way women were rendered invisible; but, ironically enough, so were gendered men. The terms *he, his,* and *man,* claimed as both grammatically masculine and neuter and allowing of no visible feminine, paradoxically also masked the particularity and materiality of their masculine referents.[5]

We have aimed in this volume to bring into sharper focus the individual particularity and the wondrous variety of Chaucerian men and in doing so to call attention to the gender issues that still affect us all.

If as an editor I have been liberal in encouraging contributors to go in their own directions with the concept of masculinity and to suggest their own definitions of the term, then I have been – as I am sure every one of the contributors will attest – pushingly conservative with matters of form. With a view to the publishing and purchasing costs of long books, I have been particularly outrageous in my insistence that the essays stay within the stipulated length requirements. With a view to a potential readership that we all hope will include undergraduate students as well as professional scholars, I have asked that contributors write in sentences and terms that non-specialist readers can understand, that they place near the start of their essays a preview of the major ideas in their essays, and that they give meaningful section headings to help guide readers through their arguments.

After hearing a tale by the aggressively masculine Miller about John's aging masculinity, Nicholas's randy masculinity, Absolon's questionable masculinity,

---

4   Laskaya, 1.
5   From "Preface: Why Men?" in Lees, *Medieval Masculinities*, x.

and the reactions of the sometimes un*lady*like Alison, the various pilgrims enjoy chatting about the tale:

> Whan folk hadde laughen at this nyce cas
> Of Absolon and hende Nicholas,
> Diverse folk diversely they seyde.   (I 3855–57)[6]

Like the Canterbury pilgrims, we are a group of diverse individuals who have different personalities, different notions about what makes a man, and different reasons for telling our tales. Like them, we never quite reach our destination, and none of us wins the free supper at the Tabard. But we have had fun on our journey. We hope we have given others some reason to be glad that they listened to what we have had so "diversely" to say to one other, and we encourage them to join us as we continue our journey.

---

[6]   All the quotations in this volume are from the *Riverside Chaucer*, ed. Larry D. Benson (Boston: Houghton Mifflin, 1987). Readers should keep in mind that other editions may have slightly different readings, and that virtually all of the punctuation in modern editions is inserted by the editor. We have indicated the fragment, book, and line numbers parenthetically after quotations, though sometimes, when it is obvious what the fragment number is, we have omitted fragment designations after the first few references.

I. *Canterbury Tales*

Mirth and Bourgeois Masculinity in Chaucer's Host

MARK ALLEN

Chaucer's Host is a descendent of Deduit of the *Roman de la Rose*, but unlike his literary antecedant, he is a figure of bourgeois masculinity. Masters of ceremonies and leaders of revels in their respective fictions, Deduit and the Host both provide their constituencies with diversion or "myrthe," the term used in the Middle English *Romaunt of the Rose* to translate the name "Deduit" into Middle English and the word Chaucer uses recurrently to introduce his Host. One an aristocratic garden-owner and the other a middle-class innkeeper, the two characters differ radically in social class and, as I will argue here, this class difference manifests itself in parallel differences in gender or kind of masculinity. My point is not that Chaucer set out to show us how class inflects gender. Instead, I want to explore how the interrelationships between class and gender are initially evident in the transformation from Deduit or Sir Myrthe to Chaucer's Host and how they play out in the Host's roles in the rest of the Canterbury fiction.

Mirth and commerce

In creating his Host, Chaucer converted the upper-class grace and courtesy of Sir Myrthe – note the title in *Romaunt of the Rose* (725, 733–34, etc.) – to a middle-class domineering presence.[1] Both characters are male, of course, but

---

[1]   There is no parallel to the title in the original French, but its use in the Middle English translation – perhaps by Chaucer himself – reflects contemporary awareness of the aristocratic status of the figure. On the possibility that Chaucer himself translated the *Roman* (or

their masculinities are quite different. Much of the difference resulted, no doubt, from transporting the traditional figure of the master of revels from the aristocratic garden to the commercial inn. Sir Myrthe simply does not belong in Southwark at the Tabard. In the *Romaunt*, Myrthe is introduced as "lord of this gardyn" (601), a place of solace (613, 621, 735) for himself and his "folk," a "fair and joly companye / Fulfilled of alle curtesie" (622, 639–40). The garden excludes all those who are sorrowful, and those included are attractive and without worry. Myrthe himself is described by the narrator as an ideal of masculine beauty. He is young and marked with physical attributes less reminiscent of the Host than the Prioress – an apple-round face, red-and-white complexion, "metely mouth and yen greye," fashionable dress, and recurrent use of the intensifier "ful" (eight times in thirty-two lines [817–48]). The highly conventional portrait is static, except that Myrthe dances with Gladnesse, holding her by the finger in a gesture more elegant than intimate. We are told only that "gret love was atwixe hem two"(854) and "bothe were they faire and bright of hewe" (855).

Partners in the dance, Myrthe and Gladnesse are cast as sexually male and female, although they are barely distinct in gender: both fair and beautiful, both gracious and graceful, both taking solace in the pleasures of the garden. They share what can be called feminine qualities and no strong sense of social distinction separates them or the other participants in the dance. The only distinguishing feature of Myrthe is his lordship over the garden, since it was he who had brought to it all the trees "fro the land of Alexandryn" (602) and had them enclosed within the decorated wall.

The dance of Myrthe sets the scene as the narrator enters the garden of the *Romaunt*, establishing its courtly, aristocratic atmosphere, but disappearing before the narrator is stricken by Love's arrows, the enactment of his passion for the Rose. The dance ends – and the dancers disappear from the fiction – as the various paired lovers go "awey / Undir the trees to have her pley" (1317–18). Envious of their dalliance, the narrator sets out to inspect the garden where he gazes into the fountain of Narcissus, conceives his love for the Rose, and is pierced by Love's arrows. During his subsequent quest for the Rose, he does not meet Myrthe again, so that Myrthe is perhaps best understood as part of the setting of the poem, a psychomachiac personification who helps to

a portion of it) as the existent *Romaunt of the Rose*, the introductory note to the *Romaunt* in the *Riverside Chaucer* says simply that there is "some doubt," although fragment A, which includes the material on Myrthe, "is Chaucerian in style and language and has been accepted by most scholars as an early work of Chaucer's" (686). For convenience, I cite the Middle English translation throughout this essay, except when it is helpful to recall, following Charles Dahlberg and Barbara Nolan, that "Deduit," and hence "Myrthe," denotes both "having a good time" and "turning away from a course." See Charles Dahlberg, trans., *The Romance of the Rose* (Hanover and London: University Press of New England, 1983), 361, 590n, and Barbara Nolan, " 'A poet ther was': Chaucer's Voices in the General Prologue to the *Canterbury Tales*," *PMLA* 101 (1986): 165.

establish the mental condition of the narrator that leads to his falling in love with the Rose.

The Host, of course, is not a personification, and the atmosphere he establishes for the Canterbury pilgrims is another form of mirth altogether – competitive and commercial rather than courtly or aristocratic. Unlike Sir Myrthe, he appears among a variety of social types and, as the *Canterbury Tales* develops, his continued interaction with the pilgrims effects some depth of characterization.

Unlike the other descriptions in the General Prologue, that of the Host was not apparently constructed from estates satire, but social status and economic gain are recurrent concerns which underlie the description, both functions of class distinction and class competition. Yet the Host is initially reminiscent of Myrthe. He extends his "chiere" to "everichon" (I 747), addressing one and all as "lordynges" (761, 788), and devising a plan (a "myrthe" [767]) that will provide diversion ("myrthe" [766]) alike for all. The reminiscences of Myrthe in the Host's description and initial speech include four instances of "myrthe," four of "myrie," two each of "pley" and "confort," and one each of "chiere," "ese," and "disport" (747–83).[2] Competing with the mirthful egalitarian surface here, however, is a cross-current that is less merry and distinctly commercial and competitive, antithetical to the rarified social harmony of the dance of Myrthe. The description of the Host is preceded by the narrator's apology for not setting "folk in hir degree" (744), a comment that focuses the economic and social differences among the preceding sketches, much as the similarities of detail and diction disallow such differences in the descriptions of Myrthe, Gladnesse, and their entourage. We are then told that the Host "served" food and strong drink to all the company alike, and we are given the impression that he somehow simultaneously presides as he proposes his

---

2   No material on innkeepers is included in Jill Mann's *Chaucer and Medieval Estates Satire* (Cambridge: Cambridge University Press, 1973), and though Barbara Page asserts a "vast reservoir" of applicable criticism from estates literature, she depends for the most part on a twentieth-century general critique of the bourgeoise by Felix Colmet Daâge. See Page, "Concerning the Host," *ChauR* 4 (1970): 10–11. On issues of class and economy in the characterization of the Host, see Patricia J. Eberle, "Commercial Language and Commercial Outlook in the General Prologue," *ChauR* 18 (1983): 161–74; Walter Scheps, " 'Up roos oure Hoost, and was oure aller cok': Harry Bailly's Tale-Telling Competition," *ChauR* 10 (1975): 128n8; Nolan, 164 (as in note 1 above); and Linda Georgianna, "Love So Dearly Bought: The Terms of Redemption in the *Canterbury Tales*," *SAC* 12 (1990): 103–05. Peter Brown, *Chaucer at Work: The Making of the Canterbury Tales* (London and New York: Longman, 1994), 44, suggests that Chaucer's transformation of Myrthe into the Host enabled him both to burlesque the aristocratic pretensions of the *Roman* and to critique his own society. J. V. Cunningham laid the groundwork for comparing Myrthe and the Host when he discussed the "literary form" of the General Prologue as the "dream-vision prologue in the tradition of the *Romance of the Rose*," in "Literary Form of the Prologue to the *Canterbury Tales*," *MP* 49 (1952): 172–81. Loy D. Martin shows how Chaucer adjusted the dream-vision prologue to the economic realities of his contemporary society, in "History and Form in the General Prologue to the *Canterbury Tales*," *ELH* 45 (1978): 1–17.

diverting "myrthe." This combined ideal of service and mastery may trigger deep religious associations (Christ as servant and lord),[3] but the tension between the two roles is more apparent here than the resolution. In the Host's case, both his role as servant and his role as leader have a commercial basis and economic motivation. He profits while serving food and drink, and he stands to profit again if he can lead them back to his inn. The Host addresses the group only after "we hadde maad oure rekenynges" (760), and the language of "cost" (799, 804), spending (806), and "pris" (815) is apparent in his proposal to the pilgrims. As Patricia Eberle succinctly puts it, the Host knows "how to turn a tidy profit from a religious occasion like a pilgrimage."[4]

Of course, the very game by which the Host sets out to achieve mirthful social harmony (and personal profit) takes the form of a competition with the economic reward of a supper, and as the tale-telling contest plays out, the competition is sharpened by class differences and professional antagonism, most obvious in the Miller's challenge to the Host's authority, and the quarrels between the Miller and Reeve, Friar and Summoner, and Cook and Manciple.[5] These class- and profession-based upheavals are paralleled by the Host's concerns with gender – e.g., his comments on the virility of the Monk, his accounts of his own marital turmoil, and his confrontation with the Pardoner. The parallel between class turmoil and gender tensions indicates similarity and a kind of interdependence: both are threats to the Host's authority and, in turn, means to characterize the limitations of the outlook upon which his authority is based.

[3] John Leyerle suggests that the Host's profit motive indicates that he "is a parody of the true Host," in "Thematic Interlace in the *Canterbury Tales*," *Essays and Studies* 29 (1976): 116. For connections between commercial imagery and the imagery of redemption, see Georgianna, 85–116, as in note 2 above.

[4] Eberle, 169. Robert Lumiansky, in *Of Sondry Folk* (Austin: University of Texas Press, 1955), 221, comments that the "high regard for a 'grote' is one of Harry's predominant traits."

[5] The classic discussion of professional antagonism among the pilgrims is Frederick Tupper, "The Quarrels of the Canterbury Pilgrims," *JEGP* 14 (1915): 256–70. Of the critics mentioned in the notes above, Scheps considers the Host's struggle for authority most directly. See also L. M. Leitch, "Sentence and Solaas: The Function of the Hosts in the *Canterbury Tales*," *ChauR* 17 (1982): 5–20. David R. Pichaske and Laura Sweetland assess the Host as a figure of good governance in "Chaucer and the Medieval Monarchy: Harry Bailly in the *Canterbury Tales*," *ChauR* 11 (1977): 179–200. More persuasively, Judith Ferster reads the Host as a figure of an unsuccessful tyrant who overreaches himself and fails because judgment and interpretation are slippery businesses; see her *Chaucer on Interpretation* (Cambridge: Cambridge University Press, 1985), 139–49.

The Host's masculinity in the General Prologue

In the fourteen lines of introduction before the Host begins to speak of "myrthe" in the General Prologue we are told that he is a "semely man" (751), a "large man" (753), a "myrie man" (757), and that "of manhod hym lakkede right naught" (756). This introduction contrasts markedly with the stylized presentation of elegance in Sir Myrthe. In the Host, Chaucer confronts us with a distinctly male master of ceremonies whose particular brand of masculinity is less elegant than domineering, indicated not only in the repetition of "man" and the suggestion of virility, but in the adjective "large" and the additional details that he had "eyen stepe" (753) and was "Boold of his speche" (755). As others have pointed out, the "eyen stepe" link the Host with that "manly man," the Monk (167, 201), and they differentiate his masculine gaze from the wantonness of the Friar's twinkling eyes (264–67) and the vexed sexuality of the Pardoner who in his "glarynge eyen" is "as an hare," an animal thought to be hermaphroditic in the Middle Ages (684; see *Riverside* notes). For Chaucer's contemporaries, William Keen has shown, "eyen stepe" also brought to mind the superior physical presence and prowess of the traditional aristocratic military heroes of Middle English romances.[6] The "manhod" of which the Host "lakkede right naught" does not necessarily have the same connotations as modern "virility," but at "manhed" 2.c the *Middle English Dictionary* cites John de Trevisa's translation of Ranulph Higden's *Polychronicon* where "manhode" translates Latin "virilitas," so the modern connotation was not far afield. The primary meaning of "manhod" in the Host's description appears to be something closely akin to general "manliness" or even "chivalric demeanor" (*MED*). These nuances, the repetition of "man" in the immediate context, and the juxtaposed declaration of his occupation as a tradesman – a "burgeys" (754) – bring together social rank, masculine gender, and commercial enterprise.

The initial indications of the Host's masculinity are consistently intertwined with reminders of class and commercial economics. He is a "semely man . . . / For to been a marchal in an halle" (751–52), where "marchal" raises some of the same aristocratic associations that can be seen in "eyen stepe" or "manhod." [7] The term is a chivalric one that associates the Host with a high aristocratic office, just before the qualifier recalls that his arena of operation is a hall rather than the lists or battlefield. In tension with its aristocratic associations, the adjective "stepe" rhymes with "Chepe" (753–54), the name of medieval London's best-known business district and a word that is etymologically linked with trade. The other "thynges" besides "myrthe" that the Host

---

6   See William Keen, " 'To doon yow ese': A Study of the Host in the General Prologue to the *Canterbury Tales*," *Topic* 9, no. 19 (1969): 5–19, esp. 9.

7   *MED* "marshall" 2 cites Chaucer's use of the word as the first in which the meaning does not have any specific aristocratic or military connotations; we can infer, therefore, that such resonances were available. See Keen, 13.

speaks of rhyme with the "rekenynges" (760) which he apparently insists upon before introducing the competitive diversion of the tale-telling contest. In short, the portrait of the Host is touched by indications of aristocratic masculinity that are undercut by reminders of his bourgeois occupation. As a result, we are presented with a new masculinity, one without a tradition of literary conventions to support it, and one, therefore, that Chaucer was relatively free to explore. Indeed, we might even take for granted that Chaucer had to imagine – initially at least – his masculine master of ceremonies in the aristocratic terms of Sir Myrthe since literary tradition provided few, if any, parallel masculine models that were not aristocratic.[8] But the Host is as emphatically not an aristocrat as he is emphatically masculine. Commerce and sexuality are two of the Host's most insistent concerns, and it is from these emphases that much of the Host's interaction with other characters arises in the links throughout the *Canterbury Tales*.[9]

Before turning to the links, however, one other instance of gender/class affiliation may be included from the General Prologue – the Host's role as judge and "aller cok" (I 823) on the pilgrimage. Walter Scheps has made the convenient point that the "act of judgment itself is traditionally associated with men," linking it with Biblical and political judgment.[10] In aggressive fashion, the Host lays claim to "juggement" (I 778) and threatens punishment in exorbitant commercial terms to anyone who challenges his authority: "And whoso wole my juggement withseye / Shal paye al that we spenden by the weye" (I 805–06). Although his authority is later successfully challenged by the Miller and others, the Host's claim to judgment of the contest is made with characteristic masculine boldness and economic motivation.

Not only judge but also expeditor of the tale-telling contest, the Host gets the contest going after he awakens the pilgrims the next day: "Up roos oure

---

[8]   Christ comes to mind as an obvious exception, but as noted above (note 4), the possibilities of religious associations with the Host are muted by social concerns. Anne Laskaya, *Chaucer's Approach to Gender in the Canterbury Tales* (Cambridge: D. S. Brewer, 1995), 15ff., posits four medieval ideals of masculinity (heroic, Christian, courtly, and intellectual). The Host clearly does not fit any of them.

[9]   S. S. Hussey has argued that the Host was a character very much under continuing development as Chaucer worked on the Canterbury fiction, assessing him as a realistic character and a structural device throughout the work. See "Chaucer's Host," in *Medieval English Studies Presented to George Kane*, ed. Ronald Waldron and Joseph S. Wittig (Cambridge, and Wolfeboro, NH: D. S. Brewer, 1991), 153–65.

[10]   Scheps, 114, cites Ewart Lewis, *Medieval Political Ideas*, 2 vols. (New York: Knopf, 1954), 1.39, 122, and esp. 182, 282. On the legal aspects of the Host's role as judge, see Elizabeth Dobbs, "Literary, Legal, and Last Judgments in the *Canterbury Tales*," *SAC* 14 (1992): 31–52. The hallmark study of the Host as a figure of limited aesthetic judgment is Alan Gaylord, "*Sentence* and *Solaas* in Fragment VII of the *Canterbury Tales*," *PMLA* 82 (1967): 226–35. The majority of recent critics follow Gaylord, especially Scheps, Leitch, Nolan, Ferster, and Lisa Kiser, *Truth and Textuality in Chaucer's Poetry* (Hanover, NH: University Presses of New England, 1991), esp. 123–29.

Hoost, and was oure aller cok, / And gadrede us togidre alle in a flok" (I 823–24). The gender opposition of cock and hens underscores the masculine nature of the Host's claim to authority, and it also starts a pattern that develops later in the *Tales*, that of the Host as a figure of haste, charted by Cynthia Richardson,[11] and characterized by Eberle as the commercial view that "time is money and idleness a waste of time." Eberle neatly contrasts the world of commercial *"negotium"* in the *Tales* with the *"otium"* ("leisure") of the *Roman*, observing that it is "Ydelnesse" (original French "Oiseuse") who invites the narrator into the garden of Myrthe or Diversion.[12] In direct contrast with idleness, the Host busily establishes the mirthful diversion of the tale-telling contest, beginning the movement toward Canterbury, and, along the way, hastening progress by reminding the pilgrims of the passage of time. In the *Roman*, Ydelnesse, personified as feminine, leads the narrator to the masculine Myrthe, whereas in the *Tales*, haste and mirth combine in a way that effaces the feminine to produce the newly-competitive masculinity of the Host. In a proto-capitalistic gesture, the Host leads toward his own profit even while he moves society forward.

Comedy and male bonding between the Host and the pilgrims

Characteristically, the Host's method of moving the tale-telling contest forward takes the form of some kind of homosocial bonding through which the commercial basis of his own masculinity becomes apparent. He offers the straws first to the Knight, defers to the Knight's authority when squaring off with the Pardoner, and, most tellingly, echoes the Knight's very words when chiding the Monk's mirthless catalog of tragedies (VII 2767 and 2788). We will return to these. Earlier in fragment VII, in his response to the *Shipman's Tale*, the Host wishes the teller the good commercial fortune of long sailing, and in distinctly masculine terms jokingly warns his fellow men not to allow monks into their "inns":

> "Now longe moote thou saille by the cost,
> Sire gentil maister, gentil maryneer!
> God yeve the monk a thousand last quade yeer!
> A ha! Felawes, beth ware of swich a jape!
> The monk putte in the mannes hood an ape.
> And in his wyves eek, by Seint Austyn!
> Draweth no monkes moore unto youre in."   (VII 436–42)

---

11 See Cynthia C. Richardson, "The Function of the Host in the *Canterbury Tales*," *Texas Studies in Literature and Language* 12 (1971): 325–44; and Page, 9–10.
12 Eberle, 167–68.

The contrast between the masculine perspective here and the Host's ensuing speech to the Prioress when he speaks "as curteisly as it had been a mayde" (446) underscores the masculine nature of his mirth, and his economic well-wishes to the Shipman combine with the reference to an inn to indicate a related commercial preoccupation.

In a similar way, before the Monk tells his tale, the Host flatters the cleric's virility in extravagant terms, concluding with the diction and imagery of payment that overtly aligns male sexuality and commerce:

> "This maketh that oure wyves wole assaye
> Religious folk, for ye mowe bettre paye
> Of Venus paiementz than mowe we;
> God woot, no lussheburghes payen ye!"   (1959–62)

The much poorer Nun's Priest receives equivalent sexual approval – but without the commercial imagery – only after he has told a tale which thoroughly pleases the Host:

> "I-blessed be thy breche, and every stoon!
> This was a murie tale of Chauntecleer.
> But by my trouthe, if thou were seculer,
> Thou woldest ben a trede-foul aright."   (3448–51)

Similarly, the Host applies a more condescending comparison to the lowly (and poor) Clerk: "Ye ryde as coy and stille as dooth a mayde / Were newe spoused, sittynge at the bord" (IV 2–3). To the Host, the Physician is a "propre man" (VI 309), while the presumably less-well-to-do Chaucer-pilgrim is "a popet in an arm t'enbrace / For any womman" (VII 701–02). Clearly, sexuality is a recurrent concern of the Host, and for ecclesiastical and secular men alike, his approval of their sexuality seems to parallel their economic standing.

Carolyn Dinshaw has pointed the way to recognizing another combination of gender and economy in the Host's language in the Introduction to the *Man of Law's Tale* and its Epilogue. Following Eberle in noting the economic basis of the Host's concern with time, Dinshaw observes the alignment of time and virginity in the Host's encouragement that the Man of Law tell his tale. After warning the pilgrims that the "fourthe party of this day is gon" (II 17), the Host says of time, more generally, that

> "It wol nat come agayn, withouten drede,
> Namoore than wole Malkynes maydenhede,
> Whan she hath lost it in hir wantownesse.
> Let us nat mowlen thus in ydelnesse."   (29–32)

To Dinshaw, the Host's juxtaposition of the "unprofitable conduct of life" (wasting time) with the "unregulated body of women" (Malkin's virginity) sets the scene for his approval of the Man of Law's presentation of a "heroine as a will-less blank."[13] The so-called poverty prologue of the Man of Law (99–133) and the particular fact that he learned the tale from a merchant (132–33) align commercial concerns with a tale in which Constance is shipped, commodity-like, from father to husband, husband to husband, and husband to father by Divine Providence. The Host approves of the tale, addressing "Goode men," while standing in his stirrups and declaring it "a thrifty tale for the nones" (1163–65). It may not be stretching a point to read the Host's stirrup-standing and address to males only as homosocial behavior in support of an antifeminist tale. Certainly, the term "thrifty" had economic nuances even in Middle English, so that economics and gender come together once again.[14]

The Host's response to the *Physician's Tale* has resonances similar to his invitation to the Man of Law to tell a tale. After the Physician finishes, the Host bemoans both the death of the tellingly-named Virginia who "to deere boughte" beauty (III 293) and the fact that the "yiftes of Fortune and of Nature" (III 295) bring to men "ful ofte moore for harm than prow" (VI 300). The economic language of purchase ("boughte") and profit ("prow") is by this time characteristic of the Host, and the fact that he applies it to the tale of Virginia aligns female chastity and commercial concerns in a way similar to his reference to Malkin's maidenhead. The opportunity for production (sexual or commercial) is gendered female in each case and, in the case of Virginia, the loss of opportunity is generalized to the broader notion that what is not worked for brings harm rather than profit.

The logic whereby the Host first considers "beautee" as something bought "to deere" and then as one of the (presumably) free gifts of Nature and Fortune is impossible to follow, but it is no more slippery than the Host's introduction of Fortune into the Physician's concern with Nature. In the beginning of his tale, the Physician comments on the physical and spiritual perfections Nature has given to Virginia, speaking primarily of her beauty and virginity (VI 30–71). In his response, the Host speaks not only of Nature's gifts, but of Fortune's also. The Parson speaks of the gifts of Fortune as "richesse, hyghe degrees of lordshipes, preisynges of the peple" (X 454), concerns of economy and class that have little to do with the plight of Virginia. The Host's allusion to such gifts reinforces his commercial language, and, in equating Virginia's natural gifts with her fortunate gifts, it commodifies the former. Beauty and chastity become

13 Carolyn Dinshaw, *Chaucer's Sexual Poetics* (Madison: University of Wisconsin Press, 1989), 94 and 136.
14 In the *MED*, "thrifty" ranges in meaning from rich or prosperous to suitable. See also Peggy A. Knapp, "Thrift," in *Art and Context in Late Medieval English Narrative: Essays in Honor of Robert Worth Frank, Jr.*, ed. Robert R. Edwards (Cambridge: D. S. Brewer, 1994), 193–205.

like riches and lordship, possessions that can cost one dearly and, when not worked for, often bring more harm than good.

Other responses of the Host to tales or to their tellers also fuse gender and economic concerns. In his wishes that his wife had heard both the *Clerk's Tale* and the *Melibee*, he says that he would prefer her hearing the tale to his own having a "barel ale" (IV 1212c and VII 1893), a matter of some economic importance to the innkeeper. He not only wishes his wife has "swich pacience" (VII 1895) as Prudence (and we presume Griselda), but he is also willing to pay for it. At the end of the *Merchant's Tale*, the Host critiques the "sleightes and subtilitees" (IV 2421) of women and critiques his own wife for being "povre" (2427) in all but her tongue. He fears that if he should "rekenen every vice / Which that she hath" (2433–34) it will be reported to her by an unnamed woman among the pilgrims, "Syn wommen konnen outen swich chaffare" (2438). The economic diction of poverty, reckoning, and wares is clear here, fused with male anxieties about female subtlety and female discourse. The combination represents a comic middle-class masculine outlook, a man of business unable to escape from commercial and sexual worries.

Notably, the comedy of the scene is at the Host's expense. The joke about Malkin's maidenhead and the teasing of the Clerk may be the Host's own form of mirth, rooted in his sexual and commercial outlook, but this outlook itself is the object of comedy or mirth elsewhere in the fiction. In the domestic drama that follows the *Melibee*, the comedy is pointed as the ironically named Goodelief and her husband are depicted as switching gender roles. Goodelief takes the Host's characteristic masculine role of speaking boldly when she encourages him to "Slee the dogges everichoon, / And brek hem, bothe bak and every boon!" (VII 1899–1900). She speaks here of the "knaves" who presumably have been remiss in their responsibilities as employees or servants at the inn. Goodelief's threat to trade her distaff for the Host's knife (1906–07) is also linked to their socio-economic status, as it results from her rage over the matters of rank and precedence involved in attending church. As others have pointed out, these scenes enable us to characterize the Host as hen-pecked, but the characterization is also consistently linked with the language and imagery of middle-class economics.[15] Indeed, the Host/Goodelief drama is a precursor of today's comic-strip sexualities of Andy Capp and his wife or Maggie and Jiggs.

[15] The sketch of the Wife of Bath in the General Prologue emphasizes that precedence at church was an important issue among bourgeois women, or at least an aspect of the social stereotype; see the corroborating evidence cited in the *Riverside Chaucer*, 818, I 449–51n. The fact that the Wife is also characterized as "masculine" in several ways (bold of face, hat like a shield, wearing spurs) may also indicate that switching gender roles is part of the tradition. On the Host as henpecked, see, among others, Kemp Malone, *Chapters on Chaucer* (Baltimore: Johns Hopkins, 1951), 188; Lumiansky, 95; and Pichaske and Sweetland, 179.

Displacing bourgeois masculinity: Pardoner, Knight, and Parson

If the Host's bourgeois masculinity generates a form of mirth and, in turn, becomes the object of comedy, it has darker dimensions that are unmirthful indeed. His response to the Pardoner is the clearest indication of the malevolent dimension of the sexuality represented, evident in the violent scatology of his reference to castrating the Pardoner: "Lat kutte hem of, I wol thee helpe hem carie; / They shul be shryned in an hogges toord!" (VI 954–55). The homophobia implicit in the excessiveness of the threat is the obverse of the homosocial bonding that elsewhere typifies the Host's efforts to move the contest along.[16] Furthermore, the scene involves a tension that is as much commercial in nature as it is sexual, for the Pardoner's offer of his "absolucion" (924) and his "pardoun" (926) is an offer of nothing for something that depends upon a commercial mentality even while it runs directly counter to the commodity basis of any trade. The Pardoner offers admittedly bogus relics and false pardons for money, implicating not only Church practices but the commerciality upon which they are based. His sermon against gluttony, swearing, and hazardry – the so-called "tavern vices" – challenges the Host's occupation as innkeeper specifically, and his request for money in exchange for pardon challenges commercial exchange more generally. In this way, the Host-Pardoner opposition can be seen as a microcosm of an opposition between productive commerce and the vacuity of the Pardoner's ventures. At the same time, it places virility – or obsession with virility – in opposition to sterility. Confronting the Pardoner, the Host faces commercial and sexual unproductivity, and his inordinate rage at the confrontation indicates the reductiveness of his outlook on both.

Haste and homosocial bonding are the Host's means to move the pilgrimage along, but in this scene, movement begins again only when the Knight imposes a kiss of peace between the Host and Pardoner:[17]

> "Namoore of this, for it is right ynough!
> Sire Pardoner, be glad and myrie of cheere;
> And ye, sire Hoost, that been to me so deere,
> I prey yow that ye kisse the Pardoner.
> And Pardoner, I prey thee, drawe thee neer,

---

[16] Eve Kosofsky Sedgwick comments on the continuity of homosocial bonding and homophobia in *Between Men: English Literature and Male Homosocial Desire* (New York: Columbia University Press, 1985), 1–2.

[17] Glenn Burger has examined the kiss for the way it complicates our responses to the Pardoner and the Host. See his "Kissing the Pardoner," *PMLA* 107 (1992): 1143–56. I have commented elsewhere on the symbolic possibilities of the Pardoner's offer of absolution to the pilgrims while they are halted on the Canterbury road; see my "Moral and Aesthetic Falls on the Canterbury Way," *South Central Review* 8 (1991): 36–49.

And, as we diden, lat us laughe and pleye."
Anon they kiste, and ryden forth hir weye.   (VI 962–68)

The Host's ability to keep things moving is insufficient here, a representation of the limits of his authority and an indication that his bourgeois masculinity is, under the conditions, insufficient as well. In simplest terms, he loses his sense of humor with the Pardoner, and the Knight is required to renew both the mirth of the contest and the progress toward Canterbury. The figure of middle-class commerce gives way to the superior authority of the aristocrat, and aversion to the Pardoner's queerness gives way to a kiss that transcends the blunt masculinity the Host has come to embody as the pilgrims "laughe and pleye" again.

The Knight later interrupts the *Monk's Tale* in language reminiscent of his intervention in the Host-Pardoner squabble, language that the Host parrots as a means to reestablish his control. But the Host's "namoore of this" (2788) to the Monk does not achieve the same potency as the Knight's uses of the phrase (VI 962 and VII 2767), and the Host's authority is compromised by his deference to the Knight in both scenes. The Knight – not the Host – invokes again a form of mirth in place of the Monk's tales of woe, reminding him that the opposite of misfortune is "joye and greet solas" (VII 2774), a "gladsom" thing, "goodly for to telle" (2778–79). The Knight's mirth is not the sexual jocularity of the Host, but the philosophical conviction that weal follows woe. Similarly, the Parson will finally supplant the insufficiency of the Host's mirth with his spiritual "myrie tale in prose" (X 46). In both cases, as the Host gives way to superior authority, the limitations of bourgeois masculinity give way to more exalted outlooks. The Knight's and Parson's outlooks are, it is true, masculinist, and behind them lie long traditions of gender politics, but with the Host Chaucer exposes the politics of gender in combination with middle-class commerce.

The fact that the interrelationships between class and gender are so clear in the Host evinces a "constructivist" view of gender before modern theorizing of such a view and, in doing so, reminds us that particular views of gender *are* historically based, products of social conditions. More specifically, modern gender theory attributes – and at times even blames – western gender roles on the commercial competitiveness of capitalism,[18] and insofar as the Host can be seen as a figure of proto-capitalist competition and commercial concern, Chaucer's work anticipates the attribution. His replacement of the Host's authority with that of the Knight and the Parson emphasizes the insufficiency

---

[18] Elisabeth Badinter provides a convenient summary of differences between "essentialist" and "constructivist" views of gender in *XY: On Masculine Identity*, trans. Lydia Davis (New York: Columbia University Press, 1994), 21–27. For alignments of capitalism, competition, and modern masculinity, see Kenneth Clatterbaugh, *Contemporary Perspectives on Masculinity: Man, Women, and Politics in Modern Society* (Boulder, CO: Westview Press, 1990), chapter 7, and R. W. Connell, *Masculinities* (Berkeley and Los Angeles: University of California Press, 1995), 185–203.

of his bourgeois masculinity, just as the comedy of the domestic scenes lampoons it, and the confrontation with the Pardoner exposes its potential for malevolence. Still, finally, Chaucer does not indict bourgeois masculinity. For all its absurdity and danger, the Host's masculinity is the major moving force of the pilgrimage. It may be insufficent to move the pilgrimage to completion, but it gets the pilgrimage started and, in many instances, keeps it going. In Chaucer's mirror of society, bourgeois masculinity is a potent force, one to laugh at, one to be cautious of, but certainly one not to be ignored.

Homosociality and Creative Masculinity in the *Knight's Tale*

PATRICIA CLARE INGHAM

Chaucer's Knight tells a tale about death. Of course, and as the critical history of the tale shows, death and destruction are only one side of this story,[1] for the Knight finally rearranges the dirges of a warrior's funeral into the harmony of wedding anthems. And despite Arcite's gruesome exit from what Duke Theseus calls the "foul prison of this life," Theseus's famous final exhortation to "make a virtue of necessity" helps transform Arcite's mourners into Palamon's wedding guests. When the witnesses to the spectacle of gruesome knightly demise (after a period of years) turn their tears into songs of joy, the necessity of funeral pyres gradually mutates into a celebration of marriage, an event constituted, according to medieval sacramental theology, by the consent and choice of the willing participants.[2]

---

[1] Critical history has long debated the tale's representations of "chaos" and "order." Recently this debate has turned on the question of the extent to which Chaucer's *Knight's Tale* offers a critique of the destructions wrought by chivalric culture. See, for example, Robert Hanning, " 'The Struggle Between Noble Designs and Chaos': The Literary Tradition of Chaucer's *Knight's Tale*," *The Literary Review* 23 (1980): 519–41; Charles Muscatine, *Chaucer and the French Tradition* (Berkeley: University of California Press, 1957); H. Marshall Leicester, Jr., *The Disenchanted Self: Representing the Subject in the Canterbury Tales* (Berkeley: University of California Press, 1990). On the relation between historical writings on chivalry and the *Knight's Tale*, see Lee Patterson, *Chaucer and the Subject of History* (Madison: University of Wisconsin Press, 1991), 171–76. For a review of critical tradition about the *Knight's Tale*, see Anne Laskaya, *Chaucer's Approach to Gender in the Canterbury Tales* (Cambridge: D. S. Brewer, 1995), 55–77.

[2] Louise Fradenburg has examined the importance of consent for medieval culture in its understanding of the relationship among men and women as well as those between rulers and their subjects; more recently she links the subject's desire for "the gift of death" with

The end of the *Knight's Tale* joins death with consent, two elements not usually imagined together. The movement from death to marriage implies that, for Theseus, and perhaps for Chaucer's Knight, necessity (or fate) can become beautifully desirable. It implies as well that the prospect of heterosexual union can compensate somehow for the inevitability of extinction. Necessity, and philosophical exhortations that we accept and even desire it, have a long history in western culture,[3] a history which, as the *Knight's Tale* can remind us, has pertinence for relations of gender. In these pages I will argue that the representations of masculinity in Chaucer's *Knight's Tale* need to be read in relation to that text's representation of necessity and its virtues. In the sections that follow I examine how Chaucer's tale represents masculine suffering, that is, the relationship between the necessity of loss and the willingness and ability of men to bear loss stoically. In the first part of this paper I examine the masculinity of fallen warriors Palamon and Arcite, their homosocial rivalry and the power of their violence for Duke Theseus's creative governance. In the second part I offer Theseus's representations in Book I as a counterpoint to the victimizations of Palamon and Arcite, and as testimony to state rule as a masculine power. And in the third part I explore further how a ruler's masculinity requires both the victimization of his soldiers and the excessive mourning of his women. As we shall see, Theseus's stoic masculinity depends upon a series of losses suffered more directly by his subjects than they are by himself. Indeed, the suffering of others – both male and female – becomes the basis for Theseus's ability to create, to move his populace from funerals to weddings, while himself remaining safely distant from the liabilities of suffering. I argue that Chaucer's text imagines Theseus's creative power, and perhaps creative power more generally, as a masculine attribute.

Victimized doubles: The masculinity of Arcite and Palamon

While we may be used to imagining masculinity as the embodiment of power and victory (a representation we will eventually witness in the representation of Theseus in Book I) the *Knight's Tale* troubles the assumption that an unfettered and victorious power attends masculinity as such. Our first view of Palamon and Arcite, for example, provides a striking image of the masculine

---

the "sacrificial structure" of Chaucer's *Knight's Tale*. These important cultural analyses are crucial to my reading of masculinity in this tale. On consent see "Sovereign Love" in *City, Marriage, Tournament: Arts of Rule in Late-Medieval Scotland* (Madison: University of Wisconsin Press, 1991), 67–83, on knighthood's sacrificial structure see "Sacrificial Desire in Chaucer's *Knight's Tale*," *Journal of Medieval and Early Modern Studies*, forthcoming.

3   On the politics of death's association with ontological necessity, see Herbert Marcuse, "The Ideology of Death," in *The Meaning of Death*, ed. Herman Fiefel (New York: McGraw Hill, 1959), 64–76. For its pertinence to the *Knight's Tale*, see Fradenburg (forthcoming).

warrior as victim; the text introduces us to these two cousins just as their bodies are poised together, on the edge between life and death:

> And so bifel that in the taas they founde
> Thurgh-girt with many a grevous blody wounde,
> Two yonge knyghtes liggynge by and by,
> Bothe in oon armes, wroght ful richely,
> Of which two Arcita highte that oon,
> And that oother knyght highte Palamon.
> Nat fully quyke, ne fully dede they were,
> But by hir cote-armures and by hir gere
> The heraudes knewe hem best in special
> As they that weren of the blood roial
> Of Thebes, and of sustren two yborn.   (I 1009–19)

In this description these warriors embody complete powerlessness, their agency so compromised that they can move neither into life nor into death. The scene evokes a double effect: on one hand, it reminds us that conquerors like Creon and Theseus need male warrior bodies (as well as female Amazonian ones) willing to suffer grievous woundings; on the other, it implies the value, even beauty, of knightly unions on the field of battle. Indeed, the poetic descriptions link the wounding of warrior bodies with a fellowship between soldiers. Arcite and Palamon's intimacy with death is written here upon their intimacy with one another. Warrior homosociality (unions between fighting men) merges here with a knight's body in pain.[4]

Strikingly, the poem emphasizes the former more than it does the latter. We do not hear the precise nature of Palamon's or Arcite's woundings, but instead are privy to the details of their relation couched in a way that accentuates their affections for one another. Despite the horrifying image of these young men disguised in a heap of bloody corpses, the language of the description seems remarkably gentle. Two knights lie "by and by," in a figuration that evokes the intimacies of sleep as much as it does the sacrifices of the grave. And in contrast to the grisly enumeration of lesions, lacerations, and dismemberment we will later witness at the Temple of Mars in Book III (see 1195–2009), or the

---

[4] Eve Sedgwick describes unions between men, unions often mediated through their mutual desire for a particular woman, as "homosocial." I both borrow her term and extend it: as we will see shortly, Palamon's and Arcite's homosociality will soon be mediated through their mutual desire for Emily; but I am suggesting as well that Chaucer's *Knight's Tale* indicates that battlefield violence can also mediate homosocial desires "between men." I have argued elsewhere that such chivalric bonds remain haunted by homoerotic desire pertinent to the character of knightly brotherhoods. See Ingham, "Masculine Military Unions: Brotherhood and Rivalry in the *Avowing of King Arthur*," *Arthuriana* 6 (1996): 25–44, and Eve K. Sedgwick, *Between Men: English Literature and Male Homosocial Desire* (New York: Columbia University Press, 1985).

gruesome biology of Arcite's death in Book IV (see 2743–60), this description of Palamon and Arcite foregrounds the wartime homosociality of knighthood, the valuable unification of knights. Indeed the gentle tone marks the scene of knightly togetherness with a fond poignancy often reserved for lovers.

Scholarly accounts of chivalric culture also emphasize a unity of brotherly affections in battle, where images of male-to-male intimacy in war signify both masculine community and military virility. In his *Memorials of the Most Noble Order of the Garter*, for example, G. F. Beltz links the kind of intense identification between brothers-in-arms – so like Chaucer's depiction of Palamon and Arcite together – with the strength and power of the ruler. Beltz writes

> As if members of one family, [knights] wore similar apparel and armour, desirous that, in the heat of battle, the enemy might mistake one for the other, and that each might participate [in] the dangers by which the other was menaced. By brotherhoods of this character, the sovereigns, under whose banners they enlisted, were able to achieve the most daring warlike operations.[5]

This account of knighthood marks knightly unions as both permanent (that is, comprising brotherhoods beyond the grave, despite the dead bodies war produces) and productive (that is, able to produce a superlative daring army). For Beltz, the substitution of knight for knight proves desirable because it can create a sovereign's "most daring warlike operations." These knights together display their ruler's military potency and virility. Knightly relations produce the pleasures of violence not for their own sake, but for the sake of the sovereign, channeling the excitement of aggression through the potency of a warrior-king. But, as Louise Fradenburg has recently argued, the structure of this relationship, while conceived as generative and immutable, rests on the principal of mutability, on the soldier's willingness to sacrifice. Knighthood manages a mutual participation in one another's lives through a participation in the possibility of one another's death, that is, through the apparently noble act of renouncing one's life for the life of a brother knight.[6]

The likelihood of wartime death and wounding, while not immediately emphasized in the description of Palamon's and Arcite's bodies together, continues to haunt the scene of battle carnage within which the vanquished cousins lie. In fact, the twinning resemblance between the two, lying in a mass of wounded flesh, provides an eerie reminder of death, the great equalizer. Poised on death's edge, these two knights seem uncannily alike, bereft of individuation, the particular differences and personal specifities that grant them separate identities. In fact, the confluences between Palamon and Arcite are so

---

5   G. F. Beltz, *Memorials of the Most Noble Order of the Garter* (London: W. Pickering, 1841), xxviii.
6   See Fradenburg (forthcoming).

deeply woven here that this description has prompted a number of critics to wonder if these two characters are really different from each other at all. As doubles surrounded by their slain fellows, Palamon's and Arcite's war-appareled bodies gesture at the terrifying loss of individuation a warrior risks in battle. Their doubling image amidst an assemblage of bodies cut through with many a grievous, bloody wound reminds us that as bloody corpses, warriors horrifically resemble one another.[7]

In Palamon's and Arcite's union on the edge of death the possibility of sacrificial death haunts the masculine image of a soldier at the very moment that testimony to a homosocial brotherhood of brave knights offers its consolations. The connection between the pleasures of the homosociality of knighthood and the violent risks knighthood offers to particular soldiers continues to drive the plot of Chaucer's tale. Rivalries between Arcite and Palamon provide a view of the exciting spectacles knightly relations can produce while simultaneously endangering the integrity of each of the knights themselves. Emily, for her part, apparently figures as the singular object of their desire. Her continual presence (frequently as a backdrop to their actions) has at least two implications: it identifies rivalry between knights as pertinent to categories of masculine sexuality, and it testifies that the exciting physical relations between these cousins have heterosexual limits.

Of course, the *Knight's Tale* also suggests that heterosexual desire can have tragic consequences for the future of knights together. It may be, thus, no coincidence that the tale's denouement displays state-sponsored heterosexual union as a compensation for the losses to chivalric fraternity. Still, if the ending of the *Knight's Tale* ties things up rather neatly, earlier portions of the tale cause some readers to remain unconvinced by this final resolution. Chilling reminders of the risks and dangers that war offers to male bodies recur throughout, suggesting a preoccupation with the horrors of biological death – with the savage elements that threaten to overcome even the order and civilization offered in the end of the tale itself. To be sure, critics have long emphasized Theseus's creative fortitude in attempting to cope with the uncontrollable destructions of violence. When, for example, Palamon's and Arcite's rivalry results in a brutal man-to-man affray in the wood, Theseus transforms the

---

[7] In "The Uncanny," Sigmund Freud, following the work of Otto Rank, describes the "invention of doubling" as "preservation against extinction." He links fantasies of doubleness to "all those strivings of the ego which adverse external circumstances have crushed and all our suppressed acts of volition which nourish in us the illusion of free will" (141–42). That is, Freud identifies the appearance of doubles with the desires for, and struggles to find, agency amid constraint. That struggle, I am arguing, is part of the *Knight's Tale* and can help us understand the representations of masculinity therein. Freud's essay "The Uncanny" is found in *On Creativity and the Unconscious: Papers on the Psychology of Art, Literature, Love, Religion* (New York: Harper, 1958), 122–61. On the relation between such fantasies and the apotropaic protection of gender see Elisabeth Bronfen, *Over Her Dead Body: Death, Femininity and the Aesthetic* (New York: Routledge, 1992), 59–75.

brutality of wild hand-to-hand combat into the apparent civility of chivalric tournament.[8] In an impressive (and impressively narrated) display of state power, Theseus commands the creation of an amphitheater (a Chaucerian addition to Boccaccio's story) convening a magnificent state festival to settle the dispute between the two soldiers.

While critics continue to debate whether the resolution of this text satisfies our doubts or merely redirects them (and whether Chaucer, or his Knight, criticizes Theseus or admires him) we can at least note how impressively Theseus uses the violent rivalry of the Theban cousins to his own ends. The rivalry between two enemies of Athens becomes, in Theseus's capable hands, a display of monumental Athenian wealth (read in the amazing building of the amphitheater, in Arcite's lavish funeral, in the final wedding feast) and power (read in the efficacy of Theseus's ability to civilize the private battle in the grove into tournament game, and in his skill at transforming death into marriage, sorrow into joy). In the process, Theseus lays claim to the energy, power, and virility of both cousins. Their fighting becomes a testimony to his masculine power, as conqueror and as governor. In harnessing the masculine violence of rivalry to undergird his power as ruler, Theseus shows us that the violent risks warriors suffer can be useful to a sovereign's power and prestige. In fact, Theseus's power as ruler has, from the text's inauguration, been linked with his masculinity. We turn then to an examination of that masculinity and the various victimizations upon which it depends.

Conquering masculinity: Theseus of Book I

Gendered identities and their relation to victimization and loss inaugurate Chaucer's *Knight's Tale*. Our first introduction to Duke Theseus describes his position as triumphant military leader and sovereign ruler in distinctly masculine terms:

> Whilom, as olde stories tellen us,
> Ther was a duc that highte Theseus;
> Of Atthenes he was lord and governour,
> And in his tyme swich a conquerour,
> That gretter was ther noon under the sonne.
> Ful many a rich contree hadde he wonne;
> What with his wysdom and his chivalrie,
> He conquered al the regne of Femenye,

8   We would not wish to overestimate the differences between battle and tournament, however. On their similarities see Maurice Keen, *Chivalry* (New Haven: Yale University Press, 1984); Fradenburg, "Soft and Silken War," in *City, Marriage, Tournament* (1991), 192–224.

That whilom was ycleped Scithia,
And weddede the queene Ypolita,
And broghte hire hoom with hym in his contree
With muchel glorie and greet solempnytee.   (859–70)

Theseus's role as conqueror poetically parallels his position as "lord and governour" of Athens; both those roles, by the eighth line, sit parallel to the "regne of Femenye," a phrase which also denotes a kind of sovereign rule and conquest. The parallel structure of these lines may suggest at first that the Amazonian warriors with whom Theseus fights are enough like him to be suitable adversaries; after all both Theseus and the Amazon queen count militarism among their arts of rule.

Yet the next few lines circumscribe any comparison initially suggested here. Indeed Chaucer decided to begin his story after Theseus's battles with the Amazons are over – scenes available to Chaucer by way of his source, Boccaccio's *Teseide*, which could have supplied images of valiant, brave, and impressive fighting women. Chaucer's elimination of these representations of Hypolita as a soldier like Theseus implies that he is not as interested in comparisons between Theseus and his Amazonian adversaries as he is in their contrasts. Conqueror of a "regne of Femenye," Theseus appears, by implication, a virile and masculine ruler, utterly different from his female captives. For one thing he is the conqueror, they the conquered. For another, he stands as the male husband whose rule domesticates aggressive soldiers into respectable Athenean wives. In fact, by the time we hear the Amazon queen's name, Theseus has already "weddede" her, figuring her position in a way that emphasizes both Hypolita's subjection to Theseus's rule, and Theseus's gendered difference from her. We are not encouraged to dwell long upon Theseus's similarities (as warrior, as ruler) with "his" Amazonian Queen.

When Chaucer's text begins by contrasting Theseus's conquering power with his new wife's victimization it offers, as Susan Crane has put it, "a familiar instance of defining gender by differentiation."[9] More precisely, the difference of male to female in the opening of this text is solidified and crafted through violent activity, albeit violence that takes place off stage.[10] As *fait accompli* produced by Theseus's virile conquest, male and female literally begin this tale violently opposed. More precisely, we feel the strength of their opposition precisely because the violent encounter that produces such difference takes

[9] Susan Crane, *Gender and Romance in Chaucer's Canterbury Tales* (Princeton: Princeton University Press, 1994), 20.
[10] Teresa de Lauretis has argued compellingly that gender distinctions are always made through violence. As she puts it, "The representation of violence is inseparable from the notion of gender." See "The Violence of Rhetoric: Considerations on the Representation of Gender," in *The Violence of Representation*, ed. Nancy Armstrong and Leonard Tennenhouse (London: Routledge, 1989), 240.

place off stage. On one hand, the allusion to war inscribes the difference of duke to Amazon with the apparently absolute terms of military enmity; on the other hand, the elision of the scenes of battle from the text makes the images of brave, violent Amazonian women – images that stress not their differences from Theseus so much as their similarities with him – nearly illegible.[11]

This violent opposition of male to female, however, as a number of critics have noted, is soon qualified by another representation of the female. Theseus's masculinity borrows "womanly" qualities from another subjected female group, this time the Argive widows. Theseus's victorious difference from his Amazonian captives merges with a similarity across gender; again as Susan Crane puts it, a "counterprocess" of gender representation "recuperates for [Theseus's] masculinity some of the traits associated with women."[12] When the "compaignye of ladyes, tweye and tweye" (897) beg that Theseus " 'lat oure sorwe synken in thyn herte' " (950), the widows display a compassion here defined through women's sorrow. The poignant (and extended) description of these "wrecched wommen" crying out in lamentation (mournful voices that, the narrator momentarily seems to worry, might be troublingly ceaseless) foregrounds the importance of female woe for the tale before us. It suggests, too, that Theseus needs wailing women to mediate his warrior masculinity. The Argive Widows who interrupt Theseus "in his mooste pride" (895) allow him to gain compassion, an attribute required of the virtuous king. The masculine heart of a conqueror needs access to the compassion that a woman's woe can inspire; yet the earlier representation of Theseus as himself a conqueror of women may imply that he is not wholly unlike the tyrant Creon in his willingness to victimize females.[13] There are, to be sure, important differences between the Amazonian warriors and the Argive widows. Indeed, the gender implications of the contrasts between the Amazons and the Widows suggest some crucial attributes of the version of femininity offered by the *Knight's Tale*. The victimization and domestication of the Amazons is, apparently, a legitimate victimization of aggressive femininity; the victimization of the Argive widows is not. Such contrasts suggest that the representations of femininity in this tale place women always outside the legitimate powers (and pleasures) of aggression.

From the beginning of the tale, then, Chaucer presents us with a representation of Theseus the masculine ruler marked both by his triumph over

11 On the extent to which this structure obscures what I call elsewhere the "military intimacies" of enemies, see Ingham, 27–29.
12 Crane, 20.
13 For an especially fine reading of the similarities between Theseus's actions and Creon's as an implied critique of Theseus's activity in Book I, see H. Marshall Leicester, Jr., 221–382. While Theseus is contrasted with Creon here, in pursuing that tyrant, Theseus's behavior is not unlike his adversary's. Leicester notes, moreover, that Theseus's identity as conqueror is troubled by the horrific representation of "Conquest" in the iconography of the Temple of Mars in Book III.

vanquished women and by his willingness to adopt the so-called "womanly" qualities of the vanquished. This image of medieval masculinity should not surprise us. Sovereign figures like Theseus – compassionate and conquering – are as common in medieval literature and medieval theology as are images of interceding ladies and queens who entreat those sovereigns on their suffering subjects' behalf.[14] Yet the combination of difference and similarity here (the image of a vanquished Hypolita alongside the poignant figures of the mourning ladies) also reminds us that for all his willingness to remake his warrior heart with compassion and pity, Theseus is not himself "feminized" as a victim. His family's dead bodies are not lying unburied, and he remains the conqueror throughout. Indeed, he will soon display himself as conqueror again, this time over Creon, the king whose tyranny the Argive widows lately lamented. For all his proximity to death and wounding, Theseus's position throughout Book I of the *Knight's Tale* – unlike the various positions of Hypolyta, Emily, the Argive widows, Palamon or Arcite, even Creon – remains that of the victor. His masculine presence invites feasting rather than mourning.

Of course, Book IV of the *Knight's Tale*, despite its final (apparently happy) resolution in the marriage of Emily to Palamon, also registers the limits to Theseus's sovereign agency. Arcite's death springs up, unbidden, despite Theseus's promise that the contest between cousins will end peaceably. The scene of brotherly affection and wounding we examined as a part of Book I recurs in Book IV as tragedy. Palamon howls; Arcite dies. With Arcite's death the scenes of the rivalry and discord between the cousins are finally resolved in a display of remarkable singularity mediated by Theseus, who now appears less the conqueror than the "philosopher king."[15] In the denouement of the tale Palamon becomes a singular hero; with Palamon's marriage to Emily, Theban and Athenian wartime enmity become reconciled into the nearly absolute unity of matrimony.[16]

Theseus's ability to resist chaos – or perhaps, to put it more precisely, his willingness to reinterpret chaos in the service of an apparently more beautiful future – constitutes a power this text links with a masculine attitude toward loss.

[14] Feminist scholars have analyzed the intercessory role of powerful women during the middle ages. The model for such figures is, of course, the Virgin Mary. See, for example, Marina Warner, *Alone of All Her Sex: The Myth and Cult of the Virgin Mary* (New York: Warner, 1982).

[15] The phrase is borrowed from Paul Olson who argues that Theseus becomes the image of the virtuous monarch who strives to reconcile divergent interests in "a community of interest." See his "Chaucer's Epic Statement and the Political Milieu of the Late Fourteenth Century," *Mediævalia* 5 (1979): 61–87. I argue that Theseus's masculinity is a crucial, yet in Olson's reading unanalyzed, attribute of this role. A "philosopher queen" seems here a cultural impossibility.

[16] According to medieval sacramental theology, marriage legally and sacramentally created a single person where there had previously been two. The wife was subsumed into the person of her husband. See Fradenburg (1991), pp. 67–90; Anne Middleton, "War by Other Means: Marriage and Chivalry in Chaucer," *SAC: Proceedings*, vol. 1 (1984): 119–33.

In the final sections of the poem, Theseus's masculinity remains set apart from the victimized masculinities of Palamon and Arcite, masculinities upon which his governance nonetheless has depended. Theseus's ability to recover from loss, to "make a virtue of necessity," moreover, is here related to the poignant and apparently more excessive mourning of a female victim, Emily. We return by Book IV to an image of Theseus's masculinity again wrought through the combination of his difference from a woman and his simultaneous relation to a woman's sorrow. I turn now to the resolution of Chaucer's *Knight's Tale*, the final scenes of Arcite's death and Palamon's marriage.

The masculine virtues of necessity

Arcite's death erupts chaotically into Theseus's otherwise well-ordered state festivities, causing all the town to cry and weep at their unanticipated loss. The turn of events reminds the reader (as it must remind Theseus himself along with all the men and women ruled by him) that even the most prodigious of rulers and conquerors cannot control death. Yet in the midst of the disaster, Theseus remains apart from the rest. As Theseus compassionately copes with what the figures of Emily and Palamon register as the most monumental of losses, we see a ruler's stoicism represented in contrast to the moans and swoons of women:

> Shrighte Emelye, and howleth Palamon
> And Theseus his suster took anon
> Swownynge, and baar hire fro the corps away.
> What helpeth it to tarien forth the day
> To tellen how she weep bothe eve and morwe?
> For in swich cas wommen have swich sorwe,
> Whan that hir housbondes ben from hem ago,
> That for the moore part they sorwen so,
> Or ellis fallen in swich maladye
> That at the laste certeinly they dye.   (2817–26)

The description presents us with a spectrum of responses to the fact of death: from Emily who shrieks and weeps ceaselessly, "bothe eve and morwe," to Palamon who howls and then falls silent, to Theseus who apparently subordinates his grief in the compassionate care of his excessively grieving "suster," an Amazon woman he recently conquered. The narratorial voice of Chaucer's Knight, moreover, moves immediately to contextualize Emily's hapless mourning as an attribute of gender: "Wommen have swich sorwe," he tells us, and are "fallen in swiche maladye" that "at the laste certeinly they dye." Women's mourning is here identified as inevitably lethal. Female mourning, in its excesses, can apparently be dangerous to women themselves and useless to those who hear it second-hand. "What good does it do," the Knight asks rhetorically, "to waste the day by telling of woman's weeping?"

While Chaucer's Knight avers that woman's sorrow is to no avail, the gender relations in the tale belie that assertion. For when, at the moment of greatest tragedy, the Knight links ceaseless sorrowing with the tears and moans of women, he offers to men a different series of responses. At the level of our story, Theseus's moderate mourning, in contrast to Emily's woeful shrieks, comes to seem both productive and masculine. He comforts his grieving sister; he plays the compassionate, resilient, and wiser paterfamilias. We might well remember here Theseus's relation to the sorrowing Argive widows at the beginning of Book I. Fresh from battle, Theseus then requires a compassion borrowed from a woman's heart to sustain his difference from the tyrant Creon. Here, I would argue, he likewise requires access to Emily's sorrowing. Without it, the stoical philosophizing that follows might appear hard-hearted. Emily's uncontrollable mourning is useful to Theseus's masculinity because he can again merge gender difference with gender similarity. He is thus marked as both sensitive and manly, neither overrun by the lethal excesses to which mourning women like Emily are subject, nor coldly immune to their pleas.

Emily's weeping, moreover, serves other masculinities as well. Immediately before his narration of the piteous Emily, Chaucer's Knight registers his own verbal inabilities when confronted by such senseless tragedy:

> [Arcite's] spirit chaunged hous and wente ther
> As I cam nevere, I kan nat tellen wher.
> Therfore I stynte, I nam no divinistre;
> Of soules fynde I nat in this registre,
> Ne me ne list thilke opinions to telle
> Of hem, though that they writen wher they dwelle.
> Arcite is coold, ther Mars his soule gye!
> Now wol I speken forth of Emelye.   (2810–16)

In his important aside Chaucer's Knight records his own speechlessness before the fact of death. His story is halted. Indeed, he repeats a number of times his inability, or unwillingness, to tell his audience the meaning of Arcite's fate. We find instead a litany of what the teller of this tale will not, or cannot, do: he cannot tell where Arcite has gone; he threatens to stop entirely; he does not desire to say any more about it. We hear instead only the bald facts: Arcite is cold.

The threat of muteness implied here registers the mutability of authorship. How can one (the Knight? Chaucer?) speak before death's inexplicability, ineffability? Yet one can, or so the Knight's next words imply, move forward by describing the pitiful shrieks of women. In what seems a remarkably sudden shift in tone and content the Knight moves quickly to a more comforting subject, describing a (female) subject in need of comforting. Perhaps not ironically, and despite his assurances about the futility of its narration, the image of Emily's weeping has, in fact, helped the Knight a good deal. It has enabled him to get beyond his silence before the face of death, a silence that has the dangerous power to end his story prematurely.

The Knight's power to create, like Theseus's power of creative governance, is gained in part through its relation to the power of a woman's sorrow. The Knight, like Theseus, luxuriates in his description of sorrowing women while avoiding further mention of the problems death raises for his own art, the way death's baldness threatens the telling of this tale. Theseus, for his part, cannily moves Athens beyond Arcite's death and into a new alliance with his former enemy, and his statecraft comes to seem compassionate and wise because he has previously shown such care for female woe. And, of course, Theseus the compassionate philosopher is also Theseus the conquering hero. He uses the virile power and the contests between Palamon and Arcite to display his own powerful masculinity. Yet such uses, in this tale, never position the body of the Duke as victimized by the vicissitudes of battle. We do not much attend to threats to Theseus's body. And this quality of Theseus's masculinity is both a deeply admired attribute of power and one envied by Chaucer's Knight.

Chaucer's *Knight's Tale* thus provides us with a view of governance as dependent on both the power of the masculine knight and the woe of weeping women. A decidedly masculine ruler, Theseus harnesses the potentially destructive and violent energies of his male prisoners-of-war for the glory of his rule and his state. Yet the figures of Hypolita and Emily point to Theseus's own interest in militarism and its destructions. Indeed, the masculinities in this tale could offer consolation to a tarnished veteran like Chaucer's Knight, providing him with a vision of a "mature" male ruling potency and agency that can outlive the humiliations and victimizations (as well as the adventures) of battle. Chaucer thus provides us with a view of how chivalric culture clings to images of an ordered masculine agency amid the destruction and chaos of war; along the way he points to creativity itself (and perhaps to the poet) as a power in masculine terms.

"Convictions about gender," writes Susan Crane, "underlie choices in every social context, from the public and private behavior of a young knight to the ground plan of a nunnery, to law of primogeniture, and the sacrament of marriage."[17] Crane's list of medieval examples reminds us that understandings of gender, of masculinity and femininity, affect the way a society wages its wars, builds its edifices, passes its wealth on to future generations, and structures its sexual relations. Gender relations have material consequences. Representations of gender, thus, are not only descriptive but proscriptive: that is, they tell us not only what men or women do, but what they ought, or ought not, to do. And those prescriptions and prohibitions pertain to questions of necessity – to how,

[17] Crane, 6.

when, where, and what must be suffered, and to which particular people must do the suffering.

Such consequences (more tragic for some bodies than they are for others) remind us that our efforts at analyzing masculine gender must do more than merely set out the variety of forms masculinity can, or does, take. As feminist scholarship has long since taught us, an appreciation of the implications of gender requires attention to the material consequences of one representation or another. In Chaucer's *Knight's Tale*, diverse masculinities have very different (yet ultimately related) consequences: the victimization of Palamon and (especially) Arcite sponsors the conquering virility of Theseus. When it does so the *Knight's Tale* allows us to read the dependence of one kind of male virility upon the victimizations of another.

If Chaucer's Knight seems well aware, perhaps even critical, of the victimizations Theseus's masculinity requires of soldiers like Arcite, he seems less analytical toward the image of weeping women to which Theseus's compassionate male rule is also indebted. We return finally, then, to the persistent presence of weeping women throughout Chaucer's *Knight's Tale*. Representations of Emily's shrieking and of the woe of the Argive widows as dangerously excessive inscribe in women a victimization beyond escape while laying the blame for such victimizations at the feet of the women themselves. The image of an inevitably lethal mourning of women,[18] moreover, disciplines the rest of us: we will, like Theseus, order our responses to loss more moderately. Yet a willing acceptance of, even gratitude for, loss – an ability, as Ralph Waldo Emerson once put it, to "build altars to the beautiful necessity" – endangers our abilities to resist injustices, especially those perpetrated by the philosopher King.[19] These representations of Emily and the Argive widows, moreover, imagine women (even former Amazons) as finally unable or forbidden to defend themselves, or to return violence for violence; inscribe in women the necessity of their victimization; and render female suffering as pathetic and unheroic. To make a virtue of such putative necessity would be tragic indeed.

[18] On Chaucer's preoccupation with mourning (and the implications for an important new understanding of Chaucer's poetry), see Fradenburg, "Voice Memorial: Loss and Reparation in Chaucer's Poetry," *Exemplaria* 2.1 (1990), 169–202.
[19] See Ralph Waldo Emerson, "Fate," in *Selections from Ralph Waldo Emerson* (Boston: Houghton Mifflin, 1960), 352.

Negotiating Masculinities:
Erotic Triangles in the *Miller's Tale*

MARTIN BLUM

In Chaucer's *Miller's Tale* a number of things seem to go wrong: characters end up in situations they would rather not find themselves in, private parts are revealed where they are usually not exposed, and a kiss is placed where it was not intended. All these "misunderstandings" are part of the generic makeup of the *Miller's Tale*, which places the narrative in the topsy-turvey world of the fabliau tradition. While these confusions have frequently been taken for granted and have been discussed in their historical function of making the audience laugh, the underlying reasons why these mishaps are in fact perceived as confusions seem to have as frequently eluded critical attention. I want to draw attention to the structural foundation of the *Miller's Tale*, which relies on the use of two erotic triangles. The first consists of Alison, John, and Nicholas, the second of Alison, Nicholas, and Absolon. The significance of these erotic triangles as the departure point of my analysis lies in their ability to register the various obvious and hidden dependencies that exist between the tale's major characters. I will concentrate in particular on the positions the three male characters inhabit within these two constellations. I want to demonstrate that all three male characters are in some way feminized, and thus, according to the Miller, fall out of their role as men. Alison, however, it turns out, is far from the passive female frequently encountered in other texts belonging to the fabliau-tradition. In fact, her take-charge attitude makes her not merely the most successful, but also the most masculine character in both erotic exchanges. Her distinctive position is reflected in the conclusion of the tale: of all the significant characters in the *Miller's Tale*, Alison alone gets away unpunished. She is, it seems, rewarded for being the most successful "man" of the tale, whereas her male counterparts all receive their individual lessons for failing to fulfil their expected roles as men.

Unstable gender roles

One of the obvious signs of the social riot depicted by the fabliaux is that the roles men and women are expected to play in medieval society are frequently upset, which indicates a deeper-running instability of gender roles within the genre.[1] Are these violations of norms as accidental as they look at first glance, or is it possible to identify an alternate subset of rules which designate these very mishaps as infractions? Can these mishaps, in turn, shed light on this instability of gender roles as well as ultimately serve to make sense of at least some of the confusions depicted in the tale?

Symptomatic of this general precariousness is that in particular the roles played by the male characters in the *Miller's Tale* are not filled in any straight-forward way, since none of the men plays only one single part, be it as husband, lover, or rival. In the course of the events each man will be forced to adopt other roles, depending on his degree of involvement as a more active or passive participant in the ensuing action. One of the most obvious consequences of this multiplicity of roles is that each one of them enters into his own negotiation of masculinity. These negotiations are characteristic for the concept of masculinity as an intrinsically troubled category, lacking any biological foundation and thus depending very much on socially and culturally determined negotiations of its own definition:

> Masculinity is, like femininity, a concept that bears only an adventitious relation to biological sex and whose various manifestations collectively constitute the cultural, social, and psychosexual expression of gender. . . . Furthermore, given that almost all anthropologists and ethnographers agree that masculinity appears transculturally as something to be ac-quired, achieved, initiated into – a process often involving painful or even mutilating rituals – there is ample evidence to suggest that there never is, never was, an unproblematic, a natural, or a crisis-free variant.[2]

Drawing on the notion of masculinity as a highly unstable and ultimately arbitrary signifier of manhood, I understand the concept as defined by the sum of a number of individual enactments of maleness, which are culturally and historically sanctioned, or for that matter, disciplined and thus foreclosed from the repertoire of roles expected to be fulfilled by men.[3]

---

1   See for instance Linda Lomperis, "Bodies that Matter in the Court of Late Medieval England and in Chaucer's *Miller's Tale*," *Romanic Review* 86 (1995): 243–64.

2   Abigail Solomon-Godeau, "Male Trouble," in *Constructing Masculinity*, ed. Maurice Berger, Brian Wallis, and Simon Watson (New York and London: Routledge, 1995), 71.

3   Compare also Jo Ann McNamara, "The *Herrenfrage*: The Restructuring of the Gender System, 1050–1150," in *Medieval Masculinities: Regarding Men in the Middle Ages*, ed. Clare A. Lees (Minneapolis: University of Minnesota Press, 1994), 3, who claims that "the masculine gender is fragile and tentative, with weaker biological underpinnings than the

The fabliau's generic characteristic of overthrowing established or expected notions of order finds its equivalent expression in the structure of the first fragment of the *Canterbury Tales* when the Miller disturbs the intended orderly succession of the Knight by the Monk and insists that he has a suitable story to "quite" his predecessor: "I kan a noble tale for the nones, / With which I wol now quite the Knyghtes tale" (I 3126–27). This interruption of the planned sequence of the pilgrim narrators is an indication of the Miller's attempt to disrupt the seemingly clear cut erotic relationships depicted in the *Knight's Tale*. The Miller's own admission that he is "dronke" (3138), and hence cannot be held responsible for his words, allows the suspicion that what is to come is a "cherl's" version of the chivalric tale, his very own, decidedly impolite, perspective on sexual relationships. Despite his facetious claim to tell "a legende and a lyf" (3141), the Miller is quite aware that he is telling a story of a rather different calibre when he lashes out at the Reeve and simultaneously imparts his wisdom on husband-wife relationships: " 'Leve brother Osewold, / Who hath no wyf, he is no cokewold' " (3151–52). The Miller's words are evidence enough that what is to follow will indeed be a "cherles tale" (3169), and that stories of this kind inevitably involve marital unfaithfulness. He sums it up very succinctly in his concluding *sententia*: "An housbonde shal nat been inquisityf / Of Goddes pryvetee, nor of his wyf" (3163–64).

By poking fun at the Reeve, the Miller shows his intimate familiarity with and wisdom about the nature of husband-and-wife relationships, which almost by necessity invite trouble, since in the background there usually lurks a hopeful lover, just waiting for the appropriate moment to make his move and try to gain the wife's sexual favors, which, in case of his success, will turn the husband, as predicted, into the cuckold.[4] The pattern that forms the structural underpinnings of poems and narratives dealing with one man's challenging of another man's claim to a woman is the erotic triangle. As a graphic representation of this tenuous system of social relationships played out in the scenario of the erotic exchange, the triangle assigns a specific position to each of the agents involved. These are, first, the position of the woman as the desired object, second, that of the husband who has a legitimate claim to the woman as object, and who at the same time fulfils the function of a mediator of desire, and, finally, that of the rival attempting to challenge the husband's claim to his object.[5] While both men are seemingly pitted against each other, the one in his pursuit of the

---

feminine." For this reason "it requires strong social support to maintain fictions of superiority based solely on a measure of physical strength."

4   Derek Brewer, "The Couple in Chaucer's Fabliaux," in *The Making of the Couple: The Social Function of Short-Form Medieval Narrative*, ed. Michel Olsen (Odense: Odense University Press, 1991), 129–30.

5   My notion of the triangle as a mimetic representation of the type of erotic relationships discussed in this essay is indebted to René Girard's concept of "triangular desire" in his *Deceit, Desire, and the Novel: Self and Other in Literary Structure*, trans. Yvonne Freccero (Baltimore and London: Johns Hopkins University Press, 1966), 1–52. For a detailed but

lady, the other in his attempt to retain control over her, both men, albeit unknowingly, have also entered into a precarious relationship with each other, based on a bond of rivalry and erotic enticement, of simultaneous aggression and attraction which in their intensity often equal that of their ties with the object. The intricacies of the various bonds existing between both men and the woman betray the locations on the erotic triangle not as fixed, but rather as inherently dynamic and unstable demarcations of the interplay between notions of gender, desire, power, and identification, themselves highly contested *loci* in the economy of erotic exchanges. In my own use of the erotic triangle as an interpretative tool I want to emphasise its nature as a register of instability,[6] noting the constantly shifting positions inhabited by the various characters taking part in this exchange. One of the most salient ramifications of this lack of finite positions within the triangle of desire is that each new development of the narrative upsets its already precariously unstable balance of gender and desire, thus prompting its characters as well as its readers each time to enter into a new negotiation of femininity and masculinity.

Acting like men: the first love triangle

To return to Chaucer's tale, the Miller, instead of leaving it with a simple husband-rival story, ups the ante and, unlike the Knight, presents not one, but two erotic triangles by introducing two hopeful lovers, Nicholas and Absolon, who are both competing for Alison, the young wife of John, the third man. John, the elderly husband, considers himself lucky to have married recently such a young woman, who is likely to arouse other men's envy. While Alison's youth may be very flattering to John's status as a husband, the interest other men are likely to show in his wife at the same time presents an inherent threat to his own position, both as spouse and man, a threat he is only too aware of:

> Jalous he was, and heeld hire narwe in cage,
> For she was wylde and yong, and he was old
> And demed hymself been lik a cokewold.   (3224–26)

The only means to keep his wife under control, and her potential suitors at bay, is closely to guard her since her sexual drive is no match for his own waning powers, a fact the narrator alludes to when he points out John's ignorance of

highly schematic study see also Michel Olsen, *Les Transformations du Triangle Erotique* (Copenhagen: Akademisk Forlag, 1976), 5–60.
[6] I draw here on Eve K. Sedgwick, *Between Men: English Literature and Male Homosocial Desire* (New York: Columbia University Press, 1985), 27, and her critique of Girard's model, which she proposes to modify "as a sensitive register . . . for delineating relationships of power and meaning, and for making graphically intelligible the play of desire and identification by which individuals negotiate with their societies for empowerment."

the proverb that "youthe and elde is often at debaat" (3230), found in the *Facetus*, a collection of maxims attributed to Cato. John, the *senex amans*, may not be familiar with Cato's warning, but he is by no means oblivious to his own physical shortcomings, his incipient impotence, and he quite correctly predicts that his failure to fulfil his proper male role and keep his young wife sexually satisfied will inevitably lead to her unfaithfulness.[7] When the already weak biological underpinnings of men start to fail, the only alternative is to cover up this failure as husband and man.

John's attempts to lock away his young wife may display the traits of a jealous husband, only too aware that there are other, more able males out there, but he can also be seen as acting merely in defense of his own status, since he certainly lacks the rancor of other fabliau-husbands, who often physically abuse their wives. In addition, John also exhibits a caring side, made obvious when Nicholas confronts him with his concocted story about the flood, and John's first care is not about his own safety, but that of his wife:

> "Allas, my wyf!
> And shal she drenche? Allas, myn Alisoun!"
> For sorwe of this he fil almoost adoun.   (3522–24)

The concern John shows for Alison stands in clear opposition to the selfish possessiveness of other husbands in his situation, and almost seems to betray a "maternal" side in him. Against the background of John's lack of sexual power, his jealousy, along with his pronounced protectiveness towards Alison, reveals how a weakening of the biological underpinnings of the male have a profound impact on his social perception: the lack of sexual performance goes hand in hand with an exclusion from the community of more virile men, and in its last consequence means that he is perceived as feminized. The social category for men like John is that of the cuckold. His impotence as a purely physiological phenomenon is perpetuated as a form of social impotence, meaning that he has to adopt a largely passive role. That role designates him as a potential victim, open to the attack of other men. In this respect the older man's place is equal to that of the socially enforced passivity of medieval women, who by reason of their gender were largely barred from taking on more active roles.[8] As a fabliau-figure, the cuckold is punished primarily for not being a "real," meaning primarily a sexually functional, man, and not so much for his jealousy

---

[7]   Vern L. Bullough, "On Being a Male in the Middle Ages," in *Medieval Masculinities*, 41, claims that being sexually active was an indispensable part of maleness: "It was part of his duty to keep his female partners happy and satisfied, and unless he did so, he had failed as a man."

[8]   A particularly strident example of enforced female passivity is given by Constance in Chaucer's *Man of Law's Tale:* "Wommen are born to thraldom and penance, / And to been under mannes governance" (II 286–87).

and possessiveness, which are merely its visible consequences. John becomes the butt of the joke not for what he does, but for what he *is*, essentially a failed man, lacking wholeness. In the grand finale of the tale, John's fall out of his tub and the fracture of his arm are highly symbolic means of punishment: the broken limb can be read as a public confession of his impotence,[9] and his fall pays tribute to his premonition that indeed he was "fallen in the snare" (3231).

Although John's impotence might make him a predominantly passive partner in the relationship with his wife, he is nevertheless very much part of the ensuing action. Even though he sleeps through most of the events, his mere presence necessitates that Nicholas has to go to great lengths to come up with the story of the imminent flood in order to gain access to Alison. John, although he is not aware of it, has become a partner in the first love triangle, consisting of himself, Alison, and Nicholas. In his function as a mediator of desire, John's presence alone, as well as his legitimate claim to his wife, makes it necessary that Nicholas first has to form a bond with him, although for quite ulterior motives. Nicholas has to establish a position of trust with John, which enables him to convince the unsuspecting husband of the "truth" of his premonition about the deluge, and to ensure the success of his strategy. The way to gain the husband's trust is to impart some invaluable piece of information to him, and to stress at the same time the privilege John enjoys by being the only other partner in this bond, based on an exchange of knowledge, as elaborated by Nicholas when he indicates that he has something important to say:

> "Fecche me drynke,
> And after wol I speke in pryvetee
> Of certeyn thyng that toucheth me and thee.
> I wol telle it noon oother man, certeyn." (3492–95)

Nicholas's ploy, of course, falls on fertile ground since by means of his pretended insanity he makes sure that John will be receptive to the knowledge entrusted to him. The traits John displays when he is worried about the well-being of his lodger are remarkably similar to the "maternal" concern he shows towards his wife. His unselfish and ultimately unsuspecting nature makes it easy to manipulate him, and furthermore to ensure that he will honor the secrecy of the details of the flood, a scheme that is imperative for the success of Nicholas's ruse. Knowledge or its absence becomes symptomatic in this context for the widely different positions of power held by both men. Nicholas's effectiveness as a ruthless and skillful, but above all well-informed, manipulator of knowledge, which merits him the epithet "hende," ensures that he can achieve his goal of sexual satisfaction, and thus prove his "manhood," while John, on the other hand, admits to his impotence and powerlessness by

---

[9]   See Derek Brewer, *Chaucer: The Poet as Storyteller* (London: Macmillan, 1984), 114.

conceding his ignorance.[10] The dismay he voices about Nicholas's studies shows not only his anti-intellectual attitude, but is also an admission of his own powerlessness, which designates him as the victim *par excellence*:

> "Men sholde nat knowe of Goddes pryvetee.
> Ye, blessed be alwey a lewed man
> That noght but oonly his bileve kan!" (3454–56)

Nicholas, it seems, is in charge here. His plan, once put in motion, runs with the smooth precision of a well-oiled clock, and it certainly has its desired effect on John, who will spend the rest of the time fast asleep until his rude awakening.

With the jealous husband safely out of the way, Nicholas seems to embody the successful, aggressive, "go-get-it" type of male, who can achieve anything if he sets his mind to it, regardless of the consequences for others. But I want to reconsider here for a moment the events that lead up to this situation. It is not entirely by his own design that Nicholas resorts to the trick he plays on John, since he has had an earlier chance to try his luck with Alison when her husband was away at Osney on business. Nicholas shows little hesitation when the opportunity arises, and immediately starts his advances on Alison: "And prively he caughte hire by the queynte, /. . . And heeld hire harde by the haunchebones" (3276, 3279). In his first attempt, however, Nicholas has definitely gone too far and has overstepped the bounds of appropriate behavior. His approach to Alison is coarse, violent, and above all, threatening, which makes his advances look more like the attack of an animal than the wooing of a lovesick suitor. Alison's resistance to his brutality pays tribute to her tenacity not to accept Nicholas's terms, and instead forces him into a negotiation which takes her own wishes into account as a condition for granting him her sexual favors. Her strategy proves to be astonishingly successful and his demeanor immediately changes: "This Nicholas gan mercy for to crye, / And spak so faire, and profred him so faste" (3288–89). Nicholas's sudden change in attitude shows that Alison represents much more than a passive object of exchange, who is passed from one man to another. Her determination to change the rules of the game assigns her a position of power which enables her to curtail Nicholas's aggressive masculinity and forces him to make concessions, first by putting off his plans until a more suitable opportunity arises, and secondly by concocting the story to deceive her husband. Nicholas, it seems, has found his master in an eighteen-year-old woman. While John has been comparatively easy to deal with, Alison, on the other hand, shows a great deal of dexterity as an independent player in the market-place of erotic exchanges, and her refusal to surrender unconditionally to male sexual aggression consequently

---

[10] Sedgwick, 50, sees ignorance as the distinctive feature of the cuckold: "Most characteristically, the difference of power occurs in the form of a difference of knowledge: the cuckold is not even supposed to know that he is in such a relationship."

destabilises the previously assumed firmly demarcated positions within the first erotic triangle. By offering her resistance and taking an active part in Nicholas's plans, Alison trespasses into male territory and usurps a more masculine role than Nicholas has bargained for. A meek, passive, somewhat feminized husband might be no match for him, but a rebellious and active woman is indeed able to show him his limits.

To complicate matters for Nicholas even more, Absolon, a second hopeful young lover, appears on the scene and demands his fair share of attention since he also has set his eyes on Alison. Absolon, however, demonstrates an entirely different type of male behavior from his competitor. Nicholas's aggressive pursuit of his goal, based on his strategy of manipulating his opponents, stands in sharp contrast to Absolon's seemingly ineffectual flaunting of the role of the courtly lover. Instead of concentrating on the end of his pursuit, sexual satisfaction, Absolon makes the means his end. Any action he takes to win his lady becomes self-serving. Instead of being a lover, he derives his satisfaction from impersonating one. There is even some doubt whether it is really a sexual union he is after since it seems that a kiss is reward enough for him: "Thanne kysse me, syn it may be no bet" (3716). Similarly, his serenading underneath Alison's bedroom window makes little practical sense as long as she is there together with her husband. The only thing he achieves is to declare his love to Alison, and more importantly to declare himself a lover. It is clearly his intention before he sets off to "tellen al / My love-longynge" (3678–79), to Alison and to everyone else who happens to be within earshot, one might add. The candid nature of his approach, which stands in stark contrast to Nicholas's "derne love," exemplifies the importance Absolon places on his acting out of his favorite part, which almost by necessity demands an audience. Absolon's self-definition as a male is entirely based on this notion of performing the part of the courtly lover. He even manages to use some of his other activities to pursue his "paramours" (3354). Most notable among them is his role as a "real" actor, in which he enacts the part of Herod (3384) to show Alison "his lightnesse and maistrye" (3383). In addition, he makes use of his more mundane chores, such as waving the censer during mass, to court the ladies present, as he does of his playing of the guitar in any pub in town, that has "any gaylard tappestere" (3336). All these attempts to court pretty women are symptomatic for Absolon's behavior. Flaunting and role-playing are second nature to him; instead of defining himself, like Nicholas, as a man by his activity, in order to "make things happen," Absolon's masculinity is primarily defined by the *performance* of a number of activities, such as his acting, his singing, and his dancing, which are all part of his favorite role as the refined courtly lover. The culmination of his attempts to become a credible lover is the selection of the text of the biblical Song of Songs (3698–3707)[11] for his performance

[11] See Robert E. Kaske, "The *Canticum Canticorum* in the *Miller's Tale*," *SP* 59 (1962): 479–500.

underneath Alison's window. As the outcome of the tale shows, however, all his efforts are in vain: Absolon's aspirations are rudely snuffed out, and the dream of the courtly lover is revealed as a failed one.

The reasons for Absolon's eventual failure are to be found less in his lack of ability to perform any of his individual activities, than in his own misconceptions, both about the nature of Alison's wishes and, more importantly, about his own notion that impersonating a lover is an adequate substitute for actually being one. The first mistake that Absolon makes is that he fails to acknowledge that John's house in Oxford is as far from a noble household as Alison is from a courtly lady. In this setting,[12] dominated by carpenters, their wives, and student-lodgers, his courtly manners are quite simply out of place. This incongruity between his own, assumed role and the social class of his "audience" is also continued in the character of Absolon, whose duties as barber and clerk are hardly compatible with the persona of the courtly lover into which he tries to fashion himself. The other reason for Absolon's failure is equally tied to his person. As signaled by his biblical namesake,[13] Absolon personifies a type of male beauty that is as much out of place in the decidedly uncourtly setting as his previously mentioned occupations. A look at the text reveals that the Miller's description of his physical attributes (3314–25) is heavily dependent on the tradition of the *effictio*,[14] which conventionally served as a model to describe female beauty. Apart from his fashionable clothing and his long, blond, curly hair, which merit him the epithet "joly," his rosy complexion and grey eyes in particular provide the feminizing touch to his appearance. As E. Talbot Donaldson phrased it many years ago, it is by "possessing a 'rode' – that is a peaches-and-cream complexion recommended by fourteenth-century Elizabeth Ardens, [that] Absolon places himself in the almost exclusive company of Middle English damsels."[15] Although he defies the stereotype of the passive effeminate, since the pursuit of his "paramours" seems to keep him busy during the day and for the best part of the night, his activity is nevertheless largely ineffectual, since at no point is there any confirmation of the success of his efforts. Absolon's failure as a lover, and by implication as a man, can ultimately be attributed to his reluctance to seek actual sexual satisfaction, instead of merely pretending to do so. An explanation for the curiously asexual nature of

---

[12] On the aspect of class in the tale see Lee Patterson, " 'No man his reson herde': Peasant Consciousness, Chaucer's Miller, and the Structure of the *Canterbury Tales*," *The South Atlantic Quarterly* 86 (1987): 469–72.

[13] Paul E. Beichner, C. S. C., "Absolon's Hair," *MS* 12 (1950): 222–33.

[14] On the rhetorical tradition of the *effictio* / *notatio* as a model for the description of female beauty see Valerie Allen, "Blaunche on Top and Alisoun on Bottom," in *A Wyf Ther Was: Essays in Honour of Paule Mertens-Fonck*, ed. Juliette Dor (Liège: Université de Liège, 1992), 23–29.

[15] E. Talbot Donaldson, "Idiom of Popular Poetry in the *Miller's Tale*," in *Explication as Criticism: Selected Papers from the English Institute 1941–1952*, ed. W. K. Wimsatt, Jr. (New York: Columbia University Press, 1963), 39.

all his "paramours" can be found in the Miller's comments on his person, when he varyingly refers to Absolon as "myrie child" (3325), or at the moment of his humiliation as "a child that is ybete" (3759). These comments are an indication of Absolon's perception as an adolescent, rather than as a man. His playfulness and his feminine appearance pay tribute to his child-like state as a pretty but largely inexperienced boy, which removes him, like John, from the sphere of a sexually defined masculinity.

Failing as men: the second love triangle

For the second love-triangle, Absolon's appearance upsets the previously established positions within the first constellation. It forces the participants into a new negotiation to define their relations once more. With his claim to Alison's favors challenged by Absolon, Nicholas suddenly finds himself in the role of the mediator, and, like John before him, he has to defend his position against his competitor. This time, however, the other man poses no real threat, since Alison makes it sufficiently clear that Absolon's antics do little to make him a serious contender for her love. Alison's rather rude dismissal of the unwanted suitor and her threat to "caste a ston" (3712) echo her previously exhibited determination, and, if anything, confirm her refusal to be the passive object of exchange between men. These men have precious little to say in this exchange since, again at a crucial moment, Alison changes the rules of the game and leaves no doubt that the final decision is up to her. Nicholas's plans for his night with Alison might initially be interrupted by the appearance of the annoying, lovesick youth, but of greater consequence is the shift of power that simultaneously takes place within the relationship of the three characters: Alison becomes a more and more dominant part in this exchange, while Nicholas, previously nothing short of the embodiment of the domineering male, quite unobtrusively fades into the background.

The plot of the tale is now dominated by the verbal exchange between Absolon and Alison, and it is entirely on her own initiative that Alison tells the unwanted lover off. She is to be credited with the idea to get rid of Absolon once and for all by granting him his kiss. During the whole exchange, Nicholas does not even so much as get a word in, and he finds himself suddenly reduced to the role of the passive watcher of the spectacle when Alison announces to him her intention to perform the joke on what in reality is *his* competitor: "And unto Nicholas she seyde stille, / 'Now hust, and thou shalt laughen al thy fille' " (3721–22). The joke works out as planned, and Absolon's disgust, caused in part by his confusion about who precisely it was he has kissed, is the visible sign that the positions within the second triangle have been upset by Alison's refusal to accept her expected passive role. Absolon's outrage and disgust after "he kiste hir naked ers" (3734) can be traced back to the ensuing general confusion about who is who in this exchange of kisses. Although he in fact kissed a part of Alison's anatomy, the Miller's comment, "For wel he wiste a womman hath no berd" (3737), suggests that to Absolon the only plausible explanation of what has happened is that he has kissed another man.[16] His frantic attempts to cleanse himself after the encounter by rubbing his lips are supposed to erase all traces of physical contact with another male.

His confusion is due in large part to his sexual inexperience, and his interpretation that "a thyng al rough and long yherd" (3738) is a part of a male body is compounded by his expectation that females in this situation are, at best, passive spectators, and not the instigators of jokes. This fact is borne out by almost all of the other extant versions of the *Miller's Tale*, which adhere to the conventional distribution of power, activity, and gender within the triangular structure, since in these examples the figure represented by Nicholas in both cases exposes himself to his competitor.[17] The consequence of Chaucer's change is epitomised by Alison's "Tehee!" (3740), which flies into the face of Absolon, who is caught out by the confusion. By substituting a woman for a man, Chaucer has once more upset the conventional expectations of male and female behavior. By making Alison the perpetrator and thus the author of the first joke, Chaucer has invested Alison with a degree of power usually reserved for the male characters of the tale, and she thus acts in a way far more masculine than any of the other males present. At this moment her position in relation to the other characters reflects very much that of the active instead of the passive party, a place which, I would argue, she has traded with Nicholas, who in turn finds himself in the largely passive role of the spectator of the spectacle, merely acting as a commentator on Absolon's misdirected kiss: " 'A berd! A berd!' quod hende Nicholas, / 'By Goddes corpus, this goth faire and weel' " (3742–43). Nicholas's gloating over his opponent's blunder underscores his position on the margin, removed from any significant development of the plot. His reinstatement as an active part of the tale, however, occurs soon afterwards, when the call of nature doubles as his own wake-up call:

> This Nicholas was risen for to pisse,
> And thoughte he wolde amenden al the jape;
> He sholde kisse his ers er that he scape.   (3798–3800)

The idea of sex with Alison suspended, Nicholas thinks he can do one better, and to add insult to injury, make Absolon actually kiss another man's body. The question is, however, whether Nicholas is for once not too clever and gets

---

16 Contrastive readings of this scene are offered by V. A. Kolve, *Chaucer and the Imagery of Narrative: The First Five Canterbury Tales* (Stanford: Stanford University Press, 1984), 194–97, and H. Marshall Leicester, Jr., "Newer Currents in Psychoanalytic Criticism, and the Difference 'It' Makes: Gender and Desire in the *Miller's Tale*," *ELH* 61 (1994): 487. Kolve and Leicester both claim that Absolon is aware that he has kissed a woman.
17 See for instance Peter G. Beidler, "Art and Scatology in the *Miller's Tale*," *ChauR* 12 (1977): 91–94.

carried away by his own "jape." It can be argued that his joke actually cuts both ways, since not only will Absolon be kissing another man, but Nicholas in return will also be the recipient of another man's kiss.[18] By substituting his own body for that of Alison, he has maneuvred himself into the place of woman, a position that allows him virtually no control over what is going to happen to his own, male body. Moreover, Nicholas's prank, a seemingly ingenious duplication of Alison's, puts him into a passive role, since all he does is cite Alison and confirm her as the true author of the joke, an act which undercuts his newly resumed activity. Against that activity, his fart is a somewhat ineffectual gesture, since he does not take into account that Absolon has learned from his previous experience.

Absolon's visit to Daun Gerveys brings him back not only with the "hoote kultour" (3776), but also with a completely novel kind of knowledge. The experience of the first kiss has not merely taken the fun out of his role-playing, but moreover has initiated a learning process with the effect that his notion of performance as an adequate substitute for action is once and for all dispelled. Giving up old habits, however, does not come easy, as Absolon's complaint shows:

> "Allas," quod he, "allas, I ne hadde ybleynt!"
> His hoote love was coold and al yqueynt;
> For fro that tyme that he hadde kist hir ers,
> Of paramours he sette nat a kers.   (3753–56)

His "healing"[19] not only has the consequence that he swears off his "para-mours," but also stirs him to action, which becomes obvious when he pays his friend the smith a visit. He ignores Daun Gerveys's ribbing about some "gay gerl" (3769) since Absolon has other things on his mind. The sole purpose of his visit is to borrow the weapon of his revenge, the "hoote kultour."

Upon Absolon's return, Nicholas, assuming that he is still dealing with the incompetent flaunter, makes the serious mistake of putting himself into a vulnerable position, and in anticipation of a repetition of the first kiss prepares to answer the kiss with the fart. Nicholas's plan, however, fails miserably since he is now dealing with a revenge-seeking opponent instead of the inexperi-enced, easily duped youth of before:

---

18 For the implications of the same-sex kiss on the delimitations of masculine and feminine positions see Glenn Burger, "Kissing the Pardoner," *PMLA* 107 (1992): 1147–48.

19 On Absolon's healing from his lovesickness see Edward C. Schweitzer, "The Misdi-rected Kiss and the Lover's Malady in Chaucer's *Miller's Tale*," in *Chaucer in the Eighties*, ed. Julian N. Wasserman and Robert J. Blanch (Syracuse: Syracuse University Press, 1986), 223–33.

And he was redy with his iren hoot,
And Nicholas amydde the ers he smoot.
Of gooth the skyn an hande-brede aboute,
The hoote kultour brende so his toute,
And for the smert he wende for to dye.   (3809–13)

Nicholas, it turns out, has to pay dearly for his joke. His burning is severe and his pain excruciating. The hot coulter, although intended by Absolon as a malicious response to Alison's "tehee," has, nevertheless, in the narrative economy of the tale, met the intended target. Nicholas has not only made the grave mistake of underestimating his adversary, but also of transgressing his possibilities as a male by offering his own body to another man in a sexually charged scene, an act of transgression that the fabliau forestalls. On the textual level, Nicholas's quotation of Alison's joke is a sign that his own body, used in the joke's execution, has become the citation of another, of a female body, and thus a troubled version of a male body. This possibility, namely that a man's body becomes the object of desire for another man, is not tolerated by the narrative, and is consequently foreclosed by means of the punishment.[20] And yet, it is precisely this possibility which is hinted at early on in the beginning of the tale when the audience learns that there is also another side to this clever student, who is at times "lyk a mayden meke for to see" (3202). Despite his demonstrated ingeniousness when it comes to using John's credulity for his own end, Nicholas, by blindly following Alison's example, is equally prone to being manipulated into a situation where he relinquishes control over his own body, and thus leaves his masculinity to the discretion of others, who will show no mercy and take advantage of his own position of weakness. With his severely burned backside, Nicholas joins ranks with the other two males in the tale and has to accept that in his failure he is no different from them.

Subverting masculinity: the case of Alison

In contrast to her male counterparts, Alison is the only character in the *Miller's Tale* who escapes unscathed from this turmoil. Although early on in the tale it seems that she is just a pawn in the game, fought over by two men, she very soon makes it clear that she is not willing to accept this role quietly. On the contrary, in the course of the tale it becomes evident that Alison takes an increasingly active part in the events, and finally beats all three men at their own game. The Miller gives an inkling of Alison's vitality when he introduces

---

[20] On the discursive strategy of foreclosing transgressive sexual desires see Judith Butler, *Bodies that Matter: On the Discursive Limits of "Sex"* (New York and London: Routledge, 1993), 111–18.

her and in the course of her description makes reference to a number of animals, such as the weasel (3234), the swallow (3258), the kid, the calf (3260), and the colt (3263), which in their wild and untamed nature highlight one of her most significant traits: her determination and her unwillingness to submit under someone else's dictate. This characteristic is borne out for the first time when she fends off Nicholas's initial advances, and she is once more compared to the young colt:

> And she sproong as a colt dooth in the trave,
> And with hir heed she wryed faste awey,
> And seyde, "I wol nat kisse thee, by my fey!"   (3282–84)

Alison's refusal to accept Nicholas's terms sets the tone for their future relationship: if Nicholas wants to gain her sexual favors, it will happen only on her terms. Nicholas's subsequent compliance with her demands shows that her determination proves her right and serves only to strengthen her position. It is, however, in her dealing with Absolon that Alison shows the true extent of her ability to take charge and to pursue her own interests. In this second triangle Alison, in effect, assumes Nicholas's role, and thus acts in a far more "masculine" way than he himself does by taking on what is essentially *his* competitor. In so doing she fulfils two functions at the same time: on the one hand she is still the object of Absolon's desire, but on the other hand she has also become the mediator of his desire. By assuming the control over her own body and making it unattainable to the wooing would-be lover, she takes on what is usually the role of the male, exercising his control over a woman's body. Alison's defiance of the stereotype of the passive and available female whose possession is negotiated between two men is precisely the reason for the conflation of both functions, and is thus at the heart of the ensuing confusion of gender roles in the tale.[21] As a woman who shows that she has a will of her own, as well as the determination to get what she wants, Alison has no need for a male "helper" to fend off competitors. Nicholas's conspicuous silence during the episode is testimony enough to his lack of importance in this exchange. Alison develops strength in the tale, which places her in sharp contrast to Nicholas: while he initially appears to be the one in charge, and hence the most active player, his dominant role soon becomes challenged by Alison, who subsequently beats the men at their own game and almost monopolizes the action. Not only does she demonstrate to all three men her independence, but, more importantly, by subverting the roles she is expected to play, she debunks

---

21 In contrast to Lomperis, 253, who essentially confirms the notion of fixed gender roles and explains Alison's apparent masculinity by suggesting that she is in reality an "impersonated woman, a man in woman's clothing," I maintain that the issue of masculinity is not necessarily tied to sexed positions.

the myth of masculinity as being exclusively tied to the male gender. The reason for her success may well be found in her determination to defy the very roles all three men have designed for her: she is neither John's idea of the young and controllable wife, nor Absolon's courtly lady, nor the available mistress to Nicholas, the deft lover. What unites the three men is less their pursuit of the same woman than their underestimation of Alison's virile womanhood, a mistake which contributes to their individual failures as men, so succinctly summed up by the Miller:

> Thus swyved was this carpenteris wyf,
> For al his kepyng and his jalousye,
> And Absolon hath kist hir nether ye,
> And Nicholas is scalded in the towte. (3850–53)

No doubt, the conclusion to the tale, which doubles as the Miller's "moral" *lectio,* brings home to his male fellow pilgrims the knowledge that masculinity is a preciously tender thing indeed: one wrong move and its foundation on "fictions of superiority," to invoke Jo Ann McNamara's words once more, will expose them as the sham they are. All three men in the tale are guilty of exposing the true nature of these fictions as arbitrary conventions of behavior, which can only be upheld if their trespass is penalized: John's "swyved wyf," as well as his broken arm, are the punishment for his being a sexually dysfunctional man who has taken on more than he can handle. Absolon gets a lesson in the physical reality of human bodies which he, in his enactment of the courtly lover, so desperately tried to avoid. Nicholas, the clever manipulator of husbands, receives a painful impression on his backside which, although it will seriously interfere with his ability to sit down and study, will nevertheless add a new dimension to his existing *corpus* of knowledge. While it may be easy to "bigyle" (3300) a carpenter, overestimating one's own cleverness and under-estimating a woman like Alison might prove to be equally devastating to one's own position as man. But I also want to suggest that the Miller not merely punishes the shortcomings of John, Absolon, and Nicholas in their roles as men, but that he also creates his fabliau world as a "little hell"[22] in order to bring each of his male characters back in line by subjecting each of them to some form of "painful or even mutilating ritual," a necessary prerequisite for their (re)initiation into manhood. The project of the *Miller's Tale* shows that masculinity requires carefully controlled narratives, serving as the parameters to define the socially acceptable behavior for men. Breaking the rules is not to be

---

22 Paul A. Olson, "Poetic Justice in the *Miller's Tale,*" *MLQ* 24 (1963): 234, also argues that each of the male characters receives the form of punishment specific to his transgression, but differs by identifying the deadly sins of lechery, pride, and avarice as reasons for the punishment.

tolerated, and the "failed" man is subjected to an individual and painful learning process, which will inscribe the sentence on his own body, driving home the fact that masculinity is never to be taken for granted, but always a state of existence to be carefully negotiated.

Performing the Perverse:
The Abuse of Masculine Power
in the *Reeve's Tale*

DANIEL F. PIGG

Much of the scholarship on the *Reeve's Tale* has called attention to its dark tone and revengeful actions. John Plummer observed that "what persists in the *Reeve's Tale* is a slight but real sense of injustice, of pathos, and bitterness of afterthought which fits uncomfortably with the fabliau form."[1] What is often regarded as verbal and artistic violence against the teller of another tale, the Miller, should more accurately be attributed to Chaucer's attempting to negotiate issues of masculinity well-known in the Middle Ages through the competing discourses that we call the *Miller's Tale* and the *Reeve's Tale*. The reaction of the Reeve to the *Miller's Tale* demonstrates that the Reeve's masculinity has been threatened. The tale that he tells, differing from its primary French source in several key moments, is his response to that threat in ways that both confirm suspicions about his own status as a male and become a mark of his revenge. In the introductory essay to *Performativity and Performance*, Andrew Parker and Eve Kosofsky Sedgwick begin with two questions: "When is saying something doing something? And how is saying something doing something?"[2] These are important questions to consider in the *Reeve's Tale*, for as I assert below, the verbal performance of violence in the act of fiction-making is equivalent to an actual violent encounter.

---

[1] Plummer, "Hooly Chirches Blood: Simony and Patrimony in Chaucer's *Reeve's Tale*," *ChauR* 18 (1983): 58.
[2] Parker and Sedgwick, *Performativity and Performance* (New York: Routledge, 1995), 1.

The issue central to discussions of medieval masculinity, according to Carol Clover and Thomas Laqueur, concerns performance in the gender role.[3] Both the Reeve in his prologue and the two young scholars in his tale must come to terms with their gender roles, yet the way they handle their performance moves the conception of masculinity into the perverse: literal and symbolic rape. In this prologue and tale, Chaucer explores the dark side of masculine power and identity. "Quiting," an act of literary agency and of generic determination in Fragment I, is very much connected with the medieval notions of masculinity as well as with tale telling.

In this essay I assert that in the *Reeve's Tale* Chaucer presents an image of the perversion of the power of masculinity by directly connecting both the action of fiction-making and the fiction itself with performativity and performance. I examine the construction of masculinity in the *Reeve's Tale* as a way of understanding one facet of experience, particularly an abusive one, very much like rape, where gendered identity becomes an issue in an attempt to preserve power as well as destroy it. In developing my ideas, I shall consider first certain ideological underpinnings to my discussion, then examine the attitudes and actions of the Reeve and the two Solar Hall scholars in his tale. I shall, return finally, to the Reeve to show how in "saying" his tale he is not merely talking, but also metaphorically "doing" something quite perverse to his adversary, the Miller.

Ideological underpinnings

Before examining the *Reeve's Tale*, we need to consider the ideological notions of gender that underlie the text. In the last five years, many feminist scholars have shifted part of their focus in recovering the history of women's experience in the Middle Ages. In the introductory essay to *Medieval Masculinities: Regarding Men in the Middle Ages*, Clare A. Lees notes that the presentation of women is inextricably bound up with men and that there are "many different male experiences that still need to be recovered."[4] Without question much medieval scholarship has focused on male writers and male characters, yet for the most part, attention has not been paid to their gender in any directly psychological or biological way; maleness was merely assumed as a way of approaching other points connected with male power in the family, political alliances, feudal relationships, and religious vocations. Work by such scholars as Carol J. Clover, Nancy F. Partner, Clare A. Lees, Vern L. Bullough, James

---

3   Clover, "Regardless of Sex: Men, Women, and Power in Early Northern Europe," *Speculum* 68 (1993): 363–87; Laqueur, *Making Sex: Body and Gender from the Greeks to Freud* (Cambridge: Harvard University Press, 1990).

4   "Introduction," *Medieval Masculinities: Regarding Men in the Middle Ages*, ed. Clare A. Lees (Minneapolis: University of Minnesota Press, 1994), xvi.

Brundage, and Jeffrey Cohen has recently demonstrated the need to re-examine the presentation of masculinity in medieval texts in general and Chaucer's text in particular.[5]

One of the most significant issues in the representation of masculinity is the ideological understanding of the human body in medical or biological terms, as Joan Cadden has recently demonstrated.[6] Earlier, in a groundbreaking study, Thomas Laqueur demonstrated that to the eighteenth century a single-sex model was dominant in western society. Drawing on the works of Galen and Aristotle, he demonstrates that the perfect image of the human body was the male body; women were perceived as inferior or underdeveloped males.[7] As Laqueur notes, biology was tied to power: "In a public world that was overwhelmingly male, the one-sex model displayed what was already massively evident in culture more generally: *man* is the measure of all things, and woman does not exist as an ontologically distinct category."[8] Carol Clover extends Laqueur's study in Old Norse literature to show that a dividing line existed in society as a result of this ideological model.[9] The perfect form was the virile male. Non-assertive women, children (even boys before adulthood), eunuchs, and impotent males occupied a space of "other" in the model. Males, in particular, had an unstable relationship to this model. As they grew older, their status moved to "other" as a result of biological changes. Models for the study of gender in the twentieth century favor a distinction between sex and gender and also differentiate between essentialist and constructionist models of gender (nature vs. nurture), but, as Joyce E. Salisbury notes, "medieval thinkers did see biology as destiny."[10] A civilization that would allow an annulment on the basis of impotence duly affirmed by an examination by medical experts clearly demonstrates the importance of performance, and probably contributed to the anxiety of that performance.[11] Vern L. Bullough states the issue directly: "Though what constitutes manhood has varying definitions according to a

---

[5]   Clover, "Regardless," 363–87; Partner, "No Sex, No Gender," *Speculum* 68 (1993): 419–43; Lees, ed., *Medieval Masculinities*; "On Being Male in the Middle Ages," *Medieval Masculinities: Regarding Men in the Middle Ages* (Minneapolis: University of Minnesota Press, 1994), 31–45; Bullough and Brundage, eds., *Handbook of Medieval Sexuality* (New York: Garland, 1996); Cohen, "Medieval Masculinities," *Interscripta*, October 1993.

[6]   Cadden, *Meaning of Sex Difference in the Middle Ages: Medicine, Science, and Culture* (Cambridge: Cambridge University Press, 1993).

[7]   Laqueur, 27–62.

[8]   Laqueur, 62.

[9]   Clover, 365–81.

[10]   Salisbury, "Gendered Sexuality," *Handbook of Medieval Sexuality*, ed. Vern L. Bullough and James A. Brundage (New York: Garland, 1996), 81.

[11]   Jacqueline Murray, "Hiding Behind the Universal Man: Male Sexuality in the Middle Ages," *Handbook of Medieval Sexuality*, ed. Vern L. Bullough and James A. Brundage (New York: Garland, 1996), 139.

society and culture or time period, the most simplistic way of defining it is a triad: impregnating women, protecting dependents, and seeming to provide to one's family."[12]

Oswald's male honor

The prologue to the *Reeve's Tale* may well be one of the most introspective of all the prologues. While we do find personal comments preceding other tales, such as the Merchant's references to his marital problems, except for the Wife of Bath and the Pardoner we do not find any character but the Reeve fully personalizing any tale to himself and particularly noting his own inadequacies, all of which he announces. No doubt hearing a tale about John's cuckolding is provocative enough in terms of gender, age, and vocational identification, but he might have perceived what Laura Kendrick observes as an icon of castration in the careful construction of the tubs in the roof of the carpenter's house.[13] The Reeve describes himself in biological terms to be an aged man no longer able to bring physical violence on the Miller. His "fodder is now forage" (I 3868); he has white hair and a moldy heart, yet he notes of old men that "in oure wyl ther stiketh evere a nayl" (3877). He is now in a state of oxymoronic rotten ripeness, but he is still able to articulate a level of emotions given to an old man: "Avauntyng, liyng, anger, coveitise" (3884). Any of them could become a driving force both behind and within the fiction of tale telling. All of these are sublimations of his own sexual energies. He has "alwey a coltes tooth" (3888), has the ability to speak "right in his cherles termes" (3917), and utters a prayer for physical violence to the Miller. Believing that his own masculinity has been called into question, he has no alternative except to act – to perform. His own performance of his masculinity can only be verbal, yet it is equivalent to fighting, to "bleryng of a proud milleres ye" (3865). The Reeve's honor as a man is at stake, and he punches back.

Performing in the tale

Stewart Justman notes that the tale itself has to do with maintaining male honor, and that honor is demonstrated by the way Symkin has constructed his house-hold.[14] Much of the world Symkin creates is shot through with irony, some of which has caused scholars to miss the abusive and perverse male perform-ance by concentrating instead on the bogus and superficial world of social

---

12 Bullough, "On Being Male," 34.
13 Kendrick, *Chaucerian Play: Comedy and Control in the Canterbury Tales* (Berkeley: University of California Press, 1988), 6–8, 67–68.
14 Justman, *"The Reeve's Tale* and the Honor of Men," *Studies in Short Fiction* 32 (1995): 14.

superiority. Symkin's wife affects the forms of a noble lady even though she is "digne as water in a dich, / And ful of hoker and of bisemare" (3964–65). That his daughter is a "wench" who has a "kamus nose and eyen greye as glas, / With buttokes brode and brestes rounde and hye" (3974–75) certainly makes her sound like the lusty women of many of the fabliau. But throughout the tale, the implicit concern of Symkin is to set up a household whose patriarchal control is manifested through his own biological superiority and class consciousness. His family becomes the central emblem of his own masculine self, and it is precisely patriarchal control that he loses through theft and rape, both crimes against property, and by extension, against himself. That the tale concerns itself with law in its own perverse way, as Paul Olsen and Joseph Baird have noted, should again call our attention to the fact that laws were produced to maintain the power of male authority.[15]

After Aleyn and John arrive at the mill, they desire to see what the milling process entails. During the experience, which is fraught with sexual innuendo, as Ian Lancashire has noted, the Miller releases the horse, which immediately runs toward the fen to make "wehee" with the mares.[16] Here we meet one of Chaucer's most intriguing changes from his primary French source *Le meunier et les .II. clers*. Changing the gender of the horse to male has usually been interpreted in connection with an anticipation of the lusty play of the bedroom involving John, Aleyn, Malyne, and Symkin's wife. Certainly, animal imagery appears frequently in Chaucer's fabliau, but here it is ambiguous. Its associations could be those of positive, natural activity as connected with Alison in the *Miller's Tale* or perhaps contain shades of darker revelation in the destruction of Symkin's family romance. Sandy Feinstein, examining the history of animal references in the Middle Ages, suggests that the scholars' horse probably was a gelding and that such an animal would retain some interest in the mares but not be able to perform sexually.[17] If so, then the horse would represent the Reeve instead of the scholars, with desire and ability being disconnected. Whatever the horse's actual association may be, the change of gender alone suggests that performance is a key issue. The horse demonstrates his own performance, though it is shrouded in mystery for us, just as all of the males in the tale, and the teller himself, are shrouded through literal and symbolic means.

The events in the bedroom are more revealing of the performative abuse of masculine power. In both the French source and in Chaucer's tale, one of the clerks decides to approach the Miller's daughter, but in Chaucer's text, he ravishes her in specifically legal terms. Aleyn notes that "gif a man in a point be agreved, / That in another he sal be releved" (4181–82). In the French original, the daughter takes part in her own sexual encounter by opening the

[15] Olsen, "Law and the *Reeve's Tale*," *NM* 70 (1969): 679–83; Bairn, "*The Reeve's Tale*: Chaucer's Measure for Measure," *SP* 59 (1962): 1–17.
[16] Lancashire, "Sexual Innuendo in the *Reeve's Tale*," *ChauR* 6 (1972): 159–70.
[17] Feinstein, "The *Reeve's Tale*: About that Horse," *ChauR* 26 (1991): 100–05.

bin where she is locked for safe keeping. She is thus a type of the fabliau woman, as Tamarah Kohanski observes.[18] Chaucer, however, represents the start of the encounter differently. Depending upon how ironically one reads the sequence as well as the entire tale, very different meanings can present themselves:

> This wenche lay uprighte and faste slepte,
> Til he so ny was, er she myghte espie,
> That it had been to late for to crie,
> And shortly for to seyn, they were aton.   (4194–97)

Medieval law required the person against whom the crime of rape was committed to raise the "hue and cry," just as John did when he found the horse had disappeared.[19] The scene described in the Chaucerian text sounds very much like a rape, a crime that places much weight on the victim to prove. Henry de Bracton noted a legal process, quite lengthy in its administration, which began with the victim raising the hue and cry.[20] Since Malyne cannot do that, the incident in the sight of the legal authorities does not constitute a rape. Chaucer, however, would have known the law regarding rape, and he encoded it into the incident.

That "they were aton" (4197) seems on the surface to mitigate against regarding the meeting as a rape, but as Kohanski notes, we do not know what Malyne felt about the incident.[21] Medieval authorities, obviously male, sometimes contended that the woman's response might change during the rape. The writer of *On Human Generation*, a pseudo-Galenic text, notes that

> If in the beginning the act displeases the woman raped, yet it pleases [her] because of the weakness of the flesh. For there are two wills in humans, namely the rational and the natural, which we often see fighting within us.[22]

Even law, again male conceived, saw duplicity in female action and desire regarding rape. A statute of 1382 provided husbands or fathers the right of redress against a rapist even if the act were consensual.[23] How the victim might have felt seems to have had little impact on the interpretation of the experience. That Malyne weeps when Alayn departs might reflect her sadness at her lover's departure, but could also be seen as a recognition that she could not possibly

---

[18] Kohanski, "In Search of Malyne," *ChauR* 27 (1993): 228–38.
[19] John Marshall Carter, *Rape in Medieval England: An Historical and Sociological Study* (New York: University Press of America, 1985), 93–96.
[20] Carter, 94–96.
[21] Kohanski, 235–38.
[22] Translated in Cadden, 95.
[23] Joseph Allen Hornsby, *Chaucer and the Law* (Norman, OK: Pilgrim Press, 1988), 116–17.

perverse performances
of masculinity and
power

"has something to prove"

violence

they take it a step
further; not only use
women but beat Synkyn,
where John was unintentionally
hurt

prove the rape now. At the same time, under the Reeve's vengeful fictive eye, what was rape could be treated as insignificant, thus increasing the revenge against the Miller in both fictive layers. The first level is the tale as an independent story, in which the revenge comes in the form of stealing the goods of another. The second level that I will explore later is the tale as the speech act of the Reeve, who can use it to gain revenge against Robin the Miller for his having insulted the Reeve through his tale of an old carpenter's cuckolding.

At the level of the tale as independent story, the most significant issue is that Aleyn's act not only brings about the restitution of stolen goods but garners an extra portion through the perverse performance of his own masculinity. He literally has made contact with the miller's property and has destroyed it as a commodity. That the miller is aware of this theft when he awakens can be heard in his question, "Who dorste be so boold to disparage / My doghter, that is come of swich lynage?" (4271–72).

Although a part of the French source as well as in the *Reeve's Tale*, the second act of violence is also significant in the abuse of masculine power. Realizing that his failure to act may render him a "daf, a cokenay" (4208), John must assert his own masculinity. He indeed has something to prove. While it is certainly unlikely that Symkin's wife could have been mistaken that her bed companion was not Symkin, the narrative focuses on the act of violence in a more significant way. The Reeve's comment that John "priketh harde and depe as he were mad" (4231), transforms the sexual coupling into an act of violence, at least in John's mind. His violent act against the Miller's wife is designed to save his reputation, to give vent to his own masculinity however perversely and abusively conceived. Again he asserts himself symbolically and literally in the destruction of property as he threatens the neat world of social hierarchies which Symkin, proud as a peacock, has attempted to establish in Trumpington.

Performing with the tale

On the next morning as the tale concludes, the two scholars beat Symkin after his wife has knocked him out by mistake, or perhaps intentionally, as Gay L. Balliet contends.[24] Again they have demonstrated their contempt for the miller through an act of violence. The sequence of events of violence – first against Malyne, next against Symkin's wife, and finally against Symkin himself – bring together the two levels of symbolic and literal action. The two scholars demonstrate their masculinity through abusive assault, and in doing so, destroy Symkin's domain. Having the tale serve as an exemplum for the proverb "Hym thar nat wene wel that yvele dooth" (4320) seems an ironic justification for violence in the story. The Reeve also notes that "A gylour shal hymself bigyled

[24] Balliet, "The Wife in Chaucer's *Reeve's Tale*: Siren of Sweet Revenge," *English Language Notes* 28 (1990): 1–5.

be" (4321), which on the surface seems to refer to Symkin, but language, especially that of linguistically conceived revenge, is far more unstable. Is it not possible that the Reeve may be referring to himself as well? He has narrated a story from the start whose words are products of "avauntyng, liyng, anger, coveitise" (3884), but no male in the story is free from these vices.

Telling a story of rape, however conceived, is a potentially ambiguous act. Sexual acts in the tale are described in terms of gaining "easement" or of appeasing anger. The women in the story are certainly important, and overlooking their participation and victimization is an oversight too long made by readers of Chaucer's tale. At the same time, however, it is also fair to say that this is a story of male violence – male against male. It is a tale of symbolic rape. We might argue that male power has been abused and made perverse in at least two ways. Dolores Warwick Frese has noted homoerotic elements in the *Miller's Tale*, but with regard to the *Reeve's Tale*, she observed that the "heterosexual encounter is remarkably non-erotic, and the corresponding homoerotic underside is consequently nonexistent."[25] She is indeed correct that the sexual encounters are "non-erotic," most likely as a result of their being rapes. At the same time, since the effects of male-against-male violence is to destroy the power of the female and male victims, it is possible to see the experience as containing shadows of homosexual rape.

Medieval records are all but silent on the issue of homosexual rape, not because it did not happen, but because it was ultimately an attack on the world of male authority. Throughout the Middle Ages, but particularly from the High Middle Ages on, homosexual activity was seen as breaking natural patriarchal boundaries. How much of a threat homosexual rape was will probably remain unclear, but it was certainly enscribed in the cultural mind. During the Crusades, there were many reports of alleged homosexual rape by Turks against Christians.[26] What seems clear is that the act itself was seen as separating one from community in addition to feminizing the victim. On the symbolic level of the tale, the Reeve has merely substituted the clerks' attack on the two women for his own verbal attack on the Miller. Since the Miller has been careful to construct his world of patriarchal control around biology and class, it is possible to see that *raptus* has been enacted upon his body of goods – even upon his body. He has been made to feel in words the pain that the Reeve, now an old man whose biological functions have diminished, knows. That the Reeve would tell this tale to get revenge on the Miller would thus give the tale a darker, more sinister tone. It would become impossible to separate justice from revenge in the text, and therein lies the ambivalent mood the tale creates.

To return to the questions that Parker and Sedgwick pose about performance

---

25 Frese, "The Homoerotic Underside in Chaucer's *Miller's Tale* and *Reeve's Tale*," *Michigan Academician* 10 (1978): 148.
26 James A. Brundage, *Law, Sex, and Christian Society in Medieval Europe* (Chicago: University of Chicago Press, 1987), 213.

and performativity and to apply them to the Reeve's prologue and tale provide some interesting insights. The question "when is saying something doing something?" is answered with the tale itself. The Reeve is no longer able to pursue physical violence against Robin the Miller, who is Chaucer's representation of the hypermasculinized male. Words become his means of attack. They are his weapons used to penetrate the image that the Miller sets for himself. The question "how is saying something doing something?" is answered in the Reeve's perverse performance. Specifically, that performance resonates through the violence of the Solar Hall scholars as well as through his own emotional commitments in verbally creating the performance. Chaucer has presented his readers with the darker, more perverse side of male power in this tale. The raucous humor of the *Miller's Tale*, which precedes it, is answered by a tale filled with the abuse of masculine power, performed in all its perversity.

A Wife, a Batterer, a Rapist:
Representations of "Masculinity" in the
Wife of Bath's Prologue and *Tale*

ELIZABETH M. BIEBEL

A variety of literary scholars have commented on the so-called masculinity of Chaucer's Wife of Bath. George Englelhardt compares Alisoun to a "virago, who is 'mannish.' "[1] By process of association, Robert Hanning types Alisoun as a masculine woman when he assesses that she hates herself for having to adopt the practices of her oppressors.[2] And by process of elimination, David Williams, who directly incorporates Alisoun into his reading of her tale, believes that the only true representative of womanhood in the *Wife of Bath's Tale* is the "aggrieved maiden seeking justice."[3] Having come under critical censure for not adhering to socially prescribed gender roles for femininity, Alisoun is also reproved for what she has done to men. For example, many scholars have expressed dissatisfaction, outrage, or contempt when discussing what they perceive to be Alisoun's instigating a physical assault against her fifth husband Jankyn when she is annoyed by his reading from his Book of Wikked Wyves. While these critics react negatively to Alisoun's expression of violence, they have not devoted particular attention to Jankyn's physically abusing Alisoun. Likewise, while the knight in Alisoun's tale rapes a young woman, certain critics are more upset with the hag (with whom Alisoun is frequently linked) for stripping away the knight's will. As Norman Holland

[1] Engelhardt, "The Lay Pilgrims of the *Canterbury Tales*: A Study in Ethology," *MS* 36 (1974): 321.
[2] Hanning, "From Eva and Ave to Eglantyne and Alisoun: Chaucer's Insight into the Roles Women Play," *Signs* 2 (1977): 599.
[3] Williams, *The Canterbury Tales: A Literary Pilgrimage* (Boston: Twayne, 1987), 70.

states, "raping the girl breaks one taboo. . . . But we are not repelled by those violations as we are at the knight's being asked to perform sexually for the old crone."[4]

From these statements we might assume that there is something wrong with the things that Alisoun says and does, yet this is hardly the case. The Wife of Bath is a prototype of a modern woman in that she maintains a loose construction of socially prescribed gender roles. For example, we see in her portrait in the General Prologue that she rides her ambler astride. While some critics have theories as to why she does so, we can imagine that Alisoun puts aside the more "lady-like" style of riding for her own convenience while traveling the road to Canterbury. How she chooses to travel, though, is just a minor aspect of her crossing the lines of cultural gender expectations. Alisoun is an efficient business person, she is not afraid to verbalize her desires, and she frankly admits that she delights in sex. As a result of this behavior, the Wife of Bath may be seen as a threat to the medieval hierarchy of power relations between the sexes because she violates the conception of what a woman should be according to the medieval estates tradition. She has chosen not to be passive, silent, obedient, or chaste. What is striking about the above quotations, however, is that they come from twentieth-century literary scholars, people whom we would ideally assume have more open views on what it is to be a woman, and thus, conversely, what it is to be a man. What we can gather from these assessments is that our culture still maintains specific and unequal gender roles and behavioral expectations for men and women. This inequity can be and has been used for "men's subordination and denigration of other men as well as men's exploitation of women."[5]

In this paper I will examine these so-called masculine mannerisms of Alisoun in order to understand both why such actions have been used by Western culture as a definition of masculinity and why society tends to be critical of such actions when they are performed by a woman. In response to those who feel that Alisoun becomes a ridiculous figure in the world of men, I suggest that we should add to our perspective of Alisoun's struggling to achieve self-governance in an unegalitarian society a critical view of the hierarchy of gender. In addition to studying Alisoun, then, I will also analyze the primary male characters in Alisoun's prologue and tale, Jankyn and the rapist-knight. In doing so, I read the Wife of Bath's performance as a critical evaluation of a social system that not only disempowers women but that also victimizes men through its construction of rigid gender roles. It is only through the events of Alisoun's fictional tale of romance that men and women both gain recognition and respect as individuals who are free from the limitations of a culture that emphasizes male dominance.

---

4   Holland, *The Dynamics of Literary Response* (New York: Oxford University Press, 1968), 14.
5   Judith Lorber, *Paradoxes of Gender* (New Haven: Yale University Press, 1994), 4.

The "masculine" Wife?

Throughout her life, Alisoun struggles to maintain her independence in a culture that perceives women as being inferior to men. In this quest for self-governance she comes to value the effectiveness of what many might call the means of men: wealth, power, and aggression. Alisoun becomes a part of the economic sphere of men, and she both challenges the scholarly world of men and manipulates their textual authority for her own purposes. She also renounces woman's relegation to being a passive sexual creature and becomes an active agent of her own sexuality. We cannot call Alisoun "masculine," however, simply because of her participation in these traditionally male-dominated fields and her rejection of dictated codes for women. Let us examine Alisoun's attitudes towards sex and money, her aggressive behavior, and her challenging of masculine authority in order to find out why she has been criticized for implementing them.

Alisoun's candid revelations about her love of sex have caused some critics to label her a carnal figure and a nymphomaniac.[6] The root causes behind these accusations may very well be the double standard that society has long employed regarding female and male sexuality. Western culture has maintained a definition of masculinity that asserts that men have highly-charged sexual drives. Conversely, women are supposedly less interested in sex. A man's sexual activity is thus legitimized, while a woman is required to maintain a chaste persona. While all of Alisoun's liaisons are legitimate in that they have been sanctioned by marriage, her frank discussion of them contradicts the discourse that alleges women's weaker sex drive. Her candor about intimacy with her husbands is subversive, because she complains about the performance of her first three husbands. Through illustrating the sexual inefficacy of these older men, Alisoun threatens the genderized myths concerning sex.

While male-dominant society has worked to maintain women in the role of sex object, Alisoun has learned to make use of this objectification for her own benefit. Realizing the worth of her sexuality, Alisoun commodifies her attractiveness, using it to appeal to a man's sexual desires in order that she can maintain herself in one of the more common occupations open to women in her time, that of being a wife.[7] In doing so, she has amassed the fortunes of her late husbands. Her combined sexual and economic promise as a mate most likely held great appeal for her fourth and fifth husbands. While these subsequent marriages to a peer and to a younger man may have brought more promise to her bed, Alisoun had to cope with the frequent absences and the infidelity of her fourth husband and the beatings she received from her fifth. Unfortunately

---

[6]   D. W. Robertson, Jr., *A Preface to Chaucer* (Princeton: Princeton University Press, 1962), 317; Beryl Rowland, "Chaucer's Dame Alys: Critics in Blunder land?" *NM* 73 (1972): 393.
[7]   For further reading about Alisoun's commodification of sex, see Sheila Delany, "Sexual Economics, Chaucer's Wife of Bath, and *The Book of Margery Kempe,*" *Minnesota Review* 5 (1975): 104–15.

for Alisoun, none of her marriages has been a healthy union based on equal partnership.

While some might find ethical flaws in Alisoun's practice of sexual economics, there is one practical dilemma. When women are viewed as commodifiable sexual objects, as they have been for so long in our social system, their marketability severely declines with their advancing age. Since Alisoun at the time of the pilgrimage to Canterbury is in her forties, she no longer manifests the fresh beauty of a younger woman. Thus, she learns to value the wealth she has acquired, for she knows that while some men desire beautiful women, others lust for gold. Indeed, Alisoun hints that she used her economic assets to attract Jankyn. In her professional life, Alisoun has become a successful business woman, and she has learned that accruing personal wealth can attribute power and prestige. This wealth gives her pride in making charitable offerings at church. The most valuable thing that money has done for Alisoun, however, is that it has made her an independent woman. It gives her licence to exercise her will, and it allows her to travel. She need not be a dependent wife. When she becomes older, she will not have to place herself at the mercy of other people's charity, which may or may not be forthcoming. Since the patriarchy has denied women their autonomy, Alisoun seeks to gain her freedom by making use of her culture's worship of wealth, and she does so effectively.

Alisoun's strong drive for independence is one of the factors that has given rise to the accusation of her being an aggressive woman. While society's gender expectations not only encourage a man to be aggressive but also cast aspersions on a man who is not aggressive, aggressiveness in a woman is not acceptable. At times, what we might consider to be merely *assertive* in a man may be viewed as being *aggressive* in a woman. Alisoun needs to be aggressive, however, in order to maintain her independence. A case in point is evident in the dynamics of Alisoun's fifth marriage, for the one scene that usually comes to mind when we reflect on the *Wife of Bath's Prologue* is the climactic fight in which Alisoun damages Jankyn's book and knocks him into the fireplace, and Jankyn, in turn, fells Alisoun with a blow to the head so powerful that she permanently loses hearing in one ear. As a result of her actions, Alisoun has been accused by many literary critics of being too aggressive.[8] We might well ask why Alisoun's hostility is viewed as being inappropriate when Jankyn's violence is not. It appears that those who find Alisoun's behavior to be distasteful are relying on the double standard that the physical demonstration of power is in keeping with the definition of a man, while in a woman it is perceived as being unfeminine, a violation of woman's traditional role of passivity.

8   Such opinions may be found in John Davenant, "Chaucer's View of the Proper Treatment of Women," *Maledicta* 5 (1981): 153–61; Robert M. Lumiansky, *Of Sundry Folk: The Dramatic Principle in the Canterbury Tales* (Austen: University of Texas Press, 1955), 118; Kemp Malone, *Chapters on Chaucer* (Baltimore: Johns Hopkins Press, 1951), 215–16.

Sadly, it has often been overlooked that Alisoun is an abused spouse. Regarding Jankyn, she tells us:

> And yet was he to me the mooste shrewe;
> That feele I on my ribbes al by rewe,
> And ever shal unto myn ending day.   (III 505–07)

Physical violence against women was culturally condoned in the Middle Ages. A medieval theological dictionary states, "Moreover, a man may chastise his wife and beat her for her correction; for she is of his household, and therefore the lord may chastise his own."[9] A husband could beat an overly independent wife into submission as he might break his high-spirited horse. This relegation of women to the status of mere property is another damaging example of patriarchal power, and it should be emphasized here that mere social acceptance of an ignoble practice is a poor excuse for its justification. In addition, it is clear that Jankyn's violence towards Alisoun teaches her the necessity of using physical force in order to recover power over her own life. The angry fight and the book-burning scene are the result of Alisoun's refusal to be abused. They are examples not of an aggressive, unprovoked attack but of self-defense.

Along with her role in the fight, one of the more common pieces of evidence used to highlight Alisoun's aggressive tendencies is her horoscope, in which Mars, the planet dedicated to the god of war, is the ascendant in Taurus. Scholars Chauncey Wood, J. D. North, and Beverly Kennedy inform us, however, that such a reading is a misinterpretation.[10] "According to both classical and medieval astrology, the appearance of Mars in Taurus at a woman's nativity means simply that she will have a strong sexual desire and will therefore be sexually active."[11] It was not written in the stars, then, that Alisoun should be a violent and aggressive person. Rather, Alisoun comes to learn that violence must sometimes be met with violence if a person wishes to survive.

In addition to having come to appreciate the power of physical aggression, Alisoun has also learned the power of both the spoken and the written word. While some women of Alisoun's day had been taught to read and write, they were by no means encouraged to make their voices heard. In the "educational" book of conduct for women, *The Book of the Knight of the Tower*, Geoffrey de la Tour-Landry stresses the importance of a wife's silence when he tells the story of an outspoken woman who is punished for her impropriety when her angered husband breaks her nose. Because the written word has been

---

[9] G. G. Coulton, *Life in the Middle Ages, III* (New York: Macmillan, 1910), 119.

[10] See Chauncey Wood, *Chaucer and the Country of the Stars: Poetic Uses of Astrological Imagery* (Princeton: Princeton University Press, 1970), 175; J. D. North, *Chaucer's Universe* (Oxford: Clarendon, 1988), 292 and 299; Beverly Kennedy, "The Variant Passages in the Wife of Bath's Prologue and the Textual Transmission of the *Canterbury Tales*: The 'Great Tradition' Revisited," in Lesley Smith and Jane H. M. Taylor, eds., *Women, the Book, and the Worldly* (Cambridge: D. S. Brewer, 1995), 89.

monopolized by men, women have often been misrepresented in texts. Jankyn's Book of Wikked Wyves is a primary example of an antifeminist tract, and we witness the damaging influence it has had on both Alisoun and her scholarly husband. The misogyny that the book preaches reinforces Jankyn's "right" to beat his spouse, and for a time Alisoun endures the painful consequences. The injustice of these antifeminist sentiments causes Alisoun to complain,

> Who peyntede the leon, tel me who?
> By God, if wemmen hadde writen stories,
> As clerkes han withinne his oratories,
> They wolde han writen of men moore wikkednesse
> Than all the mark of Adam may redresse.   (III 692–96)[12]

Alisoun uses a major portion of her story-telling time in Harry Bailly's contest to expose the way she has been treated in her marriages. She is out to set the record straight, and her performance becomes a rallying cry to other women to stand up for themselves and seek independence as she has done. In her prologue Alisoun reveals the need for women to speak out against their position within a male-dominated society and also shows how capable a woman can be at public speaking. Indeed, she earns the praise of her fellow pilgrim, the Pardoner, who believes she is "a noble prechour" (III 165). Not all of the Canterbury company are pleased with Alisoun's words, however. While the Friar criticizes her for her long-windedness, we must wonder if it is not the length but the content of Alisoun's performance to which he truly objects.

Alisoun has made use of sex, money, aggression, and the power of the spoken word in order to escape the limitations that unequal gender stereotypes have placed upon women. A wife, as the property of her husband, is dependent upon him for her survival, and if that husband is not a kind master, the wife's existence will be a painful one. Alisoun has learned this bitter lesson from first-hand experience, and so she has resolved to make sure that she need not be dependent upon a husband, to make sure that she may have mastery of herself. If the patriarchal system objectifies women as sexual creatures, then Alisoun will play up this misrepresentation and use it to her advantage. Since wealth is a key to power, she will accrue as much money as she can. If violence is the only effective way to react to violence, Alisoun will not hesitate to become physically aggressive. Since men have maligned women with their words, she will not remain silent about the bad experiences of her marriages.

As Judith Lorber tells us, "most societies rank gender according to prestige

---

11 Kennedy, 89n.
12 While many literary critics have subsequently discussed this passage and its implications, the initial article that addresses the issue of female misrepresentations is Mary Carruthers, "The Wife of Bath and the Painting of Lions," *PMLA* 94 (1979): 209–22. Carruthers also shows how Alisoun uses her economic resources to gain independence.

and power and construct them to be unequal, so that moving from one to another also means moving up or down the social scale."[13] Alisoun's success in employing tactics and attributes that our culture stereotypes as belonging to men may therefore be perceived as threatening to the status quo. A woman's acquisition of power and prestige attacks the cultural imbalance of power and symbolizes the possibility of a more egalitarian world. It is because of this threat that Alisoun has been labeled as being "unfeminine" or "masculine," for if women and men are taught to perceive Alisoun's actions as aberrant, gender inequity will remain intact.

We have just seen how gender inequity works toward disempowering women. Culturally prescribed definitions of femininity encourage a woman's passivity. Institutionalized "personality structures, sexual exploitation, and physical violence help maintain men's control over women."[14] This imbalance of power, however, does not promote the victimization of only women. Men have also been disempowered by this social arrangement. Through the illustrations of the major characters in Alisoun's performance that Chaucer provides, we may witness how cultural expectations of masculinity exploit men.

The "real men" in Alisoun's performance: the batterer and the rapist

If we look to the most fully-developed representatives of the male sex in Alisoun's performance, Jankyn in her prologue and the knight in her tale, for a possible definition of masculinity, we are provided with two sorry examples of manhood.[15] While Jankyn is evidently good-looking and an excellent performer in bed, these "positive" traits provide a shallow interpretation of what it is to be a man. Furthermore, Jankyn is both psychologically and physically abusive towards his wife and has spent most of his life studying and evidently believing in the antifeminist writings of the Fathers of the Church. The knight, as well, is a "lusty bacheler" (882), and while he too may be outwardly appealing, he abuses his power, strength, and rank when he rapes a young maiden. Obviously, these men are no friends to women, but we should examine what has made them so violent. As we shall see, cultural expectations of masculinity lie at the heart of this matter.

We have already looked at the book-burning fight in order to show how

13 Lorber, 27.
14 Lorber, 291.
15 While I have not chosen to focus on all the men in Alisoun's life and tale for gathering insights into society's definition of manhood, a few factors deserve some attention. That Alisoun discredits her first three husbands for being old and thus no longer fully virile reveals to us how the Wife of Bath, as a representative of her society, has been taught to value men as sexual machines. An old man, then, is of little value in such a culture in spite of all the wisdom he may have for future generations. Alisoun's fourth husband, the adulterer, also serves to underscore the sexual aspect of manhood. While Alisoun was not pleased by his actions, her world permits a man's promiscuity while condemning promiscuity in a woman.

Alisoun learns the harsh lesson that violence is her only recourse in defending herself against Jankyn's physical attacks. What we should now examine are the factors that have formed Jankyn into an abusive husband. If we compare the specifics of Alisoun and Jankyn's marriage to case studies reported by sociologists and psychologists who have studied the occurrence of family violence in contemporary society, we can find striking examples that may serve to explain why Jankyn beats Alisoun. In addition to the socialization of violence demonstrated in the licensing of medieval clerks to discipline their wives that Coulton recounts, the non-traditional elements of Alisoun and Jankyn's marriage also add to domestic tensions. Several specific conditions of the marriage may be interpreted as a threat to Jankyn's masculinity. Sociologist Murray Straus notes that "sexism is also grounded in institutional arrangements – such as the expectation that men will marry younger women – that make male domination a reality."[16] Since Jankyn is married to a woman who is twenty years his senior, he does not have this traditional, chronological advantage of "superiority" that many husbands have over their wives. Since experience plays such a crucial role in Alisoun's value system, we can most likely assume that Jankyn has been made aware of his lack of life experience in comparison to that of his wife. Like Symkyn's lack of respect for the college education of the clerks in the *Reeve's Tale*, Alisoun's lack of respect for authority would ensure that she would not accept Jankyn's life of studying as a worthy substitute for the experiential education that life provides. Indeed, Alisoun speaks out strongly against authority throughout her prologue. In addition to their difference in age, while Alisoun has given Jankyn control of her finances, it is *her* accrued wealth, *her* entrepreneurship in the textile trade, that guarantees their financial security. There is no evidence in the text that Jankyn's Oxford education serves the couple as an economic resource. This factor plays into the sociological studies of Allen and Straus who note, "the wife's possession of superior resources can undermine the ability of the husband's resources to validate superior power, thus leading to the substitution of a resource in which wives can rarely be superior to their husbands: physical violence."[17] If this observation is found to be true in modern society, we must consider how intensified such feelings would have been on Jankyn's part in a time when not so many women participated in the economic life of the middle class.[18] Age difference, conflicting value systems,

16 Murray A. Straus, "Sexual Inequality and Wife Beating," in Murray A. Straus and Gerald T. Hotaling, eds., *The Social Causes of Husband-Wife Violence* (Minneapolis: University of Minnesota Press, 1980), 86.
17 Craig M. Allen and Murray Straus, "Resources, Power and Husband-Wife Violence," in *The Social Causes of Husband-Wife Violence*, 203.
18 As Hotaling and Straus put it, "Logically, we would assume that the increasing breakdown of the sexist organization of the family would also lead to a decrease in husband-wife violence. But this decrease may not be the case, at least in the short run. During this transition period, as the family restructures its power distribution, conflict and violence may actually be increased as men feel threatened by their loss of power. Ironically, attempts by women

and Alisoun's success in the business world may all contribute to the emasculation of Jankyn and his consequent need to assert his maleness through force.

After observing these underlying factors in the marriage, we cannot view Jankyn as being intrinsically evil. I do not, however, mean to try to exonerate him for abusing his wife, for ideally he should be psychically strong enough to overcome socially-imposed feelings of inferiority and not resort to venting his frustrations through violent physical actions. But Jankyn is also a victim of his culture's construction of manliness: breadwinner, head of the household, superior in intellect and strength to the so-called weaker sex. As a man living in a male-dominant system, he should be able to maintain power and control over his wife. We should note how Jankyn is supposed to define his own self-worth by setting himself above, and thereby dominating, women. There is little logic in attempting to define the self by incorporating only external factors into this definition without seeking one's inner strengths.

In the *Wife of Bath's Tale*, the knight provides us with another example of a man who incorporates power over women into the definition of masculinity. Rape has frequently been misperceived as a crime of sexual passion. The motivations of rapists, however, are not sexual but rather involve issues of power and control. Rape is "an assault against personhood which has its origins and maintenance in a system of social inequality that victimizes all, but some more than others."[19] In his analysis of men who rape, A. Nicholas Groth analyzes three particular types of sexual assault: anger, power, and sadistic rapes. While we have little textual background concerning the knight, and the rape scene in Alisoun's tale is dealt with in just a few lines, we can assess the knight as a power rapist, a man who abuses sex "as an expression of conquest."[20] Unlike anger rapists and sadistic rapists, the power rapist uses just enough force to subdue his victim,[21] and we are given no evidence of the knight's excessive brutalizing of the maiden. Chaucer's mentioning that the rape victim is a maid can lead us to assume that she is a relatively young woman. That a power rapist selects a victim who "tends to be within the same age range as the offender or younger" and that "the choice of a victim is predominantly determined by availability, accessibility, and vulnerability,"[22] also fit the rape

---

to increase their power in society and the family may serve to victimize women further, at least temporarily" ("Culture, Social Organization, and Irony in the Study of Family Violence," in *The Social Causes of Husband-Wife Violence*, 19–20). While this quotation refers to the Women's Movement of the 1970s, it can be applied to the age of Chaucer. As an emerging emancipated woman, Alisoun is a direct threat to Jankyn and the cultural and academic ideologies with which he has been indoctrinated.

[19] Joyce E. Williams and Karen A. Holmes, *The Second Assault: Rape and Public Attitudes* (Westport: Greenwood Press, 1981), xiii.

[20] A. Nicholas Groth, *Men Who Rape: The Psychology of the Offender* (New York: Pelnum Press, 1979), 13.

[21] Groth, 25.

[22] Groth, 28.

scene in the *Wife of Bath's Tale*. The knight is young, and the solitary setting underscores the helpless predicament of the maiden.

In his profile of the power rapist, Groth reports that "one of the dynamics in the assault is reaffirmation of his manhood. Such offenders feel insecure about their identity." Groth also asserts that "the quest for power, mastery, and control appears to be an unresolved life issue operating in this offender that he acts out in his sexual assaults."[23] While we are given very little information concerning the knight's background, we can use what we do know of him to examine why he feels the need to reaffirm his masculinity in such a destructive manner. One trait that is common among rapists is "social isolation."[24] While our rapist-knight ostensibly is a part of a community, Arthur's court, he is conspicuously alone throughout the text. We never see him in the company of peers, and when he must solve the riddle we receive no account that he consults a friend or a mentor for advice. Instead, he wanders the country in search of an answer, going to "every hous" (919) and not to a specific home. That the rapist is a knight is also telling about him, for "military history allows the clinician to explore the offender's self-image, his male peer relationships."[25] We have just examined how, despite his belonging to a highly fraternal organization such as the Round Table, the knight is bereft of male companionship. As a young knight in a society that upholds gender inequality the knight can evaluate his existence "as one of conquering women and competing with men."[26] In the feudal system, the rapist-knight must bow to the superior power of his liege lord as well as to that of more established, older knights. This apparent lack of control he experiences can make him feel victimized and insecure about his status as a man. Thus he desires to gain compensational control over others in order to reaffirm his masculinity. He rapes, then, out of "non-sexual needs."[27]

My above assessment is not intended to *excuse* the knight for committing rape. Its function is to help us *understand* his situation and expose how cultural expectations of masculinity contribute to motivations for rape. The rapist's "perception of the masculine role is one of incurring increasing and various obligations and responsibilities to an extent that will prohibit any independent choice of activities."[28] Because the knight has resorted to rape, it is extremely likely that he will rape again if he remains unreformed: "His sense of victimization, his reliance on sexual aggression as a way of counteracting his distress, and the failure of sexual assault to remedy the situation makes the likelihood of this individual's being a repetitive offender very high."[29]

While employing capital punishment would certainly ensure that the rapist-knight would never become a repeat offender, we should ask how his death might act as a preventative strike against rape. Obviously, the threat of death

---

23 Groth, 28, 30.
24 Groth, 198.
25 Groth, 197.
26 Groth, 198.

27 Groth, 13.
28 Groth, 50.
29 Groth, 109.

did not deter the knight from committing rape. As Groth informs us: "The consequences of his behavior, what may happen to him or to others, have no meaning at the time. Therefore, he is not deterred by such logical considerations as punishment, disgrace to his family, injury to his victim, etc."[30] Because a rapist's motivations are linked to socially constructed notions of gender, the women in Alisoun's tale set out to rehabilitate the knight, who has been strongly influenced by his culture's definitions of masculinity and femininity. As the romance progresses, we come to witness an ideal relationship based on mutual respect. Let us now read the *Wife of Bath's Tale* as a promotion of gender equality that is brought about by the rehabilitation of a rapist.

Gender equity: The ideal vision in the *Wife of Bath's Tale*

The *Wife of Bath's Tale* reveals to us Alisoun's idealized picture of personhood and community. In order for such a society to evolve, the hierarchy of gender must dissolve, for we have witnessed not only the damaging effects it has brought upon women, such as being reduced to property and having no autonomy, but also its detrimental consequences for men. In the final portion of Alisoun's performance, we see the evolution of a world in which women can dispense justice and where the wisdom of an old woman can serve to reform a man who has been misled by his society's rigid definition of gender roles.

If we read the rape scene as an example of how the current value system has misrepresented both men and women, we can view the remainder of the tale as an example of how society may be improved. When the knight is brought to court for punishment, the queen disagrees with the death penalty that Arthur would employ and seeks to preserve the rapist's life, despite his apparent disregard for the quality of the life of others. In her wisdom, she does not intend to provide dispensation for the rapist without the assurance that he is truly converted, thereby endeavoring to make sure he will not go out and rape again. The sentence of the year-and-a-day long riddle quest returns the knight to the real world where he will have contact with women. As Asher Pacht notes,

> The artificial environment of the typical correctional institutional setting is not the most conducive for achieving a meaningful psychological change. It is incongruous for an individual who may have primary problems in his relationship with mature women to be sentenced to the all-male environment of the typical prison. That is hardly an ideal atmosphere for the development of the social-sexual skills necessary for establishing such relationships.[31]

[30] Groth, 6.
[31] Pacht, "The Rapist in Treatment: Professional Myths and Psychological Realities," in Marcia J. Walker and Stanley L. Brodsky, eds., *Sexual Assault: The Victim and the Rapist* (Lexington: Lexington Books, 1976), 94.

On his quest the rapist-knight encounters his "primary counselor," the loathly lady, whose "treatment program" includes both making the assailant fully aware of the role of victim when he himself is placed in a situation of victimization and making him listen to the sermon on *gentillesse*.

When confronted with his impending marriage to the loathly lady, the knight utters a plea that we can imagine has crossed the lips of many a woman facing an attacker, "Taak al my good and lat my body go" (1061). Here the knight's true lesson, brought about through experiencing what gender inequity has done to women, begins. Having been reduced to a piece of property, he attempts to barter other possessions so that his most precious one, his personhood, might not be victimized. He comes to understand what it feels like to be forced into a marriage that is not of his choosing. His protests against what he views as his "dampnacioun" (1067) are not listened to. He is stripped of his power and his will. To him, his wedding night will be a rape. Thus the loathly lady reveals to the knight what it is like to be marginalized and to be stripped of self-governance.

When the newlyweds are alone, the loathly lady lectures the knight about socially constructed values. As an ugly, old woman, the loathly lady is a contradiction to most of the cultural ideologies with which the knight has been infused. Because of the aging process she is ugly in the eyes of the knight, who has been influenced by the opinion that "physical ugliness as the worst of sins in a female, overriding all compensating qualities of virtue, kindness, or intelligence, because these qualities are more or less irrelevant in a sex object."[32] That an older woman expresses her sexual desires conflicts with both the notions that women should be passive and the notion that an old woman, one who is beyond her child-bearing function, desires pleasure from sex is "a moral evil."[33] The loathly lady also discusses the social inequity brought about by the high priority placed on class and wealth.

In order to find out if her disciple has truly listened to her words, at the end of her lecture the loathly lady offers him a difficult choice: she can remain in her old and ugly form yet be a faithful wife to him, or she can transform herself into a beautiful, young bride who may be unfaithful. The old woman's offer is indeed a test of the knight's progress, because it involves two traits that the system of male dominance values in women: beauty and fidelity. According to the loathly lady's options, however, the knight cannot have both qualities in his bride. The line "This knyght avyseth him and sore siketh" (1228) realistically indicates the struggle that the knight has in renouncing the gender roles with which he has been indoctrinated since his childhood. Yet he triumphs in this struggle, as is indicated by his following speech:

[32] Barbara G. Walker, *The Crone: Women of Age, Wisdom, and Power* (San Francisco: Harper and Row, 1985), 121.
[33] Walker, 90.

But atte laste he seyde in this manere:
"My lady and my love, and wyf so deere,
I put me in youre wise govenance;
Cheseth youreself which may be moost plesance
And moost honour to yow and me also.
I do no fors the wheither of the two,
For as yow liketh, it sufficeth me."   (1229–35)

Here we witness the power rapist's relinquishing his need for absolute control, placing his fate in the hands of another person. In choosing an alternative solution to this test, the knight proves that he has learned the lesson of individual will. He has realized that it is not for him to impose any personal preference in determining something so private as how a woman should appear and, subsequently, recognizes the flaws in a system of gender inequity. While his desire to impose his own definition of woman was his initial fault in that he objectified a maiden to the extent of committing sexual violence, the knight does not make the same mistake twice. As a husband he places self-governance in the hands of his wife and renounces the patriarchal "right" of domination. Having thus received proof that the knight has learned his lesson, the loathly lady transforms herself into a young, beautiful woman who will also be faithful to her spouse. The transformed couple in their nuptial bed represent a world in which individuals share mutual respect and equality.[34] The only sorrow to be found in the happy closure of the story is that it is the ending to a fairy-tale romance. Even modern audiences of Alisoun's performance are still steeped in socially prescribed notions regarding gender and will therefore view this final scene as a pretty, but fictional, tale of happy-ever-after.

By examining the gender roles illustrated both in Alisoun's world and the fictional setting of her romance, we can perceive the misrepresentations of what it is to be a woman or a man that occur when inequitable definitions of masculinity and femininity are applied. This unegalitarian society has rightly been accused of devaluating women, yet it is not often assessed for the injustice it does to men. We come to understand, however, through the harmonious ending of her romance, that Alisoun knows that there is more to being a decent human being, whether male or female, than what the prescribed definitions of the patriarchal power system dictate. In order for people to realize their full potentials, she suggests, they should work to dispel prescribed gender notions. Eradication of stringent gender roles is the key to human fulfillment. Unfortunately, few in Alisoun's world were ready to accept the answers presented in her tale, so Alisoun must continue her struggle. Centuries later, too many facets of gender inequity are still prevalent in our own society. Are we prepared to make Alisoun's fiction a reality?

---

[34] Jill Mann, *Geoffrey Chaucer* (Atlantic Highlands: Humanities Press, 1991), 92, reads the ending of Alisoun's tale as a vision of mutuality between the sexes.

Ambiguous Brotherhood in the
Friar's Tale and *Summoner's Tale*

JEAN E. JOST

Chaucer's Friar and Summoner are in many ways as antagonistic as the first biblical brothers, Cain and Abel. Yet these natural enemies are also bonded together in a complex love-hate relationship that neither fully acknowledges, understands, or appreciates. To show how the concept of brotherhood grows increasingly complex in the last two tales of Fragment III, I shall first discuss Chaucer's concept of brotherhood growing out of the Western Biblical tradition, then consider the relationships between the yeoman-devil and the foolish summoner in the *Friar's Tale,* and between the friar, old Thomas, and the young squire in the *Summoner's Tale.* After exploring the relationships between the most anal-oriented pair of tales in Chaucer, I shall close with a suggestion that the Friar and the Summoner, despite their apparent antagonism, may simultaneously feel more than a fraternal attraction, in fact a sexual attraction to each other, with which neither is comfortable.[1]

[1] I am most grateful to Michael D. Sharp, whose paper " 'To telle his harlotrye': Sodomitical Discourse in the *Friar's* and *Summoner's Tales*," delivered October 11, 1996, at the conference of the Medieval Association of the Midwest, in Terre Haute, Indiana, stimulated some of the ideas in this essay. To quote from a written copy of the paper that he kindly shared with me, Sharp finds the Friar and Summoner to be "arguing about the relationship between sexuality and the proper performance of religious offices. In the Friar-Summoner rivalry, each man tells a tale in which his rival's professional corruption is signified by his improper intimacy with another man. The Friar and Summoner exchange tales which are specifically about the perversion of fraternity, each man emphasizing the social and spiritual threat his rival poses to the Christian laity by occasionally but pointedly evoking the specter of the sodomitical." My argument is unrelated to the professional or religious offices of the Friar and Summoner, and does not focus on spiritual threat. Sharp offers some interesting observations about the hare (and, by implication, the Friar's summoner)

"Am I my brother's keeper?"[2] Lies and deception. The first Biblical story of brotherly love reveals men at their worst: sons born of the same mother poised in deadly rivalry. Cain and Abel, jealously battling for God's favor, offer no amicable human paradigm. From its very inception, western myth thus paints a negative model of male bonding in this closest of familial relationships. Why has such an intimate relationship as brotherhood been perverted, as in the Genesis tale, in the most deceitful and pernicious ways? As the concept of fraternity, conceptually framed as positive, supportive, and even affectionate, has grown to encompass lesser masculine bonds, they too are often countered by a hypocritical reversal: an honest shake of the hand masking a duplicitous stab in the back.

The context of brotherhood in Chaucer

Chaucer's concept of brotherhood is broad, comprising the following bonds, from strongest to weakest: (1) literal brothers of the same mother such as Placebo and Justinus in the *Merchant's Tale*; (2) closely related kin such as the cousins Palamon and Arcite in the *Knight's Tale*; (3) the putative "cousins," the monk and the merchant, in the *Shipman's Tale*; (4) the three comrades who pledge sworn brotherhood in the *Pardoner's Tale*; (5) men connected in some affectionate or emotional bond such as the philosopher and his "leeve brother" in the *Franklin's Tale* (V 1607); (6) those bound together in a religious confraternity such as the Franciscans in the *Summoner's Tale*; and (7) simple acquaintances who acknowledge the other's friendship, as does Harry advising the Miller, "Robyn, my leeve brother" (I 3129). This last instance may be a weak tie which someone wishes to enhance for his own self-interest, akin to the depression-era song request, "Brother, can you spare a dime?"[3] Here, the forced intimacy of "brother" to a near-stranger is either an attempt to create bonding where there is none for a self-serving end, or an apparent but false acceptance of a brother, laid over an underlying foundation of hostility and contention. The *Canterbury Tales* encapsulates these and other notions of brotherhood, but the last two, in which fraternity is subversively upended and surreptitiously perverted in both primarily religious and somewhat more secular contexts, control character, narrative action, and meaning in the *Friar's Tale* and the *Summoner's Tale*.

At yet another level of subversion, these tales may hint at what Carolyn Dinshaw calls "the potential for a representation of male-male sodomitical relations" within Chaucer's strongly heterosexual norm, suggesting an "alterity," an "otherness," in their "unorganized sexual behaviors – because the

as sodomitic and hermaphroditic, and about the friar in the *Summoner's Tale* using his glossing skills to solicit money from Thomas in a kind of "homosocial courtship."
2   *The Holy Bible*, Genesis 4:9 (Douay Version), New American Catholic Edition (New York: Benziger Bros., 1950).
3   Song Lyrics by E. Y. Harburg, music by Jay Gorney. ©1932.

hetero norm keeps them that way."[4] In other words, in contrast to the normative, heterosexual mode encouraging generation which permeates the General Prologue, and is similarly epitomized in most tales, this pair of tales is as conspicuously counter-cultural and anti-normative as their deceptive, misleading males who feign brotherhood but offer malign camaraderie. This exploration will "out" both the subversively hostile underbelly of "polite" brotherhood and the latent homosexual implications in the *Friar's Tale* and the *Summoner's Tale*.

Eve Kosofsky Sedgwick describes this complex masculine relationship symbolized by a dichotomous love-hate, attraction-repulsion syndrome as "male homosocial desire."[5] Such homosociality must be "pointedly dichotomized" because, as she explains in citing Gayle Rubin, " 'obligatory heterosexuality' is built into male-dominated kinship systems . . . [and] homophobia is a *necessary* consequence of such patriarchal institutions as heterosexual marriage."[6] Thus in reinforcing masculine patriarchal dominion, seemingly a positive endorsement of maleness, ironically one simultaneously endorses homophobia which threatens the patriarchal status quo. On this continuum of homosocial desire comprising "male friendship, mentorship, entitlement, rivalry, and hetero- and homosexuality . . . [then may also be found] intense homophobia, fear and hatred of homosexuality":[7] a schizophrenic love-hate bifurcation. Sedgwick is right in "using 'desire' in a way analogous to the psychoanalytic use of 'libido' – not for a particular affective state or emotion, but for the affective or social force, the glue, even when its manifestation is hostility or hatred or something less emotively charged, that shapes an important relationship."[8] This claim does not, however, deny the very real affective state, or states, given the conflicting emotions of the relationship this glue often bonds. Both social male bonding and its emotional manifestation are implicated. On the other hand, in the *Friar's Tale* and the *Summoner's Tale* the glue is in fact both hostility or hatred and attraction simultaneously.

Similarly elusive are the precise liminal boundaries of "masculinity," both medieval and modern, as nebulous as those of "brotherhood." In reviewing Jeffrey J. Cohen's network publication, the "Interscripta" collection *Medieval Masculinities: Heroism, Sanctity, and Gender*, Clare A. Lees remarks: "That there is no single hegemonic construction of masculinities but rather a gender continuum of masculinities in the Middle Ages conforms neatly with the current

[4]   Carolyn Dinshaw, "Chaucer's Queer Touches / A Queer Touches Chaucer," *Exemplaria* 7 (1995): 82, 82n14.
[5]   Eve Kosofsky Sedgwick, *Between Men: English Literature and Male Homosocial Desire* (New York: Columbia University Press, 1985), 1.
[6]   Gayle Rubin, "The Traffic in Women: Notes Toward a Political Economy of Sex," in *Toward an Anthropology of Women*, ed. Rayna R. Reiter (New York: Monthly Review Press, 1975), 174; cited in Sedgwick, 3.
[7]   Sedgwick, 1.
[8]   Sedgwick, 2.

gender theory and with other studies of masculinity in the period."[9] The varied approaches and definitions employed in this volume attest to the "multivocality of gender," in Lees' words, which informs the Middle Ages. Attempting to box general concepts into rigid artificial categories surely does them violence, but some working definitions are useful in examining the *Friar's Tale* and the *Summoner's Tale*. Among other traits, "masculine" stereotypically encompasses that quality of maleness vis-à-vis either men or women which is protective, strong, assertive, dominant, courageous, firm, and daring – easily falling into the nomenclature of "heroic." Alternatively, the relatively less-realized "feminine" typically signifies that which is gentle, passive, reticent, subservient, patient, obedient, and docile. Because of these cultural suppositions, gender expectations of characters delineate and shape discourse: the speaker's gender conditions audience interpretation. When the expected discourse pattern is broken, we must re-examine gender assumptions: are both males in the dialogue playing masculine roles? Has one of the two male interlocutors accepted the female role? Do gesture and behavior – active or passive – reinforce this broken stereotype? What is the significance of this counter-normative dialogue? Can homosociality, the relationship between males marked by latent sexual, often aggressive overtones, be read from the type of language employed by the speakers when compounded by reinforcing body language and behavior? And, what if the language and gestures conflict? Similarly, is it possible for the surface structure of dialogue to be complimentary and affirming while the deeper meaning is injurious and insulting, or vice versa?

A Complete Concordance to the Works of Geoffrey Chaucer[10] lists 82 occurrences of the word "brother," 3 of "broother," 2 of "brotheres," 11 of "brethren," and 3 of "bretherhed" or "bretherhede" in the *Canterbury Tales*, suggesting the concept's strong linking function throughout the work. But not all of them are unadulteratedly positive. Although brotherhood is repetitively featured and highly touted throughout the *Tales*, in the Friar-Summoner contest this ambiguously figured bond regularly proves deceptive and underhanded for one of the players. Often set up as an ideal paragon of the desired male relationship, of camaraderie and mutual respect, brotherhood is initially or subsequently undercut by a counter-relationship distinctly subversive. What you first see is *not* what you get. The brother is regularly set up, anticipating a congenial interaction, only to discover he has been "had." Why is unbrotherly conduct so often presented as the norm in these two tales? Is it, in the nature of men, an inevitable testosterone reaction? Surely some male-male relationships

---

9   Clare A. Lees, review of "Medieval Masculinities: Heroism, Sanctity, and Gender," Jeffrey Jerome Cohen and Members of Interscripta. See website http://www.george-town.edu/labyrinth/e-center/interscripta/mm.html.

10   *A Complete Concordance to the Works of Geoffrey Chaucer*, ed. Akio Oizumi, programmed by Kunikiro Miki. Hildesheim, Zurich, New York, 1991. See vols. I (esp. 349) and IV.

are true friendship, but for the Friar and Summoner, competitive jealousy, on any number of levels, is an overriding motivation. In their tales, the brotherhood bond is as ambiguous as an emotional love-hate situation, and almost always, overtly or covertly, laced with an element of sexuality. Buried barely below the surface of the discourse and embedded within this bipolar love-hate tension is a darkly figured attraction, strangely and perversely expressed in hostility and cruelty.

The historic rivalry between mid-thirteenth-century Parisian mendicants (friars) and secular clergy (summoners) noted by Thomas Tyrwhitt[11] is financial, a template of the vitriolic animosity between *this* Friar and Summoner, vying for the lucrative profits of soul-shriving. No wonder the Summoner is angry: if the Friar or his band absolves sins in confession – for a pretty price – he is left with nothing to extort. And if a sinner absolved by a friar cannot be charged with the sin again, his bribing days are done. His very livelihood and security are at stake, his profession rendered useless. This professional animosity is a given. It underlies the Friar-Summoner confrontation. But a darker and more "privy" antagonism, secret and surreptitious, permeates these stories of deception. Their subtly but aggressively sexual nature casts yet another ambiguous shadow over the very issue of sexuality.

The Friar's prologue

The Friar prefaces his tale with open hostility against the Summoner, expressed both in his "louryng chiere" (III 1266) and in his contention that "of a somonour may no good be sayd" (1281). As a financial rival, he can hardly be expected to endorse the work of his opponent. Interestingly, he directs his remarks to the last teller, the Wife of Bath, who only moments before had begun her tale with an antifraternal invective: friars endanger young women today as incubi had done a century ago. The comparison blatantly equates the moral status of the two. Quiting is thus by no means an exclusively male prerogative, as this emphatic woman proves. The Host attempts to interrupt the Friar's direct, confrontational taunt, until the putatively hostile Summoner grants the Friar's story licence, with the proviso that he be allowed reprisal.

Even before the *Friar's Tale* begins, the Summoner sexualizes the context by interjecting a highly loaded sexual comparison: Friar Huberd's claim that he is free to reveal the fictional summoner's "harlotrye," being safely out of his jurisdiction. Seemingly a criticism, the Summoner's association places the fictional summoner, and thereby himself, in a sexual role, reiterating the Friar's iconographic image of "this Somonour wood . . . as an hare" (III 1327). Janette Richardson glosses the proverb as "referring to erratic behavior during the

---

[11] Thomas Tyrwhitt, ed., *The Canterbury Tales of Chaucer*, 5 vols. London: T. Payne, 1775–78.

breeding season. In iconographic representation, the hare was frequently symbolic of lechery."[12] The Summoner thereby ambiguates the Friar's character of "summoner," and by extension, possibly himself. The connection may or may not be negative, but certainly it is sexual. Huberd himself extends the sexual association by mentioning that the summoner "hadde alwey bawdes redy to his hond" and "wenches at his retenue" (1339, 1355) who bribed and confided their secrets to this long-term acquaintance unbeknownst to his archdeacon. This patriarchal figure of male authority is implicated in the deeds, for he also hypocritically extorts and reinforces the dishonesty of his ward, if not the backbiting of the brothers. Further, well he "knew a sly lecchour, / Or an avowtier, or a paramour" (1371–72) whose contact implicates him in sins of lechery. Thus, secrecy and eroticism, as well as Judas's greedy betrayal, mark the fictional summoner's character, directly or by association. His deceitful trickery, "pile the man, and lete the wenche go" (1362), only to feign friendship by saying "I am thy freend, ther I thee may availle" (1366), foreshadow the devil's quiting response he will soon earn. The Friar's ostensible antagonism toward the pilgrim Summoner and his created summoner is yet expressly sexual, perhaps double-edged, and even seductive. Further, the pilgrim Summoner, who appears hostile on the surface, has nevertheless colluded with the Friar by also associating Hubert's created summoner with sexual irregularities and innuendos. Is he not simultaneously admitting to them himself by his acknowledged association with the Friar's summoner? What unspoken words might these two tellers be saying to each other under the guise of anger?

The *Friar's Tale*

More subtle and underhanded than the spoken, openly antagonistic bargain initiating the tale, however, is the fiction employed by both tales, as their characters subversively hoodwink their "brothers" under pretense of affection and co-operation. Although the audience is privy to the double-dealing chicanery, the naively trusting characters are soundly duped.

The *Friar's Tale*, a manly tale of men, begins with a stupid summoner who encounters a yeoman: "A bowe he bar, and arwes brighte and kene" (1381). Besides foregrounding an obvious phallic representation on his person, this seemingly attractive young man is presented as unmitigatingly positive: the two engage in pleasant banter, the yeoman at first speaking reticently, but finally firmly directing the discourse. With intimate admissions, the yeoman sycophantically sucks in his companion in several ways. First, he affiliates with him through their putative mutual occupation of bailiff: " '*Depardieux,*' quod this yeman, 'deere broother, / Thou art a bailly, and I am another' " (1395–96).

---

12 *Riverside Chaucer*, ed. Larry D. Benson (Boston: Houghton Mifflin, 1987), 875, note to line 1327.

Second, he claims to be a stranger, perhaps suggesting loneliness and a desire for friendship: "I am unknowen as in this contree" (1397). Third, he specifically requests his acquaintance, " 'Of thyn aqueyntance I wolde preye thee, / And eek of bretherhede, if that yow leste' " (1398–99). If this were not sufficient, the bribe of gold and silver he offers to share is too sweet to refuse. The rather naive summoner too readily accepts the yeoman's invitation. With a handshake, the deal is sealed: "Everych in ootheres hand his trouthe leith, / For to be sworne bretheren til they deye" (1404–05): a devil's bargain with a fool.

Their mutual attraction, their physical contact, the Friar's innuendoes, the summoner's interest in the yeoman's abode, inquiring " 'Brother . . . where is now youre dwellyng / Another day if that I sholde yow seche?' " (1410–11), the yeoman's "softe speche" (1412) and invitation " 'Brother . . . fer in the north contree, / Whereas I hope some tyme I shal thee see' " (1413–14) all hint of a strongly personal relationship. The summoner's intimate request for advice or subtle tricks, " 'In myn office how that I may moost wynne; / And spareth nat for conscience ne synne' " (1421–22), suggests mutual trust, collusion, partnership, affiliation – only a short step to deeper intimacy. The yeoman's equally familiar response admits that he lives by extortion, deception, violence, serious offenses which bond the two in private and dangerous acts. His trust is reciprocated in the summoner's equally damaging admission: unless it is too heavy or too hot, I steal too. Similarly lacking conscience, extorting for sustenance, and eschewing penance, the summoner concludes that he is well met in his companion. Discovering the true identity of the playfully seductive yeoman-fiend, who slowly and teasingly reveals his corruption with a flirtatious, demure little smile and a provocative deferral, " 'wiltow that I thee telle?' " (1447), the summoner feels even closer kinship. They are brothers in crime and immorality, deceiving for profit, regardless of how. In the fiend's words, " 'Looke how thou rydest for the same entente' " (1452). The entranced summoner listens to the fiend's catalogue of vices, identifying with his brash and callous boasting. For his part, the fiend is equally engaged, and even committed, promising, " 'I wole holde compaignye with thee / Til it be so that thou forsake me' " (1521–22). The summoner's passionate response seals the bargain in a kind of marriage "trouthe":

> "Nay," quod this somonour, "that [forsaking] shal nat bityde!
> . . .
> My trouthe wol I holde, as in this cas.
> For though thou were the devel Sathanas,
> My trouthe wol I holde to my brother,
> As I am sworn, and ech of us til oother,
> For to be trewe brother in this cas;
> And bothe we goon abouten oure purchas.
> Taak thou thy part, what that men wol thee yive,

> And I shal myn; thus may we bothe lyve.
> And if that any of us have moore than oother,
> Lat hym be trewe and parte it with his brother."
>
> (1523, 1525–34)

In fact, the commitment is for fidelity and worldly possessions, stronger than the standard sworn brotherhood. The fiend's plighted trouthe, his matrimonial "I do," is equally serious: " 'I graunte . . . by my fey' " (1535). When their congenial travel takes them to the next adventure, the summoner, ever eager to please, intimately "neer the feend he drough . . . / Ful prively, and rowned in his ere" (1449–50) so that the fiend might profit from the carter. The tone of personal collusion and physical nearness describes a brotherhood of body as well as spirit. Again, at the old woman's door, the whispering summoner intimately suggests extortion. But the tables are now turned, and all of the yeoman-fiend's pledges of fidelity mean nothing: when the furious old woman curses the summoner to hell, without batting an eye, the fiend traitorously assents. He roughly escorts his "brother" to hell, exclaiming, " 'Thy body and this panne been myn by right' " (1635), a markedly suggestive, homoerotic statement. His next claim carries ambivalent overtones, both sexual and destructive, as he asserts, " 'Thou shalt with me to helle yet tonyght' " (1636). Despite the apparent affectionate affiliation of partners in crime, and the façade of gentile politeness, the vow is a deadly affair. This intense homosocial relationship, erotic in its innuendos, is an injurious double-dealing mask, a perversion of the bonds of friendship, and a destruction of the naive summoner's welfare through foreswearing. The yeoman's deceptive manipulation under the guise of intimate brotherhood, boldly occurring twenty times in one of its various forms, but most often as "myn owene deere brother," ultimately proves spiritually fatal.

What is the real seduction here? Perhaps it is both the wooing by the empowered (masculine?) double-dealing yeoman, luring his summoner into admissions, extortions, and hell with offers of amicable erotically-tinged brotherhood, and the reciprocal wooing by the disempowered (femininized?) summoner with pledges of faithful comradeship to his ideal extortionist. The very concept of "brotherhood" as a supportive, equal relationship is perverted in this self-serving, acquisitive, surreptitious, libidinous bond.

The Summoner's prologue

The trembling Summoner fully perceives that the approbation heaped upon the Friar's fictional summoner is a lightly disguised insult: "Upon this Frere his herte was so wood / That lyk an aspen leef he quook for ire" (1666–67). His first quiting is to accuse the false Friar of lying, and boasting of his knowledge of hell. He associates the friars and fiends who are but "lyte asonder" (1674), just as the Friar has bound the summoner and the fiend in sworn brotherhood in his tale. He thereby subtly connects friars and summoners, both allies of the devil. Through his raging ire, he is yet affiliating the mendicants and lay clergy, and by extension, the two of them as their representatives, in a hateful union. His vengeance is a Dantesque scatological vision of hell, graphically anal, and not far removed from the homoerotic. He recounts that "a frere ravysshed was to helle" (1676) in a vision, a remarkably sexual verb indicating both "abducted" and "enraptured," with overtones of the physical, possibly even sexual, pleasure of the mystics. His guide reveals to the "ravysshed" friar the habitat of his fellow friars by urging Satan, "Shewe forth thyn ers, and lat the frere se / Where is the nest of freres in this place!" (1690–91). The subtle, surreptitious pleasure of voyeurism in "letting the friar see" into this dark cavity heightens the forbidden and the titillating. As twenty thousand friars swarm forth, and quickly back again, sexual connotations are unavoidable. The friars are the cause of this erotic experience. But for the trembling friar, privy to these secret pleasures, "So was the develes ers ay in his mynde" (1705). The realms of scatological and homoerotic have been fused, as the friars have been both defamed and eroticized in one fell swoop.

Whereas in some instances within the *Friar's Tale*, seemingly affectionate terms of fraternal camaraderie (the term "brother" is used 18 times in the prologue and tale[13]), and even wooing behavior suggestive of positive sexuality mask an underlying hostility, in this instance, seemingly otiose feelings of resentment mask the highly charged sexual imagery, indicating more ambivalent emotions than those on the surface suggest.

The *Summoner's Tale*

Obsession with anal penetration continues in the *Summoner's Tale*, which is about a religious brother and his patron who victimizes him mentally and perhaps sexually. The Summoner does not begin his tale with more invective against friars, as his prologue has done, and as Friar Hubert did against summoners. Rather, he straightforwardly describes a "lymytour" (1711) doing as he should: preaching and begging. One day, "excited he the peple in his prechyng" (1716), yes, to prayers, but he uses an ambivalent verb at best, containing undeniable sexual associations. Interestingly, *both* friar and patron play seduction roles, and although they seem to be working at cross purposes, despite John's putative anger, the result may be more erotic than hostile. Friar John is depicted ostensibly as a solicitous cleric encouraging prayers for "freendes soules, as wel olde as yonge" (1725). But this is not the whole story. His greedy nature soon emerges as he scours his parish for meal, cheese, corn

---

[13] *A Complete Concordance to the Works of Geoffrey Chaucer*, vols. 1 and 3.

or whatever provisions he can unearth. This first inversion of expectation foreshadows what follows.

Stopping at his favorite house offers another satisfaction, as John embraces, kisses, and compliments the wife with some sexual innuendo, chirping like a lecherous sparrow, and claiming she is the fairest in all the church. Interestingly, one of her complaints about her husband is that their sex life is lacking: " 'Oother desport right noon of hym have I; / I may nat plese hym in no maner cas' " (1830–31). Thus sex is foregrounded first by John's overly affectionate greeting to her, and then by the wife herself, like the merchant's wife in the *Shipman's Tale*, acknowledging her dissatisfied state. Friar John's method of wooing the couple for his gain is ingratiating and hypocritical: he feigns personal interest, while seeking financial remuneration, particularly through John's appellation, "leeve brother" (2089), to the husband Thomas, seemingly a positive, even affectionate term. But again irony creeps in to figure the term much more dangerously, and also sexually. Thomas's ambiguous word choice is revealing, claiming other clerics are "ful necligent and slowe / To grope tendrely a conscience" (1816–17). While the Riverside edition of the *Canterbury Tales* glosses *grope* as "examine (a penitent's conscience)," the complete glossary offers "grope" and "feel about" as first suggestions. The primary physical, tactile implications of the word are impossible to ignore. Thomas will soon grope around all right. Although other clerics may be remiss, the friar John will grope well when Thomas, astute detector of hypocrisy and horse manure, turns the double-dealing John into the receptor of that horse manure.

With the threat of Thomas's gold diminishing, John moves into second gear, putatively begging not for himself, but for his convent and the building of a church, a kind of financial wooing that spurs the hot-blooded Thomas into retaliation. Additionally, the friar offers "brotherly" advice laced with misogyny for the dual purpose of alienating him from his wife while purporting to do the opposite, thereby cementing their masculine bonds. He warns:

"Be war, my sone, and herkne paciently
That twenty thousand men han lost hir lyves
For stryvyng with hir lemans and hir wyves,
Now sith ye han so hooly meke a wyf,
What nedeth yow, Thomas, to maken stryf?
Ther nys, ywys, no serpent so cruel,
Whan man tret on his tayl, ne half so fel,
As womman is, whan she hath caught an ire."   (1996–2003)

Given the wife's recent complaints to John, we question his sincerity in praising this "holy, meek wife" and recognize his misogyny as attempted male bonding. His injunction against ire, the wife's very accusation against Thomas, begins with *women's* purported ire. After (1) John's thinly disguised appeal for money (claiming of his cloister "unnethe the fundement [with the revealing double

entendre, meaning both 'foundation' and 'anus,'] / Parfourned is" [2103–04]),
(2) John's disingenuous bonding with Thomas against women, and (3) his
interminable series of sermons, Thomas is ready for revenge. If the ever-
glossing friar has been attempting seduction, Thomas now supersedes him. The
patient first woos enticingly through claim of mutual brotherhood with his
religious order, but he also suggests brotherly affection: " 'Ye say me thus, how
that I am youre brother?' " (2126). The bait is dropped, the hook is in:
gold-hungry John anticipatingly retorts: " 'Ye, certes . . . trusteth weel' "
(2127). Thomas continues in the mode of kindly brotherhood perverted with
his own disingenuous "my deere brother" (2133), followed by John's tactile
handshake sealing the sworn promise to share, much like the fiend and summoner's clasp in the *Friar's Tale*. Two lines later, the physical touch turns
ambiguous with Thomas's directions for retrieving his "gift" to be dispensed
to all the other brothers:

> "Now thanne, put in thyn hand doun by my bak,"
> Seyde this man, "and grope wel bihynde.
> Bynethe my bottok there shaltow fynde
> A thyng that I have hyd in pryvetee."   (2140–43)

It is a strange hiding place, but John is a willing partner in the hide-and-seek
game. So blinded is his desire for gold that he no longer thinks critically, delving
below with nary a reservation. Further, the Summoner is no shy shrinking violet,
reluctant to describe the consenting John's immediate acceptance: " 'That shal
go with me!' " (2144). He seems to relish describing Thomas who "felte this
frere / Aboute his tuwel grope there and heere" (2147–48). At some deeper
unconscious level he may well realize and accept the unspoken, secretive
invitation to the masculine *privitee* he himself has called forth. This bizarre
seduction is triply figured. First, it appears to be positive and inviting, the
offering of a present. Second, it is in fact the prelude to an insult. And third,
that insult may well be a mask for a deeper sexual invitation, namely Thomas's
withholding of monetary gratification (traditional correlate to sex) which
actually disguises a tantalizing physical gift or satisfaction. This richly provocative act, then, signifies layers of purposeful misrepresentation through a perversion of the terms of brotherhood. Perhaps at some level, John's earlier
misogynist suggestions have indeed stirred the concomitant homoerotic response he sought, albeit in unacknowledged manner. And yet his apparent
reaction is hostility at having been taken advantage of, and an immediate
promise of requital, " 'Thou shalt abye this fart' " (2155), for the fraudulent
treatment: no gift – of any sort. In arousing him, but denying him monetary or
sexual satisfaction, ignoring his greed and eroticism, Thomas tantalizes; he
maintains the power advantage through elusive withholding of pleasure.

Although they are quiting each other, Thomas, the "false cherl" (2153) who
does not fulfill expectations, ultimately wins the game of seduction. Friar John,

summarily chased away, cannot find satisfaction from the worthy lord of the village, for in his rage he becomes impotent to speak, or at another level, to admit to the true nature of his deprivation. Testosterone nourishes both his ire and his desire. Finally, when John reveals his insult, the lord's wife vicariously and voyeuristically experiences his erotic behavior and rejection, doubling its effect. This prelude to the shame John must acknowledge to his brother friars in "sharing" his reward anticipates his repeated humiliation at the monastery. He vows to slander back.

Ironically, true brotherhood comes where it is least expected. Friar John's anguish, heard by the lowly meat-carving squire, Jankyn, is resolved through the squire's reasonable, logical, helpful suggestion. How to part a fart? Easy. The twelve-spoked cart-solution funnels off anger, masculine rivalry, and sexual energy from which John had previously all but disintegrated. The squire, then, deferentially posing a solution, is the true friend, the real brother of the irous friar, saved from his own embittered pain of rejection and shame. The final execution reiterates the sexual theme, but now is bound by control and rationality: "Thanne shal this cherl, with bely stif and toght / . . . make hym lette a fart" (2267, 2270). The language of arousal persists, although the passion is gone in the practicality of the deed. Further, the malice is contravened in a Bakhtinian carnivalesque inversion. The once-dreaded fart has been trans-formed into an idealized sought-after quality whose first fruit is afforded the most worthy men of great honor. Now John privileges its odor as desirable, and he who receives it "bereth hym so faire and hoolily" (2286). This is a case of appropriating what the enemy sees as evil, and renaming it as ideal, for one's good. Only in this way can the irate friar reclaim his dignity and diffuse the power held by the controlled Thomas.

In both the *Friar's Tale* and the *Summoner's Tale* the title "brother" serves as a cover for deceptive protagonists to suggest co-operative, friendly, suppor-tive interaction, although their intent is often more sinister. Specifically devoid of obvious sexual connotation, the term may yet mask ambiguous homosocial attitudes or emotions. The speaker has an ambiguous axe to grind and wields it against his so-called brother. The perpetrator is thus underhandedly quiting his rival in a most pernicious way because his cards are not on the table, and his sexual intent is masqueraded. His opponent, unaware of the competition, is thereby kept at a severe disadvantage through the ruse of kindly "brother-hood," and deceived by the equally ambivalent sexual innuendoes which accompany these seemingly innocuous, innocent attempts at male bonding.

Why do Chaucer's tellers create such complicated and ambiguously figured men involved in an attraction-repulsion syndrome which is fraudulent at best, and destructive at worst? Perhaps the answer lies in actual masculine interaction visible at the time, and the social attitudes toward male bonding. The medieval church's position toward homosexuality is remarkably inconsistent, and nearly as ambiguous as the seduction driving these tales. But later medieval attitudes generally prohibit and condemn sodomy between men and women, or men and men, because no offspring is produced through the holy office of procreation. David Greenberg comments that:

> Hostility toward homosexuality intensified during the twelfth and thirteenth centuries. . . . Under Pope Innocent III (1198–1216), the twelfth-century penalty for heresy was increased from exile and confiscation of property, to death. . . . As heretics were believed to practice sodomy, the Inquisition [created by Gregory IX in 1233] gained jurisdiction over sodomy only where heretical beliefs were at stake, but later, as antihomosexual sentiment grew it was less restrained. . . . [Yet] the highest levels of the church hierarchy responded cautiously to the growth of hostility toward homosexuality. . . . [t]he medieval church courts rarely prosecuted sodomy cases; if the English church dealt with sodomy at all it was through the confessional. . . . Court records show that no one was convicted, much less executed for sodomy in the secular courts during the reigns of Louis IX (1226–70) and Philip IV (1285–1314).[14]

Thus, while earlier homophobic attitudes still permeated much of the fourteenth-century social fabric, with the passage of time this past harshness was woven into a somewhat gentler pattern of the present, an unstable blend of rejection and tolerance. This ambivalence Chaucer represented through his "brothers," those exemplary religious who tell the tales and live the lives of uncertain sexuality and fraternity.

The elaborate game-playing between competitive males shown in the obvious quiting combats represents only one level of male interaction. Far more pernicious is the less obvious rivalry, the unspoken but deadly subversive contention infiltrating the *Friar's Tale* and the *Summoner's Tale*. This contest is shot through with dangerous, if fascinating games of erotic intrigue and sexual invitation. The homophobic self-hatred too often exhibited by the homosexual, grounded in shame and self-revulsion, here irrationally explodes in a furious vendetta against the chosen partner. Like Groucho Marx's famous joke that he would not join any club that would have *him* in it, the homosexual often despises what he is and whom he is attracted to, and he often perversely makes his paramour the object of his hostility. Self-loathing and its extension, transference to the beloved, thus undermine the ostensively affectionate term "brother," and provide a subversively antagonistic attitude to a seemingly well-loved comrade. Fraternity is thus exploited in this doubly figured construct. Apparently co-operative, it is actually contemptuous. A relationship

---

[14] David F. Greenberg, *The Construction of Homosexuality* (Chicago and London: University of Chicago Press, 1988), 268, 271, 269, 274. On the other hand, Greenberg points out that "A knifemaker was burned to death in Ghent in 1292 for a homosexual act. Jehan le Bal records an instance of total castration for sodomy and heresy in his mid-fourteenth-century chronicle of the Hundred Years' War" (274).

defined as supportive and collegial is here inverted in a Bakhtinian reversal of roles, functions, and affection. Its fraudulence is more malicious than carnivalesque. But that is not the end of the story, for beyond the contempt emerges an unspoken, unacknowledged attraction, a homophobic but also seductively inscribed invitation, simultaneously smacking of self-loathing and sexual desire. Above and below the surface of the texts, the Friar's and Summoner's narratives weave contradictory messages to their characters, the mouthpieces by which these characters telegraph each other equally ambivalent messages. The love-hate conflict of the unresolved homophobic infuses their narrative dialogues. A doubly ambiguous pattern of contradictions – in the deceptive kindness of brotherhood turned treacherous, and in the masked, seductively erotic posture of desire – lies hidden within the hearts of their tales.

Sight and Sexual Performance in the *Merchant's Tale*

CAROL A. EVEREST

In the medieval medical understanding of gender roles, anatomy was, to a large extent, destiny. Formed in the right side of the womb by masculine sperm and plentiful heat, the male fœtus enjoyed a longer gestation period than his feminine counterpart, and he was born hotter, dryer, and more fully formed than the inferior female. His masculinity was evident in the external male genitalia, of which the female reproductive system was an underdeveloped replica. As he matured, his manliness would be measured by his virility and potency, signs that his physiology was indeed masculine. The truly masculine man possessed great body heat and natural moisture, indicated by his hairy body, his bold temperament, his sexual ability. As Vern Bullough argues, "male sexual performance was a major key to being male. It was a man's sexual organs that made him different and superior to the woman. But maleness was somewhat fragile, and it was important for a man to keep demonstrating his maleness by action and thought, especially by sexual action. It was part of his duty to keep his female partners happy and satisfied, and unless he did so, he had failed as a man."[1] In addition, he had to demonstrate his sexual prowess by engendering progeny, especially male children. Aristotle, for example, claims that of the 72 children Hercules fathered, only one girl was produced,[2] and Avicenna, Constantine, and Haly Abbas all agree that hot, hairy men who show a marked

---

[1] Vern Bullough, "On Being a Male in the Middle Ages," in *Medieval Masculinities: Regarding Men in the Middle Ages*, ed. Clare A. Lees (Minneapolis: University of Minnesota Press, 1994), 41.

[2] Aristotle, *De historia animalium*, vol 6. of *Aristoteles opera cum Averrois commentariis* (1562, Frankfurt: Minerva Underveranter Nachdruck, 1962), bk. VII, ch. VI.

interest in sex and who do not appear to be debilitated by it produce male offspring.[3]

In Chaucer's *Merchant's Tale*, therefore, the stakes are clearly high for the aged January, married to young and nubile May. The test of his manliness lies in his ability to satisfy his bride sexually and to provide an heir for his estate. Yet January is old; medically, his vital warmth and moisture are in decline, and with them his sexual prowess. He may attempt to restore his humoral balance through stimulating potions, and he may deceive himself that he is as sexually competent as a younger man, but the proof of his failures lies in May's dissatisfaction and in the suggestion that a younger, more virile man must produce his heir. January's pretentions to youth elicit mockery from narrator and reader alike, but his self-deception cloaks a more sinister reality. Sexual activity is dangerous for elderly men. It depletes already-diminishing stores of vital bodily moisture and *spiritus*, the mysterious life-giving breath which permeates all living things. January refuses to admit his own susceptibility to the changing physiology of age. According to medical theory, his folly in doing so may well be fatal.

Dangerous sex

The aphrodisiacs to which January resorts on his wedding night comprise the nexus of a complex series of medical teachings relating to his sexual and procreative abilities. Speaking of the "ypocras, clarree, and vernage / Of spices hoote" (IV 1807–08) with which January fortifies himself, Paul Delany provides a useful analysis of the therapeutic effects offered by warm, spiced wine. By referring to Constantinus's *De coitu*, Delany demonstrates that January's tonic drinks illustrate his desire to achieve the right balance of humors for effective and fertile intercourse by countering the cold dry constitution of old age.[4] As Emerson Brown, Jr., states in "Januarie's Unlikely Elde," however, the scientific theories of the time pronounce sexual activity for the elderly "nearly a physical impossibility."[5] Medical writings current in the Middle Ages further reveal that January's sexual excesses, his advanced years, and his blindness all combine to signal his dangerously debilitated condition.

Physicians from the classical period onward equated loss of sight with excessive sexual indulgence and with a perilous physiological decline. In clearly delineating the intricate connections between the eyes and the production of semen, medical texts suggest that blindness can indicate a serious depletion of both natural moisture and *spiritus* due to intemperate sexual

3   Vincent of Beauvais, *Speculum naturale*, vol. 1 of *Speculum quadraplex* (1624, Austria: Akademische Druck-u. Verlagsanatalt, 1964), bk. XXXI, ch. XXXVII.
4   Paul Delany, "Constantinus Africanus and Chaucer's *Merchant's Tale*," *PQ* 46 (1967): 560–61.
5   Emerson Brown, Jr., "Januarie's 'Unlikely Elde,' " *NM* 74 (1973): 99.

activity. When exacerbated by the normal losses attendant upon old age, such a diminution can become life-threatening. Coitus constitutes a danger even to the young and fit, excessive sexuality always leading to disability or death. It is therefore far more dangerous for the elderly and infirm. January's vulnerability is demonstrated in his blindness which shows that none of his attempts to warm and moisten his aged body have met with any success. In fact, the physiological condition indicated by January's symptoms suggests that his very life may be threatened by his carnal appetites.

In documenting January's loss of sight, the Merchant likens Fortune to a scorpion which entices yet stings, and which has caused the ancient knight's disability:

> O sodeyn hap! O thou Fortune unstable!
> Lyk to the scorpion so deceyvable,
> That flaterest with thyn heed whan thou wolt stynge;
> Thy tayl is deeth, thurgh thyn envenymynge.
> O brotil joye! O sweete venym queynte!
> O monstre, that so subtilly kanst peynte
> Thy yiftes under hewe of stidefastnesse,
> That thou deceyvest bothe moore and lesse!
> Why hastow Januarie thus deceyved,
> That haddest hym for thy fulle freend receyved?
> And now thou hast biraft hym bothe his yen,
> For sorwe of which desireth he to dyen.   (IV 2057–68)

Though in medieval writings the poisonous scorpion often serves as an image of Fortune's vagaries, it also frequently refers to the sexual improprieties of a wicked woman, sometimes even representing lust itself. Ecclesiasticus 26.10, for example, observes that consorting with an unfaithful woman resembles holding a scorpion: "As a ӡok of oxen that is moued, so and a shreude womman; who holdith hir, as he caӡte a scorpioun." The Wycliffe Bible glossses this verse with a definition: "*a scorpioun*; that makith fair semelaunt with the face, and prickith with the tail; so a wickid womman drawith by flateryngis, and prickith til to deth, as Dalida dide to Sampson in xvij cº. of Judicum."[6] In an interpretation clearly indebted to the reference in Ecclesiasticus, the *Ancrene Riwle* more specifically identifies the scorpion with the sting of carnal pleasure, listing the scorpion of lechery in its catalogue of the seven deadly sins:

> whi Leccherie is likned to þe scorpioun Loo here þe skille. Þe scorpioun is a worme þat haþ sumdel þe heued likned to womman and nedder it is bihynden and makeþ fair semblaunt & fikeleþ wiþ þe heued and styngeþ

---

6   John Wycliffe, trans., *The Holy Bible*, ed. Josiah Forshall and Frederic Madden (Oxford: Oxford University Press, 1850), 3: 173.

wiþ þe tayl. . . . Qui apprehendit mulierem est quasi qui apprehendit scorpionem. (Who so takeþ a womman on honde he takeþ as he toke a scorpioun þat wolde styngen hym.) Þis leccherie is þat deuels best.[7]

The link between lustful practices and the scorpion's sting suggests an obscene pun in the Merchant's use of the word "tayl" which is reinforced by its proximity to the exclamation, "O swete venym queynte!" and through the growing implication that the wicked woman particular to this story is not only Fortune, but the "fresshe May" herself.[8]

In words that can easily suit the adulterous May, the Merchant condemns Fortune as a monster who covers her deception with promises of steadfastness. May panders to her husband's jealous self-interest, flattering him with protestations of fidelity before his humiliating betrayal. Her insincere blandishments disguise a scorpion's sting:

> I prey to God that nevere dawe the day
> That I ne sterve, as foule as womman may,
> If evere I do unto my kyn that shame,
> Or elles I empeyre so my name,
> That I be fals.   (IV 2195–99)

Like the scorpion, however, she soon stings him with her "tayl," although the destruction caused by her venomous "queynte" is not restricted to the arboreal exploits that make her husband a cuckold. The scorpion sting depriving January of his sight alludes both to the instability of earthly joy and to the more concrete effects of his carnal appetites, for medieval doctors caution that excessive coitus leads to blindness and eventual death. The Merchant may despise January for his senile lustfulness, but in this passage he equally condemns May as the agent of her husband's disability. The identification of Fortune with the scorpion and consequently with May leads to a causal relationship between the stinging tail and January's sudden blindness, a relationship which receives further emphasis through the context of the Merchant's lament. Occupying a privileged position by initiating the final act of the domestic drama, the Merchant's mocking apostrophe to the Goddess Fortuna immediately follows his voyeuristic report of January's activities in his enclosed garden:

> In somer seson, thider wolde he go,
> And May his wyf, and no wight but they two;

7   *The English Text of the Ancrene Riwle, Edited from Magdalene College, Cambridge MS. Pepys 2498*, ed. A. Zettersten, EETS, OS 274 (Oxford: Oxford University Press, 1976), 95. All other manuscripts of the *Ancrene Riwle* contain a similar passage.
8   Paull F. Baum ("Chaucer's Puns," *PMLA* 71 [1956]: 243) writes that the double meaning in these lines is unmistakable.

And thynges whiche that were nat doon abedde,
He in the gardyn parfourned hem and spedde.   (IV 2049–52)

This narrative connection with the garden of love augments the suggestive diction in extending the image of the scorpion to the illicit sexuality attributed to the wicked woman of the scriptures.

Necessary moisture

Although the female animal escapes the debilitating effects of sexual activity because she possesses a cold, moist constitution, sexual congress with her seriously depletes the male animal's vital heat and moisture. Commenting on Aristotle's observation that salacious males die sooner than their more temperate brothers, Averroës observes that, because life depends on heat and moisture, the complexion of youths is hot and moist, and that of the elderly is cold and dry: "and the proof of this is that those who engage in frequent intercourse live less long, and those who are castrated live longer than those who are not."[9] Medieval physicians and philosophers similarly depict sexual union as a necessary and deceptively pleasant danger. For example, in enumerating the harmful effects of coitus, Constantinus Africanus refers to Galen's teachings:

Galen says the same thing in his book on semen, when he speaks of those who have intercourse too often: not only does a humor come from the organs, but the vital spirit also leaves with the semen through the arteries. So it is hardly surprising that someone who has intercourse too often will be weakened. For when the body is drained of these two substances, and lustful man thinks only of pleasure, the vital spirit is dissipated; many have died in this way, and no wonder. Galen shows that when any animal has intercourse too often it soon dies, but will live longer than usual if it has intercourse rarely.[10]

Not all the sexually incontinent die outright from their excesses, however. When natural moisture and vital spirit become sufficiently depleted, blindness results,

---

[9] Aristotle, *De longitudine et brevitate vitae*, vol. 6 of *Aristoteles opera cum Averrois commentariis*, ch. 3. Aristotle's original comment states: "Quapropter salacia & multi seminis senescunt cito semen enim excrementum & amplius exsicat emissum. Et propter hoc mulus est longioris vitae equo & asino, ex quibus genitus est: & foeminae maribus, si salaces sint mares. Quapropter & passeres masculi breuioris vitae foeminis." [This is why those who are salacious and those who produce much semen grow old quickly. The semen is a residue, and its emission causes dryness. And because of this the mule lives longer than the horse or the ass from which it is generated, and females live longer than males, if the males are salacious. This is why male sparrows have a shorter life than females.]

[10] Paul Delaney, "Constantinus Africanus' *De Coitu:* A Translation," *ChauR* 4 (1970): 61.

for the eyes, the brain, and the genital secretions are closely connected. The loss of sight is both a warning that the body has become overtaxed, and a harbinger of imminent death should the reckless behavior continue.

Through comments not found in any of the sources or analogues to the tale, Chaucer carefully establishes that, although January had remained "wyflees" for sixty years, he had certainly not pursued celibacy, following "his bodily delyt / On wommen, ther as was his appetyt" (IV 1249–50). Having decided to marry, January emphasizes his interest in the carnal aspect of conjugal relations, declaring that abstinence or even temperance within marriage holds little attraction for one who feels his "lymes stark and suffisaunt / To do al that a man bilongeth to" (IV 1458–59). Although he piously intends children as part of the joys of wedlock, January clearly focuses on the pleasure involved in their begetting. According to his philosophy, the elderly man should "take a yong wyf and a feir, / On which he myghte engendren hym an heir" (IV 1271–72). January fully adopts medieval society's criteria for proof of masculinity. He congratulates himself on his ability to satisfy even a young and lusty wife, and he emphasizes his intention to beget a male child to inherit his estates and possessions. In this emphasis, Chaucer's character differs markedly from the husband in the analogues who, although jealous of his wife's affections, never exhibits the lascivious nature attributed to January.[11]

Having indulged in salacious fantasies about the young woman who will become his bride, January emphasizes his manliness by celebrating his sexual stamina and prowess in pitying the innocent May:

> "Allas! O tendre creature
> Now wolde God ye myghte wel endure
> Al my corage, it is so sharp and keene!"   (IV 1757–59)

Nor does his ardor abate after the exertions of the honeymoon, for lust forms the basis of every encounter between the old lecher and his young wife. Boasting, "I feele me nowhere hoor but on myn heed" (IV 1464), January declares his resolute intention to ignore chronological age and to demonstrate what he believes to be youthful virility.

Because the analogues to the *Merchant's Tale* devote little space to the psychology of the deceived husband, neither his lecherous history nor his present lasciviousness receive any attention. In addition, although other renditions of the story identify the husband as rich, none presents him as old. Unique in emphasizing both January's advanced years and his life-long lustfulness, Chaucer provides physiological clues that explain the blindness which occurs without comment in most other treatments of the story. January suffers from

11   Larry D. Benson and Theodore M. Anderson, eds., *The Literary Context of Chaucer's Fabliaux* (New York: Bobbs-Merrill, 1971), 204–05.

old age and the deleterious effects of excessive sexual activity, each of which, according to medical wisdom, can precipitate a loss of vision.

Albert the Great details the effects of carnal overindulgence on both the eyes and the brain by recounting an exemplum told to him by his teacher, Clement of Bohemia. A certain grey monk, he says, approached a beautiful lady and, like a famished man, he made love to her sixty-six times before the matins bells were rung. He collapsed that morning and died the same day. At his autopsy, his whole brain was found to have shrunk to the size of a pomegranate, and the moisture in his eyes was similarly diminished.[12] This story illustrates the intricate connection between brain, eyes, and semen which originates in classical medicine and which permeates all medieval explorations of the source of sperm. Later in his work, for example, Albert posits a special relationship between the encephalic system and the members of generation. Sperm, he writes, is derived mostly from the brain, which is white and soft and moist, similar to the substance of sperm. Proof of his explanation lies in the observation that through excessive coitus the brain is diminished and the eyes which are like the brain are also drained and greatly debilitated.[13] In this opinion, Albert agrees with earlier sources. Hippocrates describes how the foamy sperm passes through the body to the testicles: "This humor is diffused from the brain into the loins and the whole body, but in particular into the spinal marrow: for passages extend into this from the whole body, which enable the humor to pass to and from the spinal marrow."[14] Connected to the brain and extending the length of the body to the members of generation, the spinal cord contains cerebral matter which provides a major component of sperm. Hippocrates proves this affinity by observing that "those who have had an incision made by the ear, can indeed have intercourse and emit sperm, but the amount is small, weak and sterile. For the greater part of the sperm travels from the head past the ears into the spinal marrow: now when the incision has formed a scar, this passage becomes obstructed."[15]

Following Hippocrates, Aristotle equates the nature of genital secretions to that of the brain, explaining, like his source, that specific veins carry seminal

[12] "Et quidem narravit mihi magister Clemens de Bohemia, quod quidam monachus griseus accessit ad quandam dominam pulchram et sicut famelicus homo eam ante pulsam matutinarum expetivit sexaginta sex vicibus, in crastino decubuit et mortuus est eadem die. Et quia fuit nobilis, apertum fuit corpus eis, et repertum est cerebrum totum evacuatum, ita quod nihil de ipso mansit nisi ad quantitatem pomi granati, et oculi similiter annihilati." Albertus Magnus, *Questiones super de animalibus*, vol. 12 of *Opera omnia* (Aschendorff: Monasterii Westfalorum, 1955), 268; bk. XV, qu. 14.
[13] "Et ideo ab illis partibus magis derivatur sperma et maxime a cerebro, quia cerebrum est album et molle et humidum, et in hoc convenit cum substantia spermatis. Et huius signum est, quod per superfluum coitum extenuatur cerebrum et profundantur oculi, qui conveniunt cum cerebro et debilitantur multum." Albertus Magnus, 268; bk. XV, qu. 14.
[14] Hippocrates, "On the Nature of the Child," *The Hippocratic Treatises*, ed. and trans. Iain M. Lonie (New York: Walter de Gruyter, 1981), 1.
[15] Hippocrates, 2.

matter from the brain to the testicles.[16] He offers as proof that the brain becomes diminished by intercourse the observation that eunuchs do not become bald because they have a large amount of cerebral matter with abundant moisture to stimulate hair growth. Their success in preserving this vital substance stems from their inability to ejaculate. Brain and genitals are therefore linked.[17]

As Jacquart and Thomasset demonstrate in their study, *Sex and Medicine in the Middle Ages*, the teachings of both ancient and contemporary physicians were readily available to the literate laity in the great medieval encyclopedias.[18] Vincent of Beauvais' *Speculum naturale*, for example, contains a full range of opinions about the origin of semen, providing arguments both from those who contend that it derives from the brain and those who state that it is drawn from the whole body. After establishing that semen, produced in the fourth and final digestion, mingles with *spiritus* in the seminal plexis described by Galen, Vincent quotes Hippocrates' dictum that semen derives from the brain and that veins passing behind the ears transmit seminal matter.[19]

The eyes, connected to the brain and hence through the backbone to the genitals, form another important component of semen. In his discussion of the formation of the embryo, for example, Aristotle explains the congruence of eyes and brain by observing that, "the purest fluid around the brain is carried away through the ducts which are visible running from the eyes to the membrane around the brain. A proof of this is that there are no other moist, cold parts in the head except the brain and the cool, moist eyes."[20] Through this affinity with the brain, the eyes maintain a close relationship to semen because, as Aristotle

---

16 "Sunt item quae de utraque proferantur ad testes, per dorsi medullam tenues: atque etiam aliae quae subditae cuti tendant per carnem ad renes, cessentque ad testes viris, ad vterum mulieribus ... quae seminariae nominatur." [There are also two other delicate veins running on each side (of the neck) through the spinal marrow, which are directed to the testicles. There is another pair which are called the seminal veins running a little under the skin through the flesh to the genital regions, terminating at the testicles in men and at the uterus in women]. Aristotle, *De historia animalium*, bk. III, ch. II.

17 "Cur spadones calui effici nequeant? An eo quam multum cerebri obtinent: quod sane his contingit, quia rem veneream non agunt: semen enim labi per spinam ex cerebro videtur." [Why is it that eunuchs cannot become bald? Is it because they have a great deal of cerebral matter and this surely happens because of their inability to have intercourse: for it is seen that the semen flows through the spine from the brain.] Aristotle, *Problematum*, vol 7. of *Aristoteles opera cum Averrois commentariis*, bk. X, no. 56.

18 D. Jacquart and C. Thomasset, *Sexuality and Medicine in the Middle Ages*, trans. Matthew Adamson (Princeton: Princeton University Press, 1988), 38.

19 "Hippocrates ait, quod plurimum materiae spermatis est a cerebro, & quod descendit ex duabus venis, quae sunt post ambas aures." [Hippocrates says that the material of sperm mostly comes from the brain and descends by way of two veins which are behind both ears.] Vincent of Beauvais, bk. XXXI, ch. XI.

20 "Ab humiditate que circa cerebrum segregatur purissimum per poros, qui videntur ferentes ab ipsis ad miningam eam que circa cerebrum. Huius autem argumentum: neque enim alia particula humida et frigida est in capite preter cerebrum, oculusque frigidus et humidus." Aristotle, *De generatione animalium*, trans. William of Moerbeck, ed. H. J.

goes on to explain, "The passage around the eyes is the most closely connected to the sperm of any of the passages which go around the head. This is abundantly clear in that in sexual intercourse it alone is changed and the eyes are clearly sunken in after too much intercourse."[21] The pseudo-Aristotelian *Problems* confirm the belief that coitus diminishes vision by referring to the dessication attendant upon sexual activity: "Why is it that those who are sexually active and eunuchs who never have sex both lose their sharpness of vision? Is it that in the former because of their desire and the latter because of their excision, the upper parts become drier than usual, and this is most easily seen in those organs which perform delicate work, such as the eye?"[22]

Galen greatly expands Hippocratic and Aristotelian descriptions of the relationship between eyes and genitals, observing from his anatomical dissections that large, soft nerves from the encephalon (the brain, spinal cord and the nervous system) extend into the eye. As the chief instrument of vision, the crystalline humor or lens must receive quality nourishment from the body. Because blood in an unrefined state will not suffice to feed this radiant humor, the body forms an intermediary, the vitreous humor which moistens and nourishes the delicate lens. This specialized humor, or white of the eye, derives its sustenance from the encephalon itself, being of similar constitution.[23] The dessication concurrent with old age dries all parts of the eye, including the important vitreous humor. With its source of nourishment impaired, the lens solidifies and darkens until sight diminishes.

The *Speculum naturale* likewise links cerebral matter to the physiology of the eye: "Eyes are the most precious part of the body. None of its members are cold and moist except the eyes and the brain."[24] Quoting Avicenna's *Canon*, Vincent further explains that cerebral matter and *spiritus* descend to the eye

---

Drossart Lulofs, vol. 17.2.5 of *Aristoteles Latinus* (Leiden: E. J. Brill, 1966), 71; bk. II, ch. I.

[21] "Circa oculos enim porus eorum que circa caput maxime spermaticus est. Declarat autem in coitibus transformatus manifeste solus, et utentibus pluribus venereis operibus deprimuntur oculi manifeste." Aristotle, *De gen. an.*, 78; bk. II, ch. VIII.

[22] "Quam ob rem & qui concumbunt, & spadones, qui re minime vtuntur venerea, in acumine oculorum offenduntur? An quam alteris ob libidinem, alteris ob excisionem partes superiores plus iusto exiccantur: quod perspicuum in iis est, quorum opus exquisitius administratur, aspectus autem tale est." Aristotle, *Prob.*, bk. IV, qu. 3.

[23] "Eadem porro ratio est in nervis oculorum: duri quidem in ipsorum musculos inferuntur, alii vero in primum et principalissimum visus instrumentum, humorem scilicet crystallinum." [So too the hard nerves of the eyes are inserted into the muscles, the other truly into the first and most important instrument of vision, that is the crystalline humour.] Claudius Galen, *De usu partium corporis humani*, vols. 3–4 of *Opera Omnia*, ed. C. G. Kühn (1822, Hildesheim: Georg Olms, 1964), 635; bk. X, ch. 1. For an English translation, see Margret Tallmadge May, trans., *Galen: On the Usefulness of the Parts of the Body* (Ithaca: Cornell University Press, 1968).

[24] "Oculi sunt pars corporis preciosissima. Nullumque in eo membrum est frigidum & humidum nisi oculi & cerebrum." Vincent of Beauvais, bk. XXVIII, ch. XLVII.

through two nerves.[25] Although Vincent refrains from providing the kind of moral exemplum given by Albert, according to his view of anatomy the brain, eyes, and members of generation share both substance and *spiritus*.

Chaucer's old knight clearly faces risks to his eyesight simply by virtue of his age; he increases his susceptibility, however, in his foolish insistence on sexual pleasure as a measure of his manliness. Even in youth, sexual activity reduces the body's moisture, especially in the eyes and brain which demonstrate a constitutional affinity to semen. In advancing years, too much sex further dims the vision of those who already experience the natural dessication of the body.

Vital spirits

The entire encephalon including brain and eyes also differs from other bodily organs by its plenitude of *spiritus*. Because the sense of sight depends heavily on sufficient *spiritus* in the eye, sexual activity which depletes this essential ingredient in addition to necessary moisture is doubly harmful. Originally denoting both air and wind, the word *spiritus* evolves in medical writings to describe the complex merging of the material substance of air with the body's vital force.[26] Bartholomaeus Anglicus identifies *spiritus* as a "sotille spiritual substance and aery kind," commenting, "and þat is iclepid *spiritus [naturalis]*, for kindeliche by þe myȝt þerof he makeþ þe blood sotile, and by liȝtnes þerof he meueþ þe blood and sendiþ it aboute into alle þe lymes. And þerfore þis spirit propirliche reuliþ and gouernyth þe kinde vertu of lif."[27] Although he mentions three separate varieties of *spiritus*, Galen stresses mainly two kinds, that which is carried to all organs by the arterial blood and that which permeates only the brain and nervous tissue, including the bone marrow and the spinal cord. Essential to maintaining life, the vital *spiritus* which infuses the whole body differs in both production and purpose from the cerebral *spiritus* which specifically carries messages relating to nervous and mental activity. Bartholomaeus likewise divides *spiritus naturalis* into two distinct varieties. Maintaining life in all parts of the body, the *spiritus vitalis* originates in the heart whereas the brain manufactures *spiritus animalis*.[28] Bartholomaeus goes

[25] "Virtus autem visus & materia spiritus visibilis a cerebro procedit ad locum per viam duorum neruorum concauorum." [But the virtue of sight and the *spiritus* providing the material for vision proceeds from the brain to that location (i.e., the eye) by way of two concave nerves.] Vincent of Beauvais, bk. XXVIII, ch. XLVIII.

[26] James J. Bono traces the evolution of the term *spiritus* from its simple denotation in Greek medicine to its far more complex meaning in the medicine and philosophy of the Middle Ages. See "Medical Spirits and the Medieval Language of Life," *Traditio* 40 (1984): 92–130.

[27] John Trevisa, *On the Properties of Things: John Trevisa's Translation of Bartholomaeus Anglicus De proprietatibus rerum* (Oxford: Clarendon Press, 1975), 1: 122.

[28] "For out of a denne of þe lift side of þe herte comeþ a veyne and in is meuynge is departid in tweye braunches. Þe on þerof goþ donward and sprediþ in many bowes and sprayes by

on to point out that this spirit travels via the backbone to the various parts of the body.[29]

Of all sensory organs, the eye requires the largest amount of *spiritus* to operate effectively, vision depending heavily on the action of this vapour within the structure of the eye. Explaining that large quantities of cerebral *spiritus* are needed to fill the empty spaces of the eye socket as well as to enable the iris to open and close, Galen suggests an experiment to verify his belief: "if we close one eye and keep the other open, we see that the pupil becomes dilated and expanded, as if it were inflated. Now reason makes evident that it is in this position because it is full of *spiritus*."[30]

In old age, the supply of *spiritus*, like the supply of blood, diminishes for a variety of reasons. The lungs dry out, drawing in less air to be used as raw material,[31] the moisture in the brain lessens because of general dessication, and the soft, flexible nerves, conduits for *spiritus*, harden and narrow. Whereas drying and wrinkles of the transparent humors of the eye contribute to loss of vision in old age, Galen explains that a decrease in the amount of available *spiritus* constitutes the major cause of senile blindness.[32]

þe whiche þe spirit *vitalis* of lif is ibrouȝt to ȝeue þe lif to alle þe ne ir lymes of þe body. Þe oþir bow goþ vpward and is departid in þre braunches. Þe rizt bow þerof goþ to þe riȝt arme and þe lift bowe to þe lift arme and spprediþ in diuers sprayes. And so þe spirit *vitalis* is isprad into al þe body and makeþ þe veynes þe puls of lif. Þe middil bouȝ strecchiþ to þe brayn and ȝeueþ lif to þe ou[er] parties and spprediþ þe spirit *vitalis* in alle þe parties about. Þe same spirit perischiþ and passiþ furþere to þe dennes of þe brayn and þere he is iruled and imade sotile and bicomeþ *spiritus animalis*. And þis spirit is so ichaungid, it is more sotile þan oþir." Trevisa, 1: 122.

[29] Trevisa, 1: 123.

[30] "Quin et si alterum oculorum clauserimus alterum aperientes, amplificatam ac dilatatam et veluti inflatam pupillam intuebimur. Proinde non ratione modo constat, pupillam quidem spiritu refertam sic affici." Galen, 782; bk. X, ch. 5.

[31] In old age, the lung becomes hard, dry and unable to draw in the necessary air. See Aristotle, *De iuuentute et senectute, vita et morte, et respiratione,*vol. 6 of *Aristoteles opera cum Averrois commentariis*, ch. XIV. In his second book on the organs of respiration (bk. VII, ch. 1) Galen also describes the flexible, blood-filled lung necessary for adequate respiration. In old age the amount of blood decreases and the lung dries, a process which depletes the supply of *spiritus* available.

[32] "Quin et valde senibus cornea tunica interdum adeo fit rugosa, ut alii quidem prorsus nihil, alii ver male ac vix adhuc videant. Incidentibus enim aliis super alias rugis, tunicaque ob eam causam duplicata, crassitiemque acquisititiam assumere, spiritu praetera superne ad pupillam parciore affluente, proportione oculi iis impediuntur; id ipsum enim, quod spiritus parcior a principio affluat, in causa potissimum est, ut pupilla corrugetur. Ex quibus omnibus intelligi potest, spatium omne, quod est post humorem crystallinum, spiritu simul et humore tenui assidue repleri; num, quodque in caeteris partibus humor, in ipsa vero potissimum pupilla spiritus inest plurimus. [Moreover in old people the cornea frequently becomes wrinkled so that some of them have no sight, others see poorly or with difficulty. When the wrinkles overlap each other, and for this reason the cornea is doubled in thickness, and when less *spiritus* flows into the pupil from above, the eyes are impaired proportionally.

The production of semen similarly requires an abundant source of *spiritus* to facilitate both erection and ejaculation. Frequent coitus therefore depletes the body's supply of this vital breath. January's eyesight is already endangered by virtue of his age, but according to medical teachings linking sex and *spiritus*, his excessive carnal appetite increases the likelihood of blindness. In discusssing the role of *spiritus* in male sexual performance, Aristotle notes the unique ability of the male organ to expand or decrease naturally, attributing this facility to the presence of airy *spiritus* which fills hollow chambers and allows erection.[33] In addition, sexual intercourse further depletes the body's supply of *spiritus* because it is emitted with the sperm.[34] Building on Aristotle's teaching, William of Conches lists *spiritus* as among the three necessary prerequisites to successful coition.[35] He continues his explanation of sexual union, linking the male genitalia with the sensory system.[36] Later he proves that all sensory organs originate in the brain, being therefore replete with cerebral *spiritus*.[37] Thus, in addition to dessicating the body's natural moisture, primarily that of the brain and eyes, the production and emission of semen draw on the supply of cerebral *spiritus* contained mainly in the members of the encephalon. Of all bodily organs, the eye holds the greatest amount of this vital breath because it is necessary for adequate vision. Excessive sexual activity therefore saps this important component of sight, intensifying the already deleterious effect of moisture loss.

From this, then (it is understood that), less *spiritus* flowing from the brain is the greatest cause of the wrinkling of the pupil. From all of this it can be understood that all the space behind the lens is filled with *spiritus* and a thin humour. In the rest of the eye the humour prevails, but most of the *spiritus* exists in the pupil itself.] Galen, 783–84; bk. X, ch. V.

33 "Augetur etiam, et minuitur hoc vnum membrum, sine vlla morbi mutatione. . . . Constat hoc membrum ex eiusmodi partibus, vt eorum, quam modo dixi, vtrunque possit euenire partim enim neruum, partim cartilaginem habet, itaque & contra hi potest & extendi, atque entflatus capex est." [This organ, again, is the only one that, independently of any morbid change, admits of augmentation and of diminution of bulk. . . . For it is partly sinewy, partly cartilaginous, and thus is enabled either to contract or to become extended, and is capable of being inflated.] Aristotle. *De partibus animalium*, vol. 6 of *Aristoteles opera cum Averrois commentariis*, bk. IV, ch. 10.

34 "Quod virtus animae emittitur cum spermate." Albertus Magnus, 267; bk. XV, qu. 13.

35 "Sunt uero illi tria necessaria: semen quod emittatur, calor qui hominem accendit, & qui semen eliciat . . . & spiritus qui uirgam erigat & semen expellat." [These three (qualities) are necessary: semen to be emitted, heat to inflame men and to bring out semen . . . and air to cause erection of the male member and to expel semen.] William of Conches, *Dragmaticon (De substantiis physicis) Book 6* (1567, Frankfurt: Minerva, Unveranderter Nachdruck, 1967), 237.

36 "Sed quia neruosa est uirga, nerui vero sunt organa sensus." [But the penis is a nerve, and nerves are indeed organs of sense.] William of Conches, 238.

37 William of Conches, 326. Having cited Avicenna and Constantinus in defining semen as hot, moist, and full of *spiritus*, Vincent of Beauvais quotes William of Conches's three requisites for intercourse (bk. XXXI, ch. X).

Bartholomaeus also explicitly connects the eyes with sexual activity, explaining that too frequent coitus depletes both moisture and *spiritus*. He writes that blindness can be caused by both outward injuries and by inward malfunctions, including "fleischlich likinge and ofte seruyse of Venus þat corrumpiþ and dissolueþ þe spiritis and þe humour cristallyne."[38] In old men, he explains, the important bodily humors and *spiritus* are consumed by time and wasted away.[39] Coitus, therefore, places enormous demands on a physiology already heavily burdened. January's eyesight is endangered by virtue of his age alone, but according to all medieval evidence, his susceptibility is greatly increased by frequent sexual congress.

The final tableau of the *Merchant's Tale* shows January, flattered by his impending fatherhood, lovingly caressing May's abdomen. The aged knight readily accepts his wife's protestations of innocence after the affair in the tree, as well as her hint that she is about to bear legitimate offspring. The resolution of the tale suggests that May's relationship with Damian will continue to bear fruit. In addition, it implies that January's already dangerous physical condition will worsen, despite the restoration of his sight. If he persists in his lascivious ways – and the erotic undertones of the final picture leave little doubt that he intends no conversion – his already diminished supply of moisture and *spiritus* will not long sustain him. The ultimate irony of the *Merchant's Tale* may be that January's attempts to prove his masculinity, even in old age, will not only result in an illegitimate heir, but will also hasten his own demise.

[38] Trevisa, 1: 360.
[39] Trevisa, 1: 364.

Male Movement and Female Fixity
in the *Franklin's Tale* and *Il Filocolo*

ANDREA ROSSI-REDER

A discussion of masculinity in Chaucer's *Franklin's Tale* requires an examination not only of men's actions in the tale, but also of the way in which men's actions affect and contrast with women's behavior. Moreover, since Chaucer bases his depictions of masculinity and femininity on models in Giovanni Boccaccio's *Il Filocolo*, Libro IV, Questione III, the probable source for Chaucer's *Franklin's Tale*, it is important to see what Chaucer really did with gender issues in *Il Filocolo*. In Boccaccio's tale men are constantly on the move, either parading in public or traveling around the world, usually in an attempt to attract the *donna*'s attention. In the *Franklin's Tale* Chaucer incorporates this theme of mobile men, but demonstrates further that men's movements take place outside of the domestic sphere, whereas women's movements, confined to enclosed spaces, are severely limited. In Boccaccio, the *donna*'s limited mobility also limits her characterization, but Chaucer places his female lead, Dorigen, at the center of the tale despite her lack of physical movement in the story. In Chaucer the reader is privy to Dorigen's mental movements and to the plans that she makes in private, unobtrusively, that produce as much result as the obvious place-to-place movements and machinations of the men in the tale. Masculine agency in Chaucer's *Franklin's Tale* involves physical mobility while female agency entails intellectual movement, which serves as a remedy for limited physical movement and rock-like fixity.

Boccaccio's story in *Il Filocolo* opens with the would-be lover, Tarolfo, strutting before the *donna*:

Forse con sovente passare davanti alle sue case, o giostrando, o armeg-
giando o con altri atti, s'ingegnava d'avere l'amore di lei.[1]

[Maybe with frequent passing before her house, either tilting, or jousting,
or performing other feats, he would be able to earn the lady's love.]

Tarolfo remains active throughout the tale, not only prancing about, but later
traveling to the remotest parts of the world, eager to devise a way to produce
the garden that the *donna* has requested. Tebano, the magician whom Tarolfo
encounters in his travels, also moves in an accelerated manner, even flying in
a Medea-like chariot around the world in one night to create the magic garden.
Overall, masculinity in *Filocolo IV, III* points to agency through exaggerated
movement. The movement of the men contrasts with the unnamed *donna*'s lack
of movement; she remains at home throughout the tale, venturing out only at
the request of her husband to fulfill her promise to Tarolfo. House-bound as she
is, the *donna*'s method of agency involves private, inward action – thinking –
rather than outward, physical action. Privately, she devises a way of discourag-
ing Tarolfo – thus, the request for a flowering garden in December – which
eventually causes all of the men in the tale to re-act. The men's exaggerated
motions, especially those of Tarolfo and Tebano, bring the male characters to
the forefront as central characters while the *donna*, overshadowed by male
movement, becomes even more marginalized.

Like Boccaccio, Chaucer sets up the contrast between men's movement and
women's fixity. In the *Franklin's Tale* men move about freely and in an
exaggerated manner, while Dorigen remains relegated mostly to the domestic
spheres of her world. Boccaccio emphasizes the *donna*'s lack of mobility by
marginalizing her as a character, but Chaucer makes Dorigen his central
character by revealing in detail what her private thoughts and actions are.[2]
Chaucer demonstrates that Dorigen's remedy for her lack of physical mobility
is the exercise of her mental capacities. Furthermore, Chaucer highlights the
contrast between male movement and female fixity by changing the nature of
the task that the woman requests of the suitor. By substituting Boccaccio's
garden in December with removing the rocks, Chaucer has chosen an appropriate symbol, not only of Dorigen's separation from Arveragus, as many critics
have noted,[3] but of her own physical state. Like Dorigen, the rocks remain fixed

---

1   Giovanni Boccaccio, *Il Filocolo*, a cura di Salvatore Battaglia (Bari: Laterza, 1938), 311.
All translations are mine.
2   Carolynn Van Dyke, "The Clerk's and Franklin's Subjected Subjects," *SAC* 17 (1995):
53, claims that references to and by Dorigen take up 30% of the *Franklin's Tale* (she counts
270 out of 896 lines devoted to Dorigen in Chaucer). This would give Dorigen more lines
than any other character in the tale. Van Dyke points out that in Boccaccio, text related to
the wife's character takes up only about 22%, thus showing Chaucer's expansion of the
wife's role in his tale.
3   For example, see Charles A. Owen, Jr., "The Crucial Passages in Five of the *Canterbury
Tales*," *JEGP* 52 (1953): 295; Douglas A. Burger, "The Cosa Impossibile of *Il Filocolo* and

in one place and only seem to be re-moved through male agency (and even then their removal seems to be only an illusion). Although both Dorigen and the *donna* demonstrate cleverness in dealing with Aurelius and Tarolfo, the men of the tales ultimately take credit for saving the women from shame and dishonor. Women's agency remains private and unseen, while men's agency tends to be public and therefore seemingly more efficacious.[4]

Astonished women

As Elaine Tuttle Hansen points out, Dorigen is stunned, or "astoned," in the *Franklin's Tale* when she hears that the rocks have disappeared.[5] I contend that men's movements in Boccaccio and Chaucer cause the women to be "astoned" throughout both tales. Dorigen and the *donna* are part of a medieval and Renaissance literary tradition of the unmoving woman, or to borrow a term from Dante's *Rime Petrose*, the *Donna Petrosa*. Dante's *Donna Petrosa*, or "Stony Woman," in her unwillingness to love, becomes a natural force, like a mountain or rock that cannot be moved despite the male lover's attempts to move her emotionally. In the *Rime*, Dante identifies her with and absorbs her into his poetic landscape.[6] Based on earlier *stilnovisti* models, Dante's stony woman becomes a model for later "cold ladies" who appear in poems by Petrarch, Shakespeare, and others.

Boccaccio's *donna* and Chaucer's Dorigen are likewise unmovable in their affections. Committed as they are to their husbands, they both find it unthinkable to give in to their suitors. Thus, part of their "a-stone-ishment" is voluntary. The traditional *Donna Petrosa* is cold and unmovable without reason and is, moreover, compassionless. Similarly, Boccaccio's *donna* is not moved by Tarolfo, but in her annoyance she devises the garden task to get rid of him. In the *Franklin's Tale*, despite Dorigen's unwillingness to be moved to love Aurelius, his pathetic pleas move her to compassion, and she offers the rock task as a sort of solace. Dorigen's compassion allows her to present to Aurelius, along with her promise, the terms of her conditions – and the terms of her own rock-like social condition. Dorigen asks, perhaps subconsciously, for an end to

the Impossible of the *Franklin's Tale*," in *Chaucer and the Craft of Fiction*, ed. Leigh A. Arrathoon (Rochester, MN: Solaris Press, 1986), 169; Gerald Morgan, "Boccaccio's *Filocolo* and the Moral Argument of the *Franklin's Tale*," *ChauR* 20 (1986): 295; Elaine Tuttle Hansen, *Chaucer and the Fictions of Gender* (Berkeley: University of California Press, 1992), 277–78.

[4] See Hansen, 268–69; David Raybin, " 'Wommen, of kynde, desiren libertee': Rereading Dorigen, Rereading Marriage," *ChauR* 27 (1992): 66–67.

[5] See Hansen, 278–79.

[6] See Dante's so-called *Rime Petrose*, numbers 77–80. The best edition, with excellent footnotes, appears in G. B. Squarotti and others, eds., *Opere Minori di Dante Alighieri* (Torino: Unione Tipografico Editrice Torinese, 1983). See also Patrick Diehl, trans., *Dante's Rime* (Princeton: Princeton University Press, 1979).

her own "stony" situation. As a medieval woman, she has little access to the mobility and to the credit for deeds that men in her society enjoy. Since there is little hope of changing her "astoned" state in any noticeable way, Dorigen's rock challenge is illusory even before the Orleans clerk renders it so. She may try what she can to attain results, and even succeed, but by the end of the tale, men seem to have done more because their actions have been physical, public, and therefore more obvious. When both Boccaccio's and Chaucer's stories end, women easily are overlooked as potential candidates for being the "mooste fre" (V 1622), and men, who seem to have done so much more, become the focus of the debates about generosity.

The effect and influence of men's agency are particularly evident in Boccaccio's *questione d'amore*, where the debate regarding who is most generous immediately focuses on the three men, excluding the *donna* completely:

> Dubitasi ora quale di costoro fosse maggiore liberalitá, o quella del cavaliere che concedette alla donna l'andare a Tarolfo, o quella di Tarolfo, il quale quella donna cui egli avea sempre disiata, o per cui egli avea tanto fatto per venire a quel punto a che venuto era, quando la donna venne a lui, rimandò la sopradetta libera al suo marito; o quella di Tebano, il quale, abbandonate le sue contrade, oramai vecchio, e venuto quivi per guadagnare i promessi doni, e affannatosi per recare a fine ciò che promesso avea, avendoli guadagnati, ogni cosa rimise, rimanendosi povero come prima.[7]

> [Decide now who of these three showed the most generosity: The knight who allowed the lady to go to Tarolfo? Or Tarolfo, who had always desired the lady and for whom he had done so much to get to this point (yet when the lady came to him, he sent her back free to her husband)? Or Tebano, who, already old, having allowed the contract to be broken, having come all this way to earn the promised rewards and having earned them justly, and having worked to bring about all that he had promised, renounced everything, remaining as poor as before?]

In this passage Menedon (Boccaccio's storyteller) uses active verbs of giving which strongly suggest that the men have been generous. Interestingly enough, although Fiammetta and her female companions (listening to Menedon's tale) have the last say in the debate, they still choose the husband, never even considering the generosity of the *donna*.[8]

In the *Franklin's Tale*, however, Chaucer does not exclude Dorigen from the debate. Not specifying names, the Franklin merely asks who is "mooste fre" (1622), without limiting the options to the three men. In this way Chaucer

---

7   Boccaccio, 320.
8   For more on this, see Morgan, "Boccaccio's *Filocolo*," 303.

allows the reader to make the choice,[9] and the award for generosity can be as much Dorigen's as any of the three men's.[10]

Moving men

Yet Chaucerian critics, perhaps taking the lead from the *Filocolo*, traditionally have excluded Dorigen from the contest. Another factor may contribute to the omission of women from the debate in both tales: men's actions and movements are more exaggerated than women's, thus distracting the readers' attentions from the women to the men. Arveragus is off traveling for most of the tale, and when he does return home he "daunceth" and "justeth" (1098); Aurelius energetically prances about and later travels to Orleans; the clerk journeys from Orleans to Brittany and then back. In Boccaccio, Tarolfo struts, demonstrating his prowess to the *donna*. Moreover, as if identity necessarily involves physical movement and public exposure, only Tarolfo and Tebano are named – both the *donna* and her husband remain at home and anonymous. Once the *donna* has requested the garden, she more or less disappears, and the tale centers on Tarolfo's journey that eventually takes him to far-off Thessaly, where he meets Tebano. The focus then becomes Tebano's worldwide search for the ingredients to make a garden bloom in December as in May. In *Il Filocolo* and to a certain extent in the *Franklin's Tale*, physical action and generosity seem to go hand in hand. Generosity is deemed an active choice performed only by physically active men. In order to produce visible results, the men in these tales must rely on obvious physical movement. In his study on masculinity, David E. Gilmore discusses the perceived connection in certain Mediterranean countries between masculine action and result. In many cultures, he tells us, the ideals of manliness

> depend upon . . . a mobility of action, a personal autonomy. A man can do nothing if his hands are tied. If he is going to hunt dangerous game and, like Odysseus, save his family, he needs absolute freedom of movement.[11]

---

[9] Van Dyke, 49; N. H. G. E. Veldhoen, " 'Which was the mooste fre': Chaucer's Realistic Humour and Insight into Human Nature, as Shown in the *Frankeleyns Tale*," in *In Other Words: Transcultural Studies in Philology, Translation, and Lexicology Presented to Hans Heinrich Meier on the Occasion of His Sixty-fifth Birthday* (Dordrecht: Foris, 1989): 107, remarks that although the neuter pronoun in Chaucer's question ("*which* was the mooste fre?") indicates male *and* female contention, the Boccaccian source tale, by its insistence on male generosity, eliminates the *donna*.

[10] See Hansen, 10–15; Carolyn Dinshaw, *Chaucer's Sexual Poetics* (Madison: University of Wisconsin Press, 1992), 57; Mary R. Bowman, " 'Half as she were mad': Dorigen in the Male World of the *Franklin's Tale*," *ChauR* 27 (1993): 241–42.

[11] David E. Gilmore, *Manhood in the Making: Cultural Concepts of Masculinity* (New Haven: Yale University Press, 1990), 50.

Gilmore argues that manliness in certain cultures is dependent upon access to mobility, specifically acted in the public sphere and away from domestic spaces.[12] Similarly, the male characters in Chaucer and Boccaccio assert their masculinity by moving freely. Such unrestricted movement makes men more visible and thereby more likely to be held accountable for results of actions. Masculinity in the *Franklin's Tale* and *Il Filocolo IV, III* involves outward action with its perceived effectiveness, while femininity encompasses the less conspicuous action of thinking in private which falsely appears to produce fewer results.

Men seem constantly on the move, while women tend to stay close to home. The exception to the "moving man" is the husband in the *Filocolo*, who, unlike Arveragus, never leaves home during the tale. In fact, the *donna* tells Tarolfo (once she has seen the garden) that she can visit him only when her husband is away hunting or out of town. Since her husband never seems to leave, perhaps she offers this condition knowing that her spouse will never be absent, and the opportunity to "pay her debt" to Tarolfo will not arise. Indeed, when she visits Tarolfo on her husband's advice, Tarolfo, knowing that her husband has not gone away, is surprised to see her and inquires what has happened. She informs him of her husband's wish that she keep her promise, and Tarolfo is so touched by the husband's generosity that he releases her. Thus, the husband's fixity has helped to bring about a happy resolution. Ironically, although the husband remains as fixed as the *donna*, he receives Fiammetta's vote for having shown generosity, while his wife gets no credit. It seems that in Boccaccio even immobile men can still receive credit for action. (At least in Chaucer Dorigen has the opportunity to receive more credit than her Italian counterpart, the *donna*.) In sacrificing his wife's honor the husband also sacrifices his own honor. Such acquiescence, along with his fixity, may suggest to Fiammetta that he acts more like a woman should than a man, thereby earning her sympathy and the sympathy of her female companions.

Chaucer's Arveragus, despite his lack of characterization because of his prolonged absences, garners the readers' sympathy when he cries on hearing of Dorigen's dilemma. David Raybin notes that upon hearing of Dorigen's promise to Aurelius, Arveragus maintains a "nonemotive, rational distance between himself and the problem . . . until the thought of his wife's threatened violation forces him to tears."[13] Up until this point, Arveragus's physical movements have involved his trips away, but here he is "moved" physically to cry. His e-motion may suggest, especially in the context of the tale, feminine behavior, because his reaction, although physical, takes place in private. Arveragus displays true compassion for Dorigen's situation since he begins to understand her dilemma from her viewpoint. That is, he sees it from the inside

---

12 Gilmore, 42–51.
13 Raybin, 68–69.

looking out, rather than from his usual viewpoint from the outside, typically from "out of towne" (1351), or from as far away as England.

During Arveragus's prolonged stay across the channel, Dorigen advances her Boethian philosophy regarding the "grisly rokkes blake" (859) which separate her from Arveragus and symbolize her own immobile situation.[14] Significantly, Chaucer mentions several times Dorigen's immobility, especially during her philosophizing, when "ther wolde she *sitte* and *thynke*" (857, my emphasis), and "on hire *feet* she myghte hire noght sustene. / Thanne wolde she *sitte* adoun upon the grene" (861–62, my emphasis). Dorigen's friends, concerned over her loneliness, try to comfort her by coaxing her out of the house. Significantly, Chaucer uses "stone" imagery to describe the process of Dorigen's mollification by her friends:

> By proces, as ye knowen everichoon,
> Men may so longe graven in a stoon
> Til som figure therinne emprented be.
> So longe han they conforted hire til she
> Receyved hath, by hope and by resoun,
> The emprentyng of hire consolacioun,
> Thurgh which hir grete sorwe gan aswage.   (829–35)

Dorigen's friends must, in a sense, chip away at her until she is willing to change her situation even just a bit. At last Dorigen's friends bring her out to socialize in a garden. Here Aurelius finds the nerve to approach her, but she is unwilling to dance without Arveragus present. Aurelius, who "syngeth, daunceth, passynge any man" (929), moves freely, but Dorigen is physically static. At first she chides him for his boldness, then "in pley" (988) promises to be his love if he can remove the rocks – the symbol of her separation from Arveragus and of her own lack of mobility as a woman (after all, she cannot be as forward as Aurelius). In this scene, moreover, in the face of Aurelius's obnoxious and presumptuous request, Dorigen demonstrates her generosity. Aurelius has told her he will die for her, and she compassionately offers him some hope, however impossible the task. By doing so, she behaves unlike Boccaccio's *donna*, who, unwilling to inform her husband of Tarolfo's attentions, and wishing to get rid of her suitor once and for all, carefully devises the garden scheme. Dorigen, caught off guard and caught up in thoughts of Arveragus, acts impulsively yet compassionately.[15] Like a *Donna Petrosa*, Dorigen is unwilling to give her love to Aurelius. She is, however, moved slightly to pity him.

Dorigen's compassion, though, causes Aurelius some problems. Unable to figure a way to make the rocks disappear, Aurelius, once active and "fressher . . . than is the month of May" (927–28), slows down because of his

---

14 Hansen, 277–78. See also Morgan, "Boccaccio's *Filocolo*," 295, on *eutrapelia*.
15 Burger, 170.

love-sickness, until his brother finds it necessary to confine him to bed: "Two yeer and moore lay wrecche Aurelyus, / Er any foot he myghte on erthe gon" (1102–03). It is as if Aurelius has caught the "disease" of women's physical immobility. After two years, his brother revives Aurelius in order to take him to Orleans to seek the clerk. Even sick men, it turns out, travel more than healthy women. In the meantime Dorigen, her beloved Arveragus returned, steps backstage – or back into the house – momentarily. Arveragus, however, will leave again in time for Dorigen to make her crucial decision regarding surrender to Aurelius when the latter informs her that he has made the rocks disappear.

Between a rock and a hard place

Confronted with the dilemma over whether or not to sleep with Aurelius, Dorigen considers suicide by comparing her plight to that of several virtuous women from antiquity. These women, like Dorigen, find themselves, as it were, "between a rock and a hard place." The limited choices for women – suicide or dishonor – clearly demonstrate the difficulties for women in situations involving unwanted sexual relations or rape. Nevertheless, this catalogue of suicidal women does not show failure or weakness on Dorigen's part.[16] Rather, "hoom she goth" (1346), where she thinks through the situation, overcoming her petrified state and relinquishing her commitment to suicide. She demonstrates her literary-mindedness by referring to women mentioned by classical and patristic authors, including Jerome in his anti-feminist *Adversus Jovinianum* (1355–66).[17] Susan Crane points out that Dorigen, like Judith Fetterley's resisting reader, at first allies herself with literary subjects and then, ultimately, rejects them and refuses to submit to the roles standard for literary women.[18] Dorigen resists the heavy burden put upon women by gradually resisting "set-in-stone" tradition regarding "proper" female behavior dictated by men. Chaucer, unlike Boccaccio, provides insight into the heroine's intelligence and decision-making processes. Dorigen proves herself compassionate and clever – a woman who deserves not only the readers' sympathy, but also consideration for being the "mooste fre," especially since she acts graciously and selflessly throughout and even tries to save love-sick Aurelius's life with her request.

Scholars have criticized Dorigen and the *donna* for their poor foresight and rash boons, but the two women actually show better judgment than do their male suitors. Although critics applaud men in these tales for their good judgment,[19] many of the male characters, in fact, make bad judgments. Like

---

16 Morgan, "Boccaccio's *Filocolo*," 298.

17 See Raybin, 73; Gerald Morgan, "A Defence of Dorigen's Complaint," *MÆ* 46 (1977): 94.

18 Susan Crane, *Gender and Romance in Chaucer's Canterbury Tales* (Princeton: Princeton University Press, 1994), 111.

19 For instance, Morgan, "Boccaccio's *Filocolo*," 300–03; and Burger, 174.

Dorigen, Boccaccio's Tarolfo turns to literature when he is confronted with a problem. Dorigen, however, by deciding against suicide, wisely throws aside the advice of literary patriarchy, whereas Tarolfo conforms to literary advice. Tarolfo follows the teachings of Ovid to persevere in his courtship. As Chaucer likens Dorigen to a rock that is chipped away by her friends, through Ovid Boccaccio also compares the *donna* to a rock. Thus, Tarolfo finds himself:

seguendo d'Ovidio gli ammaestramenti il quale dice: "L'uomo non dee lasciare per durezza della donna di non perserverare, però che per continuanza la molle acqua fora la dura pietra."[20]

[following the advice of Ovid, who says "A man should not quit persevering because of a woman's hardness, because even the persistence of the soft water wears away the hard rock."]

In a passage that Chaucer must have had in mind when he wrote the *Franklin's Tale*, Boccaccio likens the *donna* to a *Donna Petrosa* who can only be worn away gradually like a rock. Tarolfo heeds Ovid's advice about wearing away the *donna* without realizing that Ovid's *Ars Amatoria* is a comical and amoral look at strategies for winning love, certainly not a book with principles to live by. He chooses his authoritative text unwisely.

Aurelius shows even worse judgment than Tarolfo. In his painful "aubade" on the morning after the garden encounter, although he is the "servant to Venus" (937), Aurelius turns to Apollo for consolation and aid. Critics have pointed out that the pagan gods are ineffectual in the world of the *Franklin's Tale*,[21] but those critics have failed to see that the gods fail for clear reasons. Apollo, notorious for many unlucky love affairs with women such as Daphne, Cassandra, and Marpessa, is scarcely a prime candidate for advice about women and love relationships. Aurelius also invokes the help of Apollo's sister, both as Lucrece and as Hecate. Again, he should know better, because although Diana as moon goddess controls the tides that have a hand in the rocks' disappearance, Diana also helps women to avoid love, and so Aurelius's desires are doomed. Both Tebano and Aurelius may be physically mobile, but they show poor judgment in assessing their situations and in entreating the help of the appropriate authorities or deities.

Like Aurelius, the magicians in both tales also invoke female deities. Chaucer's clerk from Orleans and Boccaccio's Tebano call upon the moon – upon Diana herself – for help. The clerk uses an astrological formula involving the moon's power over the tides to create the illusion of the rocks' disappearance. Likewise, Tebano calls upon the goddesses Hecate and Ceres when he begins his incantations. His prayers send the chariot that delivers the naked

20 Boccaccio, 311.
21 Burger, 172–73.

conjurer to various locales around the world to gather herbs and other in-gredients for his recipe. Once back on the site of his impending garden, Tebano mixes a variety of substances and sprinkles them on the earth. At last he boils a mixture of blood, milk, and water – the body fluids of pregnancy – to make the ground and dead twigs turn green and blossom. Such measures, under the protection of Hecate and Ceres, produce the garden (itself a symbol of woman) which Tebano has promised. Tebano has not promised, however, to convince the *donna* to sleep with Tarolfo. Hecate, Ceres, and female body fluids can produce a garden in mid-winter, but cannot force an unwilling woman to succumb to love. Perhaps the outcomes of the spells in both tales are fated to fail because the goddesses and even the ingredients involved normally come to the aid of women, and not men, in their distress.

It remains unclear whether the goddesses actually assist the *donna* and Dorigen; I would like to believe that they do. One would think, too, that relegated to passivity as they are, both women would immediately call upon divine powers to help them. We gain no insight into the *donna*'s prayers – in fact, it seems as though she relies solely on her own cleverness – and Dorigen complains against God, rather than asking for his aid. Many scholars criticize Dorigen for her inaction and passivity, but as Carolynn Van Dyke says of Dorigen:

> She is, moreover, a moral agent of a paradoxical sort, obliged to choose primarily inaction. Having pledged not to cause conflict (lines 754–59), she spends most of the tale doing little but waiting, so oppressed by her husband's absence "that al this wyde world she sette at noght" (line 821). . . . Unlike Boccaccio's heroine, Dorigen can analyze justice and virtue, but like her predecessor, she can do nothing good. Her monologues' futility is therefore the logical culmination of Dorigen's redundance as an agent. As the ethic of wifely self-abnegation paralyzed Griselda, the irrelevance of her will leaves Dorigen "astoned." (line 1339)[22]

Dorigen is, as Van Dyke suggests, unable to choose any situation besides immobility because of her womanhood. She does, in fact, remain "astoned," but only from a physical point of view. She can still use her mind to come up with a plan to dissuade Aurelius and later to save herself from suicide. Van Dyke also asserts that "Chaucer makes Dorigen comparable to the male characters in moral agency,"[23] agreeing with Douglas Burger that Dorigen proves herself morally and ethically sound throughout the tale.[24] For example, Dorigen shows sympathy for Aurelius and holds "trouthe" in high esteem. When one consid-

---

[22] Van Dyke, 63. See also Hansen, 278, for the connection between Griselda and Dorigen and the "astoned" state.

[23] Van Dyke, 52.

[24] Burger, 175; Van Dyke, 53.

ers that the men, particularly Aurelius, insist on physical action without considering consequences, it becomes apparent that Dorigen plays more of a moral
role than any of the men, thereby deserving recognition for her morally
grounded generosity.

Dorigen's real agency, however, is intellectual. She may appear passive
physically, but she is active mentally. Dorigen and the *donna* remain outwardly
unempowered because they are women. Chaucer, however, appropriates Boccaccio's clever woman and improves on her. The *Franklin's Tale* presents
Dorigen as an active and thinking character. Chaucer's expansion of women's
roles lies not so much in a feminist consciousness, but in his interest in the
differences between male and female agency – that is, how men and women
act and react in given situations.

Both Boccaccio and Chaucer demonstrate that masculine mobility is
grounded in female fixity. Although the heroines in both tales must remain at
home, they can assert their intellectual capacities to cause change by sending
men, however inadvertently, scrambling to accomplish tasks for them. Ironically, neither Dorigen nor the *donna* consciously wishes for Aurelius or Tebano
actually to act out the assigned tasks. The women are morally grounded –
concerned over consequence – while Aurelius and Tebano, in their insistence
on action, do not appear at first to connect agency with moral consequences.
Because of the nearly impossible natures of the assigned tasks, these men
disregard consequence and over-act in the hopes of gaining their desires. When,
with the help of the magicians, Tebano and Aurelius have accomplished their
garden and rock tasks, the women privately react with sadness and horror. Their
husbands also have negative reactions, which become public when their wives
inform the suitors that their husbands have sent them to fulfill their once-private
agreements. Ultimately, all of the men in the tales seem to have done more than
the women because of the public natures of their actions, but, in fact, the women
have been just as active, only intellectually and privately. In both Boccaccio's
and Chaucer's tales, the men assert their rights to mobility and its accompanying
recognition of generosity, while the women privately and quietly make plans,
and by delegating action to already active men, cause change and show
unobtrusive generosity.

Much of Chaucer's skill as a poet lies in his exploring and expanding upon
source tales, and such is the case with the *Franklin's Tale*. The tale's central
imagery of the rocks derives, at least in part, from Boccaccio's Ovidian
reference to the unmoving *donna* as a rock that must be worn away by the
constant motion of water (and Tarolfo). Furthermore, Chaucer follows in the
Italian tradition of the *Donna Petrosa*, the woman unwilling to be moved for
unwanted love. Chaucer cleverly introduces the rocks in the *Franklin's Tale* to
symbolize, besides Dorigen's separation from Arveragus and her unwillingness
to love Aurelius, her inflexible position as a medieval woman. Her rock-like
fixity stands in sharp contrast to the mobility allowed Aurelius, Arveragus, and
the Orleans clerk. Chaucer picks up on and further explores Boccaccio's theme

of female fixity and masculine movement, particularly by expanding Dorigen's role and giving the reader insight into her thought processes. As a result, men's public, physical actions contrast with Dorigen's private, intellectual action. Access to mobility seems to define masculinity in the tale while lack of mobility, counteracted by the exercise of intellect, characterizes the female condition. In the end, despite her decidedly non-male, non-public, and mental actions, Dorigen merits as much claim to generosity as the men in the *Franklin's Tale*.

Doing What Comes Naturally:
The *Physician's Tale* and the Pardoner

GLENN BURGER

The *Physician's Tale* has never been one of the more popular of the Canterbury narratives. Its brevity, unyielding insistence on virginity, and lack of any strongly dramatic relationship to its tale-teller don't encourage easy identification on the part of a reader. And not surprisingly, perhaps, the sensational excitement generated by the Pardoner has tended to overshadow the Physician's harsh morality.[1] But the connections made between the two tales and tale-tellers

---

[1] A brief plot summary should make this clear. Virginius, a knight of Rome, has a daughter named Virginia. Nature, Vicar General of God, made nothing better; even Pygmalion could not counterfeit such a work. Both in spirit and body Virginia is a flower of virginity: all her words are virtuous, no wine crosses her mouth; indeed she often pretends to be sick in order to avoid company that is likely to be lascivious. The Physician then interjects with advice to fathers and mothers, and to older women put in charge of young girls, about the proper governance of young women. One day Virginia goes with her mother to a temple in town. There a judge named Appius sees her, lusts after her, and is determined to have her. The devil shows him how he might have her by deceit. Appius summons a churl named Claudius, and together they plot that Claudius will claim that Virginia is actually his servant whom Virginius has falsely taken from him. Claudius appears in Appius's court as arranged, Virginius is called to account, and Appius decides in favor of Claudius. When Virginius realizes that he must give up his daughter to live in lechery with the judge, he goes home and calls Virginia before him. With "father's pity striking through his heart," but firm in his purpose, he tells Virginia that there are two options available to her: death or shame. Virginia asks time "my death to complain a little" (four lines in all), swoons, and then tells her father to do his will with his child in God's name. Virginius then cuts off his daughter's head and presents it to Appius. A throng of the people, suspecting deception, suddenly appear to save Virginius. They cast Appius in prison – where he quickly hangs himself – and sentence Claudius to public hanging. Virginius intervenes, Claudius is exiled, and "the remnant" (whoever they may be) are hanged. The tale ends with the counsel of the Physician to forsake sin before sin forsakes you (i.e., leaves you damned).

by the activities of the Host and Pardoner in the fictional frame bring the male body into view to an extent not seen elsewhere in the *Canterbury Tales*.[2] Indeed, few other sets of tales so explicitly and anxiously bear out Elaine Tuttle Hansen's contention that "in Chaucerian fictions, we cannot directly hear women's voices . . . but we can hear 'men's concern'."[3] And this fragment constitutes one of Chaucer's most complex and provocative explorations of the relationship between gender and power.

Men's concerns and the body writing

Fragment VI presents in the harshest possible light the oppressive force of the essentialized gender system lying behind medieval identity politics. In the *Physician's Tale* representation is literally a matter of life and death for Virginia; the excision of any female presence in the *Pardoner's Tale* effectively "kills off" the matter of woman that has so dominated previous Chaucerian fictions. Moreover, the repeated symbolic violence practiced by the Host and other pilgrims against the Pardoner constitutes a kind of queerbashing that, while not technically misogynist, does arise out of a similar fear of the feminine. Fragment VI, then, inscribes as *crisis* a representational strategy at the heart of the Canterbury project, that is, the desire to write on the gendered, sexualized body a new "bourgeois" identity often at odds with a previously clerically defined transcendent self. In doing so, the fragment both gestures toward, but fails to achieve, the authorial stability that, according to Hansen, has made Chaucer paradigmatic for an English literary tradition: "reading Chaucer . . . enables us to study . . . the alleged birth or infancy perhaps of 'the author' – recognized from the beginning, paradoxically, as already a father figure – as an individual and a personality who seeks to enjoy all the material and symbolic privileges of maleness while transcending the constraints of 'the body writing' to grasp the otherwise unavailable, to take a neutral or universally human position."[4] In Fragment VI, on the contrary, such a "modern" authoring of an autonomous self can be found only in the disturbingly "unnatural" activities of the Host and Pardoner. And it is instead the "medieval" identity politics of the *Physician's Tale* that appears to inscribe a masculine subject position successfully

---

2   Fragment VI is notable for its foregrounding of the pilgrimage frame: giving 286 lines to the *Physician's Tale* proper, 176 lines to the link between *Physician's* and *Pardoner's Tales* and to the *Pardoner's Prologue*, 442 lines for the *Pardoner's Tale* itself, and 64 lines to Pardoner's address to the pilgrimage group and altercation with the Host. Only the *Wife of Bath's Prologue* focuses as much or more attention on the fictional frame of the *Canterbury Tales*.
3   Hansen, *Chaucer and the Fictions of Gender* (Berkeley: University of California Press, 1992), 288.
4   Hansen, 286–87.

transcending the constraints of "the body writing" by defining its activity as "natural." [5]

Fragment VI, then, represents a tense, pivotal moment in the constitution of late medieval/early modern identity politics. What makes this moment especially interesting is that in it we can see the set of forces that will be harnessed to produce "Chaucerian" authorship and the "modern" autonomous subject (that is, a universalized category founded on sexed and sexualized bodies). But such a naturalization has not yet taken place, and as a result, what this fragment records instead is the *tension* of attempting to write oneself via another. Its attention to tactics forestalls the stable authorship, selfhood, and masculinity that is *later* written into Chaucerian texts, showing instead the need to attend to movement and process rather than stability and teleology. This fragment's performative framing of medieval identity politics as practice rather than nature brings to consciousness the internal contradictions and paths of resistance possible within such a representational system, even as it reproduces that system's hegemonic turn to stability and order.

Historicizing gender/queering identity

In order to historicize fully the gendered subjectivities of readers and writers in Fragment VI, I would suggest that we first need to explore how such a complicated past (both like and unlike "me") troubles "who I am" in the present. For isn't analysis of the other (in this case, medieval representational practices) always analysis of oneself (modern identity politics), of the things left behind in assuming identity and discoverable on the constructed body of the other? In my own case, I begin locked within a modern inheritance of identity, caught within mutually informing but often separated categories of gay and male, committed to an anti-homophobic, feminist, postcolonial analysis yet not ever "the real thing." How do I allow for continuities and contiguities in the representational practices of the modern and premodern without at the same time colonizing the past? How do I resist a dangerously presumptive knowledge of "what it really means," and thus of "who I really am"?

---

[5] Clearly there are ways in which such Chaucerian fictions both anticipate and help maintain modern representational practices that establish certain hierarchized and interrelated identities as "naturally" written on the bodies of individuals, thereby determining who those individuals "really" are. For example, a bourgeois, largely male, and often white and European subject position has often been represented as "universal"; in contrast working-class, female, homosexual, and non-white or colonial subject positions have been characterized as partial, even deviant, and thus denied "voice" in official culture and policy. In positing a medieval identity politics I want to draw attention to how similar but differently hierarchized and mutually constitutive identities are articulated by the representational practices of medieval dominant culture: organized, that is, around distinctions such as noble/non-noble, virgin/non-virgin, masculine/feminine (or effeminate or sodomitical), Christian/non-Christian, but written on bodies in real and discernible ways.

Recent queer theory, in its troubling of sex, gender, and sexuality boundaries, offers one methodology less likely, at least at the moment, to colonize and erase the differences of both the pre- and the postmodern body. Emphasizing the performativity of gendered and sexualized identities, and stressing the impossibility of proving sex, sexuality, and gender by recourse to a prior, foundational biological body, queer theory tries to map a more dynamic, less assured account of the body in motion within prevailing discourses of power.[6] And it is, perhaps, in seeking such destabilizing dis-identifications that the queer project finds points of intersection with feminist and post-colonial critique and inquiry. As Butler suggests, it ought "to be possible to assert a set of non-causal and non-reductive relations between gender and sexuality, not only to link feminism and queer theory, as one might link two separate enterprises, but to establish their constitutive interrelationship." For "no one term can serve as foundational, and the success of any given analysis that centers on any one term may well be the marking of its own limitations as an exclusive point of departure."[7]

In the title chapter of his recent book, Lee Edelman proposes a project of "homographesis" to critique the current cultural conceptualizations of gay identity. For Edelman the term homographesis maps simultaneous processes of oppression and resistance inherent in modern reading strategies. In the first instance, homographesis signifies the process by which dominant ideological strategies assign to gay bodies a visible "difference." Thus, as Edelman describes it, "the process that constructs homosexuality as a subject of discourse, as a cultural category about which one can think or speak or write, coincides . . . with the process whereby the homosexual subject is represented

---

6   One of the first theoretical engagements with "queer" occurred in the special issue of *differences* devoted to lesbian and gay issues (*differences* 3.2 [Summer 1991], ed. Teresa de Lauretis). See especially de Lauretis's introduction, "Queer Theory: Lesbian and Gay Sexualities – An Introduction," iii–xviii. The *locus classicus* for queer performativity is, of course, the work of Judith Butler in *Gender Trouble: Feminism and the Subversion of Identity* (New York: Routledge, 1990) and *Bodies that Matter: On the Discursive Limits of Sex* (New York: Routledge, 1993). See, for example, her claim that "Gender is the repeated stylization of the body, a set of repeated acts within a highly rigid regulatory frame that congeal over time to produce the appearance of substance, of a natural sort of being" (*Gender Trouble*, 33). See also Eve Kosofsky Sedgwick, "Queer Performativity: Henry James's *The Art of the Novel*," *GLQ: A Journal of Lesbian and Gay Studies* 1.1 (1993): 1–16; Jonathan Dollimore, *Sexual Dissidence: Augustine to Wilde, Freud to Foucault* (Oxford: Clarendon Press, 1991); and Jonathan Goldberg, *Sodometries: Renaissance Texts, Modern Sexualities* (Stanford: Stanford University Press, 1992). For recent engagements of queer theory and Chaucer studies, see Glenn Burger, "Kissing the Pardoner," *PMLA* 107 (1992): 1143–56, and "Queer Chaucer," *English Studies in Canada* 20.2 (June 1994): 153–69; Carolyn Dinshaw, "Chaucer's Queer Touches/ A Queer Touches Chaucer," *Exemplaria* 7.1 (Spring 1995): 75–92; Steven Kruger, "Claiming the Pardoner: Toward a Gay Reading of Chaucer's *Pardoner's Tale*," *Exemplaria* 6.1 (Spring 1994): 115–40; and Susan Schibanoff, "Worlds Apart: Orientalism, Antifeminism, and Heresy in Chaucer's *Man of Law's Tale*", *Exemplaria* 8.1 (Spring 1996): 59–96.
7   Butler, *Bodies that Matter*, 240.

as being, even more than inhabiting, a body that always demands to be read, a body on which his 'sexuality' is always inscribed." But Edelman also outlines another, resistant homographesis, a reading and writing practice that counters the labour of disciplinary inscription by resisting categorization, that is "intent on *de*-scribing the identities that [a conservative social] order has so oppressively *in*scribed."[8]

Edelman's analysis thus helps me, as a product of that modern regime, variously constructed as homosexual/gay man/queer, to disidentify and destabilize current oppressive modes of representation, to think otherwise my own place within the present. But if I want to adjust Edelman's discussion of difference to suit a late medieval context, I need both to substitute gender for sexuality categories – that is, "the feminine" for "the homosexual" – and to retheorize the relations between gender, sex, and sexuality. Thus, to paraphrase Edelman for my own project: "the construction of the feminine as a subject of medieval discourse, as a cultural category about which one can think or speak or write, coincides ... with the process whereby the feminine/feminized subject is represented as being, even more than inhabiting, a body that always demands to be read, a body on which his/her gender/sexuality is always inscribed."

Certainly there are analogies between medieval sodomite and modern homosexual as subject categories constituted as negatives by dominant culture; it may even be possible to discern the occasional utopic resistance to such representations anticipating modern "gay" liberation, as James Miller has recently argued for the newcomers who have no name for themselves in Dante's *Purgatorio* 26.[9] But at the same time, neither "the homosexual," nor his more optimistic "gay" younger brother, will likely be found reproduced exactly in medieval systems of representation because such categories are "born" out of modern, not pre-modern, axes of difference. What these absences indicate is not that it's impossible or irrelevant to talk about sexuality (in the sense of an identity organized around a bodily reading of sex, gender, sexual practice difference), only that it shouldn't be the modern hetero/homo axis of sexuality we are presuming or blindly reproducing.[10]

So too, with sex difference. The work of Cadden, Laqueur, and others is making us increasingly aware of the instabilities and slippages inherent in

[8] Edelman, *Homographesis: Essays in Gay Literary and Cultural Theory* (New York: Routledge, 1994), 10.

[9] "Dante on Fire Island: Reinventing Heaven in the AIDS Elegy," in *Writing AIDS: Gay Literature, Language, and Analysis*, ed. Timothy F. Murphy and Suzanne Poirier (New York: Columbia University Press, 1993), 265–305, esp. 279.

[10] The corollary, of course, is that neither are modern categories (and the identities they insist upon) as unified and stable as we might wish to think; "the homosexual" may be in some ways a modern "invention," as Foucault suggested, but other, older categories may also co-exist. And subjectivities and bodies in motion in the world may choose precisely the gaps and fissures this multiplicity allows as places to do things differently, to "become" rather than "be" themselves.

medieval models of sexual difference.[11] Whether a one-sex model that views the female body as an inferior male body turned in on itself or a humoral model organized around differences in vital heat, medieval views of biological sex and the difference they inscribe on the body seem far less stable and absolutist than the modern two-sex model, and less likely foundations for cultural meaning in the Middle Ages. As Laqueur reminds us, in classical and medieval medicine, the body "was not the biological bedrock upon which a host of other characteristics were supposedly based. Indeed, the paradox of the one-sex model is that pairs of ordered contrarieties played off a single flesh in which they did not themselves inhere. Fatherhood/motherhood, male/female, man/woman, culture/nature, masculine/feminine, honorable/dishonorable, legitimate/illegitimate, hot/cold, right/left, and many other such pairs were read into a body that did not itself mark these distinctions clearly. Order and hierarchy were imposed upon it from the outside."[12]

In such a scenario, obviously, neither gender, sex, nor sexuality can be securely founded on or fixed by a biological body, nor are sex and sexuality the crucial axes of difference in determining identity that they are in modern society. Instead the body registers the shifting variables of a socially defined set of distinctions around masculinity and femininity that determine successful identification and care of the self. Thus the process of identification that happens in modern discursive regimes along parallel essentializing axes of sex (male/female), sexuality (homo/hetero), and race (white/black), in medieval practice might more likely take place along the axis of gender (masculine/feminine). Essentialized gender difference provides the stabilizing foundation by which medieval dominant culture regulates "the natural." In doing so, the suppressed/oppressed category of the feminine inscribes and identifies a greater variety of othered bodies – women's, heretics', Jews', Saracens', effeminates', sodomites' – than is the case in modern Western regimes of representation.

Moreover, I would argue that the connection made throughout the Middle Ages between an essentialist gender system and a coercive narrative frame provides one of the controlling fantasies by which medieval dominant culture

---

11 Joan Cadden, *Meanings of Sex Difference in the Middle Ages: Medicine, Science, and Culture* (Cambridge: Cambridge University Press, 1993); Thomas Laqueur, *Making Sex: Body and Gender From the Greeks to Freud* (Cambridge, MA: Harvard University Press, 1990). Cadden's book is particularly useful in complicating Laqueur's over-dependence on Aristotle and a one-sex model as *the* model for sex difference in the premodern and early modern periods. See also Danielle Jacquart and Claude Thomasset, *Sexuality and Medicine in the Middle Ages* (Princeton: Princeton University Press, 1988); Carol Clover, "Regardless of Sex: Men, Women, and Power in Early Northern Europe," in *Studying Medieval Women*, ed. Nancy Partner (Cambridge, MA: The Medieval Academy of America, 1993), 61–87 and Michael Camille, "The Image and the Self: Unwriting Late Medieval Bodies," in *Framing Medieval Bodies*, ed. Sarah Kay and Miri Rubin (Manchester: Manchester University Press, 1994), 62–69.

12 Laqueur, 61–62.

constitutes and maintains its identity.[13] Such a model of "the natural" presupposes for the male or female body, or by analogy the sexualized textual body, a structuring gendered frame that either authorizes its inherent truthfulness as "the natural" or condemns its lack as perversity. Just as an unstable sexual body needs to be framed by a hierarchized and essentialist account of gender difference, so too with the analogous sexualized textual body. Rather than text or author providing the foundational moment for cultural production,[14] the instabilities occasioned by their dependence upon material, and thus ephemeral and contingent, media demand the stabilizing frame of a "higher" authority in order to make manifest an essential truthfulness and "masculine" will. Virginity (and its lesser cousin, chaste procreation) delineate the true nature of the "masculine" will for the sexes, just as citation of authorities, allegorical explication, or sententious kernel of wisdom, do for the text. The frame of gender and narrative authority then becomes the controlling presence that warrants the body's continued existence and usefulness as signifier.

In this model the feminine can signify only as a ventriloquized voice and a dummy's body, everything the masculine is not. As such, the feminine must be fantasized as Other in order to be absolutely transformed into speaking pictures of the truly masculine: as with female saints like St. Cecilia, or Saracen and Jewish converts, who all surmount their natural bodily weakness by manifesting a higher, "masculine" will. Or the feminine must be absolutely expunged (as with heretics and disobedient Jews or the effeminate Appius in the *Physician's Tale*), or exiled beyond the margins (as in Saracen kingdoms of the East), or hermetically sealed (as in the Jewish ghettos of European Christendom).[15] If this essentializing connection between gender and narrative frame constitutes

---

[13] See the useful discussions of the ideological import of the relationship of margin and text in medieval and early modern manuscripts and printed books by Michael Camille, *Image on the Edge: The Margins of Medieval Art* (London: Reaktion Books, 1992); and Evelyn B. Tribble, *Margins and Marginality: The Printed Page in Early Modern England* (Charlottesville, VA: University Press of Virginia, 1993), esp. Chapter One, "Authority, Control, Community: The English Printed Bible Page from Tyndale to the Authorized Version," 11–56.

[14] See Hansen, 284–92, for a discussion of how constructions of Chaucer – as the "first" English author and "father" of an English literary tradition – have worked to establish and maintain just such a foundational moment.

[15] Clearly here I'm not talking about "real" women's bodies, i.e., about biological sex per se, but about a representational fantasmatic of "the real." Furthermore, as fantasm it may have considerable ideological force, but at the same time not completely describe the complex ways in which individual bodies take on and resist such gendered identities (as my discussion of Fragment VI below tries to demonstrate). See Kathleen Biddick, "Genders, Bodies, Borders: Technologies of the Visible" (pp. 87–116 in *Studying Medieval Women*), for a similar fantasmatic relationship between the eucharistic body of Christ and the common body of Christendom. I also want to emphasize the ways in which this medieval inscription of gender difference as *the* crucial difference (rather than race, sex, or sexuality today) brings male/female, Christian/non-Christian bodies into relationship in ways different from (although also similar to) modern representational practices. Misogyny, queer-bashing, racism,

the coercive fantasmatic ideal of medieval dominant culture, however, the performativity inherent in its actual cultural instantiation guarantees that both masculine will and narrative authority remain far more anxious and unstable sites of meaning than their "nature" would appear to allow.

Careful masculinity and the bodies that matter

Throughout, the *Physician's Tale* focuses on the care of masculinity needed to secure the proper reproduction of masculine identity and authority. To accomplish this end, the tale enacts a series of transcendental metaphoric substitutions: Virginia stands in for Virginius, Virginius for Nature, Nature for "my lord" God, copy for original. Stabilizing and securing Virginius' name thus secures not only his individual authority as potent patriarch but the originary status of all patriarchal authority and control. Curiously, then, the sex of Virginia's body is at once central and irrelevant. For the tale seems concerned less with the inscription of sex difference than with proving the natural ability of an active and essential masculine will to frame and control the perversity of a passive and accidental feminine carnality. Any distinction between Virginius and Virginia ought to signal only accidental, rather than essential, difference.

In the *Physician's Tale*, then, conformity of the (wo)man's body to the inherent, "masculine" will of Nature thus brings about the rule of the universal transcendent will of God. Good sexual order guarantees good social order.[16] And the Physician, as a manipulator of the humours and harmonizer of the individual body with the natural order, can have a profoundly important role in knitting together nature – whether physical, social, or theological. For the essence of masculine power is its definition of subjectivity as activity. Only the properly masculine subject carries the vital energy for procreation; thus it is crucial that the effects of embodiment – in the sense of mere materiality without such power – be carried by the category of the feminine. What gives biological

colonialism, may take place under both regimes, but the ways in which power circulates will differ.
16 The *Physician's Tale* is particularly interesting in its attempts to harmonize an inherited classical medico/social model of the body with the demands of Augustinian Christianity. As Laqueur points out, the advent of Christianity both rendered classical harmonies of bodily humors more problematic and perpetuated their usefulness. For example, "in its advocacy of virginity, it [Christianity] proclaimed the possibility of a relationship to society and the body that most ancient doctors . . . would have found injurious to the health. . . . One's intimate experiences of sex, in this new dispensation, were the result not of an ineluctable heating of the body but of the fall and of the estrangement of will that the fall brought. . . . But Augustine's images for how 'impregnation and conception' might be 'an act of will, instead of by lustful cravings,' were very much still of the old one-sex body found in the classical doctors . . . [he] did not envisage the modern body in which ovulation, conception, and even male ejaculation are known to be independent of whatever subjective feelings might accompany them. Heat and pleasure remained an ineradicable part of generation" (59–60).

"women" like Nature and Virginia instrumentality in the *Physician's Tale* is their ability to stand in for and give voice to the will of the Father. And in order to do that and be properly masculine, their bodies must signal away from irrelevant material accidents of sexed and sexualized bodies ("the feminine"), back to some always already present original ("the masculine"). The "a" ending of Virginia's name therefore indicates carefully gendered grammatical control; for as subject it should point only to a virginal rootedness in the antecedent will of the Father. Conformity of the (wo)man's body to the inherent, "masculine" will of Nature thus brings about the rule of the universal transcendent will of God.

When the perverse gaze of Appius threatens to sully first the body of purity (Virginia) and then its essence (Virginius's reputation), the "natural" order must be inscribed on the physical and social body in ever more extreme ways. At whatever cost true masculinity must maintain itself as subject not object of the gaze of the other. And in order for that stable subject position to be maintained, no residue of the masculine body can be left to view for potential appropriation or reconfiguration. Because the distinction Virginius/Virginia should signal only accidental, not essential, difference, when Appius desires Virginia's female body rather than her signification as emblem of Virginius's power, he sexualizes and feminizes both Virginia's and Virginius's body, disrupting the normal homosocial exchanges within proper masculinity. Appius thereby feminizes his own signifying power as a proper man, foreclosing on his own agency as his actions objectify and bring into view his own excessive materiality. Such gender slippage, moreover, threatens the hierarchized binaries of accident/essence, lying/truth, perversity/naturalness that gender essentialism maintains, and exposes as proximate a feminizing, cupidinous perversity proper masculinity insists must always be outside itself.[17]

To deny such perversity, it seems, the tale must excise the accidental altogether – whether in cutting off Virginia's head, in hanging Appius, or in denying its own embodied state as fable – all in order to maintain the active subject position defined as proper masculinity. In particular, the tale asserts its status as authoritative text by emphasizing the absence of narrative play: "this is no fable, . . . The sentence of it sooth is, out of doute" (VI 155–57). The textual body, like Virginia's, is dispensable. Only masculine substance matters in this foundational myth of purity. At every level materiality is rendered unproblematic by a series of metaphoric substitutions that obscure the activities

---

[17] See Dollimore's discussion of the perverse dynamic and transgressive reinscription: "If perversion subverts it is not as a unitary, pre-social libido, or an original plenitude, but as a transgressive agency inseparable from a dynamic intrinsic to social process. Provisionally then, this concept of the perverse dynamic denotes certain instabilities and contradictions within dominant structures which exist by virtue of exactly what those structures simultaneously contain and exclude. The displacements which constitute certain repressive discriminations are partly enabled via a proximity which, though disavowed, remains to enable a perverse return, an undoing, a transformation" (*Sexual Dissidence*, 33).

of the various sexual/textual bodies encountered in the tale. In this world, it would seem, there is no time to complain, no allowance for individual desire, for accidents of time and place. The truth will out no matter what.

Only by extreme, coercive activity on the part of Virginius, the Physician, and the other successful men who follow their example in framing and controlling what the tale means, can the individual and the ideological be aligned as one and the same activity. For the supposedly "natural" boundaries separating Virginius from Appius, masculine from feminine, essential truth from perverting falsity, are themselves constructions requiring the continuing "work" that (1) Virginius does to maintain intact what Virginia means, notably by cutting off her head; that (2) the Physician does to the *materia* of his text, by attempting to excise its materiality as fable; and that (3) the tale's audience (Host and "gentils") do, by announcing their "proper" reception of the tale in their rejection of the Pardoner.

This perverse dynamic at work within the masculine "body" of the *Physician's Tale* is further exposed to view in two additions of the Physician to his otherwise pared down version of Livy's tale. In the twenty lines given to Nature near the beginning of the tale, she appears to speak directly to us as "I," literally enacting the kind of reproduction she is describing, where a subjectivity is naturally present and voicing the will of an anterior, superior "lord." But the last line of the speech – "Thus semeth me . . ." (VI 29) – introduces the voice of the Physician as an artist figure, who, Pygmalion-like, paints the "I" that has spoken by refracting it through his own subjective desire. Similarly, the Physician later breaks his narrative to advise "ye maistresses" hired to govern "lordes doghtres" (72–73), and "ye fadres and ye modres" in "charge of al hir surveiaunce" (93, 95), that they should make sure that their children "ne perisse" "by ensample of youre lyvynge, / Or by your necligence in chastisynge" (97–98). In creating and then closing these gaps in his narrative, the Physician emphasizes the permeability of supposedly secure boundaries, the ever-present possibility of perversion, and the need for vigilant surveillance in order to keep the relationship between original and copy intact. Yet only at such a fraught moment does it become possible to talk about "the Physician" as a "real" character in his tale.

The ostensible text of the Physician may be that the true social body inheres in proper masculine activity and that one naturally chooses such masculinity. For example, Appius's "sentence" is false because he chooses the feminizing material body. By choosing Virginia's accidental body (i.e., sexy woman) rather than her signification as emblem of Virginius's power (i.e., worthy wife), Appius objectifies himself and ceases to have proper agency as a man. But the subtext of the *Physician's Tale* says something else. There remains a residue of the personal and rhetorical, even in such a simplifying, pared down account. To that extent the body of the Physician inheres in his tale, exposing a "me" – objectifiable and appropriable – to view. His is a subjectivity hard at work to subsume itself without a trace within the ideologies of dominant culture by proclaiming such ideological configurations as "natural" and invariably active and in control. Yet the manipulations necessary to maintain such a "natural" authority, as well as the personal and present gains from such service to dominant culture, help us "see" the masculine body more clearly, and in doing so, open it to potential appropriation and reconfiguration.

Transgressive materiality/re-presenting feminine perversity

The Host's subsequent efforts to appropriate the Physician's "sothe" more actively and remuneratively for his own ends in the present Canterbury game foreground this residue of the personal even more explicitly. And the very sexual/textual boundaries that the *Physician's Tale* sought to efface by repre- senting them as transparent and irrelevant emerge ever more clearly. The "sentence" of the *Physician's Tale* would have us focus on Virginia's inner beauty and nobility, that is, on that "original" nobility in Virginius, and ultimately, in God. The Host's response, however, foregrounds the exterior vessel. His assessment that "to deere bought she beautee" (293) and "hire beautee was hire deth" (297) stresses a material, gendered body; the feminine supplement of the tale – story as story; fable's affect rather than effect. And the Host concludes, "This is a pitous tale for to heere. / But nathelees, passe over; is no fors" (302–03), even though the Physician has been absolutely explicit that his "historial thing" *is* "fors" and cannot be passed over.

What the Host so clearly admires is not simply how the Physician as tale-teller was subsumed within a "higher" masculinity and will – as the tale would demand – but rather how, in doing so, the Physician also expressed his own agency and power in shaping and regulating feminine lack and perversity. The Host responds as one man to another. He acknowledges the presence of the Physician in his tale as an embodied, desiring individual constructing a "nature" that demands constant vigilant surveillance of that body in order to avert perversity and loss of control. The Host's comments recognize and seek to reproduce the homosocial packaging of identity taking place in the *Physician's Tale*, thereby providing an insightful account of how the Physician secures agency as a true man within the masculinist economy of language and power outlined by his tale.

Thus the Host not only sets himself up as a mock-Physician to the pilgrimage body, but also seeks to reproduce a set of metaphoric substitutions similar to those enacted by the Physician in his tale. Just as the Physician's identification with Virginius provided the Physician with a means of putting the body "out there" in a supposedly safe way that would be masculine and active, so too, the Host's identification with the Physician will give the Host authority and instrumentality in shaping the pilgrimage body. The Physician inscribed the masculine, first in terms of control of a potentially dangerous female "lack" in the person of Virginia, and then in the even more dangerous feminization of masculine will in the perverse desire of Appius. Similarly, the Host attempts to write *his* masculine will, first by selecting "Thou beel amy, thou Pardoner" (318) to tell the next tale, and then by excising the Pardoner's feminized body and perverse desire after he has told his tale. The Physician's account suggested a potentially useful slippage between the "natural" desire of "the people" for the truth about Appius's actions and that of the *Tale*'s implied audience that allows both to represent their "natural" recognition of the "truth" through a necessary othering of perverse desire onto Appius/Claudius. This perverse dynamic in the *Physician's Tale* is echoed in the "gentils" later, supposedly "instinctive" recognition of the Pardoner's perversity and in their subsequent attempts to excise such perversity from the pilgrimage body. Cut off potentially feminizing cupidity, tell us some moral thing, behave like a true man, and "we" will speak the will of God. The more "we" – Host and "gentils" – fix the Pardoner as naturally absolutely other and subordinate (i.e., passively non-male, perversely sodomitical, excessive), the more "our nature" is guaranteed as central and dominant (i.e., actively "masculine," straight, "sotheful").

But the Host's stress on the Physician's potent "tools of the trade," his emphasis on his own potency by denying a proper "tool" to the Pardoner, and even his more general allusions to the medical benefits of recreative play (including storytelling), underscore the material bodies so perfunctorily "killed off" in the *Physician's Tale*. And in bringing the *materia* excised by the *Physician's Tale* back into play in this way, the Host comes dangerously close to destabilizing the Physician's absolutist account of the natural on which dominant culture relies for its hegemonic power. Moreover, any intended smooth transition from one articulation of the natural to the next is disturbed by the Pardoner's re-enactment of the ambiguous "sentence" of the *Physician's Tale* as refracted and vulgarized by the Host:

> First I pronounce whennes that I come,
> And thanne my bulles shewe I, alle and some.
> Our lige lordes seel on my patente,
> That shewe I first, my body to warente.   (335–38)

That is, the Pardoner too begins with the assumption that the sign of an originary authority (here papal) will naturally subsume any potentially perverse materiality by overwriting its masculine will on that body. The Host did something similar when he assumed the Physician's role (e.g., his choice of the Pardoner as the next tale-teller in order to provide solas after the melancholic affect of the Physician's story). The Pardoner's comments here foreground the gaps in the seamless garment of masculinity that the Host's bodily/bawdy appropriation of the Physician's story made visible. The *Physician's Tale* proclaims itself as an "historial thyng" (156) that will necessarily impose its unifying will on all who listen to it; body will "naturally" give way to "sentence." Yet ironically, it is just this absolutist claim, to produce the same effect no matter what context, that makes the tale such a useful commodity for the Physician and Host, that allows them to use the story of Virginia to gain agency within the existing configurations of ideology. And an awkwardly similar absolutism and commodification of desire characterizes the commerce between the Pardoner and his "lewed" audience. Indeed, the Pardoner underscores just such a perverse dynamic with his reminder that he uses Latin merely to "saffron" (345) his preaching and stir "lewed" (392) folk to devotion.

The Pardoner therefore makes explicit what the Physician and Host dare not acknowledge: the activity of the objectifying desire of his audience being written on him and the body of his text even as he stands in for "the father" and existing ideological configurations. The Physician purported to tell one "true" storial thing that repeats the originary name over and over without alteration, even at the risk of killing off the body itself. Whereas the Pardoner regularly tells a hundred or more "false japes" (394) in his preaching and chooses "olde stories" (436), not because they will transmit an anterior, primal will, but because they're what his audience wants to hear. And he does the same thing now for the pilgrimage audience by situating the exemplary tale that they have demanded within a dizzying series of frames that emphasize duplication and dissemination without a controlling originary subject, the copying of copies rather than a "truly masculine" procreative reproduction. Thus, when we reach the Pardoner's story "proper," the kinds of foundational binaries emphasized in the Physician's story have collapsed. Is it "false jape" or some honest thing, made up or historical, ephemeral or essential, the Pardoner's or our own? The Pardoner's excessive reproduction of the constructions of proper masculinity and the natural taking place within medieval identity politics thus "spoils identity" to the extent that it de-scribes the identities that a conservative social order has so oppressively in-scribed by means of essentialized gender difference.

If the question of how we work upon the world and constitute it as a social entity emerges as a crucial one in Fragment VI, equally pressing by the end of the *Pardoner's Tale* is our recognition of the socially and linguistically constructed "bodies that matter" that enable this representational work to take place, and that are themselves always already subjects and objects of desire. The Pardoner's queer re-presentation of the feminine, to adapt Sedgwick, "far from being capable of being detached from the originary scene of shame, cleaves to that scene as a near-inexhaustible source of transformational energy."[18] As such it constitutes that queer performativity Butler has described as:

---

[18] "If queer is a politically potent term, which it is, that's because, far from being capable of being detached from the childhood scene of shame, it cleaves to that scene as a near-inexhaustible source of transformational energy" (Sedgwick, "Queer Performativity," 4).

this relation of being implicated in that which one opposes, this turning of power against itself to produce alternative modalities of power, to establish a kind of political contestation that is not a "pure" opposition, a "transcendence" of contemporary relations of power, but a difficult labor of forging a future from resources inevitably impure.[19]

The perspective of hegemonic masculinity may seek to read in the Pardoner only the horrors of feminine non-identity, a hermeneutical dead-end that writes true identity as someone else's and elsewhere. But the Pardoner's troubling body – ceaselessly performing gender and sexuality but never getting it "right" – can also provide an important point of entry back into the perversities of a medieval politics of representation which the Physician's story of Virginia and its fictional frame both enacted and attempted to disguise. Similarly, the representational flux occasioned by our own attempt to de-scribe the complexities of such a "medieval" moment can also bring into view the modern body in different ways and help queer *its* claim to naturalness. Such a double process of historicization might thereby open up room to maneuver for postmodern bodies (and subjectivities) as more than that which is already known and represented.

---

[19] Butler, *Bodies that Matter*, 241.

Contrasting Masculinities
in the *Shipman's Tale*:
Monk, Merchant, and Wife

PETER G. BEIDLER

The term "masculine" can refer to a nest of negative qualities often associated with being male: brutality, self-aggrandizement, sexual irresponsibility, selfishness, inability to feel or express emotion, inconstancy. It can also refer to a host of positive qualities: self-reliance, leadership, generosity, loyalty, sexual performance, responsibility for one's family, independence, good business sense. In the two central male characters in the *Shipman's Tale*, Chaucer gives us contrasting masculinities, the negative aspects of masculinity being associated with the monk of Paris, the more positive aspects being associated with the merchant of Saint Denis. Throughout my discussion of the contrasting masculinities in the *Shipman's Tale*, I shall compare Chaucer's tale of the lover's gift regained with its closest analogue and most likely source, the first tale of the eighth day of Boccaccio's *Decameron*. I shall have much to say about the important differences in treatment of the male characters in these two tales, but will close with a brief suggestion that the *Shipman's Tale*, originally written for the Wife of Bath, shows us a wife who, while remaining undeniably and gloriously a woman, demonstrates traits that were in Chaucer's time usually associated more with men than with women.

The *Shipman's Tale* has not received the scholarly attention that Chaucer's other fabliaux have received. What scholarship there has been has generally focused on one of four problems: what the tale reveals about medieval business practices;[1]

---

[1]   Closely related to the mercantile quality of the tale is its punning. The following are some of the studies that deal with mercantile issues and puns: Albert H. Silverman, "Sex and

how it reflects religious symbolism;[2] its relationship to its antecedents;[3] and its possible early assignment to the Wife of Bath rather than the Shipman.[4] In most studies the monk is seen as clever but immoral, the husband as overly preoccupied with his business and not sufficiently attentive to his wife, and the wife as either a greedy prostitute or a neglected wife justified in complaining about her husband. Few scholars have touched on the issue of masculinity as it is portrayed in the tale, except to note that the merchant is inadequately manly. But let us first consider his cuckolder, daun John.

Money in Chaucer's *Shipman's Tale*," *PQ* 32 (1953): 329–36; Paul Stephen Schneider, " 'Taillynge Ynough': The Function of Money in the *Shipman's Tale*," *ChauR* 11 (1977): 201–09; Kenneth S. Cahn, "Chaucer's Merchants and the Foreign Exchange: An Introduction to Medieval Finance," *SAC* 2 (1980): 81–119; Lorraine Kochanske Stock, "The Meaning of *Chevyssaunce*: Complicated Word Play in Chaucer's *Shipman's Tale*," *Studies in Short Fiction* 18 (1981): 245–49; Gerhard Joseph, "Chaucer's Coinage: Foreign Exchange and the Puns of the *Shipman's Tale*," *ChauR* 17 (1983): 341–57; Thomas Hahn, "Money, Sexuality, Wordplay and Context in the *Shipman's Tale*," in *Chaucer in the Eighties*, ed. Julian N. Wasserman and Robert J. Blanch (Syracuse: Syracuse University Press, 1986), 235–49; and Wight Martindale, Jr., "Chaucer's Merchants: A Trade-Based Speculation on Their Activities," *ChauR* 26 (1992): 309–16.

2   See, for example, Theresa Coletti, "The Meeting at the Gate: Comic Hagiography and Symbol in the *Shipman's* Tale," *Studies in Iconography* 3 (1977): 47–56, and "The *Mulier Fortis* and Chaucer's *Shipman's Tale*," *ChauR* 15 (1981): 236–49; Gail McMurray Gibson, "Resurrection as Dramatic Icon in the *Shipman's Tale*," in *Signs and Symbols in Chaucer's Poetry*, ed. John P. Hermann and John J. Burke, Jr. (University, AL: University of Alabama Press, 1981), 102–12; Lorraine Kochanske Stock, "The Reenacted Fall in Chaucer's *Shipman's Tale*," *Studies in Iconography* 7–8 (1981–82): 135–45; and R. H. Winnick, "Luke 12 and Chaucer's *Shipman's Tale*," *ChauR* 30 (1995): 164–90.

3   See, for example, Murray Copland, "The *Shipman's Tale*: Chaucer and Boccaccio," *MÆ* 35 (1966): 11–28; Michael W. McClintock, "Games and the Players of Games: Old French Fabliaux and the *Shipman's Tale*," *ChauR* 5 (1970): 112–36; Richard Guerin, "The *Shipman's Tale*: The Italian Analogues," *English Studies* 52 (1971): 412–19; V. J. Scattergood, "The Originality of the *Shipman's Tale*," *ChauR* 11 (1977): 210–31; Lorraine Kochanske Stock, "La Vieille and the Merchant's Wife in Chaucer's *Shipman's Tale*," *Southern Humanities Review* 16 (1982): 333–39; Joerg O. Fichte, "Chaucer's *Shipman's Tale* within the Context of the French Fabliaux Tradition," in *Chaucer's Frame Tales: The Physical and the Metaphysical*, ed. Joerg O. Fichte (Tübingen: Narr, 1987), 51–66; and Carol F. Heffernan, "Chaucer's *Shipman's Tale* and Boccaccio's *Decameron VIII, 1*: Retelling a Story," in *Courtly Literature: Culture and Context*, ed. Keith Busby and Erik Kooper (Amsterdam: John Benjamins, 1990), 262–70.

4   See, for example, Richard F. Jones, "A Conjecture on the Wife of Bath's Prologue," *JEGP* 24 (1925): 512–47; Robert A. Pratt, "The Development of the Wife of Bath," in *Studies in Medieval Literature*, ed. MacEdward Leach (Philadelphia: University of Pennsylvania Press, 1961), 45–79; and William W. Lawrence, "Chaucer's *Shipman's Tale*," *Speculum* 33 (1958): 56–68.

The monk of Paris

Daun John's behavior and motives are in direct contrast to those of Gulfardo, his counterpart in *Decameron VIII, 1*, written at least thirty years before Chaucer wrote the *Shipman's Tale*.[5] Here is a summary of the key actions of Boccaccio's version of the story of a man who borrows from a merchant enough money to pay for sexual services from the merchant's wife:

Decameron VIII, 1. Gulfardo, a brave German soldier in Milan, is known for his trustworthiness in repaying loans. He falls in love with Ambruogia, the wife of a wealthy merchant named Guasparruolo, with whom he is on friendly terms. One day Gulfardo sends Ambruogia a message expressing his love, requesting her to reward his devotion to her, and affirming that he will do whatever she might ask of him. The lady considers his request, then tells Gulfardo that she will grant it, but only if he will give her 200 gold florins so that she can buy something for herself. Gulfardo is disillusioned that the woman he had come to love could cheapen that love by being so rapaciously greedy, and his love turns to hatred. He vows to punish her. After sending Ambruogia word that he will give her the money, Gulfardo goes to Ambruogia's husband and asks for a loan of 200 florins, at the usual rate of interest, for a certain business transaction. The husband readily agrees and gives him the money on the spot. Not long after, when her husband is off in Genoa on business, Ambruogia summons Gulfardo. He comes and, in the presence of a witness, gives her the 200 florins with the request that she should return them to her husband. So that the witness will not guess that the money is anything but a business matter, Ambruogia agrees, then pours the gold onto the table and counts it. She hides the money and takes Gulfardo to her bedroom. They make love that day and many others before her husband returns. As soon as the merchant gets back from Genoa, Gulfardo goes to him with the witness and reports, in the presence of the wife, that he had not needed the money after all and had given it to his wife to return to him. Since there was a witness to the transaction, Ambruogia says that,

[5] This is not the place to argue the importance of *Decameron VIII, 1* as the most likely source for Chaucer's tale. Readers who want to pursue the point can read my essay, "Just Say Yes, Chaucer Knew the *Decameron*: or, Bringing the *Shipman's Tale* out of Limbo," forthcoming in *The Decameron and the Canterbury Tales*, ed. Leonard Michael Koff and Brenda Deen Schildgen, Fairleigh Dickinson University Press. Giovanni Sercambi's *novelle* "De avaritia et lussuria" ("Of Avarice and Lust") is sometimes considered to be a contending source for the *Shipman's Tale*, but there is growing evidence that the book that contained it – which is based unquestionably on the *Decameron* – would not have been available to Chaucer in time for it to have influenced the composition of this tale. The text and a modern English translation are conveniently available in Larry D. Benson and Theodore Andersson, eds., *The Literary Context of Chaucer's Fabliaux* (Indianapolis: Bobbs-Merrill, 1971), 312–19. The notion that Chaucer's real source was a lost French fabliau is widely disregarded now.

yes, she had received the money, but had forgotten to tell her husband about it. The husband agrees to strike the loan from the books, and the wife gives him the 200 florins.

That summary of a two-page story does not reveal the extent to which Gulfardo, the German soldier, is held up for admiration. Neifile, the fictional teller, explicitly announces that she tells this tale not to criticize the male lover for his behavior but, on the contrary, to praise him for his clever way of punishing Ambruogia. Gulfardo is a brave soldier who is loyal to those who employ him, always pays his debts, is discreet, and is capable of true and lofty love. There is not a hint of irony in any of this praise. After she has completed her tale, Neifile again explicitly praises the wise Gulfardo for punishing the rapacious and depraved Ambruogia by finding a way to enjoy her sexual favors at no cost.

The narrator of the *Shipman's Tale* also praises the male lover, but the praise is laced with irony. Daun John is said to be "a fair man" (VII 25) and "so fair of face" (28), but handsomeness seems a curiously unnecessary, even harmful, quality in a monk. He is said to be "noble" (62) and "a man of heigh prudence" (64), but his actions in the story – cheating both the woman he says he loves and his life-long friend – surely suggest, at least in retrospect, that such praise is spoken with more than a hint of sarcasm.

Chaucer fundamentally reorients his version of the tale. Far from portraying daun John as a good person whose courtly love for a woman justifies his propositioning her and whose sense of outrage at her mercenary character justifies his tricking her, Chaucer portrays him as a sleazy opportunist who himself deserves to be punished, a man whose masculinity is almost entirely negative. Indeed, what Neifile sees as the positive masculinity of Gulfardo throws into appropriate contrast what the narrator of the *Shipman's Tale* sees as the negative masculinity of daun John. Gulfardo is a brave and reliable bachelor eligible for love. Daun John is a monk whose vows of chastity ought to make him ineligible for love. By making the lover a vow-breaking ecclesiast who takes advantage of his professional position to seduce wives, Chaucer drops him to a level with Absolon. Gulfardo genuinely falls in love with a married woman and then discreetly asks his lady for her favors. Daun John merely lusts after another man's wife. His subsequent professions of love are both indiscreet and insincere.

Although Gulfardo is said to be on friendly terms with the merchant of Milan, the two men come not merely from different cities but from different nations. Their friendship is business-based, so far as we can tell, deriving from Gulfardo's having borrowed from Guasparruolo and having repaid all of his past loans on time. Daun John, on the other hand, is a life-long friend of the merchant of Saint Denis, with whom he had grown up in the same village. In proposing a liaison with Guasparruolo's wife, Gulfardo proposes to cuckold a business associate. In proposing a liaison with his best friend's wife, daun John proposes to betray a lifelong friendship. Gulfardo is no kinsman to the man whose wife he loves. Daun John, on the other hand, claims to be a "cousin" to his friend – that is, until it is convenient to his lustful purposes to make hasty and unequivocal denial of that cousinship: "He is na moore cosyn unto me / Than is this leef that hangeth on the tree!" (149–50). Gulfardo has only a business connection with the merchant of Milan. Daun John, on the other hand, has actually sworn vows of brotherhood with the merchant of Saint Denis. His wickedness is more infamous because he cuckolds, without a moment's hesitation, not only his best friend and cousin, but the man whose interests he has sworn to support and protect always.

Why do the two male lovers negotiate sex with another man's wife? Gulfardo does so because he is in love. Daun John does so because he wants sex. How do the two male lovers introduce the question of sex? Gulfardo does it by sending Ambruogia a message expressing his love. Daun John does it directly, in a quasi-public garden scene and in the presence of a "mayde child" (95). He jests that the wife of Saint Denis must be tired from her husband's having "laboured" (108) her all night long. He promises to keep secret anything she confesses to him. He raises the question of love by telling his friend's wife that he has loved her "specially / Aboven alle women" (153–54). And daun John, in an action that has no counterpart in Boccaccio, grabs the wife: "he caughte hire by the flankes, / And hire embraceth hard, and kiste hire ofte" (202–03). This aggressive sexuality is very much Chaucer's addition to the character of daun John. The point here is not only that daun John's initiating the question of sex is more direct than Gulfardo's, but that for a monk to have any part at all in such talk, let alone fondling his friend's wife, is unambiguously wrong. As a monk he should have a higher love in the forefront of his consciousness than sexual love-making with his best friend's wife.

Daun John's masculinity, then, is loveless, sex-based, disloyal, self-centered, fraudulent, opportunistic, and immoral in the extreme. His immorality is based not just on his shabby treatment of both his best friend and his lover, but on the fact that, as a monk, he ought to stand above the kinds of actions he participates in. He ought, rather than engage in sexual activity himself, to caution others against the dire consequences of such rampantly destructive masculinity.

The merchant of Saint Denis

It is easy enough to see the merchant of Saint Denis in a negative light. This husband of a beautiful and demanding wife seems so preoccupied with his counting house and business dealings that he ignores his wife and so invites his own cuckolding. He seems too foolish to see that his best friend is his worst deceiver. His own wife, who ought to know, suggests that he is lacking in most or all of the "thynges sixe" (174) that women want in husbands. In doing so she gives expression to her own list of ideal masculine qualities:

"They wolde that hir housbondes sholde be
Hardy, and wise, and riche, and therto free,
And buxom unto his wyf, and fressh abedde."   (175–77)

I am particularly interested in the wife's two central complaints about her husband – that he is neither "free" with his money nor "fressh abedde" – though I shall have a bit to say also about his wisdom and the extent to which he measures up to the wife's other requirements.

The portrayal of the merchant of Saint Denis seems flatly to contradict his wife's claim that he is not free with his money. When the monk asks for 100 francs, his response is unhesitating: "My gold is youres, whan that it yow leste, / And nat oonly my gold, but my chaffare" (284–85). Unlike Guasparruolo, he does not charge his friend interest. In some ways, ironically, the merchant is the least mercenary of the three characters. Certainly he is the most generous. He specifically invites his friend to come to Saint Denis for a visit; he spends time with him; he provides good meals for him; he lends him as much money as the monk asks for and offers more; he does not charge interest; he does not ask his friend to return it when he visits him in Paris – even though he has gone to Paris specifically to raise money to cover certain expenses he has incurred.

The husband's generosity to his wife is more problematical. Before he leaves for Bruges, he appears to make full provision for his wife's household needs: "Of silver in thy purs shaltow nat faille" (248) – a statement that seems to contradict his wife's assertion to the monk that her husband is niggardly. The matter is complicated, of course, by the wife's motive of gaining sympathy from daun John so that he will give her a lot of money. In view of that goal, she can scarcely be expected not to tell the monk that her husband is stingy. The matter is complicated also by the husband's pompous-sounding lecture to her about the important work that merchants do and his exhortation to her to "kepe oure good" (243). Besides, it may be that his perception of how much silver is enough for a thrifty household may be quite different from hers. Still, the merchant's apparent generosity to both his friend and his wife reinforces in at least general ways the narrator's statement in the opening description of him that the merchant of Saint Denis is known for his "largesse" (22). That that generosity extends to his wife is evident enough in the final scene, where he allows his wife to keep the 100 francs. More precisely, he agrees to let her pay him back with sexual services – a sexual debt that she owed him in any case by virtue of being his wife.

One of the most strikingly original features of Chaucer's *Shipman's Tale* is that the merchant is masculinized – that he is given a phallus and allowed to use it. This feature of the story is simply not present in the *Decameron* version. In that brief tale the merchant is married, yes, but Boccaccio's tale gives no evidence whatever about Guasparruolo's sex life. His wife cheats on him, to be sure, but there is no hint that she does so because of any real or imagined sexual inadequacy on his part. She never complains about his lack of manhood in the marital bed. Ambruogia's motivation for granting sex to another man is entirely greed: she sleeps with Gulfardo not because she wants more sex, but because she wants more money. There is no husband-wife sex scene in *Decameron VIII, 1*. Boccaccio has essentially neutered the husband. His sexuality, or lack of it, is simply not an issue.

The husband's sexuality is very much an issue in Chaucer's version of the story. The wife of the merchant of Saint Denis seizes the initiative in the garden with her response to daun John's blushing suggestion that her husband has "laboured" (108) her all night:

> "Nay, cosyn myn, it stant nat so with me;
> For, by that God that yaf me soule and lyf,
> In al the reawme of France is ther no wyf
> That lasse lust hath to that sory pley."   (114–17)

After she has assurances of the monk's secrecy and his lustful feelings for her, she hints again at her husband's sexual inadequacy, but refuses to go into detail:

> "Myn housbonde is to me the worste man
> That evere was sith that the world bigan.
> But sith I am a wyf, it sit nat me
> To tellen no wight of our privetee,
> Neither abedde, ne in noon oother place;
> God shilde I sholde it tellen, for his grace!"   (161–66)

Although she does not describe her husband's sexual inadequacies, she hints at them so broadly that daun John cannot – and does not – mistake her meaning. He apparently believes her.

We readers are permitted to believe her also – until the final scene. There the husband performs so tirelessly in bed that even his wife can find nothing to complain about except perhaps that he is entirely too "fressh abedde":

> And al that nyght in myrthe they bisette
> For he was riche and cleerly out of dette.
> Whan it was day, this marchant gan embrace
> His wyf al newe, and kiste hire on hir face,
> And up he gooth and maketh it ful tough.
> "Namoore," quod she, "by God, ye have ynough!"
> And wantonly agayn with hym she pleyde.   (375–61)

It is perhaps easy to question the sexuality of a merchant whose interest in sex is said to be particularly keen after his successful business trip when he is "riche and cleerly out of dette." I caution, however, against reading those lines as evidence that when he is not rich, or that when his debts trouble him, the merchant is inadequate sexually. Rather than saying, "Hey, this fellow can succeed sexually only after he has succeeded financially," I prefer to say, "Like most of us, he feels particularly eager for sex after a day in which things have gone well. Surely he is not always so demanding of sexual services as he is after his financial success in Paris, but that does not mean that the rest of the time he has no energy for sexual activity."

It is noteworthy that Chaucer devotes far more space to the sex scene between the wife and her husband than between the wife and her lover. I have made a rough comparison of the number of lines Boccaccio and Chaucer devote to the sex between the wife and her lover. Boccaccio devotes some 25% of his tale to the soldier-wife sex in the *Decameron*. Chaucer reduces that to only 4%. Indeed, the 4% is an exaggeration. All Chaucer really tells us about their sexual encounter is a single and most general line: "In myrthe al nyght a bisy lyf they lede" (318). On the other hand, Chaucer devotes 14% of his version of the tale to the sex scene between the merchant and his wife. In that scene Chaucer not only gives us the generic "And al that nyght in myrthe they bisette" (375), but also devotes some 15 lines (376–81, 413–17, 422–26) to their sexual relations. Chaucer was clearly far more interested in portraying the merchant's nocturnal activities with his wife than the monk's. Indeed, it is notable that in one of Chaucer's two most explicit descriptions of sexual intercourse – the other being the pear-tree encounter between Damian and May in the *Merchant's Tale* – he celebrates the joy of marital sex.

In any case, the merchant's sexuality is shown in the closing bedroom scene to be such that we are led to infer that his wife's earlier innuendos about his inadequacies were fiction. Unlike the merchant in the *Decameron* version, Chaucer's merchant gets to prove his sexual manhood in that final scene. I must emphasize again that the final bedroom scene in which the merchant proves his sexual masculinity is entirely Chaucer's addition to the tale. It has no counter-part in *Decameron VIII, 1*. Chaucer appears to have used this scene to clear the merchant of the two main charges his wife had earlier leveled against him: that he is ungenerous and that he is not "fressh abedde." By showing the merchant both sexually active in bed with his wife and generously willing to accept the terms of her offer to pay him back with her sexual favors, Chaucer seriously undermines her earlier accusation that her husband is stingy with money and inadequate in bed.

Before moving to my discussion of the wife I want to discuss the wisdom of the merchant. There is some reason to doubt that wisdom. The merchant appears, after all, too foolish to see what is so obvious to the rest of us, that his best friend is a fraud capable of the ultimate in disloyalty. And he appears too foolish to see that his wife sleeps around behind his back. The opening lines of the *Shipman's Tale* may hint that the husband's reputation for wisdom is based more on his ability to accumulate wealth than to use common sense: "A marchant whilom dwelled at Seint-Denys, / That riche was, for which men helde hym wys" (1–2). On the other hand, the merchant may show his greatest wisdom in not inquiring too closely about the sexual dealings of his best friend and his own wife. Let me explain what I mean.

The *Shipman's Tale*, like *Decameron VIII, 1*, was almost certainly meant to be assigned to a female teller. The Wife of Bath is the only possible candidate on the road to Canterbury. Indeed, the tale fits her well enough. It is, after all, about marriage and infidelity, two interests of Alisoun of Bath. It is about a woman who uses her wits to seduce another man for her own financial gain, a woman who, quite unlike the unfortunate Ambruogia, is able by her cleverness both to convince her husband of her innocence and to keep the money. The telltale female pronouns near the start of the tale are entirely suitable to her:

> The sely housbonde, algate he moot paye,
> He moot us clothe, and he moot us arraye . . .
> And if that he noght may, par aventure,
> Or ellis list no swich dispense endure,
> But thynketh it is wasted and ylost,
> Thanne moot another payen for oure cost.   (11–12, 15–18)

Despite those words, the tale is generally assigned to the Shipman, but that appears to have been a late and unintegrated assignment.[6] The pronouns and the tale, on the other hand, are entirely appropriate to Alisoun of Bath. Indeed, the merchant of Saint Denis comes across as a showcase husband, to judge by the Wife of Bath's own criteria. Not the least of his virtues is that he is trusting, wise enough not to inquire overmuch about his wife's activities. From a lusty woman's point of view, he has the wisdom appropriate to husbands, a wisdom that does not bother about where one's wife bestows her sexual favors so long as she keeps her husband happy in bed. Alisoun puts it this way in her long diatribe to her old husbands:

> Of alle men yblessed moot he be,
> The wise astrologien, Daun Ptholome,
> That seith this proverbe in his Almageste:
> "Of alle men his wysdom is the hyeste
> That reckketh nevere who had the world in honde."

---

[6]   There have been several attempts to explain how or why the Shipman seems to speak in female pronouns, and so to question the evidence that the Wife of Bath was the original teller of the *Shipman's Tale*. See, for example, Frederick Tupper, "The Bearings of the Shipman's Prologue," *JEGP* 33 (1934): 352–72; Robert L. Chapman, "The *Shipman's Tale* Was Meant for the Shipman," *Modern Language Notes* 71 (1956): 4–5; and Hazel Sullivan, "A Chaucerian Puzzle," in *A Chaucerian Puzzle and Other Medieval Essays*, ed. Natalie Grimes Lawrence and Jack A. Reynolds (Coral Gables: University of Miami Press, 1961), 1–46. The widest opinion, however, and my own, is that the pronouns do indicate a female teller, and that this person can only have been the Wife of Bath. See William W. Lawrence, "The Wife of Bath and the Shipman," *MLN* 72 (1957): 87–88.

> By this proverbe thou shalt understonde,
> Have thou ynogh, what thar thee recche or care
> How myrily that othere folkes fare?
> For, certeyn, olde dotard, by your leve,
> Ye shul have queynte right ynogh at eve.
> He is to greet a nygard that wolde werne
> A man to lighte a candle at his lanterne;
> He shal have never the lasse light, pardee.
> Have thou ynogh, thee thar nat pleyne thee.   (III 323–36)

To be sure, such "wysdom" (III 326) can make a husband a cuckold, but the Wife of Bath seems to want to suggest that cuckoldry hurts no one unless the husband finds out about it. Some husbands deserve to be cuckolded because of their sexual inadequacies – John in the *Miller's Tale*, for example, and January in the *Merchant's Tale*. The merchant of Saint Denis, however, is apparently not one of them. Indeed, Chaucer's having given us the "mayde child" (VIII 95) – presumably his daughter – may be read as evidence of the merchant's sexual potency, just as Chaucer's having given us the bedroom scene may be read as evidence of his satisfactory sexual performance. Neither the child nor the sex scene appears in the *Decameron* version.

In dealing with the two men in the *Shipman's Tale*, in any case, Chaucer has given us, if not his own, then the Wife of Bath's contrasting opinions about masculinity. He has greatly debased the lover by having the young monk demonstrate the most negative masculine qualities: disloyalty, dishonesty, sexual immorality, selfishness. Incapable of a love that transcends sexual desire, he uses the wife of Saint Denis, then abandons her. Chaucer takes the most attractive character in Boccaccio's *Decameron VIII, 1* and transforms him into the least attractive character in the *Shipman's Tale*. If what daun John shows us is masculine behavior, Chaucer seems to be saying, then we want no part of it.

Chaucer has, on the other hand, enhanced the character of the merchant-husband, a relatively insignificant character in *Decameron VIII, 1*. Chaucer has endowed the merchant with a set of positive masculine qualities: he has good business sense combined with a generosity of spirit. He comes across as a near-ideal husband – at least from the Wife of Bath's point of view. What more could such wives want in a husband than a man sufficiently careful in business to provide a comfortable and safe home for his family, secure enough in his manhood not to be suspicious of her, sexually active enough to satisfy her in bed, generous enough to let her keep the money a debtor had repaid to him?

Chaucer, then, has retold an old story but given it a new twist. Despite his wife's petulant allegations to the contrary, the merchant seems to provide his wife with the "thynges sixe" (174) she says wives want: he is (1) "hardy" and (2) "wise" enough, at least to judge from his bold and successful business dealings; he is (3) "rich" and, so far as we can tell, (4) "therto free"; although he sometimes preaches his wife a small sermon – apparently well-deserved –

on thriftiness and solvency, he seems (5) "buxom" enough to her, letting her have great freedom in her dealings with others and indulging her penchant for spending money on fancy clothes; and, as we have seen, he is remarkably (6) "fressh abedde." Some wives might desire in a husband a man who might also be her friend and intellectual companion, but those are not qualities that either the Wife of Bath or the wife of Saint Denis list as desirable qualities in a husband. Hardy, wise, rich, generous, obedient, fresh in bed – surely if any man is a good enough husband to deserve the sexual rewards bestowed on him in that final scene in the *Shipman's Tale*, the merchant of Saint Denis is. If any husband is masculine enough to take advantage of the sexual activity she offers, he is.

The wife of Saint Denis

Even in a paper about masculine qualities shown in the *Shipman's Tale*, we must speak more of the wife of the merchant of Saint Denis. In the monk and the merchant, Chaucer offers contrasting simplifications of masculinity. The monk's corrupt masculinity is redeemed by no virtues. The merchant's brighter masculinity is balanced somewhat by his sometimes pompous and patronizing preoccupation with his financial dealings, but he has no apparent outright vices. Curiously, the character who shows the most interesting and balanced mixture of positive and negative qualities associated with these men is not a man at all.

Like the monk, the wife of the merchant of Saint Denis is unfaithful, aggressively self-centered, and mercenary, but she is, like her husband, likeable, clever, aggressive, resourceful, and apparently able to keep a spouse happy in bed. If Chaucer makes the monk more evil in adapting *Decameron VIII, 1* to his own narrative design, and if he makes the husband more sympathetic, surely he makes the wife more complex. There is no question that she is far more attractive than Ambruogia, her shallow, greedy, and not-very-bright counterpart in the *Decameron*. Neifile holds Ambruogia up as an example of a woman who deserves to be punished for cheapening love by putting a price tag on it. The wife of Saint Denis also puts a price tag on her love, but she is never punished for the deed. Indeed, we are more likely to admire her for her cleverness than to castigate her for her immorality.

The wife is, after all, in charge all the way through the *Shipman's Tale*. Unlike the passive Ambruogia, who is propositioned by Gulfardo, the wife of Saint Denis actively takes her case to daun John by coming to him in the garden, complaining about her husband, asking for a loan of 100 francs, and suggesting Sunday for the day of delivery. Whereas in the *Decameron* tale the wife had been in the position of responding to the aggressive advances of Gulfardo, in the *Shipman's Tale* the wife's aggressive advances to daun John put him in the secondary role of responding to her advances. In exchange for the money she gives the monk only one night in bed, not several, as does Ambruogia. Her crowning achievement, of course, comes in the final bedroom scene. In that scene the wife is confronted in bed by her husband with the embarrassing accusation that she had not told him about daun John's returning to her the 100-franc loan. At the parallel moment in *Decameron VIII, 1*, Ambruogia lamely reports that she had forgotten to tell her husband about the transaction, then returns the money to him. The wife of Saint Denis, on the other hand – "nat afered nor affrayed, / But boldely" (400–01) – admits that, yes, she had received certain money from the monk, but she had assumed it was a gift in repayment for all the hospitality he had received so often at the merchant's house, and she reports that she had spent the money on clothes for her husband's honor. Furthermore, she offers to repay the money in services: "Ye shal my joly body have to wedde; / By God, I wol nat paye yow but abedde!" (423–24). While we may be troubled by the commercialization of sex – and the jokes about scoring the financial debt upon the wife's "taille" (416) – we can but admire the moxie of the wife of the merchant of Saint Denis.

The Italian tale is told precisely to castigate greedy and unfaithful wives. Neifile sets up her tale by saying that any woman who sells her virtue for monetary gain ought to be burnt alive. A woman who yields her virtue for love, Neifile explains, is easily forgiven, but not one who yields it for money. After Neifile's story in the *Decameron*, the others in the company applaud Gulfardo's tricking of the greedy Ambruogia. At the end of the *Shipman's Tale*, however, there is no castigation of the wife of Saint Denis. Rather, the Host warns his fellow travelers to "draweth no monkes moore unto your in" (442). Boccaccio wants his readers to dislike Ambruogia and admire her soldier-lover. Chaucer and the Wife of Bath, by contrast, seem to want readers to admire the wife of Saint Denis and dislike her monk-lover. In the process of bringing about that fundamental change in the story, Chaucer has given the wife of Saint Denis an engaging mix of qualities often associated with men.

The wife of Saint Denis is without doubt a woman. She is aware of her sexuality as a woman. She knows that as a woman she has very little she can trade on except her sexuality. And she uses that female sexuality to bring about most of the key actions in the tale. So strong and important are her feminine qualities that we cannot use the term "masculine" to describe either her character or her actions. It is interesting to note, however, that the Wife of Bath gives the wife of Saint Denis a full measure of the qualities sometimes associated with successful men in the Middle Ages – leadership, independence, sexual aggressiveness, cleverness, self-assurance, articulateness, and an ability to do successful business. Through the force of their own personalities, both the Wife of Bath and the wife of Saint Denis transform traits often seen in medieval times as masculine into traits that seem both appropiate to and admirable in a woman. For traditionally masculine traits to be associated in a positive way with women is common in the twentieth century. In the fourteenth century it was no less than revolutionary.

Diminishing Masculinity in Chaucer's
Tale of Sir Thopas

Fragment VII of Chaucer's *Canterbury Tales* sutures into a single, long narrative six stories that have long impressed critics as thematically unconnected. The narrative bridges between the tales are especially rich. Taken together, these moments in the "roadside drama" suggest that one of the unifying obsessions of the fragment is the gendering of male bodies.

The connective dialogues overflow with commentary from the robustly masculine Host, a "semely man" who "of manhood hym lakkede right naught" (I 751, 756). After the *Shipman's Tale* Harry Bailly jokes about the effusive virility of monks; after the *Prioress's Tale* he pokes fun at Chaucer the pilgrim, reducing him to an "elvyssh" freak (VII 703). Having invited the poet to tell the next story, he interrupts the performance to condemn the *Tale of Sir Thopas* as mere "dogerel" (VII 925). The Host is less bellicose after Chaucer provides a second narrative, the didactic *Tale of Melibee*, in which the good wife Prudence instructs her husband in proper male reticence when his enemies beat her and murder their daughter. Harry next ridicules the Monk, announcing that his vigorous, expansive body is wasted in the cloister. Harry insists that the religious orders have drained the world of its most masculine citizens, leaving laymen who are mere "shrympes" and "wrecched ympes" (1955–56) to carry on the work of populating it. The *Monk's Tale* is, like *Thopas*, angrily interrupted. The Knight complains that its unremitting focus on the tragic fall of great men is simply too depressing; perhaps it also hits too close to home. The Nun's Priest next relates a mock-epic fabliau in which the rooster Chauntecleer escapes a menacing fox. The Host brings the fragment to a close by praising the ridiculous vision of masculinity which the "heroic" cock embodies: the Nun's Priest himself should be just like that manly fowl, Harry says, with "seven tymes seventene" (3454) concubine hens to service his virile needs.

Male bodies of all kinds tumble along these dialogic bridges that bind the six tales: celibate, hypersexual, overly physical, otherworldly, diminutive, child-like, hen-pecked, hen-serviced, ludic, and ludicrous. Yet the final vision of masculinity which Fragment VII offers is of a rooster proudly strutting through his barnyard harem, and a priest no one calls by his proper name – even Harry addresses him as "Sire Nonnes Preest," as if he lacked an identity outside of his belonging to the Prioress. This body becomes the ironic, final, but far from stable site of masculinity in the series of tales. The Host pronounces a benediction upon its "breche, and every stoon" (VII 3448).

The exaggerations and reductions of masculinity so evident in the bridges also occur, albeit more subtly, in the tales they connect. Masculinity in Fragment VII is best described as *an economy of flows*: male sexuality diminishes and expands throughout as if it were a liquid (or humor) of which a particular body can possess too much or too little, sometimes in alternation. The six narratives of Fragment VII and their dramatic bridges explore how masculinity represents itself as something bigger than life, like a giant, a *universal*. Yet masculinity "in reality" turns out to be a phenomenon of little things: merchant bodies, elvish authors, tiny clergeons, infantalized knights, self-inflated monks, farm-house fowls. In this essay I explore the first contraction of Fragment VII as it reaches a near-vanishing point in the *Tale of Sir Thopas*, the midpoint and fulcrum of the series. Masculinity shrinks, I will argue, in order to divorce gender from the *dangers* of sexuality: the male body is diminished in *Thopas* in order to keep gender safe from the possibility of sex.

The incredible shrinking knight

When Harry demands that Chaucer tell the Canterbury pilgrims a "tale of myrthe" (706) in order to counteract the harrowing reductiveness of the *Prioress's Tale*, the poet responds with the *Tale of Sir Thopas*, an affectionate burlesque of the Middle English heroic romances. The hero is a bumbling little champion with an adorable name. Sir Olifaunt, a three-headed giant and the knight's monstrous antagonist, better fits a nursery rhyme than a medieval romance. The wilderness that Thopas traverses is full of bucks and hares rather than the expected lions and bears. The "fer contree" of the hero's birth is proximate Flanders (718). *Thopas* is a story that keeps trickling into smaller portions. Fit I has 18 stanzas, Fit II has 9, Fit III has 4.5 – each section is exactly one half the length of the preceding one.[1] Meanwhile, the poem's layout in the two most important manuscripts of the *Canterbury Tales*, Ellesmere and Hengwrt, accentuates this dwindling effect by breaking each stanza across the page into consecutively smaller portions, so that the words appear to trickle

---

1   John Burrow, "Sir Thopas: An Agony in Three Fits," in *Essays in Medieval Literature* (Oxford: Clarendon Press, 1984), 61–65.

away to nothing toward the folio's edge.[2] At the point at which the tale cannot become any smaller (because the ratio of fit lengths is 4:2:1), the Host interrupts the whole performance and condemns it as a reprehensibly meager poetic achievement rather than a charmingly diminutive one: "Thy drasty rymyng is nat worth a toord!" (950). The doubled reference to excrement ("drasty," "toord") reduces what seemed a tiny, balanced world into one without proper limit, like a body that had seemed perfect in its delicately miniature scale but ends up being infantile, a body without control, a body that soils itself.

The happy detailing of physical features which begins the tale constructs a body more cute than manly. Thopas's face is as pure as "payndemayn" (white bread), his lips are red as roses, his complexion is ruddy as scarlet dye, and he has a "semely" nose (725–29). His clothing is detailed at similar length. These stanzas are not so much like the *effictiones* of romance, those long narrative catalogues that describe a (feminine) body by breaking it into beautiful fragments – eyes like the sparkling sun, lips like rubies, and so forth. Rather, the effect is of dressing up a doll in bright clothing. Thopas is as much a "popet" as the tale's narrator.

The tight poetic control of these lines is immediately translated into an interior, bodily control that characterizes Thopas in his relation to his physicality. Despite the fact that many women pine for his love, this fastidious knight will have nothing to do with them: "he was chaast and no lechour" (745). The overall impression is of tender obliviousness, of a body too innocent to know even what part it plays in the social circuit – much like the Prioress's "litel clergeon," who seems unable to imagine that the Jews whose street he passes along each day might dislike his constant pious hymning.

Thopas's diminutive size is best emphasized through the encounter with his spatial opposite, the giant Olifaunt, whose very name suggests vastness. Something more than comic necessity dictates that Thopas face this monster. An encounter with a giant is inevitable in those romances which detail the rites of passage of a young knight.[3] Similar fights against a giant occur in *Sir Eglamour, Guy of Warwick*, and *Lybeaus Desconus*, romances with which Chaucer was intimately familiar.[4] The giant functions within romance as a monstrous embodiment of sexual violence and unrestrained aggression – of what psychoanalysis labels the pre-oedipal (orality, appetite, desire that knows neither limit nor boundary). A cultural body upon which the codes that produce a safely gendered male body have failed to adhere, this monster demonstrates what

---

[2] Helen Cooper treats this effect at length in *Oxford Guides to Chaucer: The Canterbury Tales*, 2nd ed. (Oxford: Oxford University Press, 1996), 300.

[3] I argue this point at length in "Decapitation and Coming of Age: Constructing Masculinity and the Monstrous," *Arthurian Yearbook* 3 (1993): 171–90.

[4] Loomis collects the relevant analogues in *Sources and Analogues of Chaucer's Canterbury Tales*, ed. W. F. Bryan and Germaine Dempster (New York: Humanities Press, 1958), 486–559.

masculinity must not be in order to regulate what form sanctioned gender identity will take. The young hero defeats his monstrous double in a battle whose outcome announces that the knight has learned to channel the multiple drives that traverse the body, rendering a multiplicity of desire (only the dangers of which the giant enfleshes) into a unitary being. As Susan Crane observes, this "identity is finally in the gift of the community"[5]: chivalric selfhood is an identity produced through severe cultural constraint, because the goal of romance is the formation of docile or socially unproblematic subjects.

The adventure against the giant is constructed around a set of themes that appear with surprising consistency: the hero hears that a giant has abducted a maiden, and decides to rescue her; the giant is a cultural other, usually a Muslim; the monster swears by Termagaunt, which conveniently rhymes with giant (geaunt) in both Middle English and French; the giant wields a club, and his first blow misses; the giant kills the hero's horse; the hero defeats the monster and decapitates him, then publicly displays the severed head in a ritual that announces to the world that he has conquered his own dark impulses. Unlike the monster he dismembers, the young hero's body knows boundaries, and this beheading scene inscribes them, firmly and spectacularly.

The *Tale of Sir Thopas* burlesques all of the topoi of this primal scene of romance. After Thopas decides that he will love "an elf-queene" (788), he rides into the "contree of Fairye" (802). The great giant Sir Olifaunt commands Thopas to leave immediately with the resonant phrase "prike out of myn haunt" (811). The monster's use of the word *prike* resounds with good humor, for it is Sir Thopas's favorite verb. Early in the tale, when he first rides out from home, "he priketh thurgh a fair forest" (754) and "priketh north and est" (757). A little later, as he falls into "love-longynge," he "pryked as he were wood" (774), his horse tires of "prikynge" (775), and the knight himself becomes so weary "for prikyng" (779) that he tumbles into the soft grass and dreams of his beloved. Like Thopas and his horse, *prike* has been comically exhausted from over-use, and the giant's choice of words announces that this monster is safely part of the text's comedy of verbal play.

The monster swears by the Saracen god "Termagaunt," just as the threatening giants of other romances do. But whereas Amourant (*Guy of Warwick*), Grander's brother (*Bevis of Hampton*) and Maugis (*Lybeaus Desconus*) pose serious peril to the heroes of these narratives, and in fact carve bloody wounds deep into the bodies of their chivalric adversaries, Olifaunt never quite manages to menace. He announces that, should Thopas not depart Fairyland immediately, he will slay his steed with a mace, as if the worst fate awaiting the knight were the inconvenience of having to walk home. Brave warrior that he is, Thopas replies in kind:

5   *Gender and Romance in Chaucer's Canterbury Tales* (Princeton: Princeton University Press, 1994), 29.

> "Also moote I thee,
> Tomorwe wol I meete with thee,
> Whan I have myn armoure."   (817–18)

"Sorry, I don't have my armor right now – I'll come back tomorrow" really doesn't cut it as a performance of heroic masculinity.

The giant's vow to crush Thopas's horse seems silly, and in the context of the tale it is. But like the oath by demonic Termagaunt, the threat is lifted directly from the gigantomachia (battle against the giant) of romance. Giants in *Beves of Hampton, Eglamour, Guy of Warwick, Lybeaus Desconus,* and *Torrent of Portyngale* all kill their adversary's steed, an act calculated to undermine the hero's chivalric identity by reducing him to unmounted combat or even wrestling. Olifaunt's weapon is also *de rigeur*: the traditional giant nearly always attacks with a mace or club, its brutal and crushing force a blunt contrast to a knightly sword's neatly slicing blade. Giants in Middle English romance are often called "gluttons," for they resemble the personified sin of Gluttony: with their gross corporeality, they threaten to devour any identity materialized through the rigor of Christian self-control. Thopas's threat to strike the giant through his "mawe" (823) is wholly appropriate; his intention to commit this act of bravery with a "launcegay" (a parade or costume lance, a prop [821]) is not. As Thopas retreats, the giant pelts him with stones. These are not the deadly missiles hurled at passing ships by the Homeric cyclops, but rocks shot from a "staf-slynge" (slingshot [829]). Thopas and Olifaunt are David and Goliath in reverse, with Thopas as the retreating giant.[6] Later, when Thopas narrates his adventure against the monster to his "myrie men" (839), Olifaunt suddenly sprouts two more heads (842). Either the narrator of the romance is not very observant and failed to convey a vital signifier of the giant's monstrousness, or else the knight's little tale is growing in the telling.

The arming scene which follows is long and fragrant, featuring an extended description of the spices mixed into Thopas's wine. As his naked, white "leere" (flesh [857]) is clothed, the effect is again ridiculously doll-like, so that when Thopas suddenly swears an oath upon "ale and breed" that the giant shall die, the only worse thing that could happen to the romance would be a loss of poetic control. The stanza immediately ends with an inane filler line, "Bityde what bityde!" (874), the second fit soon terminates, the third fit tries desperately to get started but ends up in a slough of chivalric comparisons from which Thopas never escapes. The heroes Horn, Ypotis, Beves, Guy, Lybeaus, "Pleyndamour," and Perceval are cited in rapid succession. Overwhelmed by these exemplary bodies beside which Thopas can seem only ridiculously diminutive, the poem trickles to an end. Harry Bailly breaks in, shouting, "Namoore of this, for Goddes dignitee!" (919).

---

[6] See Laura Hibbard Loomis, "Sir Thopas and David and Goliath," *MLN* 51 (1936): 311–13.

The poem's last, revealing line is the simple and unfinished "Til on a day –" (918). The phrase gestures toward a future at which Thopas cannot possibly arrive. What logically comes next is the postponed battle against the giant, an encounter unthinkable for this narrative. The gigantomachia in romance is aways an erotically charged episode, usually fought for the body of a maiden, and the outcome of the fight is the knight's indoctrination into proper sexuality. The "chaast" and innocent body of Thopas is characterized throughout the tale by a relentless narrative protection from the mere *possibility* of sex.

Sex and giants

The *Tale of Sir Thopas* translates the performance of masculine, heterosexual identity from romance into comedy. The encounter with Sir Olifaunt is exemplary of what gets lost in the Chaucerian translation. The episode contains nearly all the topoi connected with the romance gigantomachia, carefully elaborated in order to render them harmless, ridiculous. Yet an important subtraction fundamentally transforms the romance formula. Wholly missing from the adventure against the giant is any kind of sexual menace.

Indeed, sexuality is strangely absent throughout the tale, as the very *impossibility* of "an elf-queene" (788) as love object underlines. Those medieval narratives in which a fairy mistress has captured the heart of the hero explore the incommensurability of knighthood (a performance of masculinity that is relentlessly public) with "derne love" (a private bond between the fairy and her lover). In Marie de France's lai *Lanval*, the hero must swear to keep the identity of his fay beloved secret. Rebuffed for her seductive advances, Guenevere accuses Lanval of sodomy with his men, so removed from a public sexuality does he seem. In *Lanval, Launfal*, and *Thomas of Erceldoune*, the fairy mistress has a physical presence, and the knight she takes as a lover joyfully consummates the relationship. Thopas is content to encounter his queen within the insubstantial mists of a dream. She never speaks or even appears in the text, outside of what Thopas and the giant relate on her behalf.

Thopas enters the story without a "lemman" (mistress [788]) for whom to perform his deeds of arms. The scores of wakeful women who "moorne for hym paramour" (743) are better off catching up on their missed sleep (744) because, like Chaucer the pilgrim, Thopas "unto no wight dooth . . . daliaunce" (704). One could hardly imagine Guenevere attempting to seduce Thopas, and then accusing him of sodomy with his knightly friends. The possibility of any kind of fleshly desire is never attached to his diminutive body, rendering the quest for a fairy mistress appropriately ludic. Even the gem for which Thopas is named is noted in the lapidaries for its power against that most carnal of sins, lust.[7] I would not

---

7   *English Medieval Lapidaries*, ed. Evans and Serjeantson, EETS os 190 (London: Oxford University Press, 1933): 19, 106, 122.

go as far as Lee Patterson and argue that Thopas is actually a boy playing at being a knight,[8] but Thopas is certainly developmentally arrested – child-like and therefore asexual. If "Sir Thopas is all Don Quixote in little" (as Richard Hurd observed in 1765),[9] this "little" leaves out much, and renders even the giant a diminished figure.

Chaucer's reductive poetics drain romance of its libidinal force, transforming the genre from an exercise in the excitation of desire to an exposition of the body's innocuousness. The David and Goliath story, diminished to a children's fable, is no doubt Chaucer's primary reference as he describes Thopas fleeing the shower of stones hurled upon him by the belligerent Olifaunt. Another, previously unremarked analogue for this narrative moment occurs in Geoffrey of Monmouth's *History of the Kings of Britain*. Here the giant of Mont-Saint-Michel kidnaps a maiden and carries her to his mountain home:

> This giant had snatched Helena, the niece of Duke Hoel, from the hands of her guardians and had fled with her to the top of what is now called the Mont-Saint-Michel. The knights of that district had pursued the giant, but they had been able to do nothing against him. It made no difference whether they attacked him by sea or by land, for he either sank their ships with huge rocks or else killed them with a variety of weapons.[10]

The encounter with Olifaunt absurdly repeats this giant's horrifying narrative intrusion. Both abduct a woman and keep her against her will, both are pursued to their lair by a would-be rescuer, and both defeat approaching knights by hurling rocks. Desire in romance is represented as dangerous because it is bigger than the human body: exorbitant, inhuman in its full expression, capable of sweeping up the whole of the world in its obscene enjoyments. Desire in Chaucer's burlesque is laughable, a ridiculously small part of a miniaturized realm in which bodies and desires are always something less than meets the eye.

Romance logic dictates that the giant's body ought to display just the opposite of Thopas's meticulous self-regulation. That Olifaunt has abducted the Elf Queen and holds her in his lair suggests that he is the traditional giant of romance, intent on demonstrating his lack of bodily control upon his unwilling "lemman." The expectation is quickly defeated, however, as Olifaunt reveals that he keeps the Elf Queen in a happy, musical place: "Heere is the queene of Fayerye, / With harpe and pipe and symphonye" (814–15). The

---

[8] " 'What man artow?': Authorial Self-Definition in the *Tale of Sir Thopas* and the *Tale of Melibee*," *SAC* 11 (1989): 129–30.
[9] *Hurd's Letters on Chivalry and Romance* (1765), ed. Edith J. Morley (London, 1922), cited by Loomis in *Sources and Analogues*, 486.
[10] *Historia Regum Britanniae*, ed. Actom Griscom (Geneva: Slatkine Reprints, 1977); *The History of the Kings of Britain*, trans. Lewis Thorpe (London: Penguin Books, 1966), 238.

symphonic accompaniment to the Queen's abduction effectively dismisses the possibility of a dark, sexual intention behind the kidnapping.

Or does it? The absurdly pleasant conditions under which the Queen is held deserve contextualization. Chaucer's audience, avid readers of romance, would know that giants usually inhabit the periphery of civilization – grim, haunted landscapes full of dark skies, dense trees, and infernal flames. Olifaunt's melodious dwelling should be compared to the horrible crag to which the giant of Mont-Saint-Michel drags Helen in Geoffrey of Monmouth's *Historia*, a text which in its various reworkings profoundly influenced the representation of medieval giants. Robert Mannyng of Brunne completed an English translation in 1338.[11] Here the marauding giant Dinabroke seizes Helen "to do hir schame" (11856). Arthur's knight Bedevere is the first to reach the giant's lair, a gloomy mountaintop where a mysterious fire blazes. A crying woman sits "nere all naked" (11969) atop a new grave, the tomb in which the Helen's corpse is interred. This woman, Helen's nurse, says that once the giant carried them to the isolated crag he attempted to rape Helen, but he was so gross that he crushed the life from her (11971–74). The monster keeps the frightened nurse prisoner by the grave, where he rapes her each night. Geoffrey of Monmouth's original is even more graphic. The nurse is an elderly woman whose venerable body is supposed to be culturally removed from the *fedus coitus* ("filthy copulation" [471]) that the giant forces upon her.

As the heinous Dinabroke demonstrates, giants are rapists in the double sense of the word: they abduct innocent women, and they threaten these captives with sexual violation. This aggressive sexuality is a parental inheritance. According to both the Bible and popular tradition, giants are engendered upon women by the demons or incubi who ravish them. Giants receive this sexual violence as part of their genetic inheritance. They literally embody rape. Ideally, the young hero fights this monster in order to free the woman he holds in his castle or cave, the giant's "lemman." The rescued damsel then becomes the victor's bride. But as Geoffrey of Monmouth's *History of the Kings of Britain* illustrates, and as Mannyng reaffirms, sometimes the *fedus coitus* occurs before the hero can prevent the act.

The horrifying spectacle of the woman's violated body haunts romance. Menaced and abducted women become, after Geoffrey's *Historia*, a constant feature of the gigantomachia. Yet the giant's threat of sexual violation dwindles as the *Tale of Sir Thopas* shrinks. A similar diminishing of masculinity as reduction of a potentially dangerous sexuality also animates the prologue to the

---

11 Robert Mannyng of Brunne, *The Chronicle*, ed. Idelle Sullens, Medieval and Renaissance Texts and Studies, vol. 153 (Binghamton, NY: Binghamton University Press, 1996). In fact Mannyng was translating Wace's French *Brut*, but it is clear that he also had a copy of Geoffrey's Latin *Historia* in front of him as he worked. Although Chaucer may not have known Mannyng's *Chronicle*, he was certainly familiar with the legendary history of Britain that it contained.

tale, where Chaucer the narrator becomes by rhetorical and thematic contiguity connected to both the presexual "litel clergeon" of the *Prioress's Tale* and to Sir Thopas himself. Recall Harry's words to Chaucer, which construct a body completely exterior to the social circle of the Canterbury pilgrims ("unto no wight dooth he daliaunce" [704]). This diffident, "litel" Geoffrey Chaucer cannot meet the eyes of those who look upon him, but stares constantly at the ground (697). Chaucer positions himself as object of the gaze rather than its point of origin, a nonsensical position for an observant narrator to occupy. The Host summarizes this strange but apparently harmless being with the sentence, "This were a popet in an arm t'enbrace / For any womman, smal and fair of face" (701–02). Chaucer is a perfectly safe love-object, as doll-like as Sir Thopas, a kind of toy or a tiny child that any woman can scoop up and hug. To arrive at this miniaturization, sexuality has been subtracted from both male bodies.

A poet in an arm t'enbrace

In 1381, in immediate reaction to an onerous poll tax, violence erupted in Essex and Kent. The cathedral at Canterbury was stormed, the archbishop's quarters sacked. On June 11 and 12, a former roof tiler named Wat Tyler led an armed multitude into London, seizing control of the streets. Once the gates of the city were thrown open, scores of Flemings were beaten to death. Writers who witnessed these events had no easier a time interpreting them than modern medievalists do. Sometimes the English Rising was represented as the incoherent actions of inarticulate men.[12] Walsingham described the rebellion in biblical terms, transforming events into rather inconsistent moral *exempla*. The first book of John Gower's *Vox Clamatis* depicted the rebels as hybrid freaks, beasts in men's bodies.[13]

The English Rising is a historical trauma, an event so fundamentally challenging to a society's symbolic system that no easy way exists to integrate it into meaning. Inarticulateness, exemplarity, and monstrousness were three cultural rhetorics that contemporary authors used to give the rebellion a stable signification, but the fact that each was able to offer at best only a temporary narrative suturing suggests that the events themselves are too powerfully overdetermined to be reduced to a single or permanent meaning. Given the traumatic significance of 1381, critics of Chaucer have long been puzzled that, except for one allusion, the English Rising is almost completely ignored in his

12 See Susan Crane, "The Writing Lesson of 1381," in *Chaucer's England: Literature in Historical Context*, ed. Barbara A. Hanawalt (Minneapolis: University of Minnesota Press, 1992), 202, 207–12.
13 Walsingham's and Gower's poetics of representation are discussed by Derek Pearsall, "Interpretative Models for the Peasant's Revolt," in *Hermeneutics and Medieval Culture*, ed. Patrick J. Gallacher and Helen Damico (Albany: SUNY Press, 1989), 65–66.

works. The *Nun's Priest Tale* shrinks the traumatic real of history by diminishing the revolt into a barnyard chase: the explosive volatility of the event – armed men streaming through the city gates, blood and corpses on the London streets – is reduced to a literary device.[14] It would be wrong to conclude from this miniaturization, however, that this social upheaval simply did not concern Chaucer. After all, the rebels burst into the city by passing directly under his home atop Aldgate. The English Rising of 1381 shrinks in the *Nun's Priest's Tale* so that its dangerous significance as an undermining of the prevailing social order recedes. Diminution is a characteristically Chaucerian way of avoiding the real of trauma.

The diminishing of sexuality in the *Tale of Sir Thopas* ought likewise to sound a warning bell that something traumatic is being reduced in order to avoid the fullness – the *gigantism* – of its potential signification. That event is, perhaps, the very possibility of rape that has, until a recent article by Christopher Cannon,[15] been much diminished in Chaucer criticism. Is it too much to suggest that the *fedus coitus* which has vanished from the encounter with the giant in the *Tale of Sir Thopas* has its counterpart in the *de raptu meo* of Cecily Chaumpaigne?

Diminishing masculinity could be a way of avoiding a traumatic encounter with the historical real of May 1, 1380.[16] A release bearing this date was brought by Cecily Chaumpaigne into the Chancery of Richard II and there enrolled on the close rolls.[17] The document released Geoffrey Chaucer from "all manner of actions such as they relate to my rape [*de rapto meo*] or any other thing or cause."[18] It had been witnessed three days earlier by some of the most powerful members of the king's court. The document is obviously of supreme importance, but its exact meaning has long puzzled Chaucer scholars. Its problematic relationship to three other legal records does not help much, but these two additional releases and a subsequent acknowledgment of debt apparently trace a vast sum of money as it circulates from Chaucer through two intermediaries to Cecily Chaumpaigne, perhaps as a payment for her proceedings at Chancery.

Chaumpaigne's deed of release is a legally binding promise not to bring the

---

[14] At the end of the tale, as the widow who owns the farm and all her animals are chasing the fox that carries Chauntecleer in his mouth, the commotion is likened to the noise made by "Jackke Straw and his meynee" when "they wolden any Flemyng kille" (3394, 3396). Jack Straw was one of the leaders of the Rising.

[15] Christopher Cannon, "Raptus in the Chaumpaigne Release and a Newly Discovered Document Concerning the Life of Geoffrey Chaucer," *Speculum* 68 (1993): 74–94.

[16] No evidence exists that would date the *Tale of Sir Thopas*; it is certain, however, that it found its place in Fragment VII well after 1380.

[17] Cannon, 74. The closed (sealed) letters sent by the king are recorded on these parchment sheets. The release was enrolled on May 4, three days after it was written.

[18] *Chaucer Life-Records*, ed. Martin M. Crow and Clair C. Olson (Oxford, 1966), 343; Cannon, 74. I have reproduced Cannon's translations throughout for consistency's sake, since it is upon his understanding of the documents that my argument depends.

charge of rape [*raptus*] against Chaucer, and speaks nothing about the truth value such a charge would have. The impossibility of verification has usually been accepted within Chaucer criticism as an invitation to ignore it. Ever since F. J. Furnivall discovered the Chaumpaigne release in 1873, critics have taken their lead from the *Tale of Sir Thopas*, its prologue, and the "Envoy to Scogan," accepting Chaucer's own rhetorical construction of a Geoffrey whose body announces that he is exterior to the world of sexuality. The standard Chaucer life-story erases the possibility of rape from his biography. The *raptus* of Chaumpaigne's release shrinks in the critical literature to " 'strange case,' 'escapade,' 'incident,' 'distressing incident,' 'experience' and, simply, 'case.' "[19] For a long time the argument that *raptus* meant "abduction" and carried no sexual connotations was widely circulated, but Cannon's contextualization of the word through reference to other legal documents demonstrates that "*raptus* was reserved for describing forced coitus."[20]

If Chaucer critics have attempted to diminish the trauma of rape in their subject of study, they are only following the poet's own practice. On May 7, 1380, a memorandum of the Chaumpaigne release was recorded in the *coram rege* rolls. These records of the Court of King's Bench would have been the most likely place where a copy of the document would be read during Chaucer's lifetime.[21] Here the concise *de raptu meo* of the first recording of the release becomes the verbose *de feloniiis transgressionibus compotis debitis quam aliis accionibus quibuscumque* ("concerning felonies, trespasses, accounts, debts and any other actions whatsoever"). This explosion of the single phrase into a giant body of legalese conveys very little meaning despite its expansiveness. Rape, actual or possible, diminishes from Chaucer's life-record, engulfed by a wide expanse of Latin. As in the movement from the roomy structure of romance to the narrow strictures of comedy in *Thopas*, much is lost in the transformation.

We cannot know whether Chaucer committed rape, but we can see in the possibility, in the very accusation, the precipitation of a trauma that haunts his work. Through a close reading of the short poem "Adam Scriveyn," Carolyn Dinshaw demonstrates that Chaucer "represents himself as the victim of scribal rape," a positioning of himself as feminine that recurs throughout his work.[22] Elaine Tuttle Hansen argues that in Chaucer's work "even the most egregious cases of rape are normalized and trivialized."[23] The writing of rape is obviously connected to Chaucer's writing of his narratives, and to the writing of his own body. The casual sex crime that begins the *Wife of Bath's Tale* suggests this

---

[19] Cannon, 93.
[20] Cannon, 87.
[21] Cannon, 93.
[22] *Chaucer's Sexual Poetics* (Madison: University of Wisconsin Press, 1989), 10.
[23] *Chaucer and the Fictions of Gender* (Berkeley: University of California Press, 1992), 262.

154 Masculinities in Chaucer

connection as easily as the Chaumpaigne releases do. But what are we to make of a work like the *Tale of Sir Thopas*, where the possibility of rape seems to vanish as a consequence of the narrative's insistent reduction of sexuality?

The shrinking of masculinity into the inoffensive, child-like forms of Fragment VII, especially in the *Tale of Sir Thopas*, postpones but cannot completely avoid the encounter with the giant. Because this monster is rape incarnate, Sir Olifaunt is contained, diminished, by a pervasive rhetoric of desexualization. Yet to cite the giant even in a burlesque of romance is to activate a powerful chain of resonance, a whole horizon of expectation that the audience brings to the genre – if only to have those expectations raised in defeat. The possibility of rape haunts the *Tale of Sir Thopas* in the act of its forced banishment. The giant as rapist reinscribes that very body out of control that the tale tries frantically to exclude.

Sir Thopas is named after a precious stone, a highly unusual appellation. Indeed, the only other name in all of romance tradition that bears some similarity is "Amourant." This title is adopted by Owein, squire to Amiloun, as he accompanies his leprous master into exile in the Middle English romance *Amis and Amiloun*, where it suggests something like "steadfast lover," in imitation of the names of the romance's protagonists. Significantly, Amourant is also the name of the wicked giant defeated by Guy of Warwick in the romance that was, along with Lybeaus Desconus, Chaucer's primary source for the *Tale of Sir Thopas*.[24] Amourant is an especially nasty monster, perfidious in the extreme. He reveals in battle that he fights in order to gain the hand of the Sultan's daughter, whom he describes as his "leman."[25] The giant aims not for chivalric glory, but for the pleasures of the body. He battles to obtain the very thing that Dinabroke took by force. The name "Amourant" in *Guy of Warwick* could again mean something like "lover," an ironic resonance in this context. It is a word that also means "emerald." This monster, among the most infamous giants in the romance tradition, is named after a gem, just as Sir Thopas is.

"Emeraude" is the very word used to describe the "litel clergeon" of the *Prioress's Tale*, a small body that has much in common with those of Thopas and of Chaucer. When all of these identities are connected to the familiar giant of romance, the dangers that their diminished physicalities hide become more obvious. The innocent boy causes a massacre through his relentless repetition of an expanse of Latin words that hold no direct meaning for him. His steadfast obliviousness is his guarantee that the bodily violence so impossible to attach

24 See Loomis in *Sources and Analogues*, 487. The encounter against the giant in *Guy of Warwick*, Loomis states, is the seminal rendition of the gigantomachia for all of Middle English romance (531 n1; "Sir Thopas and David and Goliath," 311 n1) and Chaucer's single most important source.

25 *The Romance of Guy of Warwick: The First or Fourteenth-Century Version*, ed. Julius Zupitza, EETS ES 42, 49, 59 (London: Oxford University Press, 1883, 1887, 1891); Auchinleck version, 126.8.

to him will erupt elsewhere in the "litel" world he inhabits. Geoffrey the pilgrim and Thopas the diminutive knight likewise seem a great deal less precious than they at first appeared. Violence, specifically sexual violence, is the absent presence which haunts both diminutive bodies.

The defeat of the giant is a powerful textual moment which announces that the knight's tightly controlled body has no tincture of monstrousness. The ritual of defeat culminates in a decapitation scene when, as in *Guy of Warwick*, the severed head of the giant delivers a powerful message about the proper construction of the hero's masculinity. The *Tale of Sir Thopas* cannot stage such a triumph. Its insistent reduction of sex ensures that Thopas will never progress much beyond the miniature identity with which he enters the story. Thopas cannot conquer the giant, cannot enact the chivalric ritual of decapitation, cannot exorcise the phantom of rape. Unique in all of romance, Oliphaunt has three heads, making the idea of a beheading scene laughably comic, and finally impracticable.

"Personal" traumas are never very distant from social ones. If I may be permitted one last, grand gesture in closing, I will suggest that the fight against the giant in Chaucer's *Tale of Sir Thopas* never takes place because England in the late Middle Ages was always haunted by the violence it committed against women's bodies. We will never know whether Chaucer raped Cecily Chaumpaigne (and that helpless lack of a firm epistemological footing is always a component of trauma, which exists outside all questions of veridicality). Nonetheless, what can be said with certainty is that the crimes against female bodies which romance describes (sometimes to celebrate, more often to protest) and which Chaucer diminished were undeniably real. The male body can be vastly comedic. Fragment VII of the *Canterbury Tales* is proof enough of that. But the same male body is also a source of great cultural danger, as the figure of the giant – and the giant of self-figuration – reveal.

The Five Wounds of Melibee's Daughter: Transforming Masculinities

DANIEL RUBEY

Chaucer's *Tale of Melibee* is a debate between two contrasting modes of masculine behavior – revenge and mercy, the old law of Moses and the new law of Christ. Melibee is transformed by the rhetoric of his wife Prudence but also by the spectacle of his daughter's wounded body, a body allegorically transformed into his own sinful body and also the suffering body of Christ, the model for a new mode of behavior based on mercy and forgiveness. But this process of transformation raises a number of questions and anxieties centered on gender, and Chaucer rejects any applicability of the tale to his contemporary world in the link to the *Monk's Tale*. This rejection can be explained by the tale's political context – Richard II's long struggle with the appellant lords and their attacks on him as young and immature. That struggle explains Chaucer's deletion of an attack on young kings in his source and points to the tale's special relevance for England in the mid-1380s.

The *Tale of Melibee* is one of two tales Chaucer assigned to the fictional narrator of the *Canterbury Tales* and the only one completed; the other is *Sir Thopas*, the parody of tail-rhyme romance judged "nat worth a toord!" (VII 930) by the Host. Some modern critics have extended that judgment to the *Melibee* as well, but the tale was very popular in its time.

Chaucer's *Melibee*[1] is a prose translation of *Le Livre de Mellibee et Prudence*

---

[1]   A broad outline of events in the tale may be useful. Melibee is a young man, rich and powerful. While he is away, three old enemies break into his house, beat his wife Prudence, and wound his daughter Sophie with five mortal wounds in five places. Melibee's followers advise war; Prudence urges patience and peace. Through the course of a long debate buttressed on both sides by references to authority, Prudence tries to persuade her husband

written sometime after 1336 by the Dominican friar Renaud de Louens. Louens's work translates and freely adapts the *Liber consolationis et consilii* of the Italian judge Albertanus da Brescia, written in 1246 for his third son. Originally written to criticize the lawlessness of feudal nobles in Northern Italy and their unwillingness to submit settlement of their feuds to legal institutions set up by the bourgeoisie of the Lombard communes, the work is generalized enough to apply to almost any kingdom at any period in the Middle Ages. Louens's adaptation was one of at least four different French versions which popularized the tale during the thirteenth and fourteenth centuries, and Brescia's Latin text was also translated into Italian, German, and Dutch during that period.[2]

It is risky to speculate about reasons for the popularity of a medieval work, but surely a large part of the appeal of this tale for contemporary audiences must have derived from the spectacle of a wife teaching her husband and modifying his behavior, transforming it from anger and revenge to forgiveness and reconciliation, from the old law of Moses to the new law of Christ. The tale raises issues of gender and hierarchy – of a husband learning from his wife instead of instructing her. The length of the debate underscores the difficulty of this process and the anxieties it raises; the popularity of the work suggests the urgent desire in late medieval societies for the reasonableness and flexibility shown in the tale on the part of those in positions of power.

One way of understanding Melibee's transformation would be to see it as resulting from the good influence of feminine behavior on masculine, to argue that Melibee acts like a man in desiring revenge and Prudence acts like a woman in desiring peace and reconciliation. But Chaucer specifically rejects the essentialism of such an interpretation in the link to the *Monk's Tale* which follows. In that link, the Host, already described in the General Prologue in terms of his masculinity ("And of manhod hym lakkede right naught" [I 756]), points out that all women are not alike in their desire for peace and forgiveness:

> "I hadde levere than a barel ale
> That Goodelief, my wyf, hadde herd this tale!
> For she nys no thyng of swich pacience
> As was this Melibeus wyf Prudence."   (VII 1893–96)

to turn from vengeance to mercy. At midpoint the debate turns overtly allegorical: the house becomes Melibee's body made vulnerable by sin and entered by his old enemies – the World, the Flesh, and the Devil – through the windows of his body, his five senses. In the end, Melibee accepts the guidance of his wife and forgives his enemies. A settlement is negotiated with her help, and harmony is restored.

2   J. Burke Severs, "The Tale of Melibeus," in *Sources and Analogues of Chaucer's Canterbury Tales*, ed. W. F. Bryan and Germaine Dempster (New York: Humanities Press, 1958), 560–614; Gardiner Stillwell, "The Political Meaning of Chaucer's *Tale of Melibee*," *Speculum* 19 (1944): 434–35; V. J. Scattergood, "Chaucer and the French War: *Sir Thopas* and *Melibee*," in *Court and Poet*, ed. Glyn S. Burgess (Liverpool: F. Cairns, 1981), 291–93.

Goodelief is more warlike than her husband, urging him to "Slee the dogges everichoon" (1899) when he beats his servants, upbraiding him at home if he will not fight with neighbors who "Wol nat in chirche to my wyf enclyne, / Or be so hardy to hire to trespace" (1902–03). Her verbal abuse uses traditional gender categories to attack his masculinity: she calls him a milksop and a coward, she offers to trade her distaff (a feminine emblem) for his knife. The issue is violent defense of what she sees as her rights in the social hierarchy:

> " 'Allas,' she seith, 'that evere I was shape
> To wedden a milksop, or a coward ape,
> That wol been overlad with every wight!
> Thou darst nat stonden by thy wyves right!' " (1909–12)

The Host is afraid she will provoke him into killing someone and is even a bit intimidated by her physically:

> "I woot wel she wol do me slee som day
> Som neighebor, and thanne go my way;
> For I am perilous with knyf in honde,
> Al be it that I dar nat hire withstonde,
> For she is byg in armes, by my feith." (1917–21)

Chaucer is not being anti-feminist: he is making the point that not all women are necessarily peaceful, just as not all men are necessarily violent. Different behaviors are available to members of both sexes. Melibee's transformation, then, is not from one gender (masculine) to another (feminine), but from one form of masculinity to another – a choice between masculinities. Using the plural "masculinities" argues that male gender, like female gender, is constructed and relational, dependent on context-bound oppositions. With its innumerable references to written authority, the *Melibee* demonstrates the textually-constructed nature of masculinity in order to imagine the possibility of change from one mode to another.

Seeing these modes as different formations of masculinity focuses on the transformation from one to the other, and on the difficult and problematic nature of that change. The return to reality effected by the Host's comments about his wife also suggests that the peaceful resolution achieved in the tale may be utopian and idealistic, given the nature of human experience. In that world not all wives are as willing to advocate peace and subordinate themselves to their husbands' interests as Prudence, and not all husbands are as willing to take their wives' advice and submit to their better judgment as Melibee, just as not all princes are willing to listen to their subordinates.

Chronological and historical context

Dating Chaucer's works precisely is difficult, but there is general agreement that Chaucer worked on the *Melibee* during the same period he translated Boethius and completed *Troilus and Criseyde*. Assuming that Chaucer finished *Troilus* in 1386 and turned to the *Canterbury Tales* in 1387–88, *Melibee* was one of the first works placed in the new narrative frame. Given that chronological proximity, the conclusion to *Troilus* may provide a philosophical and theological context for the *Melibee*.

Chaucer attempted to create a historically accurate picture of pagan Troy in *Troilus and Criseyde*, separating it from the new world of Christian revelation. Because of those two historical viewpoints the poem has two endings, one pagan and tragic, the other Christian. The pagan characters in *Troilus* are trapped by gender roles and social constraints they cannot break. The desire for revenge drives the war toward its bloody end. Diomede tells Criseyde there can be no mercy for any of the Trojans. The Greeks will take such cruel revenge on them "for fecchynge of Eleyne" that men will fear from now to the end of the world "to ravysshen any queene" (V, 890–96). The Greeks' refusal to forgo revenge for the rape of Helen freezes the poem in a tragic stasis in which the desire for transcendence through human love that Troilus represents is doomed by the weight of history. Chaucer placed his tragedy firmly in the pagan tradition of "Virgile, Ovide, Omer, Lucan, and Stace" (V, 1792), but then shifted to the Christian perspective in the last stanzas. Troilus dies and ascends to the eighth sphere from which he can laugh at human sorrow and condemn "blynde lust" (V, 1824). Chaucer urges the "yonge, fresshe folkes" (V, 1835) of his audience to turn to God, and then ends with a prayer.

Since he took the trouble to distinguish between these two historical consciousnesses, pagan and Christian, it seems reasonable to ask whether Chaucer saw the new Christian consciousness as having practical implications for political conflict and war in his contemporary world of the fourteenth century. To state the question in another way: given human nature as described in the stories of Troy and Thebes, is life inevitably tragic or does Christian revelation suggest that an end to the cycle of war is possible?

Guido's *Historia* imagined just such an end to the conflict between the royal families of Thessaly and Troy when Achilleides renounced the throne of Thessaly willingly, even though it was rightfully his, gave it to his brother Laomedon, and freed the Trojan captives.[3] The cycle of war and destruction *can* end, but only if someone willingly renounces a rightful claim in favor of the greater good. By the late 1380s in England, it was clear that the long war with France could end only if the English king were willing to give up his "just"

---

[3]   C. David Benson, *The History of Troy in Middle English Literature: Guido delle Colonne's Historia Destructionis Troiae in Medieval England* (Cambridge: D. S. Brewer, 1980), 31.

claims and negotiate peace. The *Tale of Melibee* is Chaucer's exploration of these issues.

Linking the *Melibee* to contemporary political events began in the 1940s and was revived in the 1980s. Gardiner Stillwell's 1944 article in *Speculum* defined three areas of correlation: Richard's political struggles with the English nobles; the excellence of women peacemakers like Queen Philippa, Queen Anne, and Joan of Kent; and a growing disillusionment with the French war. The war had gone well for the English under Edward III in the 1340s and 1350s. But by 1381, when Chaucer began *Troilus*, the English had been driven back to their narrowest perimeters around Calais and Bordeaux, and the French were raiding the south coast of England. The historian John Barnie says that not a single moralist or chronicler including Gower and Chaucer wholeheartedly supported the war by the 1380s.[4] After Christmas, 1384, Gaunt and his brothers pushed for a royal expedition to France at the king's council at Waltham. But Richard and his closest advisors, Michael de la Pole and Robert de Vere, were already advocating peace with France, and the council decided on an expedition to Scotland instead.[5]

The primary opposition to Richard's new peace policy came from the five lords appellant, Gloucester and Arundel in particular. The appellants fought Richard's policies by attacking his advisors (they were called "appellants" because of the charges of treason they brought against Richard's counsellors). They won a significant victory in the Merciless Parliament of 1386 at which Pole and de Vere were condemned to death in their absence, and Simon Burley, Richard's old teacher, was tried and executed. Chaucer lost two controllerships of customs because of his association with Burley's "court party," and was lucky not to have lost more.

Despite those setbacks, Richard recovered power in 1388–89, and until 1397 successfully pursued his peace policy with France while at the same time thwarting French plans in the Low Countries and Italy through skillful diplomacy. He also dealt very effectively with Ireland and Scotland during this period.[6] Richard executed Arundel and Gloucester in 1397 and exiled Henry Lancaster and Thomas Mowbray. But the appellants had the final victory: Henry returned to England in 1399, and Richard was deposed and killed.

---

[4] John Barnie, *War in Medieval English Society: Social Values in the Hundred Years War 1337–99* (Ithaca, NY: Cornell University Press, 1974), 129.
[5] Anthony Tuck, *Richard II and the English Nobility* (New York: St. Martin's Press, 1974), 90–91.
[6] Tuck, 133–37; May McKisack, *The Fourteenth Century 1307–1399* (Oxford: Clarendon Press, 1959), 496–97; J. J. N. Palmer, "English Foreign Policy 1388–99," in F. R. H. du Boulay and Caroline M. Barron, eds., *The Reign of Richard II: Essays in Honour of May McKisack* (London: Athlone Press, 1971), 75–107.

The "effeminate boy king"

Establishing this historical context does not necessarily suggest that the *Melibee* is a roman à clef or that Chaucer through the tale "rebukes both his contemporaries and his king," as one scholar has suggested recently.[7] That would have been unwise in the political climate of the Merciless Parliament, and, in any case, there is seldom a simple, one-to-one relationship between literary works and historical events.[8] But it seems likely that Chaucer followed the *Troilus* with the *Melibee* and assigned it to himself as teller because of its applicability to issues posed in his own work and to contemporary political issues, including all three raised by Stillwell: the war with France, good versus bad advisors, and the usefulness of women as mediators. An approach that ties these three threads together within the context of masculinities is the charged issue of Richard as a "boy king."

It has been a tenet of modern scholarship about the *Melibee* that Chaucer removed a passage following line 1199 about boy kings because it would have offended Richard II. Chaucer omitted these lines from his French source (in Tatlock's translation):

> And Solomon says, "Sad is the country that has a child as ruler." And the philosopher says that we do not select youthful princes, because they commonly have no prudence at all; and Solomon says again: "sad is the country of which the prince breaks fast in the morning!"

Tatlock used this omission to date the *Melibee*, believing the passage would have been insulting to Richard at any time from 1377, when he was crowned at the age of 11, until 1389, when he declared he was now at an age when "the meanest heir in the kingdom was entitled fully to enjoy his rights," and dismissed the council of regency.[9]

Richard's words showed his sensitivity on this issue, but I do not believe that Chaucer omitted the lines out of fear. After all, Gower criticized Richard on these grounds without repercussions. I think Chaucer took them out because they represented a position inconsistent with what he was trying to do with the *Melibee* and added others for similar reasons.

The issue of Richard as a "boy king" involved much more than Richard's age and did not end in 1389: the slur followed him for the rest of his life and

---

7   Lynn Staley Johnson, "Inverse Counsel: Contexts for the *Melibee*," *SP* 87 (1990): 154.
8   On the dangers of political commentary in fourteenth-century England, see Barnie, 142–45.
9   On dating the *Melibee*, see J. S. P. Tatlock, *The Development and Chronology of Chaucer's Writings* (London: Chaucer Society, 1907), 188–98, and Lloyd J. Matthews, "The Date of Chaucer's *Melibee* and the Stages of the Tale's Incorporation in the *Canterbury Tales*," *ChauR* 20 (1986): 221–34. On Richard's dismissal of the council of regency, see Tuck, 33, 137, and the *DNB* entry "Richard II (1367–1400)," 609.

beyond. The text chosen by Archbishop Arundel for his oration supporting Henry's claim to the throne on 30 September 1399 was from I Samuel ix: "Behold the *man* . . . this same shall reign over my people," and Arundel embroidered this text with others to lay every possible emphasis on the advantages of having a *man*, not a child, as ruler. It was an astonishing performance when we realize, thanks to the historian Margaret Aston, that Henry, far from being Richard's senior, was actually three months younger.

Of the five lords appellant, two were old enough to have been Richard's father, Warwick and Arundel, but two were his age, Henry and Thomas Mowbray, Arundel's son-in-law. Gloucester, Richard's uncle, was twelve years older than Richard and was Henry's uncle and brother-in-law as well. What Aston calls the "most remarkable myth to be perpetuated about Richard II . . . the myth of the king's youth" was constructed by his political enemies as a useful platform for attacking his governance.[10]

Arundel's speech and the myth of Richard's youth suggest that distinctions between the social categories "boy" and "man" have less to do with age and more with ideology and power. The anthropologist David Gilmore cites a recurring notion across human societies that manhood is different from simple anatomical maleness, "that it is not a natural condition that comes about spontaneously through biological maturation, but rather is a precarious or artificial state that boys must win against powerful odds."[11] In patriarchal societies, where money and power pass from father to son, fathers set the tests and score the results. The struggle between Richard and the appellants was a struggle about money and power, and about inheritance in particular, cloaked in the ideology of patriarchal masculinity.

The appellants were sons of lords who had prospered through Edward's war with France. The fathers died in the late 1360s and 1370s, and their sons took part in the expeditions of the last years of Edward's reign. But the sons lacked their fathers' campaign experience and association with the early successes of the war. As Richard Tuck puts it, "a new generation of magnates took the political stage in the 1370s, a generation anxious to enjoy the profits and prestige of victory as their fathers had done, but unable to do so."[12]

The beginning and end of Richard's struggle with the appellants was over inheritance, from the March inheritance early in his reign to the Bolingbroke inheritance of Lancastrian lands at the end. When Edmund Mortimer Earl of March died suddenly in December, 1381, his son and heir, Roger, was a minor and the king received custody of the inheritance. Richard gave the manors and lordships piecemeal to more than a dozen individuals, many of whom were

---

[10] Margaret Aston, "Richard II and the Wars of the Roses," in *The Reign of Richard II*, 305–07.
[11] David D. Gilmore, *Manhood in the Making: Cultural Concepts of Masculinity* (New Haven: Yale University Press, 1990), 11.
[12] Tuck, 20.

members of his household or close associates, none of them of greater rank than knight. The effect was to disenfranchise the son of a great lord and create a new nobility from Richard's close supporters, men who owed everything to him.

Richard lost this one. In December 1383, the whole inheritance was committed back to a group of Mortimer's peers who could be trusted to respect the laws of patriarchal inheritance. The incident was put down to Richard's "youth and inexperience," to his listening to "evil counsellors" instead of the lords who felt they had the right to advise the young king.[13] Near the end of his reign, it was Richard's seizure of Bolingbroke's Lancastrian inheritance that provided the justification for Henry's landing at Yorkshire in July 1399.

In political terms, then, the attacks on Richard's youthfulness and inexperience and on his counsellors were a means of opposing his attempts to take money and influence away from the lords and centralize it in the court. In this context, for Chaucer to have included the lines about youthful princes would have been to support the arguments of Richard's, and his own, bitter enemies.

The political charge of Richard's youth and inexperience was closely linked to a related attack on the supposedly unmilitary, pleasure-seeking behavior of Richard's court by opponents of his peace policy with France. Richard's peace policy raised many of the same issues for the lords as the Mortimer inheritance, since their necessary rite of passage was the pursuit of war through which their fathers had made their fortunes. "Effeminancy," the term used by modern historians in characterizing these charges, is a loaded term and may not be entirely appropriate. But it is clear that Richard and his close friends were portrayed in terms of an opposition between inappropriate pleasure-seeking behavior associated with women, on the one hand, and knightly, war-like activity on the other.

Toward the end of his reign, even Edward III had been criticized by Gower and others for being ruled by Alice Perrers, "whence he abandons honour for foolish pleasure," as Walsingham wrote. As Barnie puts it, John Erghome said Edward had been made effeminate and no longer had a taste for war, but remained at home indulging in pleasure and luxury. The same charges were brought against Richard. Froissart reported a speech by Gloucester, one of the appellants, complaining that "Richard is no true knight," that he was only interested in drinking and eating, sleeping, dancing and leaping about, when true men-at-arms should be winning honor through deeds of arms.[14]

In 1387 Walsingham jabbed at what Lynn Staley Johnson terms the "effeminacy" of Richard's court and the closeness between Richard and de Vere which kept the king from serious pursuits and undermined the chivalry of the court. He notes that "knights are more devoted to Venus than Bellona, more at home in the bedchamber than in the field, and more likely to use language than lances

13 Tuck, 88–89.
14 Barnie, 119–20, 127.

in defense."[15] According to Aston, this portrait of Richard as an effeminate weakling continued into the Tudor period. In Samuel Daniel's *Civil Wars*, Richard was still the "wanton young effeminate" at the time of Bolingbroke's banishment near the end of the reign. Just as Richard III's cruelties were mirrored in his bodily deformity, so Richard II's supposed effeminate weakness was associated with what was reputed to be his exceptional beauty.[16] In 1399, when Archbishop Arundel argued for deposing Richard, he was punishing the bad son who had not submitted to the law of the fathers and had not become a man according to their rules, and elevating the good son who had.

It should be said that despite the myth of Richard's "effeminacy," he was actually an able general as well as an effective statesman, and certainly no pacifist.[17] When the king and the members of his council at Waltham after Christmas, 1384 decided not to invade France, that decision was made not out of pacifism, but because of a political decision that the money and resources would be better spent attacking Scotland. This Scottish expedition in the summer of 1385 was Richard's first military expedition, and he proved himself as a military leader. Richard's overruling of Gaunt's reckless plan for crossing the Forth at Edinburgh and marching into the highlands without adequate supply lines provoked a bitter dispute between the two, but it also showed Richard to be the better strategist and general.[18]

In the end, Richard's deposition was not an indication of his personal weakness, but of the strength of the English medieval monarchy. As Tuck puts it in his concluding paragraph, "The nobility could not make their will prevail for long if the king was determined not to co-operate, and in the end the only effective alternative was to remove the king."[19] Richard's struggle with the lords was part of a broad cultural shift in the late fourteenth century pointing toward the Tudors and Elizabeth I, who, near the end of her reign, aging and childless, said bitterly to Lambarde, "I am Richard II. Know ye not that?"[20]

Towards a new masculinity

In light of the work of medieval historians in the 1970s like Tuck, Palmer, Aston, Barnie, and others, Richard's kingship can be seen as representing a shift away from the feudal politics of the appellants to a more diplomatically-based and sophisticated international policy, and also toward greater centralization of

---

[15] Johnson, 147.

[16] Aston, 309–10.

[17] William Askins, *"The Tale of Melibee* and the Crisis at Westminster, November, 1387," *SAC* 2 (1986): 103–12 and J. J. N. Palmer, "English Foreign Policy 1388–99," argue that pacifism was not an issue at Richard's court.

[18] Tuck, 97–98.

[19] Tuck, 225.

[20] Aston, 317.

political and economic power. The attack by his enemies on Richard's manhood was one ideological means of resisting those changes, and it suggests the possibility of a larger social dialogue on the nature of masculinity which is engaged in Chaucer's work.

Modern theoretical discussions of masculinities tend to divide them into hegemonic (culturally dominant) heterosexual patriarchal masculinity and anti-hegemonic homosexual masculinity.[21] For the Middle Ages, however, at least from the twelfth century on, it may make more sense to divide masculinities into an aristocratic patriarchal masculinity involving the production of children and heirs, and a celibate clerical masculinity. Seen in these terms, the transformation of Melibee moves him from the aristocratic patriarchal model of masculinity to a more clerical model, the distinction revolving around the issue of inheritance and the question of whether values are to be centered in this world or the next.

If Chaucer's *Melibee* is suggesting that a new or different masculinity is needed, one based on mercy and forgiveness rather than violence and revenge, what would it look like and how would we get there? The feminist film theoretician Jane Gaines has said that "the ultimate reliance on the spectacle of woman as the significatory precondition for the construction of masculine hierarchies means that the scene of gender continues to be inscribed on the female body."[22] Attempts to restructure male hierarchy must return to the female body.

The Trojan War was structured around the rape of Helen. Just as Diomede argued that Troy must be destroyed so no other man will ever ravish a queen, so Melibee argues he must take vengeance for his daughter's wounds so "they that han wyl to do wikkednesse restreyne hir wikked purpos, whan they seen the punyssynge and chastisynge of the trespassours" (VII 1432).

Melibee's debate with Prudence revolves around two issues: the difficulty of changing the historical pattern of answering violence with revenge – the response advised by his assembly of advisors – and a number of anti-feminist attacks that revolve around the question of hierarchy or "maistrie":

This Melibee answerde unto his wyf Prudence: "I purpose nat," quod he, "to werke by thy conseil, for many causes and resouns. For certes,

---

21 R. W. Connell, *Masculinities* (Berkeley: University of California Press, 1995), 67–86. In addition, my thinking about masculinities has been influenced by *Medieval Masculinities: Regarding Men in the Middle Ages*, ed. Clare A. Lees (Minneapolis: University of Minnesota Press, 1994); *Screening the Male: Exploring Masculinities in Hollywood Cinema*, ed. Steven Cohan and Ina Rae Hark (New York: Routledge, 1993); Arthur Brittan, *Masculinity and Power* (New York: Blackwell, 1989); *The Making of Masculinities: The New Men's Studies*, ed. Harry Brod (Boston: Allen and Unwin, 1987); and *Changing Men: New Directions in Research on Men and Masculinity*, ed. Michael S. Kimmel (Newbury Park: Sage, 1987).
22 Jane Gaines, "White Privilege and Looking Relations: Race and Gender in Feminist Film Theory," *Cultural Critique* 4 (Fall 1986): 59–79; quoted in *Screening the Male*, 178–79.

every wight wolde holde me thanne a fool;/ this is to seyn, if I, for thy conseillyng, wolde chaungen thynges that been ordeyned and affermed by so manye wyse./ Secoundely, I seye that alle wommen been wikke, and noon good of hem alle. For 'of a thousand men,' seith Salomon, 'I foond o good man, but certes, of alle wommen, good womman foond I nevere.'/ And also, certes, if I governed me by thy conseil, it sholde seme that I hadde yeve to thee over me the maistrie, and God forbede that it so weere!/ For Jhesus Syrak seith that 'if the wyf have maistrie, she is contrarious to hir housbonde.'/ And Salomon seith: 'Nevere in thy lyf to thy wyf, ne to thy child, ne to thy freend ne yeve no power over thyself, for bettre it were that thy children aske of thy persone thynges that hem nedeth than thou see thyself in the handes of thy children.'/ And also if I wolde werke by thy conseillyng, certes, my conseil moste som tyme be secree, til it were tyme that it moste be knowe, and this ne may noght be."

(1055–61)[23]

Melibee's reasons for not listening to Prudence are a catalogue of the gender anxieties of patriarchal masculinity: he is afraid he will look like a fool if he tries to change tradition and go against the male group decision; women are the other, unknowable, therefore wicked; to take advice from a wife would reverse the male/female hierarchy ordained by God; and, finally, never trust women, because they will betray you.

These anxieties also underlie the gender-based language of the appellants' attacks on Richard and his court. Just to be clear, I am not suggesting that the lords attacked Richard because they believed he was acting like a woman. They opposed him because of issues connected to money and power, but they and their supporters used the language of gender and antifeminism to attack his masculinity and that of his court, and to undermine his position as king. Chaucer, in his turn, uses the *Melibee* to engage those attacks and implicitly support Richard's position.

Where Melibee's arguments pose a set of absolute differences between men and women, Prudence's response deconstructs these absolute, binary oppositions and replaces them with more subtle discriminations that take individuals into account and argue for flexibility and free choice. Not *all* women are wicked, or Christ would never have been born of a woman or appeared to a woman first after his resurrection (1074–75); there are many examples of women who have given good advice to men (1095–1109).

Prudence accepts the traditional hierarchy of husband/wife and perhaps men/women, but argues that accepting advice from "lasse folk than hymself" is no shame (1072), and that being governed by Prudence's counsel would not

---

[23] The French original follows with two lines about the inability of women to keep secrets and the claim that women vanquish men with bad counsel.

give her "the maistrie and the lordshipe" over him (1081): "For if it so were that no man sholde be conseilled but oonly of hem that hadden lordshipe and maistrie of his persone, men wolden nat be conseilled so ofte./ For soothly thilke man that asketh conseil of a purpos, yet hath he free choys wheither he wole werke by that conseil or noon" (1082–83). If Melibee listens only to those above him in the hierarchy, he would seldom listen to anyone at all, and she is no different from his other advisors because she is his wife.

The wounded body of Sophie/Melibee/Christ

As Prudence confronts Melibee's objections and argues for a transformation from revenge to mercy on the level of textual authority, the tale functions on an allegorical level through images of the wounded body of Melibee's daughter, the silent woman in this tale. Through allegorical associations, her wounded body becomes the body of Melibee and finally of Christ.

To answer objections which cannot be met by reference to written authority, Prudence changes the field of debate from the secular world to the eternal world of divine revelation. A phenomenological semiotics might describe allegory as a bracketed textual space for reshuffling signifieds and signifiers. In such a space, the five wounds of Melibee's daughter necessarily call to mind the wounded body of Christ. Chaucer prepares for the connection overtly with his additions to the French, first with the narrator's reference to "the payne of Jhesu Crist" and the unified "sentence" of the four Gospels in the link between *Thopas* and the *Melibee* (943–52), and second by the name he alone gives Melibee's daughter – "Sophie" (967).

The name Sophie has been understood as derived from the Greek word for wisdom and used to allegorize the spectacle of the wounded female body into an image of Melibee's soul. The appropriateness of Chaucer's choice of the name "Sophie" is underscored by Philippa Berry's discussion of the biblical figure of a female Wisdom (Sophia or Sapientia) in Elizabethan literature. For Berry, Wisdom is always an ambiguous symbol, "probably because of her contradictory position as an image of supernatural female creativity and power within religious and philosophical systems whose fundamental assumptions were patriarchal."[24] Gender ambiguity is an integral part of the tradition behind the figure of Sophia, Berry argues, and in the Middle Ages, the originally female figure of Wisdom was regularly associated with Christ and with the Holy Spirit.

The gender ambiguity associated with the name "Sophie" facilitates the transition in the tale to the body of Melibee himself on the allegorical level, where Melibee's body is feminized – entered, penetrated, wounded by his enemies as is the body of his daughter:

[24] Philippa Berry, *Of Chastity and Power: Elizabethan Literature and the Unmarried Queen* (New York: Routledge, 1994), 10, 167 n4.

"Thou hast doon synne agayn oure Lord Crist,/ for certes, the three enemys of mankynde – that is to seyn, the flessh, the feend, and the world – / thou hast suffred hem entre in to thyn herte wilfully by the wyndowes of thy body,/ and hast nat defended thyself suffisantly agayns hire assautes and hire temptaciouns, so that they han wounded thy soule in fyve places;/ this is to seyn, the deedly synnes that been entred into thyn herte by thy fyve wittes./ And in the same manere oure Lord Crist hath woold and suffred that thy three enemys been entred into thyn house by the wyndowes/ and han ywounded thy doghter in the forseyde manere."

(1420–26)

But the allegorical process of transformation goes further, replacing the spectacle of Sophie's body with an even more powerful spectacle, the wounded body of Christ.

The gender ambiguity of Sophie's body recalls Caroline Walker Bynum's work on desire for the body of Christ as a theme in fourteenth-century religious devotion.[25] Christ's body was feminized in manuscript illuminations of the passion during this period. The wound in his side was transformed into a vagina, the opening through which the Church was born, and that wound became an object of worship and identification for pious lay women. This gender reversal parallels a shift from imagined female voices constructed by male authors to a developing voice of female lay piety. That piety often revolved around the wounds of Christ and their appearance in female bodies – the nexus of association called up by the five wounds of Sophie/Melibee/Christ.

Recalling Jane Gaines's phrase about "the ultimate reliance on the spectacle of woman as the significatory precondition for the construction of masculine hierarchies," we could say that in the *Melibee*, the substitution of Christ's body for Sophie's makes possible the reconfiguration of masculinity from a structure based on vengeance to one based on mercy and forgiveness. The penetration of the divine into the secular through the incarnation makes change possible, offering hope for an end to the human cycle of violence and revenge.

Prudence's strongest arguments often come back to the body of Christ, as when she counters with the argument that Christ would not have been born of a woman if women were wicked. When Melibee argues that not taking revenge simply invites more villainy, Prudence replies from "Seint Peter" with Christ's patience: "'Whan men cursed hym, he cursed hem noght, and whan men betten hym, he manaced hem noght'" (1504). Prudence urges patience because "the tribulaciouns of this world but litel while endure and soone passed been and goon,/ and the joye that a man seketh to have by pacience in tribulaciouns is perdurable . . . that is to seyn, everelastynge" (1507–10). This reference to the

[25] Caroline Walker Bynum, *Fragmentation and Redemption: Essays on Gender and the Human Body in Medieval Religion* (New York: Zone, 1991), 93ff.

eternal looks ahead to the end of the tale and to a final sentence added by Chaucer:

> "For doutelees, if we be sory and repentant of the synnes and giltes which we han trespassed in the sighte of oure Lord God,/ he is so free and so merciable/ that he wole foryeven us oure giltes/ and bryngen us to the blisse that nevere hath ende." Amen.   (1885–88)

The problem of inheritance

The last obstacle to peace in the *Melibee* is the question of inheritance. Melibee's enemies will submit to his absolute judgment only after being assured that the rights of their heirs will not be abridged, and the final sign of his transformation is the agreement not to exile and disinherit them. Inheritance, as has been pointed out, was a major ground of contention between Richard and the appellants. And finally, inheritance is the distinguishing difference between patriarchal masculinity, which establishes continuity in this world by passing land and wealth from father to child, and clerical masculinity, where there are no children to inherit and treasure cannot be stored up on earth.

Two centuries earlier, John of Salisbury made an explicit link between inheritance and the Christian concept of eternal life. In pagan times, he said, "the prospect of a temporal kingdom with succession from father to son was held out to men who as yet did not seek an eternal one." These days, John adds:

> since there is nought which men more desire than to have their sons succeed them in their possessions, even as men foreseeing that death is an incident of their mortal state seek to prolong their own existence in the heirs of their body, therefore this promise is given to princes as the greatest incentive to the practice of justice.[26]

Inheritance from father to son is the foundation of patriarchy because it offers eternal life in *this* world. Chaucer's new ending to the *Melibee* urges turning away from this world toward a new "masculinity" modelled on the meek suffering body of Christ.

Chaucer's "Amen" ends the tale; but then he returns to the Host and Goodelief and the gender wars because the solution of the tale is idealistic and unrealistic in his world, and because the suffering, patient, ambiguously-gendered body of Christ and the kind of masculinity it offers raises male gender anxieties. Melibee's last objection, before he finally agrees to be guided by

---

26 *The Statesman's Book of John of Salisbury, being the Fourth, Fifth and Sixth Books, and Selections from the Seventh and Eighth Books, of the "Policraticus,"* trans. John Dickinson (New York: Knopf, 1927), 48, 50.

Prudence in line 1712, is that showing Christlike meekness to his enemies will dishonor him:

> "Wol ye thanne that I go and meke me, and obeye me to hem, and crie hem mercy?/ For sothe, that were nat my worshipe./ For right as men seyn that 'over-greet hoomlynesse engendreth dispreisynge,' so fareth it by to greet humylitee or mekenesse."   (1684–86)

That suggestion about gender anxiety is impossible to document, but a kind of evidence appears in the York Corpus Christi play produced first by the Tilemakers (later by the Milliners), in which Pilate has the silent Christ brutally scourged and sent to be crucified. The pageant begins with a comically phallic episode in which the lances and banners held by Pilate's men bow to Christ in homage when he enters the court. Pilate is furious and sends for his strongest men, but even they cannot keep their lances erect in Christ's presence.[27] It is a funny scene, but it reflects deep male anxieties about the meek, silent Christ that did not begin or end in the fifteenth century.[28]

Perhaps Chaucer's point in the link and his answer to Albertanus da Brescia is that the cycle of war and revenge can never be stopped because it is impossible to realize fully the divine perspective in a secular world where even going to church is fraught with the potential for insult and violence. If Melibee's merciful but absolute kingship is an alternative to the feudal wars of patriarchal lords, it also carries the seeds of tyranny, as the final years of Richard's reign suggest.

---

[27] *York Plays*, ed. Lucy Toulmin Smith (Oxford: Clarendon Press, 1885), 325–29.
[28] Gilmore (pp. 18–19) points out that a number of Englishmen in the nineteenth and early twentieth centuries felt the need to assert that Christ was a "manly man" and no "Prince of Peace-at-any-price" in works such as Thomas Hughes's *The Manliness of Christ* (London: MacMillan, 1879) and Robert W. Conant's *The Virility of Christ* (Chicago: 1915).

Reading Chaucer's "Manly man":
The Trouble with Masculinity
in the *Monk's Prologue* and *Tale*

MICHAEL D. SHARP

In the General Prologue to Chaucer's *Canterbury Tales*, the narrator calls attention to the Monk's gender by informing us straight off that the Monk is a "manly man" (I 167), a "prikasour" (189) who loves "venerie" (166). The narrator's descriptive language has often led critics to see the Monk as "sexually driven."[1] Yet, while this language certainly conveys an implicit criticism of the Monk's professional priorities, the extent to which it conveys a suspicion of sexual misconduct remains unclear. The Monk is finally a sexual enigma, inviting speculation but never confirming it. If he is not clearly orthodox in his monasticism, neither is he in flagrant violation of his order. And if he is not celibate, neither is he necessarily a "womanizer," as some have presumed.[2] The Monk apparently rejects the cloistered life in favor of more vigorous

---

[1] Jahan Ramazani, "Chaucer's Monk: The Poetics of Abbreviation, Aggression, and Tragedy," *ChauR* 27 (1993): 271.

[2] The case for a sexualized Monk derives primarily from a figurative reading of the Monk's costume and hunting practices. For a comprehensive argument in favor of reading the Monk as sexually sinful, see Edmund Reiss, "The Symbolic Surface of the *Canterbury Tales*: The Monk's Portrait," *ChauR* 2 (1968): 254–72; 3 (1968): 12–28. Paull F. Baum, in "Chaucer's Puns," *PMLA* 71 (1956): 242, 245–6, reads "prikyng" (I 191) and "venerie" as sexual puns. Others are more cautious in their assessments of the Monk's sexuality. Jill Mann, *Chaucer and Medieval Estates Satire* (Cambridge: Cambridge University Press, 1973), 24–25, warns that "Chaucer's puns are the *only* indication we have of the Monk's sexual licence" (original emphasis). Laura Hodges, in "A Reconsideration of the Monk's Costume," *ChauR* 26 (1991): 135, argues that although many of the Monk's accoutrements, such as his "love-knotte" (197), might be read as sexually suggestive, his costume as a

pursuits, and the very indeterminacy with which the narrator describes these pursuits invites his audience to ponder a vexing question: what has a monk to do with "manliness"? Further, what has "manliness" to do with sexuality? Does the adjective "manly" suggest an active sexual desire and practice, or could a perfectly celibate monk be as "manly" as any secular man?[3] The omission of the Monk from nearly all recent studies of gender and sexuality in Chaucer's *Canterbury Tales* is surprising given the persistence with which Chaucer returns specifically to the Monk's "manliness" and the interpretive dilemmas to which it gives rise.[4]

Where the narrator remains content to describe the Monk's "manly" appearance without assigning it any fixed meaning, the Host wants answers. In the *Monk's Prologue*, the Host's invitation to the Monk to tell a tale doubles as an investigation into the mysteries of the Monk's manhood, and initiates a dialogue about the meaning and value of "manliness" as a cultural ideal. This dialogue begins with the Host's "murye words" to the Monk, continues with the Monk's tale-response, and concludes with the Knight's and the Host's interruption-commentaries. Following Ross Chambers's argument that "narrative mediates human relationships and derives its 'meaning' from them," I see the *Monk's Tale* as a response to fundamental social tensions between the Monk and his immediate audience. The narrator, the Host and the Knight at different points provide us with assessments of the Monk and his tale, but in the process reveal less about the Monk than about themselves, their own desires, and their own anxieties. And while the *Monk's Tale* might be considered in isolation as an expression of the Monk's own aesthetic and moral values, it might more fruitfully be imagined as one part of an ongoing discussion, in which the Monk's stories of emasculating wives and disgraced warriors comprise quite potent challenges both to the marital masculinity of the Host and to the martial masculinity of the Knight. Finding his own manhood under scrutiny and attack, the Monk responds with a sustained exploration of secular masculinity from a cenobitic perspective.

The Host's ambivalent approach to the Monk

The assumptions of critics that there is something actively sexual about the Monk mirror those of the Host, who, in his solicitation of a tale from the Monk, acts as a kind of surrogate interrogator for the suspicious or cynical reader. Like

whole "may be relegated to the middle ground between the designation of 'worldly' and 'ascetic.' "

3   The *Middle English Dictionary*, ed. Robert E. Lewis (Ann Arbor: University of Michigan Press, 1952–), defines "manly" in this instance as "masculine, male," a literal and conservative definition which leaves us to interpret the implications and resonances of the word for ourselves.

4   Anne Laskaya, in *Chaucer's Approach to Gender in the Canterbury Tales* (Cambridge: D. S. Brewer, 1995), 119–20, discusses the masculinity of the Monk in passing.

many critics, the Host sees the Monk in part through the lens of the medieval fabliau tradition (exemplified by the *Shipman's Tale*), in which religious men are frequently presumed to be not only unchaste but sexually rapacious.[5] In the *Monk's Prologue*, the host jokingly addresses the Monk as "daun John" (VII 1929), and thus "calls forth unpleasant association with the sly monk in the *Shipman's Tale*,"[6] who is himself named "daun John." This allusion to the adulterous monk of the *Shipman's Tale* is the first in a series of comments that suggest the Host's preoccupation with the Monk's sexuality.

The *Monk's Prologue* begins with the Host lamenting the confused state of his own marriage. Unlike Melibee's patient Prudence, the Host's wife, Goodelief, is both shrewish and violent. She chides her husband not only for failing to accomplish specific tasks (such as beating the servants properly), but more generally for failing to behave *as a man should*. Her domestic tyranny is figured as a usurpation of the Host's own masculine gender role: so deficient is he in his manly duties that she has had to assume them herself. His account of his wife's railing – "By corpus bones, I wol have thy knyf, / And thou shalt have my distaf and go spynne!" (1901–07) – highlights the gender trouble that marriage has caused him. Rather than confirm the Host's masculinity, marriage has called it into question. The Host's wife is not only stronger in speech than her husband, but stronger in body as well ("I dar nat hire withstonde, / For she is byg in armes" [1920–21]), depriving him of the one advantage that should be his by nature. Thus the Host's attempt to impugn his wife's femininity by comparing it unfavorably to that of Prudence results ironically in a detailed confession of his own emasculation.

The Host's brief diary-of-a-marriage also provides a lens through which we might view "The murye wordes of the Hoost to the Monk" and assess their implications. After revealing the ways in which marriage has compromised his own sense of masculinity, the Host moves on to comment quite explicitly on the masculinity of the Monk. What begins as apparently playful and jocular banter turns quickly into an elaborate paean to the Monk's virile body as well as an oddly impassioned argument in favor of clerical marriage. In his conversational and roundabout approach to soliciting a tale from the Monk, the Host seems to be probing the very same questions that have concerned critics and editors: what does the Monk's "manly" appearance signify? Is his professed commitment to celibacy genuine, or simply a way for him to circumvent the obligations of marriage while still remaining (secretly) sexually active? The Host moves from the violence and confusion of his own domestic life to a

[5] See Per Nykrog, *Les fabliaux: Etude d'histoire littéraire et de stylistique médiévale* (Copenhagen: Munksgaard, 1957), 62.
[6] Robert M. Lumiansky, *Of Sondry Folk: The Dramatic Principle in the Canterbury Tales* (Austin: University of Texas Press, 1955), 100.

complex and suggestive fantasy of monastic life. His desire to hear a tale thus becomes tightly bound up with his desire to establish a sexual understanding of and connection with his interlocutor, the Monk.

The Host's words to the Monk begin in a friendly, even intimate manner. Having provided us with his own version of the "wo that is in mariage" (III 3), the Host goes searching after what he imagines to be the secret joy in monasticism. The Monk is "of brawnes and of bones / A wel farynge" man (VII 1941–42), a man whose "ful fair skyn" (VII 1932) and generally impressive physique make the Host suspect that the Monk must hold some position of authority in his order. That is, the Host attempts to discern the Monk's official position in his order by reading his body. While both the narrator of the General Prologue and the Host demonstrate a curiosity in the Monk's manly appearance, the Host combines that curiosity with expressions of aesthetic appreciation.

Following this initial appraisal of the Monk, however, the tone of the Host's words shifts markedly. He curses whoever introduced the Monk into religious life and then uses his ensuing lament as an opportunity to imagine what the Monk would have accomplished had he never entered monastic orders:

> "I pray to God, yeve hym confusioun
> That first thee broghte unto religioun!
> Thou woldest han been a tredefowel aright.
> Haddestow as greet a leeve as thou hast myght
> To parfourne al thy lust in engendrure,
> Thou haddest bigeten ful many a creature."   (1943–48)

Again, the Host uses discussion of religion as a way of talking about the Monk's body, this time focusing explicitly on his sexuality. In fact, it is clear from here on out that the Host sees the Monk in almost purely sexual terms. His claim that the Monk "woldest han been a tredefowel" is a theory of masculinity in miniature: it suggests that there is an underlying, bestial procreative desire inherent in men which religion, unnaturally, thwarts. The Host condemns monasticism's celibacy requirement, yet his words are clearly tinged with an admiration for the Monk's imagined sexual talents, his powerful desire ("lust") as well as his breeding capacity. The Host's rhetoric thus remains suggestively double-edged, as he articulates his desire to hear a tale in the form of a sexual fantasy.

There is an erotic component to the interaction between the Host and the Monk that, so far as I can tell, has yet to be explored. The Host follows his misogynist caricature of his wife with a speech in praise of the Monk's manly beauty. He denies affection for his wife at the same time that he reveals affection for the Monk. Then, as if to clarify the nature of this affective shift, the Host introduces procreation as his primary concern in addressing the Monk. Thus women implicitly return, as objects of male procreative desire, to mediate the Host's relationship with the Monk, and the potentially homoerotic implications of the Host's initial remarks are deflected onto the safely heterosexual[7] discourse of reproduction. The introduction of a shared and licit object of sexual desire as the third term in their relationship authorizes and explains the sexual interest the Host takes in the Monk. By triangulating desire in this way,[8] the Host attempts to establish a sense of communality with the Monk, imagining an originary masculine identity based on natural heterosexual desire which monasticism has repressed but not eliminated.

The irony of the Host's vocal support for procreation is, of course, that procreation is ideally the result of marriage, the very institution responsible for the Host's sense of emasculation. As if the irony were not evident enough, the Host concludes his words to the Monk by not only discussing marriage, but explicitly advocating it as a masculine ideal. If he were pope, the Host claims that "every myghty man . . . sholde have a wyf" (1951, 1953). He further asserts that:

> "Religioun hath take up al the corn
> Of tredyng, and we borel men been shrympes.
> Of fieble trees ther comen wrecched ympes.
> This maketh that oure heires been so sklendre
> And feble that they may nat wel engendre.
> This maketh that oure wyves wole assaye
> Religious folk, for ye mowe bettre paye
> Of Venus paiementz than mowe we;
> God woot, no lussheburghes payen ye!"   (1954–62)

By introducing "oure wyves" (1959) as a concern of his argument, the Host reveals that his true concern is not celibacy (which he doesn't seem to believe exists), but the seductive powers that "celibates" have over laymen's wives. Whereas earlier the Host theorized about the Monk's essentially sexual nature, now he as much as accuses the Monk of putting that sexuality into practice. He does not simply declare that religious men sleep with married women. Rather, his grammar implicitly personalizes his claims: it is "ye" religious folk whom

---

[7] I use the term "heterosexual" to indicate a valence of desire rather than an essential sexual identity. On the historical specificity of the homosexual/heterosexual binary, see Jonathan Ned Katz, *The Invention of Heterosexuality* (New York: Dutton, 1995; rpt. New York: Plume/Penguin, 1996), 1–18.

[8] René Girard, *Deceit, Desire, and the Novel: Self and Other in Literary Structures* (Baltimore: Johns Hopkins, 1965), 2, uses the triangle as a "systematic metaphor" for understanding the ways that desire, particularly erotic desire, is mediated by a third party, typically a rival. Eve Sedgwick, *Between Men: English Literature and Male Homosocial Desire* (New York: Columbia, 1985), 2, develops the implications of Girard's study by focusing on the various kinds of "homosocial desire" that bind men together in social relationships. For Sedgwick, desire is not "a particular affective state or emotion" but "the social force, the glue, even when its manifestation is hostility or hatred or something less emotively charged, that shapes an important relationship."

"oure" wives seek out sexually. Though the Host generalizes about wives and monks, his previous attention first to his *own* wife, Goodelief, and then to the Monk himself makes them both an important subtext of his argument. In addressing the Monk, the Host has moved from simply admiring the Monk's body, to then imagining the Monk having sex (as a "tredefowel aright"), to finally imagining (however obliquely) the Monk having sex with Goodelief herself. The Host's fabliau-inspired interpretation of the Monk is thus in part a product of the Host's own domestic anxieties. Though his assessment of the Monk's greater generative capacity contains elements of mock self-deprecation, it also marks the Host's enduring concern with the contingency of his own masculine authority (in both heterosexual and homosocial contexts). In his "murye wordes" to the Monk, the Host rewrites his own life as a variation on the *Shipman's Tale*, in which the Monk plays the role of "daun John" not because he is in fact sexual, but because the Host's sense of his own masculine insufficiency requires that the Monk be understood as such.

Though the Host draws on satirical tradition, he does not do so in an unambiguously critical fashion. His expressions of consternation only thinly mask an underlying curiosity, admiration, and even envy. His arguments against clerical "celibacy" are indistinguishable from his fantasies about it. Rather than express a desire to join the monks, the Host proclaims that monks ought to join him and become married men. But the authority of his argument is undermined by the prefatory remarks he has already made about his own marriage. If the Wife of Bath bases her marriage sermon on "experience, though noon auctoritee" (III 1), the Host does the opposite, ignoring the evidence of his own "experience" in order to advance his case for monastic reform based on the imagined "auctoritee" of the natural world. While the Host's "sermon" is in part both tongue-in-cheek and implictly hostile, it is at the same time deeply self-revelatory, exposing the Host's own conflicted ideas about masculinity as well as the complicity of his own gender anxiety in the perpetuation of monastic sexual stereotypes.

The Host's presumption to know the sexual secrets of monks might be read as hostile, but it might also be read as a bid for intimacy, a nudge of friendly recognition, by which the Host, through "game" and "pleye," seeks to create a bond with the Monk based on a shared understanding of men's natural behavior. The Monk, however, refuses to play his scripted role in this dialogue. Resisting the Host's attempts to characterize him according to a fabliau model, the Monk does not engage the Host even on his own terms. That is, he responds only to the Host's request for a tale and appears to ignore the highly personal and potentially offensive claims that have been made about him. Rather than rush to deny the implications of the Host's speech, the Monk methodically lays out his tale-telling plans, which at first appear quite general: he proposes to tell a set of "tragedies" so that we may meditate on

"hym that stood in greet prosperitee,

And is yfallen out of heigh degree
Into myserie, and endeth wrecchedly." (1975–77)

This plan to assault worldly ideals generally, however, becomes in its execution more specifically an assault on ideals of masculinity. Though the Monk does not attack the Host directly, he responds to him indirectly by telling stories that undermine the very marital ideal the Host claimed to advocate.[9] His tragedies are both a rebuttal of the Host and, more generally, a critique of worldly masculinities as appropriate social ideals. In response to the Host's charges, the Monk does not piously proclaim his innocence or tell a tale in defense of monastic men. He sets out instead to undo the logic of masculinity altogether, by constructing his tale as a series of negative exempla featuring illustrious men whose lives nonetheless end in ruin. The Monk's critique of masculine ideals, while initially directed against the Host, extends eventually in its implications to the Knight as well, whose tale the Monk was originally invited to "quite" back in Fragment I (3119–20), before the Miller stole the floor.

Adam, Samson, and Hercules

The Monk's initial tragedies look disdainfully on two of secular manhood's defining elements: heterosexual love and procreation. In his one-stanza tragedy of Adam, for instance, the Monk vilifies human procreation by comparing it unfavorably to Divine Creation, thereby demeaning the very act which the Host had set forth as the essence of manliness. The Monk says of Adam that "With Goddes owene fynger wroght was he, / And nat bigeten of mannes sperme unclene" (VII 2008–09). The Host's appeal to nature (the "tredefowel," "corn," "trees," and "ympes") in his celebration of unfettered male sexuality is rebutted here in the Monk's appeal to Genesis. In the logic of the Adam tragedy, the semen-less propagation of textual authority (in which the Monk himself participates) more nearly approximates the original act of Creation than any amount of breeding ever could. The Host's and Monk's contrasting valuations of sexuality derive from their disparate ideas about the origins of moral authority. Where the Host's polemics are fueled by a belief in the overriding authority of nature, the Monk sees the world entirely through the lens provided by "olde bookes" (1974), the Bible and its commentaries being (at least initially) primary among them. Trumping the merely procreative power of

---

[9] Kurt Olsson, "Grammar, Manhood, and Tears: The Curiosity of Chaucer's Monk," *MP* 76 (1978): 8, also sees the struggle between the Host and Monk in terms of competing definitions of manliness, though he has a different sense of what is at stake in this struggle: "the Host identifies manhood with a capacity for fleshly pleasure and 'engendrure'; the Monk identifies it with a capacity for a knowledge that 'satisfies' curiosity."

semen with the foundational power of "Goddes owene fynger," the Monk insinuates that his own textual brand of exemplarity is both purer and more authoritative than the nature-based exemplarity of the Host.[10] The Monk reminds his audience that the Creation of *human beings* was a privileged moment in history, one that separates humankind essentially from the beasts on whom the Host would have men model their behavior.

As the Monk moves on from Adam, he continues his assault on the underpinnings of secular manhood. His focus turns to women and their role in the un-manning of two of the wisest and most powerful men the world has known: Samson and Hercules. The Monk's implicitly anti-marital focus is most evident in these tragedies. By focusing on women as a threat to both men's social stature and their physical well-being, the Monk reintroduces the association of marriage with emasculation originally set forth by the Host himself. For instance, the Monk's descriptions of Samson's unsurpassed strength and martial prowess are regularly punctuated by reminders of how the treachery of a wife ultimately brought this strong man to ruin. The following four lines from the first stanza on Samson encapsulate the logic of the tragedy as a whole:

> Was nevere swich another as was hee,
> To speke of strengthe, and therwith hardynesse;
> But to his wyves toolde he his secree,
> Thurgh which he slow hymself for wrecchednesse.   (2019–22)

The Monk does not wait until the end of the tragedy to tell us its significance. He substitutes the abbreviated logic of "Thurgh which" for a cohesive narrative in order to establish immediately the centrality of wifely treachery to his tragedy. By framing Samson's death as a suicide, the Monk suggests that the most serious damage wives do to husbands is in the end not physical, but psychic. He concludes four of the remaining nine stanzas by returning to this same theme: wives deprive husbands of their "conseil" or "secree," exposing their interiority to the outside world and thus leaving even the mightiest man weak and vulnerable.

So caught up is the Monk in his concern with the problems facing husbands that by the end he appears to have drifted from the ostensible theme of his tale; unlike his other tragedies, the tragedy of Samson concludes not with a reminder of Fortune's fickleness, but with advice to husbands on how to govern their wives:

---

10 Nature itself was frequently imagined as a book in the Middle Ages. The "book of nature" or "book of the creature" was another means (besides the written word) by which God might reveal truth to humankind. See Ernst Robert Curtius, *European Literature and the Latin Middle Ages*, trans. Willard R. Trask (New York: Harper, 1953; rpt. New York: Princeton/Bollingen, 1973), 319–26.

Of Sampson now wol I namoore sayn.
Beth war by this ensample oold and playn
That no men telle hir conseil til hir wyves
Of swich thyng as they wolde han secree fayn,
If that it touche hir lymes or hir lyves. (2091–94)

The specific treachery of Delilah (who is referred to directly in only one of the tragedy's ten stanzas) is subordinated to the more general treachery of which all wives are capable. For a brief moment, the *Monk's Tale* veers from its *contemptus mundi* ethos, as the Monk advises men how to *manage* rather than turn away from worldly obligations, in this case wives. This odd pragmatic turn recalls the Host's confessed inability to govern his own wife, and thus reinscribes the Host as the primary intended audience for these early exempla.

In the tragedy of Hercules, the Monk reprises his anti-marital (and antifeminist) theme. After a truly monotonous recitation of Hercules's trials or "werkes" (2096) the Monk begins his narration of Hercules's fall by introducing his wife (here referred to as his "lemman" [2119]), Dianira. The Monk claims that she was "fressh as May" (2120), a description which, conventional as it is, in this context is also ironic. In addition to being a springtime month, May is also the name of January's cuckolding wife in the *Merchant's Tale*, a woman whom the Merchant describes frequently as "fresshe" (IV 1886, 1955, 1977). By using the phrase "fressh as May" to describe Dianira, the Monk suggests that adultery (May's crime) and murder (Dianira's) are simply different manifestations of a single emasculating imperative shared by all wives.

Dianira's status as an exemplum of wifely treachery is compromised, however, by the Monk's awkward handling of his sources. At first the Monk explains that Hercules died as a direct result of an "envenymed" shirt given him by Dianira (VII 2124). By linking Hercules's downfall directly to the agency of Dianira, the Monk continues to undermine the marital ideal of manhood set forth earlier by the Host. He lets us know that the story of Dianira's treachery rests on good authority ("as these clerkes maken mencioun" [2121]), but then decides to qualify his original version of the story by informing his audience that not all "clerkes" agree on Dianira's guilt:

But nathelees somme clerkes hire excusen
By oon that highte Nessus, that it maked.
Be as be may, I wol hire noght accusen. (2127–29)

By demonstrating knowledge of what the "clerkes" have written on the subject of Dianira, the Monk establishes his credibility as a scholar and claims membership in an exclusive and privileged community of men, a cenobitic community founded on the ideals of chastity and learning. In displaying the depth of his reading, however, the Monk shows that there are opacities to clerkly knowledge, particularly where women are concerned. He inadvertently reveals a kinship between monasticism and the marital manhood he seeks to demean. If husbands are incapable of regulating wives' behavior, as the Monk's first tales assert, then "clerkes" are equally incapable of regulating their textual significance. After having implied that the Host was confused in his reading of nature, the Monk shows that he has reading problems of his own, and that the sharp philosophical distinction he seeks to make between himself and secular, sexually active men might not be as tenable as he imagines.

The Monk's anti-marital misogyny extends even to his portrayals of Fortune herself. At the end of the Hercules tragedy, for instance, the Monk imagines Fortune as a treacherous wife who, when she

> list to glose,
> Thanne wayteth she her man to overthrowe
> By swich a wey as he wolde leest suppose.   (2140–42)

In the tragedy of Holofernes, his portrayal of Fortune as the emasculator *par excellence* is even more vicious. The Monk claims that no one in his time suffered a worse fall than Holofernes, whom

> Fortune ay kiste
> So likerously, and ladde hym up and doun
> Til that his heed was of, er that he wiste.   (2556–58)

Fortune is now not just a seductress, but one whose seduction has a specifically homicidal intent. Again the Monk's logic is abbreviated. The "Til that" of line 2558 stands in for a coherent narrative, encouraging the reader to see a causal connection between women's sexual favors and death. The wives in the tragedies of Samson and Hercules, then, are not only agents of Fortune, but are apparently created in her image as well.

Implicating the Knight: the tragedy of Zenobia

In his characterization of marital manhood, the Monk thoroughly rejects the Host's attempt to define him, emphatically denying the benefits of sex and marriage and figuring even socially-sanctioned heterosexual practice as a misguided investment of manly desire. With the inclusion of Zenobia, the Monk shifts his criticism of secular masculinity away from the marital and begins to turn it instead toward the martial. In doing so, the implications of his tale begin to bear upon the Knight, the pilgrimage's most prominent representative of military achievement. Though Samson and Hercules are both described as "champiouns" (2033, 2119) who possess great "strengthe" (2010, 2114), the Monk concerns himself primarily with their domestic woes. It is not until Zenobia that we get a tragedy centered on the pomp and glory of a successful military campaigner.

Zenobia's tragedy is not only the longest one the Monk tells, it is also the most laudatory. Despite denying the lasting importance of military accomplishments, the Monk shows a clear respect for Zenobia, particularly her practice of marital chastity (2279–94). The Monk's denigration of military success would be insult enough to the Knight, who has spent his entire life in military campaigns all over the world; that the exemplar of military success is in this case a woman "surrounded by an aura of Oriental splendour and exoticism"[11] would have to strike particularly hard at the Knight's identity. After all, the chivalric ideology of the Knight's own tale is predicated on the dominance, capture, and domestication of the alien warrior-woman.

The Knight exemplifies Theseus's powers of governance by beginning his tale with a description of how his hero "conquered al the regne of Femenye" (I 866). The Knight then moves into an *occupatio*, wherein he refers to events which, given time constraints, he claims he cannot narrate in full. These suppressed events include all the various forms of coercion required to defeated the Amazons and wed Hippolyta. In effect, the Knight refuses to discuss Amazonian resistance. To do so would be to ascribe agency and potency to the women and thus render them potentially threatening to the profoundly paternalistic world view that the Knight, via Theseus, attempts to naturalize. As Angela Jane Weisl rightly notes, "the autonomy of the Amazon women is a profound threat to the masculine power structures of epic that Theseus espouses. In his world view, female autonomy and power is so undesirable as to be almost unimaginable."[12] The Knight begins his tale with the capture of the Amazon "queen Hippolyta" and, having reduced her to booty, assimilates her to a more stereotypically feminine role as intercessor and representative of womanly "pitee" (I 1751, 1761).

Though no Amazon, as a domesticated warrior-woman of the "orient," Zenobia is certainly a close analogue. In choosing to focus on her pre-captivity life, her valiance and morality as well as her capture and feminization, the Monk emphasizes the "hardynesse" (VII 2250) of the warrior-woman which the Knight, in his own story of female domestication, suppresses. Though the last two and a half stanzas of Zenobia's tragedy predictably tell of her downfall, this downfall does not confirm the rightness of the male-dominated world or the ultimately beneficent power of the Knight's "Firste Movere" (I 2987). Instead of glossing over the degradation that accompanies the domestication of alien women, as the *Knight's Tale* does, the Monk elevates that degradation to the level of tragedy. The Monk imbues Zenobia's fall with a sense of pathos that affirms her essential humanity, however morally misguided her life may have been. Her defeat is not an occasion for celebrating the valor of her conqueror, "this grete Romayn, this Aurelian" (VII 2361). Rather, it

11 Piero Boitani, "The *Monk's Tale*: Dante and Boccaccio," *MÆ* 45 (1976): 65.
12 Angela Jane Weisl, *Conquering the Reign of Femeny: Gender and Genre in Chaucer's Romance* (Cambridge: D. S. Brewer, 1995), 53.

perpetuates a cycle of proud rulers, all of whom (in the Monk's logic) are doomed to rise and fall at the whims of Fortune. The tragedy of Zenobia then undermines both the ideal of martial masculinity which the Knight represents and the nature of the tale that the Knight has chosen to tell.

Several of the remaining tragedies directly implicate the Knight as well. Alexander and Caesar are described as paragons of "knyghthod" and "gentillesse" (VII 2642, 2664) and "manhede" and "chivalrie" (VII 2671, 2681) respectively, before their horrid downfalls are revealed. By describing these men according to the language of medieval chivalry, the Monk implies a kinship between the values of these (doomed) men and those of the gentle Knight (who of course "loved chivalrie" [I 45]). The Peter of Cyprus tragedy might also be understood as a quite pointed attack on the Knight, who (according to the General Prologue) was personally involved in Peter's conquering "Alisaundre." One can imagine the Knight's taking offense at the brusque dismissal of Peter's military accomplishments as well as the degradation of his "chivalrie" (the Monk reminds us that, after all, Peter died not in battle, but in bed [VII 2395–96]).

It is no wonder that, facing such a multi-faceted assault on his social identity, the Knight refuses to hear any more of the Monk's tragedies. While critics have tended to read the Knight's interruption as indication of his superior aesthetic sensibilities, I would argue that his interruption indicates his anxiety about the potential persuasiveness of the Monk's tragedies. Just as the Knight is compelled to suppress the threatening Amazons, so here the Knight must suppress the Monk whose tale, however inelegant, threatens to compromise the ideality of the Knight's chivalric masculinity. Not only is military activity repeatedly exposed as a morally bankrupt enterprise, but in the tragedy of Zenobia it is no longer even the exclusive province of men. The concept of a natural gender hierarchy is essential to the Knight's vision of world order, but the tragedy of Zenobia belies that concept by emphasizing the ritualized violence and humiliation that are used to reinforce female submission.

The Knight's complaint about the one-sidedness of the Monk's tragedies is, on the one hand, a fair one. Caroline Bynum points out that the theme of *contemptus mundi* "was frequently complemented in medieval treatises by discussions of the glory of creation and of 'man.' "[13] And Renate Haas has argued that the Monk's tragedies, given their lack of "consoling vistas into the beyond," would have been particularly agonizing to a Christian audience.[14] Still, despite the Monk's short-sightedness, the Knight's preference for stories of men who "clymbeth up and wexeth fortunat, / And there *abideth* in prosperitee" (2776–77, my emphasis) shows us not a man who is looking for

---

13 Caroline Bynum, "Why All the Fuss about the Body?: A Medievalist's Perspective," *Critical Inquiry* 22 (1995): 14.
14 Renate Haas, "Chaucer's *Monk's Tale*: An Ingenious Criticism of Early Humanist Conceptions of Tragedy," *Humanistica Lovaniensia* 36 (1987): 61.

balance, but one who is as seduced by the fiction of Fortune's steadfastness as any of the Monk's tragic subjects. The Knight's own career is in its twilight, and his interpretation of the *Monk's Tale* as a "greet disese" (2771) is as much a refusal to acknowledge his own mortality, including the mortality of the chivalric value system he holds so dear, as it is a judgment against the Monk's narrative skill. The Knight's "First Movere" speech recognized the uncontrollable powers of Fortune, but implied the power of paternalistic governance to transcend any vicissitudes human beings might face. By telling tragedies that involve the ephemerality not only of human life, but of human political structures as well, the Monk effectively "quites" the *Knight's Tale*.[15] That the Knight feels compelled to interrupt thus says as much about the Monk's rhetorical success as it does about his aesthetic failure.

The Host joins the Knight in his negative assessment of the *Monk's Tale*, though he faults the Monk not for depressing his audience, but for boring it. He concludes his criticism by asking the Monk to tell a new tale, one in which he might "sey somwhat of huntyng" (2805). The reference to hunting recalls the imagery used to describe the Monk in the General Prologue; there, the narrator's language raised questions about whether hunting should be understood literally or metaphorically as an allusion to sexual behavior, and that ambiguity returns here. The Host once again attempts to coerce the Monk into confirming the Host's own fantasies about monastic behavior, but the Monk will not capitulate: " 'Nay,' quod this Monk, 'I have no lust to pleye. / Now lat another tell, as I have toold' " (VII 2806–07). In the end, the Monk remains a figure of resistance. He opposes the efforts of other men to define his identity and determine his manner of self-expression while simultaneously calling attention to the elisions and blind spots in secular ideals of masculinity. His tale is designed not to recruit secular men to the monastic life, but simply to force them to consider the inherently unstable foundations of their worldly authority. The strong reactions of the Knight and Host confirm the power of the Monk's critique, and suggest that, contrary to the Host's assertion, the *Monk's Tale* has indeed found an audience, albeit a resistant one.

---

[15] My argument here builds on that of R. E. Kaske, "The Knight's Interruption of the Monk's Tale," *ELH* 24 (1957): 266, who notes the contrast between the Monk's emphasis on mutability and the Knight's emphasis on order.

"Have ye no mannes herte?": Chauntecleer as Cock-Man in the *Nun's Priest's Tale*

PAUL R. THOMAS

As Chaucer draws us in to his *Nun's Priest's Tale*, we soon learn that Chauntecleer is the sole surviving male in an all-female household: a husband to seven of his sisters, the clock to his owner widow and her two daughters, the only animal in this mock-heroic, moated yard who does not bear offspring or yield milk or eggs for the subsistence of this dairy household. This tale will present Chauntecleer as a supernumerary to the real business of the widow's household, an unproductive, book-reading, dream-debating lover. Essentially, then, Chauntecleer is a man, for Pertelote as a woman (see VII 2912–14) accuses him after his retelling of his fearful dream of having both a beard and a cowardly man's heart (2920). This man and cock-of-the-walk presents us with Chaucer's view of masculinity as seen through mock-heroic glasses, one lens of which sees the world of beasts and the other, the world of men. Further, most of what Chauntecleer knows about his masculine role is a peculiar mixture of cocky instincts and manly texts. By the end of the tale, we will have seen how Chauntecleer has progressed from a textual seducer of Pertelote to a common-sense flatterer escaping the first fox he has ever met. Along the way in this tale of a cock, a hen, and a fox, we will see a rather different view of masculinity than Chaucer delineates in any other of the *Canterbury Tales*. Perhaps Chaucer the poet presents his masculine learning, his favorite texts or *auctorites*, differently in this tale than in any of the other tales, for those sources here which have informed Chaucer's other works in a serious way are sent up, even satirized in this mock-heroic fable. This "sending up" of valued texts is a mock-heroic version of masculinity in which Chaucer shows off both his scholastic *Sic et*

Non style of learning and his peacock feathers of parodic rhetoric in a barnyard filled with Golden Spangled Hamburg chickens.[1]

I will present here an introductory study of Chaucer's insights into masculinity in the *Nun's Priest's Tale*, hoping that the readers will further "decorate" the picture I can only sketch here. In this essay, I will concentrate on the portrayal of masculinity – mostly human masculinity – through the central character of Chauntecleer. Inevitably, I will also reflect my reading of Chaucer's insights into masculinity in this tale through his presentation of Pertelote and Russell. As we might expect in a mock-heroic work, Chaucer's view of masculinity here is sometimes obscured and filtered through the poet's persona of the Nun's Priest, a celibate who functions in an all-female priory household rather like a Chauntecleer, though, we trust, without all the cocky sexual escapades. And perhaps this witty, mock-heroic, celibate voice alone can so thoroughly undercut the hero of the piece, Chauntecleer, for the Nun's Priest knows what it is like to be the only man "at home." In addition to the possible connections between the Nun's Priest and Chauntecleer (see the Host's rude version of this in the probably-cancelled *Nun's Priest's Epilogue* at VII 3450–54), in some ways the Nun's Priest represents an epitome of Chaucer's usual portrayal of his own masculine poetic voice: a man who has observed love but who does not participate in it; a man who is capable sometimes of antifeminist outbursts but who then quickly undercuts the seriousness of what he has just said; a man who as a narrator is coolly rational and textual, who subtly paints the ironies inherent in his characters' behavior, and yet sometimes undergoes surprising and sudden changes in his own portrayal. Thus the Nun's Priest lets us see the antifeminism of Chauntecleer's debate conclusion as he mistranslates the Latin proverb of the philosopher Secundus to seduce Pertelote, but the Nun's Priest himself digresses after the manner of a preaching friar just before the temptation scene with the fox, reminding us in this outburst about woman's fatal role in history but blaming the digression on Chauntecleer.

Chaucer's changes to *Le Roman de Renart*

Let us first reflect on Chaucer's reworking of his main source for the *Nun's Priest's Tale*. The fruit of the tale can be plucked from among the Branches of *Le Roman de Renart*, the beast epic by Pierre de St. Cloud and other anonymous writers in twelfth- and thirteenth-century France.

---

[1] "*Sic et Non* style of learning" refers to the famous scholastic work by Peter Abelard in which he set out a number of doctrinal statements from the Early Church Fathers that on the surface seemed contradictory, as he paired them. The scholastic game of Sic (it is so) and Non (it is not so) is to bring harmony to these seeming opposites. The reference to the supposed breed of Chauntecleer and Pertelote comes from an overly serious examination by Lalia Phipps Boone of Chaucer's knowledge of medieval chicken breeds because of the similar colors on the throats of the cock and the hen. See her "Chauntecleer and Partlet Identified," *MLN* 64 (1949): 78–81.

Despite his devotion to *auctorites*, Chaucer changes the fable plot he received from a Branch of *Le Roman de Renart* by Pierre de St. Cloud. By so doing, Chaucer altered the masculine nature of his chicken-hero, Chauntecleer. In *Le Roman de Renart*, Chantecler's favorite wife is named Pinte (meaning pint-sized), a hen known for laying large eggs.[2] Pinte asks to hear Chantecler's dream, which has frightened him awake, in order to tell her husband what his enigmatic dream means. The sort of dream that the *Roman's* Chantecler has had that early morning was what Macrobius in his *Commentary on the Dream of Scipio* would label a *somnium*, a dream obscure enough on the surface to require interpretation, often of an allegorical sort. Chantecler has dreamed that a red sleeveless pullover shirt with a bony collar has swallowed and confined him inside it. In *Le Roman de Renart*, Pinte suggests that the bony-collared red pullover is the fox, whom she and her sister hens have seen hiding among the cabbages. Chantecler defies his wife's interpretation, saying that no fox could possibly break through the formidable spiny hedge into their yard. In essence, then, the cocky Chantecler scoffs at Pinte's accurate interpretation of his dream: that the fox is lying in wait to swallow Chantecler. Here are the relevant lines, in my translation:

In sleeping this sleep which pleased him, the cock began to dream. I don't want you to believe I lie about this, for as he dreamed (it's the truth, read the poet in the story) there came to him in the middle of the vision – I don't know what thing that was in the enclosed courtyard. Thus as he was watching him, he was very much afraid, and then he took a red pullover sweater, the border at the neckline was of bone, and he put this on by force down to his back. Chantecler was in such great pain because of that morning's dream while he slept, and the pullover amazed him because the hole in the neck of the garment was moving along until the sweater completely surrounded him. The neck opening was narrow, and he had such great distress that he awakened from fear; but even more marvelous, he was introducing himself below the chest and he entered there by the neck opening of the pullover so that his head was now in the bottom opening of the sweater and his tail was in the upper part of the garment. Because of the dream he trembled, thinking he would be ill-treated. Because of the fearful vision witnessed, he has awakened and regained consciousness, and the cock says: "Holy Spirit, keep my body today from prison and put me in safe protection." Then he returned at great speed as one who could not trust himself and came running to the hens who were under the thorn-hedge. He didn't stop until he came to

---

[2] See Mario Roques' edition of the B MS of *Le Roman de Renart* (Paris: Librairie Honoré Champion, 1972): IIIa 4130. The reader should note that the spelling *Chantecler* always refers to the cock in the *Roman de Renart*, and the spelling *Chauntecleer* always refers to the cock in the *Nun's Priest's Tale*.

them. He calls to one side Pinte, in whom he believes most: "Pinte, this is no hidden need. I am very sorrowful and distressed; I have great fear of being betrayed by a bird or by a wild beast who can soon do damage to me."

"Avoi," says Pinte, "sweet, dear sir, you ought not to say that. You do evil to say that something can frighten you. I will say to you: 'Come along!' By all the saints that I pray to, you resemble the dog who cries before the rock has fallen on him. Of what one have you had such fear? Now tell me what you have dreamed."

"What?" says the cock, "You don't know? I have dreamed just now a strange dream. Alongside the burrow of this barn I saw a very evil vision which has turned me pale. All the story that I shall tell you I shall never lie about. Will you be able to counsel me in this? I think when I was sleeping a beast that I did not know came carrying a red pullover which it made me put on by force, which was done without chisel or scissors. The border around the neckline was made of bones, all white, but it was very hard. It had turned away the skin outside. The sweater was so turned about that I was dressed in it through the upper part of the pullover first, but it was so very small that I was stuck in there. I put on the pullover in that odd way, and then afterwards I couldn't take it off because the tail was above. Then I awoke in that state. I have become very sad because of that dream. Pinte, don't be amazed if my body shakes and trembles but tell me what this dream appears to mean to you. I have been grieved so much by this dream. By that faith which you owe me, do you know what this signifies?"

Pinte, whom he trusts so much, answers: "You have told me," says she, "the dream. But, if it pleases God, that was a lie. However I am not willing to answer you in this way, for I will be very able to give you an explanation about the dream. This thing which you saw in your sleep, that carried the red pullover and distressed you before, was the fox, as you truly know. You can well perceive him in the sweater which is red and that he was clothing you in by force. The bone edging of the neckline was his teeth by which he would pull you inside. The opening in the garment where the head normally goes through, which wasn't right and which was so evil and narrow, that is the throat of the beast which pressed your head. You were entering that place without fail, as you will see, and then the tail will be above. Before that will be, if God aids me, neither silver nor gold will save you. The skin was turned out, it's true, since the skin is always pushed about when the feathers are brushed the wrong way, when it is pulled about more and reversed. Now you have heard without fail the significance of the dream. Quite surely I say this to you: before midday has passed, this will happen to you, it's the truth. If you are willing to believe me, let's retreat, for he has hidden other times in that thorn-hedge to deceive and betray us. I know that truly."

When he had heard the response that Pinte had explained: "Pinte," says he, "you were so very foolish in what you spoke when you said I would be overtaken and that the conquering beast is in the yard. I swear, cursed be 500 who ask! You haven't said anything which I myself hold to. I don't believe one bit that evil is coming to me. I shall not have evil from this dream."

"Sire," says she, "God grant that! But, if it is not as I have said to you, I grant you without contradiction that I am not at all your friend."

"Sweetheart," says he, "that doesn't matter at all. The dream has turned into a fable." (*Le Roman de Renart*, Branch IIIa 4175–4315)

In Chaucer's tale, Pertelote, unlike Pinte, is not known as she "qui plus savoit" [she "who knows the most" – see *Roman* IIIa 4129]. The clear implication of this branch of the beast epic is that Chantecler especially likes Pinte because she is so smart. Perhaps Pertelote is represented as a woman/hen that my students would label "airhead," for, after all, she only knows part of a distich of Cato as her sole *auctorite* to quote during the one-sided debate with her husband/brother. Chaucer developed this bird debate into the first major division of his tale with an argument on the efficacy of dreams far longer than in the *Roman* (compare *NPT* 2921–3156, the debate on the efficacy of dreams, to *Roman* IIIa 4263–4315, Pinte's true interpretation of Chantecler's dream followed by his sudden dismissal – in one line – of the dream as a fable). Chaucer's greatly enlarged bird debate between Chauntecleer and Pertelote shifts the portrayal of masculinity dramatically from the boastful hero who chooses to ignore his dream in *Le Roman de Renart*. Chauntecleer, on the contrary, is absolutely correct in concluding that his dream of the yellow-red beast with the black-tipped ears and tail will bring him "adversitee" (3153). And clearly too, Chauntecleer has won the debate on dreams with an overwhelming line-up of *auctorites*. Yet Chaucer shifts the vanity of Chantecler, who feels his "castle yard" is impenetrable (IIIa 4149–59), to the vanity of Chauntecleer, who is so pleased with his learning that he misses the obvious conclusion of his dream – to take cover from this hound-like beast he has never seen before. Further, the intellectual splendor of Chauntecleer's debate serves to seduce Pertelote and, perhaps, the cock himself.

Chaucer changes his beast epic source to alter Chauntecleer's masculine portrayal. In the enigmatic dream of Chantecler in *Le Roman de Renart*, he says the beast that appears with the red shirt is not really identifiable – but all the dream is unclear, really. When Pinte begins interpreting the dream, she knows at once that this enigmatic beast of the dream is Renart, for the fox had broken through the hedge into the cabbages earlier that day, a fact which she had asserted unsuccessfully earlier before Chantecler had his dream (see this discussion in *Roman* IIIa 4133–59). Pinte and the other hens who have seen the fox have had the good sense to flee the fox by going into the house (*Roman* IIIa 4127–28). In the context of Branch IIIa, Chantecler may be as cocky and self-satisfied as the rich villein who owns him, Constance des Noes. Constance has enormous supplies of food and is as rich a villein, perhaps, as Chaucer's own Franklin, all of his property being safely surrounded with oak pickets and hawthorn hedges (see lines 4069–89, which describes Constance's villa as "la forteresce.") Rather than being the knight-cock with heraldic colors that Chaucer depicts, Chantecler in the *Roman* is a self-satisfied country squire who thinks his chickenyard impenetrable, a chicken version of Constance des Noes, the proud villein. Part of the increased mock-heroic effect of Chaucer's work comes about from the mixture of cock and knight in Chauntecleer rather than cock and villein. The assumption that somehow Chauntecleer most nearly resembles the noble class is very clear in the head-to-toe description or *efficacio* in lines 2859–64. Not only is he compared to fine jewels and precious metal, but he is also compared to a standard set of heraldic coats-of-arms colors – red, black, blue, white, and gold. The dark red coral from the deeper ocean reefs was especially precious in a day before diving gear, and the jet so prized, polished, and engraved in medieval Whitby, Yorkshire, where it was found embedded in the eroding cliffs, was a hard black gemstone, midway between coal and diamond. "Asure" (2862) is not only the heraldic color blue, as gold is also an heraldic color, but like the black jet and the red coral, also heraldic colors, it represents a gemstone, *lapis lazuli*. Further proof of Chauntecleer's nobility, hidden amidst the poverty of the widow's house, is his jewel-like red comb, crenelated like the nobles' castle walls in this *efficacio*. If that head-to-toe description were not enough, his unequivocally noble description later in the tale, connected directly with his successful sexual "conquest" of Pertelote that spring morning, is so laughably chicken-like and vainly human at the same time – mock-heroic chicken-man in his essence. As he defies his dream, his pride swells to regal proportions:

> "For al so siker as *In principio*,
> *Mulier est hominis confusio* –
> Madame, the sentence of this Latyn is,
> 'Womman is mannes joye and al his blis.'
> For whan I feele a-nyght your softe syde –
> Al be it that I may nat on yow ryde,
> For that oure perche is maad so narwe, allas –
> I am so ful of joye and of solas,
> That I diffye bothe sweven and dreem."
> And with that word he fley doun fro the beem,
> For it was day, and eke his hennes alle,
> And with a chuk he gan hem for to calle,
> For he hadde founde a corn, lay in the yerd.
> Real he was, he was namoore aferd.
> He fethered Pertelote twenty tyme,
> And trad her eke as ofte, er it was pryme.

He looketh as it were a grym leoun,
And on his toos he rometh up and doun;
Hym deigned nat to sette his foot to grounde.
He chukketh whan he hath a corn yfounde,
And to hym rennen thanne his wyves alle.
Thus roial, as a prince is in his halle,
Leve I this Chauntecleer in his pasture,
And after wol I telle his aventure.   (VII 3163–86)

I have set this passage out at length because it is at the heart of the presentation of masculinity in the *Nun's Priest's Tale*. As Chaucer or the Nun's Priest builds towards the mock-heroic, pseudo-scientific pedantry of the fable portion of the tale following this description of Chauntecleer as princely hunter-gatherer, cocky lover, and the sort of proud cock found on real coats-of-arms, not only is Chauntecleer now on a level with those noble tragedies in the *Monk's Tale*, but he also has little connection with the Chantecler of *Le Roman de Renart*. Nowhere in Branch IIIa does Chantecler make love to Pinte: he only makes fun of her fearfulness in seeing a fox he is sure is not in the yard and rejects her interpretation of his *somnium*. If Chantecler is dismissive by nature, Chauntecleer is cock-sure and lusty. In the two works, there is a sort of common ground in the pride the two cocks take in their little world, but in Chauntecleer's case this pride seems to be connected to his display of sexual prowess with the favored Pertelote.

The debate between man and woman

Because the debate between Chauntecleer and Pertelote occupies 236 lines of the total 626 lines of Chaucer's tale, we will examine it carefully here for its emphasis on the textual masculinity of Chauntecleer. We must admit that Chauntecleer's shift to the male roles of scholar on dreams and devaluer of his wife's learning and experience really stems initially, after he shares his frightening dream with Pertelote, from a desire to redress the injury to his male ego in being called a fearful coward. Note these excerpts from his wife's reaction to his fear:

"Now han ye lost myn herte and al my love!
I kan nat love a coward, by my feith!
. . .
How dorste ye seyn, for shame, unto youre love
That any thyng myghte make yow aferd?
Have ye no mannes herte, and han a berd?
Allas! And konne ye been agast of swevenys?"

(2910–11, 2918–21)

One of the ways the husband's male ego counters Pertelote's charge of cowardice is to draw attention to her lack of learning. After all, has she not started her argument against dreams by drawing on her housewifely lore about upset stomachs and Chauntecleer's overabundance of this or that humor, has she not quoted in the midst of her argument only part of a distich from Cato translated into English ("Ne do no fors of dremes" [2941]), and has she not concluded with a catalogue of herbal remedies related to Chauntecleer's apparent need for a good laxative (see 2922–69)? Chauntecleer pedantically thanks Pertelote for her lore about herbal cures, but he moves right on to the main thrust of his argument which, stated plainly, runs like this: Pertelote, you paraphrase part of a distich of Cato; Cato is a schoolboy author; men (like me) have moved on to read books of much higher authority than Cato's *Distichs*; and the common-sense experience of living proves that dreams can come true (2970–83). Chauntecleer's retreat to the bookish world of men with hierarchical *auctorites* leads him to overlook not only the full distich of Cato that Pertelote cites partially (a short but also bookish answer to her citation), but also the greater wisdom of the *Disticha Catonis* in helping him avoid the dangers lurking in the chicken yard for the cock that Friday.[3] If the comment about Pertelote's not having read the legend of St. Kenelm is Chauntecleer's not-very-subtle way of saying that Pertelote cannot read at all, then the cock's urging that his wife should look carefully at the Old Testament and "reed" (3130) of Joseph is pouring salt on the wound of her deprivation of learning. Of course, Pertelote may be able to read Cato and the Old Testament, but there is something about Chauntecleer's private enthusiasm for his texts here that denotes female exclusion from his books: "By God! I hadde levere than my sherte / That ye hadde rad his legende, as have I" (3120–21). This educational exclusion is nicely epitomized by his outburst in clucking rooster terms during the second story from "oon of the gretteste auctour that *men* rede" (2984; emphasis mine). Says he,

> "And certes in the same book I rede,
> Right in the nexte chapitre after this –
> I gabbe nat, so have I joye or blis." (3064–66)

The last of these lines parallels the hen-like, monosyllabic cackle of Pertelote on herbal remedies: "Pekke hem up right as they growe and ete hem yn" (2967). These are moments when both Pertelote and Chauntecleer leave the world of fable where they represent a woman and a man and enter the world of the sudden mock-heroic drop, the world where they can only be chickens. In Chaucer's added debate, not found in the major sources, Pertelote and Chauntecleer have combined the herbal medicine lore of the noblewomen with the

---

3   Paul R. Thomas, "Cato on Chauntecleer: Chaucer's Sophisticated Audience," *Neophilologus* 72 (1988): 278–83.

textual learning of the noblemen. Yet, at the climactic moments in their bird debate, Pertelote and Chauntecleer sound more like enthusiastic chickens than noble folk.

One of the devices Chaucer uses to mock masculinity and humanity in the *Nun's Priest's Tale* relates to these chicken-like lines. In the *Roman*, the three-line description of Pinte shifts back and forth between woman and chicken: "Pinte . . . who knows the most, / she who lays the biggest eggs, / who roosts just to the right of the cock" (IIIa 4129–31; my translation). Just as these *Roman* lines describe Pinte in anthropomorphic terms (she "who knows the most") and then quickly shift in a mock-heroic way to zoomorphic terms ("She who lays the biggest eggs"), Chaucer also describes Pertelote and Chauntecleer in a shifting, mock-heroic way.

The language of *fin amor* or courtly love in these descriptions stems from the *Roman*. In Branch II of Manuscript B, as Renart gazes down at his own reflection in the well, he mistakes that "portrait" for the face of his beloved Hermeline, whom he loves with *fin amor* – "qu'aime d'amor fine" (II 3416). Chaucer builds the *fin amor* relationship between Chauntecleer and Pertelote until the hen becomes more important and more integral to the meaning of the story than Russell the fox, a major change from the emphasis upon Renart and Chantecler in *Le Roman de Renart*. Pertelote is one of Chauntecleer's seven hens with whom he did "al his plesaunce" (2866) and is "the faireste hewed on hir throte" (2869). Chaucer completes the description of the hen in terms of the ideal lady in a *fin amor* relationship in lines 2870-76. Pertelote knows all about being a fair, courtly "damoysele" (anthropomorphic) and has known this since she was "seven nyght" old (zoomorphic).

The same mock-heroic drop occurs in that mixture of masculine vanity and masculine sexual seduction at the end of the debate on dreams. Chauntecleer is sure that his dream will bring him adversity (anthropomorphic), and yet he is willing to dismiss "bothe sweven and dreem" (3171) for the beauty of Pertelote's face, "so scarlet reed" (3161) about her eyes (zoomorphic). But amid Chauntecleer's seductive talk, the male vanity mistranslates a Latin phrase to show up Pertelote's lack of learning. Chauntecleer is also seducing himself here through his clever lie. Perhaps more importantly, the pedantic cock pretends after citing a welter of *auctorites* on dreams that he needs another text to authorize his joy and bliss in making love to Pertelote. "*In principio / Mulier est hominis confusio*" becomes "Womman is mannes joye and al his blis" (3163–64, 3166). A more accurate translation of this combination of phrases would be, "In the beginning, woman is man's downfall (or ruin)." As E. Talbot Donaldson has said, "The age-old question of woman is answered – in one breath, as it were – by two equally valid if mutually exclusive commonplaces: woman is man's ruination and woman is all man's bliss."[4] Of course, these

---

4   E. T. Donaldson, *Chaucer's Poetry: An Anthology for the Modern Reader* (New York: The Ronald Press Co., 1958), 942–43.

proverbial truths need not be "mutually exclusive" if woman is man's downfall
or ruin when she is his "joye and al his blis" (3166). Since Chauntecleer is so
uxorious that he cannot pass the day in the safety of the widow's cottage – for
the Nun's Priest does lament, even if with tongue in cheek, that the cock "fleigh
fro the bemes" (3339) – Chauntecleer exposes his masculine ego to the
"*confusio*" personified by Daun Russell.

Pertelote interprets Chauntecleer's dream as an example of superfluity of
humors, that excess of bodily fluids being shown by the colors of the beast in
Chauntecleer's dream. Further, Chaucer has changed the dream in the fable
from an enigmatic *somnium* to a literal *visio*, the sort of dream Macrobius in
his classical/medieval commentary on dreams describes as revealing the future
in an exact pictorial way. We learn in Chaucer's tale that Chauntecleer has never
seen a fox before since he describes him as "a beest / Was lyk an hound"
(2899–2900). Pertelote, unlike her literary forebear Pinte, is not described as
the hen who lays big eggs but is rather distinguished from her sisters as being
"the fairest hewed on hir throte" (2869) and as possessing since one week of
age such courtly traits that label her as "curteys . . ., discreet, and debonaire, /
And compaignable" (2871–72). In *fin amor* or courtly love terms, she is a
fitting lady/sister/paramour for her knightly lord Chauntecleer. Yet in the
chicken world of her nativity, she has learned all this courtly business in just a
week!

Chaucer has redirected his characterization of Chauntecleer's favorite wife
away from wise dream interpretation and the laying of super-sized eggs to a
misinterpretation of the cock's dream based on her pragmatic knowledge of
herbal remedies and her misunderstanding of Cato's distich on dreams and to
a Pertelote who has become more of a sexual partner than a hen noted for her
production of Extra Large Grade A eggs. After greeting the day, strutting around
like a lion, and finding food for his wives, the cock leaves his *auctorites* behind
quite readily. The closeness of Pertelote on the beam while they were still in
the house has been a great motivator, but we know as soon as he mistranslates
Secundus's definition of woman that the cock's irony will rebound upon him.
Woman should not be all of the bliss and joy of man. The medieval ear would
pick up the irony of that line at once. Chauntecleer proves to be the embodiment
of Secundus's definition more than Pertelote does. Nowhere does she ask him
to make love to her; that is his doing. He confounds himself trying to run his
noble little chicken-world as usual that May morning. His excessive, perhaps
mock-heroic scale of love-making, even by fowl standards, shows him as the
"*insaturabilis bestia*" [insatiable beast] of the philosopher's definition.[5]

---

5   I quote from that portion of the *Altercatio Hadriani Augusti et Secundi philosophi* [The
Contention of the Emperor Hadrian Augustus and the Philosopher Secundus] that defines
woman, including the tag as found in *The Nun's Priest's Tale* (VII 3164): "*Quid est mulier?
Hominis confusio, insaturabilis bestia, continua sollicitudo, indesinens pugna, viri conti-
nentis naufragium, humanum mancipium.*" [What is woman? The confounding of man, an

Chauntecleer as the textual debater on dreams and as the cocky lover ("He fethered Pertelote twenty tyme, / And trad hire eke as ofte, er it was pryme" [3177–78]) contrasts with the Chantecler who wants to deny his true dream since he knows his yard is impenetrable but whose wife Pinte knows what his dream really means. The upshot of Chaucer's changes is the extended debate between the cock and hen on the significance of dreams, a sterling display of Chauntecleer as the learned man who can retell numerous *auctorites* that his wife has never read – because, as the tale implies, she can't read ("By God! I hadde levere than my sherte / That ye hadde rad his legende, as have I" [3120–21]). This cock-man has read so many texts but still has not achieved the wisdom of Pinte in the *Roman*, for though he suspects he will have "adversitee" (3153) because of his vision, he cannot postpone sex with Pertelote in order that he avoid the danger of the hound-like beast lurking in the yard that early morning.

In addition to his adding the debate on dreams between Chauntecleer and Pertelote, thereby showing cocky male learning succumbing in the end to Pertelote's overwhelmingly sexy face with its scarlet-red eyes, Chaucer has also portrayed Chauntecleer as a man who uses his learning to seduce his favorite wife. But we will see the tables turned in a proper display of poetic justice in the temptation scene. Here Daun Russell quotes from a favorite *auctorite* that our textual cock has never read, showing the fox to be much more tricky and devilishly learned than he ever is in any of the sources.

Chaucer's temptation and chase scenes

If the earlier debate has shown Chauntecleer's proud and haughty masculinity against a background of Pertelote's Cato and her knowledge of herbs and worms, the temptation scene matches the two men of the fable, the cock and the fox. And if textual knowledge that does not change the reader is arguably a chief feature of masculinity in the *Nun's Priest's Tale*, we have the same lesson illustrated in Russell's allusion to the tale of the cock from the *Speculum Stultorum* as in Chauntecleer's overthrow of all his texts for a little mirth.

Before Russell ironically alludes to his reading of "Daun Burnel the Asse" (3312), he spends much of his time engaged in the flattery that will prove his downfall with Chauntecleer during the chase scene. It is clear that Russell is relying on his previous experience with Chauntecleer's father to overpower the

---

insatiable beast, an uninterrupted disquiet, an incessant battle, the shipwreck of the man nearby, a human slave (my translation)]. The reference to "the shipwreck of the man nearby" recalls in an ironically skewed way one of Chauntecleer's many *exempla*. See VII 3064–3104. The version of the *Altercatio Hadriani* that I quote here is found in Vincent of Beauvais' *Speculum Historiale*, Book X, Chapter lxxi. See Vincentius Bellovacensis, *Speculum Maius* (Duaci: Ex officina typographica Baltazaris Belleri, 1624; rpt. Graz: Akademische Druck-und Verlagsanstalt, 1964–65) in 4 vols.

cock and carry him off to his den. In one of the most telling mock-heroic passages in the tale, Russell tries to convince Chauntecleer (and us) that a cock-a-doodle-doo is the equivalent of an angel's song:

> "I am nat come your conseil for t'espye,
> But trewely, the cause of my comynge
> Was oonly for to herkne how that ye synge.
> For trewely, ye have as myrie a stevene
> As any aungel hath that is in hevene.
> . . .
> Save yow, I herde nevere man so synge
> As dide youre fader in the morwenynge.
> Certes, it was of herte, al that he song.
> And for to make his voys the moore strong,
> He wolde so peyne hym that with bothe his yen
> He moste wynke, so loude he wolde cryen,
> And stonden on his tiptoon therwithal,
> And strecche forth his nekke long and smal."
>
> (3288–92, 3301–08)

Perhaps the angel's presence in heaven is part of Russell's characteristic irony throughout his flattery. Are we to believe that this old fox who is "worse than a feend" (3286) (since he wants to harm Chauntecleer) is one of the fallen angels who remembers the songs of the heavenly choir? Or is Daun Russell wishing a heavenly journey soon for the raucous-voiced cock whereby the cock may do his own comparing? Fortunately, most of us have heard the "song" of a rooster and can appreciate the fox's ironic sense of humor. Perhaps to us the song of man, to which Chauntecleer's heavenly voice is compared, sounds much better than a cock-a-doodle-doo, but that may be the point of Russell's comparisons: men too are vain about their voices.

In moralized fable-*exempla*, the fox or Renart is sometimes allegorized as the devil. In a reworking of a story in Branch IIIa of the *Roman* that just follows the cock and fox story, Nicholas Bozon tells of Renart's trying to convince the dove (the bird is the even smaller tit in the *Roman*) to come down from the tree to kiss him, for King Noble the lion has declared a general peace between all the beasts: no longer will large beast fight against little beast. But the dove is wary since Renart has never left his brothers alone. Just then a hunter with four dogs appears, and the fox bids the dove farewell since he does not dare remain. The dove points out that these dogs are also their brother beasts and are, therefore, surely included in the general peace the king has declared. Nicholas adds an anthropomorphic detail not found in the *Roman* original when he has the fox say that he cannot be certain that these dogs have seen the king's letters. The clear implication of this passage is that the dogs can read – they are literate hounds just as Chauntecleer and Russell are literate "men." In his *moralitas*, Nicholas Bozon allegorizes the fox as a devil:

> Thus, if the devil entices you and counsels you to sin for the purpose of improving you, thus tell him that he show you the letter that he had from God to pardon you for such sins; and I believe that it would well be necessary to seek this letter in his coffers. For St. Peter says this: "God does not spare any of his angels when they sin; how, therefore, will He spare us wretches of this time when we sin?" God has not spared the angels in their sins.[6]

The peculiar mixture between man, chicken, and fox in Chaucer's temptation scene adds greatly to the humor of the tale. According to his chicken heritage, Chauntecleer reacts instinctively as soon as he sees the fox amidst the cabbages and wants to run away:

> For natureelly a beest desireth flee
> Fro his contrarie, if he may it see,
> Though he never erst hadde seyn it with his ye. (3279–81)

Nevertheless, the Nun's Priest/Chaucer chooses to compare the cock's first sighting of a fox to a "man that was affrayed in his herte" (3278). And once Russell's flattery sets in, all traces of the "natural" cock are replaced by Chauntecleer as man.

After having read the *Nun's Priest's Tale* many times, I began observing varieties of breeds of chickens to see if Daun Russell's (and Renart's) trick of getting the cock to shut his eyes were really a possibility. From the hundreds of chickens I have observed sleeping and awake, I would conclude that none of them, cock or hen, can close his or her eyes at any time. The very fact that I have checked out such chicken facts shows the excesses Chaucer's mock-heroic tale sometimes drives critics to embrace! It is Chauntecleer, the consummate chicken-man, who is susceptible to flattery. Alert cocks and vigilant Christians may not close their eyes, but real men often do. By closing his eyes to the reality of his cock-a-doodle-doo, Chauntecleer's slender neck in this sign of Taurus (that resides in the neck of zodiacal man – see 3194) is much more easily grasped by the fiendish fox. Like many a son before him, Chauntecleer nearly loses his life by trying to outdo his father. And Chauntecleer's father – called

---

[6] See II Peter 2:4. This moralized fable is number 61 on the theme of "Quod in solo Christo spes nostra est figenda" [in Christ alone is our hope fixed] in *Les Contes Moralisés de Nicole de Bozon, Frère Mineur*, ed. Lucy Toulmin Smith and Paul Meyer, SATF (Paris: Librairie de Firmin Didot et Cie., 1899; rpt. New York: Johnson Reprint Corp., 1968), 84–85. The English translation of the *moralitas* is mine.

Chanteclin in the *Roman* – has already been captured and eaten, taken probably in the same way as the flattered, angelic-voiced Chauntecleer.[7]

If it is true that Chauntecleer fails to recognize how Cato might help him on that "fateful" Friday, it is also true that Russell's allusion to "Daun Burnel the Asse" (3312–16) ends up being the text that might have saved his chicken meal. The allusion to the *Speculum Stultorum* is a daring move by the fox, for the debate on dreams has shown what a learned cock Chauntecleer is. Part of the message about man and his pretensions here is that learning is only as valid as its application. For instance, the wildly wonderful excesses of the Nun's Priest's rhetoric as applied to the fate of the chicken are redundant as soon as Chauntecleer flies up to safety in the tree during the chase scene. The apostrophes comparing Russell to a murderer, Judas Iscariot, Ganelon, and Sinon, and cursing the day Chauntecleer flew from the safety of the beams of the widow's house (3226–31), the discussion of God's "forwityng" (3243) that invokes such *auctores* as St. Augustine, Boethius, and Archbishop Bradwardine on the subject of free choice, predestination, and simple and conditional necessity (3234–51), the antifeminist *repetitio* on women's counsels and the fall of Adam and Eve (a discussion the woman-ruled and woman-counseled Nun's Priest tries to shift to the cock's blame) (3252–66), the slyly ironic citation of Physiologus on mermaids, indicating Chauntecleer's self-deception as his own mermaid (3269–72), the *digressio* on flattery (3325–30), the further apostrophes to destiny or fate, to Venus, and to Geoffrey de Vinsauf, whose *Poetria Nova* the Nun's Priest hopes to emulate in order the "Friday for to chide" (3351), the classical comparisons of the falls of Troy and Carthage to the lamentation of the hens in the chicken yard (3355–68), the final apostrophe comparing the cries of the hens to the wives of the Roman senators massacred by Nero (3369–73), and the comparison during the chase of the noise of the beasts and humans involved to the commotion of "Jakke Straw and his meynee" (3394) as they killed the Flemish taking away their jobs during the English Rising of 1381 – all of this rhetorical outpouring by the Nun's Priest is totally inapplicable to Chauntecleer's destiny and is a part of the mock-heroic decoration of this tale without a fatal ending.

When Chauntecleer flatters Russell that he should stand up to the pursuing masses and state his intention to eat the cock, Russell shows he has forgotten the *moralitas* of his brief *exemplum* from the *Speculum Stultorum* [Mirror of Fools] to prove the wisdom, discretion, and subtlety of a beast (3312–19). Chauntecleer has apparently not read the *Speculum*, for he fails to react to this allusion. If Chauntecleer or his departed father (and, in the chase scene, Russell)

---

7   Of course, Chauntecleer's mother may have been taken at the time in the same meal (VII 3296–97). The Old French equivalent of Chaucer's euphemistic phrase "greet ese" [grant aisse], is found everywhere in *Le Roman de Renart* to indicate Renart's having just finished a great meal. See, for example, this use of "aisse" meaning the state of Renart after a large meal in two of the branches preceding Branch IIIa at I 504–07 and II 3395.

had had the wisdom, discretion, and subtlety of the cock in this *Speculum exemplum*, each beast would have experienced a different fate. Chauntecleer's ironic mannish mistranslation of *"Mulier est hominis confusio"* (3164) certainly does not surpass the fox's bravura in referring to the tale of the vengeful cock. By a neat inversion, Nigel de Longchamps' cock succeeds against Gundulfus, the priest's son, by refusing to crow and thereby not waking the household on the morning of Gundulfus's supposed ordination to the priesthood, whereas Chauntecleer fails to revenge his father's death by succumbing to Russell's blandishment to crow – just as his father did before him.

The story from the *Speculum Stultorum* is too long to set out here fully, but a summary will show the subtlety needed by Chauntecleer, the bookish man, during the temptation scene and the wisdom needed by Russell, the ironic, tricky reader, during the chase scene.

Having been injured by Gundulfus's whip when he was a tiny chick, the cock awaits the moment of his revenge – a revenge that strikes when the cock reigns as rooster some six years later (lines 1265–1312). On the eve of Gundulfus's ordination, his relatives have come to his father's house for a pre-Christmas feast to celebrate the family honor: the priest's son will soon take his father's place, just as the cock has already taken his father's place in the roost (lines 1313–30). The cock overhears Gundulfus specify to his servants the early hour he needs to be awakened for the long journey to the city the next day – an hour the servants will know by the crowing of the cock. The cock hears this, holds his tongue, and inwardly exults at the chance to wreak his vengeance on Gundulfus (lines 1331–42). Everyone in the household succumbs to their overeating and drinking, including the servants. Even after cockcrow has passed, the cock refuses to crow, calling his wife a fool for chiding him for not crowing that morning. The married chickens continue to argue (could this be where Chaucer got his idea for the man-woman debate at the beginning of his tale?) and finally the cock's wife breaks the silence of the night with an outbreak of squawking (lines 1357–76). One in the household chides the hen for invading the cock's territory for "Although a chicken cackle in the night, / No sooner will she make the sun arise" (lines 1377–80). As the household sleeps on, Gundulfus, like Chauntecleer, has a prophetic dream. Gundulfus dreams he has been ordained and is dressed in his robes to say the mass. The cock plays the role of the cantor in the dream, taking over the mass from Gundulfus, thanking the Lord in the introit for all He has done for them, draining the chalice at the appropriate moment, and then refusing to say "Depart" when the Mass was over. At this Gundulfus cried out to his servants, "Is this the day?" But they urged him to stay in bed until the cock crowed "who knows the hours / Of night and signifies each by his song" (lines 1385–1404). The servants' final words of praise for the watchman-cock are that by nature he is not capable of keeping silent (lines 1415–16). These details, of course, are chicken matters and, therefore, not seemingly germane to masculinities in Chaucer. But like a vengeful man, the cock of the story keeps quiet until Gundulfus has overslept.

Arising in a panic and rushing to the cathedral on a horse without benefit of saddle or bridle, a half-dressed, slightly tipsy Gundulfus is soon thrown by his steed and has to make his way by foot the rest of the way. Alas, he arrives too late to be ordained. The change in Fortune, of which the cock is but a minister (lines 1469–70 and 1475–76) goes far beyond the bounds of simple vengeance for the cock's broken leg, for both of Gundulfus's parents die, and he is forced to leave home and become a mendicant (lines 1495 ff.)[8]

It is significant that Chaucer has the manly learning of both the cock and the fox turn upon them as they reap poetic justice in this tale. The *Nun's Priest's Tale* is a tale that defines mock-heroic man rather thoroughly, through the words of the cock and the hen, the cock and the fox, and the Nun's Priest. In the temptation and chase scenes, the learning of the cock and the fox are contrasted: Chauntecleer has used his "mannes herte" (2920) to promulgate book learning in the cause of winning domestic arguments. Russell, as ever the tricky fox, invokes the *Speculum Stultorum* to show up the comparative textual ignorance of his prey, the cock (just as Chauntecleer has done earlier with his wife). The debater and the mocker both have their comeuppance for their misapplication of texts. The grim world of the tragedies of the *Monk's Tale* is finally reversed as Chauntecleer flies upward into the tree. Lest we take all of this chaff about men's prideful behavior too seriously, we can finally rejoice in a happy ending for a Chauntecleer who does not keep his mouth shut during the chase scene and who also finds that flattery sometimes works to his advantage. The proverbial *moralitates* of Chaucer's fable have proven again to be ambiguous when applied to man and masculine behavior.

8   I have consulted the standard edition in Latin. Nigel de Longchamps, *Speculum Stultorum*, ed. John H. Mozley and Robert R. Raymo (Berkeley: University of California Press, 1960), University of California Publications, English Studies 18. The English translation identifies Nigel by his other commonly known name: *The Book of Daun Burnel the Ass: Nigellus Wireker's Speculum stultorum*, trans. Graydon W. Regenos (Austin: University of Texas Press, 1959). Both brief translations come from page 80 of Regenos's book.

II. *Troilus and Criseyde*

"Slydyng" Masculinity
in the Four Portraits of Troilus

STEPHANIE DIETRICH

Recent criticism on Troilus's "lovesickness" and the resulting passivity suggests that if Troilus is not exactly emasculated, he is at least "feminized" by his erotic experience. While these studies have been successful at delineating gender boundaries in characterization, they have failed to recognize how much gender slippage the language of Chaucer's *Troilus and Criseyde* reveals. Although the discourses of feminist criticism and queer theory have supplied valuable tools and vocabulary for discussing gender construction in texts, ultimately evidence of Chaucer's methodology in constructing "masculinity" in Troilus must be found within the text itself. In this essay I will focus on the gender slippage achieved through linguistic slippage in the four portraits of Troilus, taking them as rhetorical units suitable for isolated and sustained rhetorical analysis. My examination will reveal that in his construction of Troilus's masculinity, Chaucer both conforms to expected literary conventions for the characterization of a male hero and invents details that resist essentialized models of gender. The result is a double-edged and culturally complex approach to characterization in which Chaucer undermines gender expectations in his presentation of Troilus's "masculinity" in the middle two portraits, where the hero "slydes" away from anticipated gender roles, while framing these with a more essentialized masculine characterization in the first and last portraits.

Portrait 1: Troilus's masculine posturing

In the first portrait of Troilus (I, 183–89), Chaucer presents a young knight clearly at ease with his status as warrior and leader. Chaucer omits, however, Benoît's emphasis on the hero as a chivalric lover, as well as Boccaccio's presentation of him as one experienced in love,[1] thus giving the overall impression that Troilus is innocent, has not been tested, and, therefore, is likely to have an "aventure":

> This Troilus, as he was wont to gide
> *His* yonge knyghtes, *lad* hem *up* and *down*
> In thilke *large* temple *on every side*,
> Byholding ay the ladies of the town,
> Now *here*, now *there*; for no devocioun
> Hadde he to non, to *reven* hym his reste,
> But gan to *preise and lakken* whom *hym leste*.[2]   (I, 183–89)

In this portrait Chaucer accords Troilus an overtly masculine posture as both prince of the city and military leader. That the men who follow Troilus are "*his* yonge knyghtes" stresses his position of superiority within the community of male warriors. Aers notes that "Troilus' performance as he leads the 'yonge knyghtes' is a representative one, part of the confirmation of gender relations and power in his culture, part of the daily making of 'masculine' identity as active, free, predatory subject."[3] The term "performance" here elucidates a point central to this portrait and reflects decidedly on the issue of gender – that Troilus's behavior, although he does not view it as such, is not an essential part of him but learned by imitating men in similar positions. First, Chaucer reinforces the masculinization of Troilus's environment by displacing the significant female role-models of both the hero and heroine. Although we know that Troilus has a mother, Troilus mentions her only once (IV, 1207), and she remains inconsequential within the action; Criseyde's mother, also mentioned once, is presumably dead, indicated by Criseyde's use of the past tense when referring to her (IV, 762). Secondly, Chaucer expands, from his sources, the role and character of Hector, Troilus's older brother, to represent the way Troilus should conduct himself as the youngest son of the king. Yet Troilus fails to act with the wisdom and nobility of Hector with regard to his support of Criseyde, and this contrast illustrates the distance between *acting* (Troilus) and *being* (Hector).

After he is smitten by looking at Criseyde, Troilus quickly attempts to hide

---

[1]   For Benoit's portrait of Troilus, see Barry A. Windeatt, *Oxford Guides to Chaucer: Troilus and Criseyde* (Oxford: Clarendon Press, 1992), 81–82. Boccaccio's Troilus says, "Io provai giá per la mia gran follio / qual fosse questo maladetto foco" (98), which Gordon (*The Story of Troilus* [New York: E. P. Dutton and Co., 1964], 33) translates as "I have found before now by my own great folly what this cursed fire [love] is." All Italian is from *Geoffrey Chaucer: Troilus and Criseyde*, ed. Barry A. Windeatt (London and New York: Longman, 1984).

[2]   The emphasis is mine here and in all quotations from the *Riverside Chaucer* in this paper.

[3]   David Aers, *Community, Gender and Individual Identity: English Writing 1360–1430* (Routledge: London and New York, 1988), 120.

his unexpected and uncontrollable reaction to her and heads to his palace straightaway. His society expects him to be the representative ideal knight, *acting* like a man regardless of the situation, yet his reaction appears to unman him far more than it unmans *his* men, who, in contrast, show a greater daring and, perhaps, a greater confidence in their masculinity, as they actively hunt the women in the temple by letting their eyes "baiten" (I, 192) on them.

That Troilus's only interaction with the women in the temple remains one of distant evaluation ("preise and lakken") signifies *his* superior "masculine" position without placing it in an evaluative position, allowing him to maintain a cavalier manner as "hym leste." The portrait, while emphasizing Troilus's masculinity, illustrates his naiveté as well. He remains unaware of the possibility that his masculinity will be tested in a manner that might challenge his ability to perform, convincingly, his role as the self-assured man. In part, Troilus lacks an awareness of himself because he plays the part of the detached and superior male, with the ironic result that, hunted by Criseyde's gaze and prostrated by love, he becomes passive, submissive, overly emotional, and irrational, characteristics which are typically essentialized as "feminine."

Troilus's patriarchal "performance" consists of his leading his men, his territorial "marking," his disinterested and proud demeanor, all of which culminate in the fulcrum of the poem – the commodification of women in the exchange of prisoners. Troilus remains unaware, however, of the serious social implications (attested to by the connection between Paris's "preise" of Helen and the Trojan War) of his masculine posturing. The emphasis on his superiority in this passage does not focus on his relationship with the other knights as much as with the women. It clearly centers on gender construction – his position as a male among females. Diamond asserts that Troilus's "explicitly masculine self-confidence, attributable to his rank and skill in battle, is linked with contempt for women, expressed in the terminology of the marketplace."[4] The spatial signifiers (up, down, on every side, here, there – all in a large temple) create a sense of the temple as a fair where women are the commodity to be obtained, but they also illuminate the compass of Troilus's "masculine" stride and territorial posturing within this male-dominated domain. Yet he does not perceive the unstable nature of *his* performative masculinity, that it is not an essential aspect of being a man, even though he does acknowledge the "folye" (I, 194) in the behavior of his knights as he mocks *their* eyeing of the women.

In the lines, "Now here, now there; for no devocioun / Hadde he to non, to *reven* hym his reste" (I, 187–88), Chaucer suggests the women's inherent danger to the male community, to their masculinity, with the word "reven." Here, as elsewhere in the poem, the context implies more than the mere "removal" of something, in this case the knight's peace because of love. Rather

---

4   Arlyn Diamond, "The Politics of Love," in *Chaucer in the Eighties*, ed. Julian Wasserman and Robert J. Blanch (Syracuse: Syracuse University Press, 1986), 97.

it connotes the taking of it by force.[5] As in Chaucer's *Knight's Tale*, the desire of the men for women is perceived as "a life-threatening adventure"[6] with the women's attractiveness being equated with aggression. Troilus's assessment of his nearness to death after seeing Criseyde for the first time parallels his shift away from "masculine" behavior, indicating a psychological rather than literal death (although Troilus insists that his physical death is imminent). Clearly he *does* experience a "death" of his belief in who he is, specifically in his masculinity. The narrator later exemplifies this loss of security in Troilus's "masculine" posturing and in the homosocial bond when Criseyde's gaze shoots and pierces through him, as she, with seemingly no effort, takes away his masculinity. Furthermore, after Troilus sees Criseyde in the temple, he chooses to close himself away in his bed chamber rather than seek solace in the company of his men. In the meantime, portrait 1 leaves the reader with an essentialized view of the masculine hero as communal, predatory, and prideful, albeit naive.

Portrait 2: Troilus's masculine vulnerability

Portrait 2 of Troilus (II, 624–644), at a glance, reveals what one anticipates: a hero dressed in armor riding back into the city after a battle with the enemy. Referring to this passage, Muscatine states that "Troilus represents the courtly, idealistic view of experience. . . . It is clear that he is conceived and constructed almost exclusively according to the stylistic conventions of the courtly tradition."[7] Similarly, Mann claims that "Troilus's physical prowess and bravery are carefully established at numerous points in the poem, most notably in the visual image created by the description of his return from the battlefield, watched by the curious Criseyde."[8] These assertions, however, do not hold upon closer inspection of the language of the portrait. Rather than giving his hero the elaborate praise accorded him by Benoît or any of his other sources or following the stylized pattern for the ideal knight, Chaucer immediately leads one to question the stability of Troilus's manliness by varying the expected trope:

[5]   *A Chaucer Glossary*, ed. Norman Davis, et al. (Oxford: Oxford University Press, 1979), 120, notes that this verb in *Troilus and Criseyde* most typically has the meaning of "take, especially by force." *Middle English Dictionary*, "to rob, plunder," 1(a).
[6]   Susan Crane, "Medieval Romance and Feminine Difference in the *Knight's Tale*," SAC 12 (1990): 50.
[7]   Charles Muscatine, *Chaucer and the French Tradition* (Berkeley: University of California Press, 1969), 133.
[8]   Jill Mann, *Geoffrey Chaucer: Feminist Readings* (Atlantic Highlands, NJ: Humanities Press International, 1991), 166.

This Troilus sat on his baye steede
Al armed, save his hed, ful richely;
And *wownded was his hors*, and gan to blede,
On which he rood a pas ful *softely*.
But swich a knyghtly sighte *trewely*
As was on hym, *was nought, withouten faille*,
To loke on Mars, that god is of bataille.

So *lik* a man of armes and a knyght
He was to seen, fulfilled of heigh prowesse,
For bothe he hadde a body and a myght
To don that thing, as wel as hardynesse;
And ek to seen hym in his gere hym dresse,
So *fressh*, so yong, so *weldy semed* he,
It was an heven upon hym for to see.

His *helm tohewen was in twenty places*,
That by a tyssew heng his bak byhynde;
His *sheeld todasshed was with swerdes and maces*,
In which men myghte many an arwe fynde
That thirled hadde horn and nerf and rynde;
And ay the peple cryde, "Here cometh oure joye,
And, next his brother, holder up of Troye!"   (II, 624–44)

As Hodges notes, this description of Troilus is atypical of those found in romances.[9] She states that "one inconvenience of errantry seldom mentioned by medieval authors depicting the ideal knight was the wear and tear of combat on pristine shining armor. Chaucer, however, recognizes this problem in his description of Troilus returning from battle."[10] Thus, Hodges categorizes Troilus and the Knight in the *Canterbury Tales*, whose gypon is "bismotered," as "working knights" because Chaucer infuses them with aspects of realism rather than the external perfection associated with ideal knights of romance literature.[11] Yet Hodges's interpretation of Chaucer's motive overlooks the matter and kind of detail in the portrait: a stain on the gypon is hardly a "helm tohewen . . . in twenty places" or a "sheeld todasshed . . . with swerdes and maces." The words "tohewen" and "todasshed" convey (and, with the morphemic intensifier "to," emphasize) the violence inherent in war and, therefore, supply an element of realism to which Hodges points. They also

---

[9] For an interesting and enlightening comparison of other knights in Chaucer's work, see the portraits of Theseus (I 975–84) and Emetrius (I 2155–86) in the *Knight's Tale*, where Chaucer provides anticipated and unequivocally flattering details.

[10] Laura Hodges, "Costume Rhetoric in the Knight's Portrait: Chaucer's Every-Knight and His Bismotered Gypon," *ChauR* 29 (1995): 275.

[11] Laura Hodges, e-mail to author, March 6, 1996.

clearly express that Troilus has been *acted upon* in an unusually brutal way; he is not idealized like the many knights in romance literature who win battles against their enemies almost single-handedly with "shining" armor intact. Furthermore, the narrative denies Troilus weapons for offensive action (clichéd phallic symbols), revealing only the hero's defensive gear – his armor, helmet, and shield. Although Blamires asserts that Chaucer's description of Troilus's " 'weldy' appearance on horseback after a hard day in the field" adds reassurances about his "manliness,"[12] Troilus's tattered gear and lack of heraldic signifiers undermine, rather than promote, an image of manliness.

The narrator further undercuts Troilus's masculinity by emphasizing the manner in which he rides – "ful *softely*" – and by praising Troilus's appearance and skill with vague modifiers that conflict with the specific and concrete image supplied by his armor: "*fressh*," "*yong*," "*weldy*." Immediately preceding this portrait, the narrator says, "And men criden in the strete, 'Se, Troilus / Hath right now put to flighte the Grekes route!' " (II, 612–13), providing a context in which to interpret the hero: he has been pivotal in winning a battle against the enemy. Although the typical idealized knight does return to court with "fresh" appearance, the specific details concerning the condition of Troilus's armor within this portrait show that, despite the narrator's attempt to present him as ideal, the hero is physically spent, leaving one to question how effective Troilus will be in protecting the city or Criseyde if she chooses to accept his affections. Indeed, the state of his armor defies the meaning of "weldy" – Troilus, if he were in control, agile, and a master of arms, would most likely not be presented in tatters.

Moreover, Troilus rides "softly," a word that implies a weariness or tentativeness atypical of a knight returning victorious from battle. Mann, in her argument that Troilus is a "feminised" hero, calls upon the essentialized gender construct that to have "vulnerability and sensitivity of feeling" is to be, in some sense, "feminine." Nonetheless, rather than emphasize what Mann calls the "generous nobility"[13] of his gentle manner, the passage illuminates the marked shift from his masculine posturing early in Book I, where he is the gazer, to a discernible insecurity at the unusual situation of being a male object of a female gaze.

Later in Book II, when Troilus rides by Criseyde's window once again, this time for the effect it will have on her, the narrator once again uses "Al *softely*" to describe his manner of passing. Although the first ride by her window is not a contrivance and the second is, Troilus's manner is consistently unself-assured, and the second "softly" further undercuts his representation as a "manly" knight. The narrator states that Troilus salutes Pandarus with "dredful chere, and oft his hewes muwe" (II, 1258), obvious signs of his unease in taking a

---

12 Alcuin Blamires, "Questions of Gender in Chaucer, from *Anelia* to *Troilus*," *Leeds Studies in English* 25 (1994): 95.
13 Mann, *Geoffrey Chaucer*, 166.

removed, but active, step in the pursuit of Criseyde. The employment of the word "muwe"[14] implies a mere attempt on Troilus's part to hide his embarrassment. The blushing, parallels that of Criseyde, who "wex as red as rose" just before Troilus's blush (II, 1256), gendering this show of emotion as feminine.

In portrait 2 Chaucer intends to shock, presenting an unusual description of a knight's armor in order to undermine one's sense of Troilus's effectiveness as a warrior and as a suitor of Criseyde by suggesting his physical, emotional and, perhaps, sexual vulnerability. Before his return from the war, the narrator establishes that Troilus has nearly lost his mind over love for Criseyde, with the extreme nature of his madness being underscored by the fact that they do not know each other, that he has seen her only once (in the temple), and that she does not return his gaze. From the first time he sees her in the temple until their rendezvous in Book III, Troilus can do little more than weep and hide beneath his bed covers. His prowess on the field, up to this point, is nothing other than a product of Pandarus's discourse. In his first conversation with Criseyde, her uncle attempts to "sell" her on Troilus by describing his fearlessness in battle:

> "Now here, now ther, he hunted hem so faste,
> Ther nas but Grekes blood – and Troilus.
> Now hem he hurte, and hem al down he caste;
> Ay wher he wente, it was arayed thus:
> He was hire deth, and *sheld* and lif for us,
> That, as that day, ther dorste non withstonde
> Whil that he held his *blody swerd in honde.*"   (II, 197–203)

Because in the poem Chaucer represents rather than presents so much of the action, sections such as this one easily contribute to one's impression that Troilus is a great warrior. Bowers asserts that "Pandarus on his own does a masterful job of manipulating Criseyde's thought and emotions. . . . He offers four detailed vignettes carefully calculated to show Troilus's courage in the field and to suggest something of his manly appearance," but a paragraph later he states that Criseyde sees the Troilus of portrait 2 "exactly as Pandarus had described him."[15] There is, however, much evidence to the contrary. The image

---

14 The *Middle English Dictionary* defines the noun form as literally "a place where hawks are put to molt" but figuratively "a hiding place," but the verb form as "of a hawk: to mew, molt, shed its plumage" and "of persons: to change (color)." Therefore, although editors tend to gloss "muwe" in terms of its noun definition (that Troilus *is* hiding his blush), the verb form definitions, especially since the word in context is a verb, more accurately reflect the situation: Troilus *attempts* to hide (in the "muwe"); however, he is "muwing" – emotionally molting, revealing his embarrassment.

15 John M. Bowers, "How Criseyde Falls in Love," in *The Expansion and Transformation*

of Troilus as a shield, given the literal physical condition of the hero's shield and the image of his brother, Hector, as "the townes *wal*" (II, 154), implies that he *is not* a good protector of the city. Pandarus's detail of the bloody sword, signifying the hero's active and aggressive role in the war and omitted from portrait 2, is a fabrication. In addition, Chaucer provides no arming-of-the-warrior scene, suppresses the scenes where Troilus leaves to go to war (his entry into a "masculine" space),[16] exaggerates the scenes in which Troilus returns from war by making them integral to Criseyde's falling in love with him (his entry into a "feminine" space), and provides obvious self-serving motivation for Pandarus's hyperbolic representations of Troilus.The arming of troops, which Brewer claims is ritualistic and signifies the importance of the warrior's mission, is used in *Sir Thopas*, indicating that Chaucer knew it quite well.[17] Furthermore, the fact that Chaucer adds two portraits that focus on Troilus as a knight makes the omission of an arming scene in *Troilus and Criseyde* puzzling.[18] The poem suggests its hero's status as a great warrior but does little to confirm it. The condition of his armor in the second portrait casts doubt on whether Troilus's tattered armor signifies that he has fought well in battle.

The battered condition of Troilus's horse in the second portrait, a unique Chaucerian invention, further hints at the hero's vulnerability through the rhetorical devices of *effictio* and *notatio*.[19] First, the knight's horse is not strictly utilitarian but rather an extension of its rider, which the linguistic connection bears out. As Edge and Paddock explain, "The close association of the knight and his horse is clearly shown by the titles by which he was known throughout Europe: in France he was a *chevalier*, in Italy a *cavaliere*, in Spain a *caballero*, and in Germany a *ritter*, from the word meaning to ride."[20] The alabaster effigy of the first Earl of Westmorland, Ralph Neville (1364–1425 AD), whose

of Courtly Literature, ed. Nathaniel B. Smith and Joseph T. Snow (Athens: University of Georgia Press, 1980), 144–45.

[16] See Diane Vanner Steinberg, "'We do usen here no wommen for to selle': Embodiment of Social Practices in *Troilus and Criseyde*," *ChauR* 29 (1995): 259–73.

[17] Derek S. Brewer, "The Arming of the Warrior in European Literature and Chaucer," in *Chaucerian Problems and Perspectives: Essays Presented to Paul E. Beichner*, ed. Edward Vasta and Zacharias P. Thundy (Notre Dame: University of Notre Dame Press, 1979), 222.

[18] Brewer, 238.

[19] See *Three Medieval Rhetorical Arts*, ed. James J. Murphy (Berkeley: University of California Press, 1971), 27–108. The section on Geoffrey of Vinsauf discusses the various "rhetorical colors," two of which are the *effictio* (physical description) and *notatio* (character delineation by trait). Marie Collins ("Feminine Response to Masculine Attractiveness in Middle English Literature," *Essays and Studies* 38 [1995]: 13) notes that medieval portrayals most commonly combine the two rhetorical devices.

[20] David Edge and John Miles Paddock, *Arms and Armor of the Medieval Knight: An Illustrated History of Weaponry in the Middle Ages* (New York and Avanel: Crescent Books, 1988), 6.

"martial demeanour is heightened by the severed head of a horse which serves . . . as a pillow,"[21] illustrates this identification.

Early in the poem, before Troilus has seen and fallen in love with Criseyde, Chaucer emphasizes the closeness of the man-horse connection by equating Troilus with a horse, "proude Bayard" (I, 218).[22] While Dares and Joseph of Exeter include the horse as a direct and active participant in Troilus's death (entangling then throwing the wounded hero), Chaucer omits this information, allowing the horse a more clearly symbolic function – foreshadowing his downfall by wounded pride and suggesting that his sensuality is impaired as well, a point reinforced by Troilus's lack of knowledge in love.[23]

Furthermore, Diomede's "unhorsing" Troilus in battle near the end of the poem and presenting the horse to Criseyde, which she eventually returns to him (V, 1038–39), clearly demonstrate Diomede's superiority over Troilus on the battlefield. While Benoît's *Le Roman de Troie* provides several important exchanges which establish an equilibrium between the two knights – Troilus's "unhorsing" Diomede and Polydamas's presentation of Diomede's horse to Troilus – Chaucer elects to omit them from his poem, indicating a textual slighting of the hero through his horse and pointing to his compromised puissance against his enemy in war and diminished virility against his rival in love.

Troilus's ability as a warrior is also questioned as the narrator compares Troilus to Mars:

> But swich a knyghtly sighte trewely
> As was on hym, was nought, withouten faille,
> To loke on Mars, that god is of bataille. (II, 628–30)

Typically, scholars[24] gloss these lines to state that Troilus is like or superior to

---

[21] Michael Jenner, *Journeys into Medieval England* (London: Michael Joseph Ltd., 1991), 175.

[22] D. W. Robertson, Jr., *A Preface to Chaucer: Studies in Medieval Perspectives* (Princeton: Princeton University Press, 1962), 476, reads the horse analogy as a sign that Troilus will succumb to his fleshly (horse-like) appetites.

[23] Chaucer completely reverses his sources' portrayals of Troilus as an experienced lover, making him consistently awkward and unable to act of his own volition with regard to Criseyde. The extent of this naiveté is made obvious during the consummation scene when Pandarus must literally push Troilus into bed with Criseyde.

[24] For example, Eugene Vance claims that "Troilus looks better to Criseyde than Mars himself" ("Mervelous Signals: Poetics, Sign Theory, and Politics in Chaucer's *Troilus*," *New Literary History: A Journal of Theory and Interpretation*, 10 [1979], 321); Melvin Storm asserts that "the narrator compar[es Troilus] to Mars *explicitly*" ("Troilus, Mars, and Late Medieval Chivalry," *Journal of Medieval and Renaissance Studies* 12 [1982], 47); and Coghill not only interprets the comparison in a favorable manner, he elevates Troilus above Mars in knightly appearance (*Chaucer's Troilus and Criseyde*, trans. Neville Coghill [London and New York: Penguin Books, 1971], 67).

Mars. Chaucer, however, clearly understates the connection of the warrior Troilus to Mars. In these lines (II, 628–30), the word "nought" suggests that Troilus is *not* like Mars since the inclusion of the intensifiers "trewely" and "withouten faille," modify "nought" in a manner that compounds a negative reading of the comparison in this section. At the very least, the awkward syntax of the passage undermines a clearly positive reading of the comparison between Troilus and Mars. Also, rather than stating "he *is* a man of arms," the narrator says, "So *lik* a man of armes and a knyght / He was to seen, fulfilled of heigh prowesse" (II, 631–2). The simile using "lik," replacing a direct statement of being, casts doubt upon Troilus's knightly prowess, only represented rather than presented in the text. He is the similitude, not the reality, of a model knight.

That Chaucer does not connect Troilus with the anticipated tropes of the ideal knight also suggests the hero's lack of ability to serve and protect his lady, as a worthy knight must do. The description of his physical appearance as he enters the gates of Dardanus functions as both *effictio* and *notatio*. He wears the signs of a difficult battle, but these signs indicate something about the character of the man. He has been acted upon rather than acting, and his head, which should be most protected, is exposed. The analogue to this battlefield vulnerability within the poem is Troilus's passive reliance upon Pandarus to become his active counterpart, almost proxy, in the wooing of Criseyde, which also subjects his lady to possible emotional abuse. Chaucer's reinvention of Boccaccio's Pandaro, Criseyde's cousin, into her uncle (who is a symbol of authority and capable of much greater harm if he abuses his position of power) exacerbates this situation through his manipulation of her.

When Pandarus visits Criseyde for the first time, it is under questionable auspices. First, the narrator alludes to the myth of Procne in which Tereus betrays his wife by raping her sister (II, 64–69), and Pandarus makes his journey to Criseyde's palace under the guidance of Janus, the two-faced god (II, 77). Both of these references portend the questionable and ambiguous nature of Pandarus's business as he assumes the role of go-between to unite his niece and his close friend. Throughout their conversation, Pandarus emphasizes that a lack of pity on Criseyde's part will result in Troilus's death as well as his own, an aspect of *Troilus and Criseyde* differing from its sources. Within ninety lines (II, 316–406), Pandarus makes reference to Criseyde's power over Troilus's life or death a total of nine times, and by the end of his speech "she began to breste a-wepe anoon" (II, 408). Pandarus uses his knowledge of the tenuous situation of Criseyde as the daughter of a traitor and anticipates her emotional reaction to being labeled a potential cause of the death of the city's prince in order to manipulate her. Troilus's lack of direct involvement in this scene not only displaces him as the "knight in shining armor," who can rescue the fair damsel, but places him, inadvertently, in the position of contributing to her victimization. At the least, Chaucer's emphasis on Troilus's passivity illuminates his folly and at most his acquiescence to the patriarchal authority of Pandarus, neither of which contributes to a flattering conception of the "masculine" hero.

Thus, Criseyde's next line, "Lo, this is he / Which that myn uncle swerith he moot be deed, / But I on hym have mercy and pitee" (II, 653–55), and her swoon seem to be motivated by fear about Troilus's vulnerability, especially since she has been made to feel responsible for the condition of Troilus's armor and his horse (undeniable signifiers of his vulnerability and possible death). Haahr's assessments that "Criseyde's response is lingering and emphatically visual" and that Crisyede is "seduced" by Troilus's masculine attractiveness"[25] ignore the details of the portrait. Although Criseyde's keenest sense is, without doubt, her "lokynge" as emphasized in her portraits (I, 169-82; 281–94), exactly what she looks at and how she assesses the information, I argue, belie Haahr's assertions. Troilus's portrait suppresses all reference to specific aspects of beauty common in twelfth-century romance portraits.[26] Despite the typically physical emphases of medieval portraits, Chaucer, who certainly could have followed Benoît's model, seems uninterested in presenting a hero who captures the eye of his lady by means of his manly "beauty." Although unquestionably Troilus is indeed a *"sight,"* *what* about the sight of him prompts Criseyde's attention remains unclear. She appears more shocked than erotically attracted to the knight of portrait 2 at this point. The ambiguity of Criseyde's reaction adds to one's sense that Troilus's gender, as illustrated in portrait 2, "slydes" away from his more traditional masculine gender construction in portrait 1.

Portrait 3: Troilus's inability to sit "on his hors aright"?

Portrait 3 of Troilus reflects Criseyde's reaction to Troilus's second ride through the streets of Troy. Both portraits 2 and 3 of Troilus are initiated by Criseyde's looking down on him from her window, as the narrator describes the knight while he is *under* her gaze, but much transpires between the two passings. From line 694 to line 812 the poem presents Criseyde's thoughts about trusting the advice of Pandarus to pity Troilus and allow him a chance as her lover. Criseyde's examination of her position as the daughter of a traitor, a widow, and a woman has a significant impact on the narrator's second portrait of Troilus. Initially, she shows concern for maintaining her freedom from love's bond and a desire to preserve her honor, all the while comprehending the restrictions placed upon her as a female in a male-dominated society. The turning point in Criseyde's decision-making occurs when Antigone enters and sings a song of love, emphasizing the great joy and security she experiences because *her* knight possesses the typical courtly traits – unceasing servitude, worthiness, truthfulness, virtue, thrift. Following this scene, Criseyde falls

---

[25] Joan G. Haahr, "Criseyde's Inner Debate," *SP* 89 (1992): 262.
[26] Alice M. Colby, in *The Portrait in Twelfth-Century French Literature* (Genéve: Librairie Droz, 1965), 15, notes the physical characteristics in Benoît's portrait of Troilus.

asleep and dreams that an eagle painlessly exchanges her heart for his own. Simultaneously, Pandarus convinces Troilus to ride past Criseyde's window again. In such a state of mind, when Criseyde looks at Troilus for the second time (II, 1257–74), her response is inevitable. Because he *must be* an ideal knight of the kind about whom Antigone sings, she rationalizes that she *must* show him pity and accept his suit:

> With that he gan hire humbly to saluwe
> With dredful chere, and oft his hewes muwe;
> And up his look *debonairly* he caste,
> And *bekked on Pandare*, and forth he paste.
>
> *God woot if he sat on his hors aright,*
> Or goodly was biseyn, that ilke day!
> *God woot wher he was lik a manly knyght!*
> *What sholde I drecche, or telle of his aray?*
> Criseyde, which that alle thise thynges say,
> *To telle in short, hire liked al in-fere,*
> *His persoun, his aray, his look, his chere,*
>
> *His goodly manere, and his gentilesse,*
> So wel that nevere, sith that she was born,
> Ne hadde she swych routh of his *destresse*;
> And how so she hath hard ben here-byforn,
> To God hope I, she hath now kaught a thorn,
> She shal nat pulle it out this nexte wyke.
> God sende mo swich thornes on to pike!   (II, 1257–74)

Unlike the second portrait, the third contains little concrete description except for references to the changing of emotion on Troilus's face. That his fear is evident and the changing of his hue cannot be hidden inform his next action in the poem, his casting up of a debonaire look. Although both the *Riverside Chaucer* and Shoaf's edition of *Troilus and Criseyde* gloss "debonairly" as "graciously," the primary definition of the word is "submissively."[27] This definition accords more with Troilus's facial expression and his subordinate physical position, emphasized by his need to cast *up* his look. Further undermining any interpretation that Troilus exhibits self-assuredness as active pursuer of Criseyde is his inability to acknowledge her as he passes. Instead of gazing up at the object of his intense desire, Troilus honors a homosocial bond and prefers an exchange of glances between men by nodding specifically to Pandarus. This facial gesture registers remarkable exactitude considering that Criseyde and her uncle are standing side-by-side in the window.

---

27 *Middle English Dictionary*, "debonair," 1(b).

Significantly, in the next stanza of the portrait, the narrator establishes a tone of doubt about his perception of Troilus. Twice within two lines the narrator says "God woot," indicating his own unwillingness or inability to interpret the hero's visual signifiers. The first instance, *"God woot* if he sat on his hors aright" (II, 1260), links the first and second portraits by way of Troilus's horse and provokes one to ask why the narrator cannot see and report what should be visible and obvious. Given the symbolic relationship between the knight and his horse, I suggest that the questionable nature of the way Troilus sits atop his steed reflects badly upon his manly presence. If the horse is a physical extension of the knight's body, his "fleshly" self, then Troilus does not appear at ease with his physical, sensual side. Troilus's unease on his horse also parallels his inability to take control of his relationship with Criseyde. The portrait intensifies the ambiguity surrounding Troilus's knightly virility by casting doubt about his ability to perform correctly the very activity that defines a professional medieval warrior and possibly his ability to perform sexually. Ironically, his sexual desire is what motivates his ride past Criseyde's window.

The second doubtful phrase, *"God woot wher* he was *lik* a manly knyght!"* (II, 1263), stresses the uncertain tone established in the first. The use of a simile in this line where a direct statement is appropriate brings into question how "he" is like (but is not) a *"manly* knyght." Furthermore, the inclusion of the word "manly" invites still more uncertainty about Troilus's ability to act according to his society's prescribed notions of male-gendered behavior. Moreover, like the equivocal "if" of the previously discussed line, the insertion of "wher" reinforces the uncertainty as it begs completing the sentence with a negative "whether or not." The total effect of these two lines is a tentative rather than a firm context in which Criseyde views Troilus. She has, at this point, justified a "change of heart" toward him, yet the portrait, thus far, does not suggest that Troilus is the type of knight about whom Antigone sings.

After examining the first three portraits of Troilus, two points regarding gender become apparent. First, in measuring medieval "knightliness," anticipated male gender roles and class are inextricably linked. To say that Troilus is a knight (a class and not merely a career in medieval society) can be equated with saying that he is male. One may find support for this assertion in *Le Roman de Troie*, in which Benoît gives considerable attention to Penthesilea, a female Amazon warrior who is pivotal in the battle between the Trojans and Greeks.[28] His omission of Penthesilea in *Troilus and Criseyde* suggests that for Chaucer the gendering of knights as a group is essentialized as exclusively masculine. Therefore, an "essentialized" construction of class attributes and gender becomes unstable in the portraits of Troilus, where the ambiguous outer aspects of the man render questionable his gender. Because of expectations based on the typical medieval romance tropes, we see what is not explicitly there — that

---

[28] In *Le Roman de Troie*, Benoît devotes 42 lines (23429–71) to a detailed portrait of Penthesilea in which she is being armed for battle.

Troilus fits the model of ideal knighthood. Secondly, Criseyde values characteristics of Troilus aside from those related to his masculinity. Nothing within
the list of what Criseyde likes about Troilus clearly points to his gender. "His
person" provides no information about how *manly* he is, which is emphasized
by the gender-neutral word choice. Her interest appears to center on his
character, what type of *person* he is, because his assertion of masculine bravado
through Pandarus has created fear and uncertainty in her rather than reassured
her of a secure future. Jill Mann states that "when left alone to reflect on the
news of Troilus's love for her, [Criseyde] is conscious of Troilus's power, as
the king's son, to hurt or assist her (II, 708-14), but even more prominent in her
mind is the fear of masculine dominance and possessiveness."[29] If Troilus is
not the "typical" male, then Criseyde can expect, or at least hope, that he will
not do to her the "tresoun" (II, 793) that men "typically" do to women and
that he will assist rather than harm her. Furthermore, Chaucer's omission of the
overt anti-feminist digressions common to two of his closest sources – Benoît
and Boccaccio[30] – softens the patriarchal / misogynist perspective in the poem,
contributing to the audience's sense that Troilus, despite his manly posturing
in portrait 1, is not the aggressive, dominating type of male more clearly
represented by Diomede.

Portrait 4: Troilus's manhood outside of the walls of Troy

The context of the fourth portrait, Troilus spending all of his time on the
battlefield searching for Diomede, suggests that Troilus's masculinity becomes
more conventional as he becomes active. Also, in his rivalry with Diomede over
Criseyde, he creates as well a homosocial bond through triangulated negotiations where the relationship between the men is central and the woman is merely
an object, commonplace within patriarchal structures. The final portrait, therefore, reveals a knight who has, without the feminizing effects of love, regained
the aspects of masculinity reinforced and expected by his society:

> And Troilus *wel woxen* was in highte,
> And *complet formed* by proporcioun
> So wel that *kynde* it nought amenden myghte;
> Yong, fressh, strong, and *hardy as lyoun*;
> *Trewe as stiel* in ech condicioun;

29 Jill Mann, "Troilus' Swoon," *ChauR* 14 (1980): 320.
30 Barry Windeatt notes that Chaucer "entirely dropped the explicit antifeminist moral that
Benoît draws from the example of Briseida: 'A woman's grief lasts a short while: one eye
weeps, the other smiles. Their hearts change very rapidly, and the wisest of them is foolish
enough' " (*Oxford Guides*, 84). One finds similar passages in *Il Filostrato*: "Why give love
to any woman: For even as the leaf flutters in the wind, so in one day, fully a thousand times,
do their hearts change" (Gordon, 33).

Oon of the beste entecched creature
That is or shal whil that the world may dure.

And certeynly in storye it is yfounde
That Troilus was nevere unto no wight,
As in his tyme, in *no degree secounde*
In *durryng don* that longeth to a knyght.
Al myghte a geant passen hym of myght,
His herte ay with the first and with the beste
Stood *paregal*, to *durre don that hym leste*.   (V, 827–40)

As befits a romance hero, Troilus has physical features created by Nature ("kynde") to perfection. Colby notes that "Nature's creative role . . . contributes to the stereotyped quality of the descriptions of general physical attractiveness"[31] in twelfth-century romance. Rather than using the language typical of Troilus's earlier portraits, which were equivocal at best in their positive rendering of the hero, the narrator in Book V says that Troilus is "wel woxen" and "complet formed." Although both phrases maintain a vagueness typical in the descriptions of the hero and heroine, they clearly connote a size and shape worthy of praise.

To reinforce the conventional composition of this portrait, Chaucer provides two similes traditionally associated with masculinity: "hardy as lyoun" and "trewe as stiel" (V, 830–31). Aside from the obvious reference to strength, both of these similes reconnect Troilus to what his relationship with Criseyde seemed to disconnect him from – his status as prince, signified by the lion which was a commonplace heraldic symbol during the Middle Ages, and warrior, represented by the material used to make the strongest weapons. These present a profound shift of perspective on Troilus, who earlier in the poem struggled within the tentative position of being even *"lik* a manly knyght." Although these new similes imply strength and manliness, they are also trite rhetorical tropes that do not provoke questioning of Troilus's masculinity.

The second stanza of Troilus's final portrait continues to counter the earlier instability of his masculinity evident in the second and third portraits. Throughout the poem, the narrator emphasizes Troilus's being second to Hector. The text notably reinforces the pitiful reality of this second-place status when Criseyde, in response to Pandarus's hinting about Troilus's desire to meet her, asks several times about Hector, whom she acknowledges as the "townes wal," while showing only a secondary interest in Troilus (II, 153–71). In marked contrast, the final portrait states that Troilus was "in no degree secounde" and that he "stood paregal" (V, 836, 840). This textual interpolation raises the status of Troilus to that described in the closest source portrait on this point, Guido,

---

[31] Colby, 28.

who tells that "for both strength and energy in war he was equal or next to Hector."[32]

Second, the narrator uses the phrase "durre don" ("dare to do") twice in the last four lines of portrait 4. Because the narrator emphasizes Troilus's inability to act from the moment he sees Criseyde and "wax therwith astoned" (I, 274) as the Trojans exchange her for prisoners, this phrase is significant. Not only does Troilus act, but, finally, he does what "hym leste," suggesting that he is a man of action who does more than what his society expects from him as a knight. That is, he finally acts upon his own desires. Moreover, this phrase connects Troilus's final portrait with his first (in which "hym leste" is also used [I, 189]), intimating that he has regained the masculine posturing which he could not retain while in the presence of Criseyde. The repetition of this phrase in the two portraits indicates that in some sense Troilus has come full circle. Yet his involvement in the action when the narrator presents the first portrait and his absence from the action during the final portrait imply a change. Troilus's character, in the end, flattens, becomes more stereotypically masculine, as his portrait is overtly represented out of context.

The final portrait of Troilus, when examined against portraits 2 and 3, reveals a surety of manner and action in keeping with essentialized views of masculinity – he "slydes" back toward the gender construction illustrated in portrait 1 before Troilus sees Criseyde. In addition, the textual positioning of a final portrait of Troilus next to that of Diomede suggests the need of outside masculine aggression to force Troilus into the gender role prescribed for a knight and a prince. When confronted with battle against Diomede, the manliest of men, Troilus clearly rises to the occasion and becomes more "masculine" than in the two previous portraits. But, alas, he rises too late to regain Criseyde.[33]

---

32 Windeatt, *Oxford Guides*, 92.
33 I would like to thank Lorraine K. Stock for her helpful suggestions in editing this essay.

"Is this a mannes herte?": Unmanning Troilus through Ovidian Allusion

MAUD BURNETT McINERNEY

The influence of one poet upon another is a subtle and delicate thing, much harder to substantiate than direct debt to a particular source. In this essay I will not be concerned, or at any rate not primarily, with identifying Ovidian sources for passages in *Troilus and Criseyde*. Rather, I hope to indicate the way particular Ovidian traces in Chaucer's text reveal not only that the English poet knew the Latin one intimately, but that he plays with Ovid – especially with the erotic elegies and the *Metamorphoses* – in ways that Ovid himself would have recognized and appreciated. Whether Chaucer's general audience would have gotten the joke must remain an open question, but the poet doubtless expected at least some of his readers to appreciate and admire the game he was playing.[1] Such playfulness, of course, is serious business; in both Chaucer and Ovid, it is concerned with revealing the paradoxical experience of the human subject in love. The Ovidian influence upon Chaucer's poem is at its most complex in the development of the character of Troilus, represented in Book III as a man trapped between two literary modes of loving, unmanned by a conflict of irreconcilable poetics.

---

[1] In *Classical Imitation and Interpretation in Chaucer's Troilus* (Lincoln: University of Nebraska Press, 1990), John V. Fleming argues that Chaucer was not only a "considerable and sophisticated 'classicist' " (xii–xiii) but one who expected or at least hoped for a similar degree of sophistication in his audience (19). Chaucer's friend and rival Gower, author of the heavily Ovidian *Confessio Amantis*, was also a serious classical scholar, and one with whom Chaucer seems to have engaged in a running game of one-upmanship.

Getting Troilus into bed

The long, central passage of Book III of *Troilus and Criseyde* is often referred to as the "consummation scene," a rather ironic description since the love-affair between Troilus and Criseyde very nearly goes unconsummated. The stage has been set by Pandarus, who smuggles Troilus into his back bedroom, where Criseyde lies weeping because she believes that Troilus has doubted her. Troilus is overcome with guilt:

> Therwith the sorwe so his herte shette
> That from his eyen fil there nought a tere,
> And every spirit his vigour in knette,
> So they astoned or oppressed were.
> The felyng of his sorwe, or of his fere,
> Or of aught elles, fled was out of towne;
> And down he fel al sodeynly a-swowne.   (III, 1086–92)

Vern Bullough has argued that in the Middle Ages "the male was defined in terms of sexual performance, measured rather simply by his ability to get an erection."[2] Bullough's definition of "maleness," while limited, provides us with a starting point from which to develop a more complex analysis of Troilus's trouble with masculinity. Troilus, at this critical moment, is unable to get an erection; the "in-knetting" of his vigour strongly suggests detumescence. It harks back to Book I, where Troilus appears as a "fierse and proude knyght" (I, 225) swaggering a bit and "byholding ay the ladies of the town" (186), playing a clearly masculine role. His first exchange of glances with Criseyde apparently threatens his maleness, if not his masculine exterior:

> And of hire look in him ther gan to quyken
> So gret desir and such affeccioun,
> That in his herte botme gan to stiken
> Of hir his fixe and depe impressioun.
> And though he erst hadde poured up and down,
> He was tho glad his hornes in to shrinke.   (I, 295–300)

The final image here is of a snail withdrawing into its shell, and suggests a flaccidity curiously at odds, as Elaine Hansen has noted, with the active, penetrating gaze which moments before pierced the crowd to light upon Criseyde.[3] The word *quyken*, furthermore, normally used of the moment of conception inside a female body, casts Troilus in the role of a fertile woman.

---

[2] Vern Bullough, "On Being a Male in the Middle Ages," in *Medieval Masculinities: Regarding Men in the Middle Ages*, ed. Clare A. Lees (Minneapolis: University of Minnesota Press, 1994), 43.

[3] Elaine Tuttle Hansen, *Chaucer and the Fictions of Gender* (Berkeley: University of California Press, 1992), 146–47.

Falling in love, for Troilus, renders *making* love impossible. For him, love and sex are incompatible. The reactions of both Pandarus and Criseyde imply that, for them, the manhood which may be indicated by knightly success must be confirmed by sexual performance. They interpret Troilus's faint as a manifestation of impotence and proceed to treat it accordingly. Pandarus

> into bed hym caste,
> And seyde, "O thef, is this a mannes herte?"
> And of he rente al to his bare sherte,
>
> And seyde, "Nece, but ye helpe us now,
> Allas, youre owen Troilus is lorn!"   (III, 1097–1101)

Love was commonly regarded as a pathological condition in the Middle Ages, and as one which was particularly common in women, whose "passionate love, figured as illness, was . . . a familiar part of thirteenth-century culture."[4] Writings on the treatment of love, however, are generally concerned with men, as though love-sickness were problematic for the male as it is not for the female. Love might increase the woman's "natural" tendencies (towards irrationality, passivity, weakness), but in the man it caused an inversion of nature: "the symptoms of the disease 'unman' the lover. As a patient he is passive, helpless and vulnerable. The signs of lovesickness . . . connote feminine and infantile behaviour."[5]

Given such an understanding of the psychopathology of love, impotence was a logical, if paradoxical, side effect of the ailment. Equally paradoxically, the prescribed remedy for the condition was sexual intercourse, which would both confirm maleness and reduce desire by sating it, thereby alleviating the incipient femininity induced by love. Thus, Pandarus urges Criseyde to help Troilus by pulling "out the thorn / That stiketh in his herte" (III, 1104–05), another image with clear sexual connotations. As Pandarus and Criseyde proceed to massage Troilus, we are being invited to see them as performing a sort of sexual first aid:

> Therwith his pous and paumes of his hondes
> They gan to frote, and wete his temples tweyne;
> And to deliveren hym fro bittre bondes
> She ofte hym kiste; and shortly for to seyne,
> Hym to revoken she did al hire peyne.   (III, 1114–18)

---

4   Mary Frances Wack, *Lovesickness in the Middle Ages: The Viaticum and Its Commentaries* (Philadelphia: University of Pennsylvania Press, 1990), 111.
5   Wack, 151–52.

The whole scene in which the lovers are observed and even aided by a third party is oddly reminiscent of Guy de Chauliac's guidelines for the investigation of claims of impotence prior to granting an annulment. In Guy's account, a matron serving as a sort of medieval sex therapist is required to observe the married couple's attempts at intercourse, and to do everything possible to encourage them. She "must administer spices and aromatics to them, she must warm them and anoint them with warm oils, she must massage them near the fire, she must order them to talk to each other and to embrace."[6] Pandarus instructs Criseyde to speak to Troilus (III, 1106); he helps her to rub her lover down and wet his temples; and finally, he withdraws with his candle to the "chymeneye" (III, 1141), where we may imagine a fire to be burning. The degree to which Pandarus's behaviour mimics that of Guy's matron reinforces our sense that the threat of impotence and the loss of manhood entailed by it is Troilus' problem. Criseyde's determined attempt to "delyver" Troilus from "bittre bondes" (III, 1116) also recalls the medical literature. Witches were believed to have the ability to cause impotence "by tying knots in threads or laces of leather, thus creating ligatures or knots in the seminal vessels; impotence so caused would remain until the hidden knots were discovered or untied."[7]

When Troilus regains consciousness, a new problem rears its head:

> And at the laste, he gan his breth to drawe,
> And of his swough sone after that adawe,
>
> And gan bet mynde and reson to hym take,
> But wonder soore he was abayst, iwis;
> And with a sik, whan that he gan bet awake,
> He seyde, "O mercy, God, what thyng is this?"   (III, 1119–24)

Troilus, it appears, has now got an erection, but does not know what to do with it, a state of affairs that provokes the second explicit reproach to his manhood: "Quod tho Criseyde, 'Is this a mannes game? / What, Troilus, wol ye do thus for shame?' " (III, 1126–27). Active participation in sexual intercourse is the "mannes game" in which Criseyde now undertakes to instruct Troilus. Pandarus, seeing that the game is afoot, leaves them to it, although it is worth noting that six stanzas elapse between his initial withdrawal, which he himself draws attention to ("This light, nor I, ne serven here of nought" [1136]), and the moment when he finally goes to sleep. He allows himself to nod off only after Troilus has "hente" Criseyde in his arms at line 1187. Even now, Pandarus cannot resist a *sotto voce* dig at Troilus's earlier incapacity:

6   Bullough, 42.
7   Bullough, 42.

And Pandarus with a ful good entente
Leyde hym to slepe, and seyde "If ye be wise,
Swouneth nought now, lest more folk arise!"   (III, 1188–90).[8]

Teaching Troilus how to love

Why *is* it so difficult for Troilus to play the "mannes game"? Most critics have
ascribed Troilus's hesitation to his inexperience, or even to his sensitivity.
Windeatt sees in Troilus's apparent lack of "manhod" evidence of an admirable
"restraint . . . associated with discretion and self-control"[9] eventually vindi-
cated by the poem. This seems to me an excessively modern version of courtly
love which deftly avoids the fact that Troilus's faint is perceived as funny not
only by every class of undergraduates which encounters it, but also by Pandarus,
who pokes fun at it as he falls asleep. It is funny precisely because it suggests
not restraint, which is voluntary, but impotence, which is involuntary, and a
favorite source of Chaucerian humour.[10]

Curiously enough, one of the clues as to why Troilus's masculinity is so
troubled can be found in C. S. Lewis's reverent assessment of the poem. In *The
Allegory of Love*, Lewis describes Book III as "a long epithalamium . . . which
contains, between its soaring invocation to the 'blisful light' of the third heaven
and its concluding picture of Troilus at the hunt . . . some of the greatest erotic
poetry of the world. It is a lesson worth learning, how Chaucer can so
triumphantly celebrate the flesh without becoming either delirious like Rossetti
or pornographic like Ovid."[11] The fact is that Ovid is a constant presence in
the poem. Fleming argues that Ovid plays an essential structural role in *Troilus
and Criseyde*, as Chaucer "makes the dialogue of the Christian classicist and
the pagan poets part of the dialectic of his poem."[12] A different dialectic may
be identified within this larger one: a dialogue, fully exploited by Chaucer,
between the ideal of courtly love as Troilus experiences it (or would like to
experience it) and the apparently pragmatic amorous counsels of Lewis's
"pornographic" poet, Ovid. Troilus is trapped between two models for erotic
behaviour and as a result, finds himself "unmanned."

The presence of the *Ars Amatoria* in the background of Chaucer's poem has

---

[8] Pandarus's role as sex therapist may account for his behavior with Criseyde the following
morning, when he begins to "prie" under the sheet that covers her (III 1571); perhaps he is
checking for evidence that intercouse has in fact taken place. The notorious line about having
"fully his entente" (1582) would then refer back to that quoted above; his "entente" is that
the relationship between Troilus and Criseyde be fully consummated.

[9] B. A. Windeatt, *Troilus and Criseyde* (Oxford: Clarendon, 1992), 278.

[10] See for instance the Wife of Bath's complaint about her elderly husbands, especially *The
Wife of Bath's Prologue*, III 394, 415.

[11] C. S. Lewis, *The Allegory of Love* (New York: Oxford University Press, 1958), 196.

[12] Fleming, 41. See also Lewis, 152–53.

often been noted. The resemblance between Pandarus and the *praeceptor amoris*, the narrator who gives young men advice on how to get girls, is a commonplace, although I will argue that Pandarus has at least one other significant Ovidian forebear. The degree to which Troilus assumes the position of the *praeceptor's* student, or fails to do so, however, has been less fully explored. A couple of examples may serve to indicate the difficulties of this position for Chaucer's hero. Take for instance the instructions in Book I of the *Ars Amatoria*:

> palleat omnis amans: hic est color aptus amanti;
> . . .
> arguat et macies animum, nec turpe putaris
> palliolum nitidis imposuisse comis.
> attenuant iuuenum vigilatae corpora noctes
> curaque et in magno qui fit amore dolor.
> ut uoto potiare tuo, miserabilis esto,
> ut qui te uideat dicere possit "amas."   (AA I 729–738)

> [All lovers should be pale; this is the most useful shade for lovers. . . . Your loss of weight will speak for your passion, and don't be ashamed to hood your shining hair. Sleepless nights and the worries and pain of great love will waste away the bodies of young men. So that you may have your wish, be wretched, so that anyone who sees you will say "you must be in love!"][13]

In Book I, Troilus appears to be following precisely this advice. He grows pale not once, but "sexti tyme a day" (I, 441). He stops sleeping and eating altogether. He has, however, missed the point of the *praeceptor's* lesson, which is that all of these symptoms are intended to be displayed to anyone who sets eyes on the lover (*ut qui te videat*), in order to arouse the beloved's sympathies to the point where she will summon her lover to her bed so that she can help cure him of his love-sickness.

For the Ovidian *praeceptor*, love-sickness is a means to an end; for Troilus, it becomes something like an end in itself (and indeed, almost ends him). He does precisely the opposite of what the *praeceptor* recommends. He tries to camouflage his symptoms, to represent them as the results of some more mundane malady:

---

[13] Ovid, *Amores, Medicamina Faciei Femineae, Ars Amatoria, Remedia Amoris*, ed. E. J. Kenney (Oxford: Oxford University Press), 140. Further references in the text will be indicated as follows: AA for *Ars Amatoria*, RA for *Remedia Amoris*. All translations from Ovid are my own.

> Therfor a title he gan him for to borwe
> Of other siknesse, lest of hym men wende
> That the hote fir of love hym brende. (I, 488–90)

When it comes to writing love letters, Troilus once again seems both aware of the *praeceptor's* instructions and incapable of performing them. The *praeceptor* urges the lover not to declaim to his mistress, but to use simple, ordinary speech, and Pandarus translates this advice almost word for word: "'Ne scryvenyssh or craftyly thow it write; / Biblotte it with thi teris ek a lite" (II, 1026–27). Troilus does so, writing to Criseyde in "ful humble wyse" (II, 1069), but once again missing the point of the exercise, which is to *seem* heartbroken, to *appear* to suffer, in order to soften up the lady's heart. Troilus actually does suffer, and weeps all over his signet as he seals the letter (II, 1086–88).

This tear-stained missive evokes a model from another Ovidian text, the *Heroides*, a collection of fictional letters from abandoned women. The *locus classicus* for tear-stained letters is *Heroides* III, Briseis's letter to Achilles, which begins:

> quascumque adspicies, lacrimae fecere lituras;
> sed tamen et lacrimae pondera vocis habent. (H III 3–4)[14]

> [The blots you see were made by tears, but tears may weigh as much as words.]

For Florence Verducci, Briseis is "a creature whose suffering and whose deformation are so coherently, convincingly realized in her letter that when we do smile at her, that smile becomes, inevitably, a wince, a reflex at once of sympathy and recoil."[15] Troilus evokes much the same reaction. We sympathize with his pain, but recoil from his easy surrender to it. We are disconcerted by the conflict between his heroic military persona and his pathetic courtly one. We may even be revolted by that singular moment when the courtly mask slips and Troilus offers Pandarus his sister, or any other woman he may have his eye on:[16]

> I have my faire suster Polixene,
> Cassandre, Eleyne, or any of the frape –
> Be she never so fair or wel yshape,
> Tel me which thow wilt of everychone,
> To han for thyn. (III, 409–13)

---

[14] Loeb Classical Library Edition, *Ovid I, Heroides and Amores* (Cambridge: Harvard University Press, 1914). Abbreviated as H.

[15] Florence Verducci, *Ovid's Toyshop of the Heart: Epistulae Heroidum* (Princeton: Princeton University Press, 1985), 121.

[16] See Hansen, 166–67, for an extended discussion of this incident.

Verducci ascribes Briseis's "deformation" to the "seeming paradox of servile love,"[17] to the conflict between her role as lover and her role as slave, a conflict developed, maintained, and manipulated by the poet in a way which reforms (or deforms) his reader's understanding of his source text, in this case the *Iliad*. The result of this parodic revisionism is a poetic subject at once more sympathetic and more antipathetic than her Homeric antecedent. Similarly, Chaucer complicates the hero he inherited from Boccacio, and does so, significantly, by playing against Ovid in some of the same ways that Ovid himself played against Homer or Vergil.

Briseis's letter carries us directly into the Troy story. What is particularly striking about the evocation of *Heroides* III is the fact that Troilus, in emulating Briseis, is casting himself in a feminine role. One of the primary effects of the Ovidian text on the Chaucerian one, in other words, is to trouble the normative gendered roles of lover and beloved. This troubling might seem coincidental were it not that this is the second time one of the *Heroides* has found its way into Chaucer's text, with a similar effect. At the end of Book I, when Pandarus discovers the true nature of Troilus's illness, he cites Apollo as an example of an unrequited lover, just like himself, drawing the example from a letter Paris is supposed to have received from his first girlfriend, Oenone. Apollo, she is supposed to have written, knew all there was to know about medicine, yet could not heal himself from the love of "the doughter of the kyng Amete" (I, 664). The problem is that this particular story about Apollo does not appear in the letter (*Heroides* V) which Pandarus cites.[18] Pandarus's intent here is to authorize himself as an appropriate confidant, but he does so by means of an example that draws our attention to a tale that has clear implications for the lovers in our story. The point, in other words, may not be the misappropriated tale of Apollo and the daughter of King Admetus, or even Pandarus's own notably undemonstrable case of unrequited love, but the letter itself, *Heroides* V. The link to Troilus is at once familial (Paris is his brother) and curiously troubled. In the Ovidian text, Paris, a Trojan, leaves Oenone, another Trojan, for a Greek, Helen. At the end of Chaucer's poem, a similar pattern will emerge as Criseyde, a Trojan, leaves Troilus, also a Trojan, for Diomede, a Greek.[19] The movement of a faithless Trojan to a Greek is preserved, but the genders of the characters are inverted. In the new triangle, Troilus assumes the role of Oenone, the abandoned heroine.

17 Verducci, 99.

18 In "Chaucer and an Italian Translation of the Heroides," *PMLA* 45 (1930), Sanford Brown Meech uses this passage to argue that Chaucer was working from a translation by Fillippo Ceffi, rather than from Ovid's original. Nonetheless, it is curious that Chaucer chooses to derive the example of Apollo as disappointed lover from such an obscure source rather than a more obvious one, such as *Metamorphoses* I, which is cited at III 726. It seems to me highly improbable that Chaucer was working exclusively from Ceffi.

19 Windeatt, 112, discusses the importance of what Pandarus does not say about this letter, but without noting the gendered implications.

The metamorphosis of Troilus

Troilus's feminization does not end with his position in this Trojan-Greek-Trojan triangle. His behavior also regularly associates him with Ovidian heroines rather than heroes: the first thing he does upon falling in love, like Medea, Scylla, or Myrrha, is to withdraw to his room and agonize. Medea debates with herself in Book VII of the *Metamorphoses*, eventually deciding that although she knows what is right, she will do what is wrong; Scylla makes a similar decision in Book VIII. Troilus appears incapable not only of making the kind of decision the *amator* of the *Ars Amatoria* would have made, to get the girl at any cost, but even of making a negative decision like that of Myrrha, who decides to kill herself. Troilus's complete submission to his own suffering marks him as a courtly rather than an Ovidian lover, even while the text insists on placing him in an Ovidian context.

Pandarus's intrusion upon Troilus's lovesickness also has echoes of the *Metamorphoses*:

> Bywayling in his chambre thus allone,
> A frend of his that called was Pandare
> Com oones in unwar, and herde hym groone,
> And say his frend in swich destresse and care:
> "Allas," quod he, "who causeth al this fare?
> O mercy, God! What unhap may this meene?
> Han now thus soone Grekes maad yow leene?
>
> "Or hastow som remors of conscience,
> And art now falle in sum devocioun,
> And wailest for thi synne and thin offence,
> And hast for ferde caught attricioun?" (I, 547–57)

When Myrrha decides to hang herself, it is her muttered words (*murmura verborum*, M X 382)[20] which attract the attention of her nurse, just as Troilus's complaints attract Pandarus's attention. Pandarus and the nurse also imagine similar causes for the distress they discover. The nurse suggests first that Myrrha may be suffering from some kind of madness (*furor*, 397), much as Pandarus imagines that fighting the Greeks may be making Troilus "leene" with anxiety. The nurse goes on to hypothesize that Myrrha's trouble may be magical or religious in nature (*sive aliquis nocuit, magico lustrabere ritu;/ ira deum sive est, sacris placabilis ira* [if something else is making you ill, it can be dismissed by magical rites; if it is the anger of some god, anger is appeased by sacrifice] (398–99)). Pandarus's suggestion that Troilus may be suffering from some unexpiated sin renders the same sentiment in a Christian idiom.

[20] Ovid, *Metamorphoses*, ed. W. S. Anderson (Leipzig: Teubner, 1977), 242. Abbreviated as M.

The presence of the *Metamorphoses* in the background of this scene is rather ironically acknowledged some lines later, when Pandarus instructs Troilus to stop feeling so sorry for himself:

> For this nys naught, certein, the nexte wyse
> To wynnene love – as techen us the wyse –
> To walwe and wepe as Nyobe the queene,
> Whose teres yet in marble ben yseene.   (I, 697–700)

Pandarus instructs Troilus to stop acting like an Ovidian heroine and assume a more sex-appropriate role, albeit also Ovidian: that of the *amator* from the *Ars Amatoria*, who, with the help of a "wyse" *praeceptor*, may "wynnene love." Troilus returns to Niobe a little later. "What knowe I of the queene Niobe?" he complains to Pandarus: "Lat be thyne olde ensaumples, I the preye!" (I, 759–60).

By the time we get to Book III of *Troilus and Criseyde*, it is clear that Troilus has either been familiar with "olde ensaumples" all along, or has brushed up on them in the intervening days or weeks. When Pandarus shows him the way to the back bedroom, he lets go with a positive torrent of allusions to the *Metamorphoses*. He prays first to Venus, to grant him her aid "For love of hym thow lovedest in the shawe – / I mene Adoon, that with the boor was slawe"(III, 720–21). Troilus continues his invocation, working in as many love-crossed Olympians as possible:

> "O Jove ek, for the love of faire Europe,
> The which in forme of bole awey thow fette,
> Now help! O Mars, thow with thi blody cope,
> For love of Cipris, thow me nought ne lette!
> O Phebus, thynk whan Dane hirselven shette
> Under the bark, and laurer wax for drede;
> Yet for hire love, O help now at this nede!
>
> "Mercurie, for the love of Hierse eke,
> For which Pallas was with Aglawros wroth,
> Now help!"   (III, 722–31)

All of these references require fuller glosses than they are generally given. The appeal to Jove, who turned himself into a bull in order to pursue Europa, sends us directly back to the proem to Book III, Lewis's "soaring invocation" to love:

> Ye Joves first to thilke effectes glade,
> Thorugh which that thynges lyven alle and be,
> Comeveden, and amorous him made
> On mortal thyng, and as yow list, ay ye

Yeve him in love ese or adversitee,
And in a thousand formes down hym sente
For love in erthe, and whom yow liste he hente.   (III, 15–21)

As Benson has noted, the Jove of the parallel passage in Boccaccio is rendered merciful by love, whereas Chaucer's Jove is "essentially predatory."[21] For Benson, Jove's behavior, as exemplified through the verb "hente," foreshadows the behavior of Diomede at the end of the poem. The same word, however, is used when Troilus takes Criseyde in his arms at III, 1187, a passage I have already discussed. Apparently, "hente," perhaps because of its implicit violence, is the only appropriate verb for the active male lover. In fact, the proem conjures up a world all too familiar from Ovid in which love is always aggression, sex almost always rape. Critics often describe the divine rapes of the first books of the *Metamorphoses* as love stories, disregarding or minimizing the terror of their mortal objects of desire.[22] When Jupiter "in forme of bole" carries off Europa, she is not simply afraid but panic-striken. *Pavet haec*, the poet tells us, the girl is terrified. The Io episode of Book I is often regarded as merely pathetic or even comic:

> . . . conata queri mugitus edidit ore
> pertimuitque sonos popriaque exterrita voce est.
> . . .
> illa manus lambit patriisque dat oscula palmis
> nec retinet lacrimas, et, si modo verba sequantur,
> oret opem nomenque suum casusque loquatur;
> littera pro verbis, quam pes in pulvere duxit,
> corporis indicium mutati triste peregit.   (M I 637–50)

[When she tried to complain a moo came from her throat and she shivered, terrified by the sound of her own voice. . . . She licked her father's hand and kissed his palms; she couldn't hold back her tears; if only words had come, she would have begged for help and told her name and what had happened. Her hoof traced letters in the dust in place of words, clues to a body sadly changed.]

---

[21] C. David Benson, *Chaucer's Troilus and Criseyde* (London: Unwin Hyman, 1990), 127.
[22] See for instance G. Karl Galinsky, *Ovid's Metamorphoses* (Berkeley: University of California Press, 1975), 162–63. Galinsky claims that Ovid represents the gods as "subhuman" in the sense of "animal" but sees this as humorous, rather than as indicating the degree to which the gods are lacking in the common virtues of humanity. His discussion of the Jupiter and Europa episode does not consider Europa's feelings, except for a single reference to her "hesitation." Joseph B. Solodow, *The World of Ovid's Metamorphoses* (Chapel Hill: University of North Carolina Press, 1988), 89ff, argues that Ovid reduces gods to the human scale, without questioning what it may mean for some "humans" to have all the power and others none.

This scene takes on a sharply different valence when read against the rape of Philomela by Tereus in *Metamorphoses* VI. Philomela too is silenced, but since her rapist is human rather than divine, he must resort to human methods:

> ille indignantem et nomen patris usque vocantem
> luctantemque loqui conprensam forcipe linguam
> abstulit ense fero.   (M VI 555–57)

> [He seized with tongs the outraged tongue that grieved, still calling upon her father's name, and cut it out with his savage sword.]

Tereus goes on to rape the mutilated Philomela again before abandoning her. Like Io, she manages to communicate her situation to her family through letters, and horrible vengeance eventually follows. The second episode, in all its stark brutality, reveals the hidden violence of the first. Jupiter is no less a rapist than Tereus, while Io's experience – rape, then enforced silence – is not substantially different from that of Philomela. Chaucer, I am suggesting, was a more perceptive reader of Ovid than most twentieth-century critics, and his choice of the verb "hente" to describe the loves of Jupiter indicates a genuine understanding of the violence beneath the surface of the metamorphic narrative.

If we return now from the *Metamorphoses* to the Ovidian invocations Troilus indulges in on his way to the bedroom, his prayers take on a dubious and sometimes even sinister cast. Jove's rape of Europa may be brutal, but it is at least successful. Troilus next appeals to Mars with his "blody cope," a curiously graphic suggestion of violence in this erotic context. The example of Apollo and Daphne is even more ominous, since not only does Apollo never enjoy Daphne's body, but her disgust for him is so profound that, even after her transformation, the wood of her trunk shrinks from his lips (*refugit tamen oscula lignum*, M I 556). The tale of Mercury and Herse (M II 708–832) is another example of non-consummation of a love-affair, as Chaucer must have known. Troilus's very first prayer, asking Venus to look kindly on him for the sake of Adonis, is, of course, the most inauspicious of all. Adonis died of a wound which classical authors explicitly interpreted as an emasculation, and which may therefore be seen as predicting Troilus's initial failure at Criseyde's bedside. The mention of Adonis, however, also predicts the dream Troilus will have in Book V, in which he sees a boar asleep in a forest, and by its side "kissyng ay, his lady bryght, Criseyde" (V, 1241). According to Cassandre,

> "This ilke boor bitokneth Diomede,
> Tideus sone, that down descended is
> Fro Meleagre, that made the boor to blede."   (V, 1513–15)

Pandarus's response to Troilus's extended series of Ovidian allusions ridicules them once and for all, and it emphasizes the degree to which Troilus fails to live up to the aggressively masculine example of Jove:

> "Thow wrecched mouses herte
> Artow agast so that she wol the bite?
> Wy! Don this furred cloke upon thy sherte
> And folwe me." (III, 736–39)

Jove took the form of a bull to seduce Europa. Pandarus turns Troilus into a mouse as he approaches Criseyde, rhetorically and maybe even sartorially, when he instructs him to put on that furry hood. The question "Are you a man or a mouse?" hangs in the air when Troilus finally finds himself standing beside Criseyde's bed.

Cures for love

One final piece of Ovidian text cries out to be considered, before I try to sum up the influence of all this Ovid on Troilus. Upon hearing that Criseyde is to be exchanged for Antenor, Pandarus tries to cheer Troilus up by telling him that "the newe love out chaceth ofte the olde" (IV, 415), a translation of the Ovidian *successore nouo uincitur omnis amor* (RA 462). Let us look briefly at what immediately precedes and follows that line from the *Remedia Amoris*, the "Cures for Love," in which the *praeceptor* gives tips to those young men who (like Troilus) have too thoroughly internalized his advice in the *Ars Amatoria* and become sick with love:

> et Parin Oenone summos tenuisset ad annos,
>   si non Oebalia paelice laesa foret...
> quid moror exemplis, quorum me turba fatigat?
>   successore nouo uincitur omnis amor.
> . . .
>   uidit id Atrides ...
> Marte suo captam Chryseida uictor amabat;
>   . . .
> quam postquam reddi Calchas ope tutus Achillis
>   iusserat et patria est illa recepta domo,
> "est" ait Atrides "illius proxima forma
>   et, si prima sinat syllaba, nomen idem." (RA 457–472)

[Oenone would have hung onto Paris forever, if she had not been cut out by her rival Helen. Why linger over examples, there are so many they wear me out! Every old love is conquered by the new. . . . Agamemnon saw this. As a victor, he loved Chryseis, captive of his war-making. . . . When Chalcas, safe with Achilles, demanded that she be returned and she was received back into her father's house, Agamemnon said "There is another as beautiful as she, and who even has the same name, except for the first syllable."]

In this single passage we thus find linked a phrase that Chaucer lifts directly into the mouth of Pandarus, who so often appears to speak for the *praeceptor*, the troubling example of Paris and Oenone we have noted before, and Criseyde herself, or at any rate her remote original, travelling predictably from one man to another.

Ovid's world, which Chaucer reproduces so painstakingly by allusion and citation, is one in which the role of men, whether divine or mortal, consists largely of the pursuit of women. Ovid complicates this scenario by his apparently sympathetic insistence upon the lack of choice of women in such a world. Similarly, Chaucer's Criseyde, Hansen and others have argued, is profoundly aware of her own helplessness. Troilus, on the other hand, regularly behaving like a heroine when he should be playing the hero, remains tragically unaware of the degree to which he is out of step with the world in which he has been placed. The rules of the Ovidian erotic elegy, which Pandarus, Criseyde, and Diomede all seem to accept and live by, betray him at every step because he, as courtly lover, is incapable of assuming in any consistent way the predatory role of *amator*. The result is that, again and again, Troilus appears ridiculous when he should appear sympathetic and sensitive.

Ovid's poems, with their emphasis on pursuit and abandonment, suggest a universe in which love is always transitory, always either unrequited or already satiated and therefore disappointing. Troilus's experiences suggest that the courtly lover may be as self-deceived as the *amator*. But Chaucer, while at pains to depict an Ovidian world, is a Christian poet. His poem goes to great lengths to "unman" his hero by catching him between incompatible models for erotic and poetic behavior, but when Troilus is irremediably unmanned by the spear of Achilles, he finds himself translated into an "eighthe spere" the Latin poet could not have imagined. From this vantage point both the ultimate erotic satisfaction which always eludes the *amator*, and the romantic bliss which always betrays the courtly lover, are revealed as "blynde lust, the which that may nat laste" (V, 1824). Chaucer goes on to revile Troilus's earlier models for "manly" behavior:

> Lo here, of payens corsed olde rites!
> Lo here, what alle hire goddes may availle!
> Lo here, thise wrecched worldes appetites!
> Lo here, the fyn and guerdoun for travaille
> Of Jove, Appollo, of Mars, of swich rascaille!   (V, 1849–53)

The disjunction between this passage and the poet's earlier evocation of the heavenly "steppes where as thow seest pace / Virgile, Ovide, Omer, Lucan, and Stace" (V, 1791–92) is brutal. The sexual and textual pressures upon Troilus's identity as a lover end by calling into question not only the construction of his masculinity and the nature of love, but also the ability of poetry to deal with either subject. The end of the poem is finally not simply about the translation of Troilus from the sphere of human, heterosexual, aggressive love to that of divine, assexual, merciful love, but about the painfully conditional love of the Christian poet for his pagan models, which must always disappoint him, just as Criseyde disappoints Troilus.

Troilus's "Gentil" Manhood

DEREK BREWER

All three main characters in *Troilus and Criseyde* have been judged variously according to the preferences and prejudices of their critics. This variation is in itself eloquent testimony to Chaucer's genius in creating characters whom the reader engages with as with living persons. The last fifty years in particular have seen extraordinary varieties of response and judgment as our own society has oscillated in value-judgments and has largely abandoned those of previous centuries. Judgments of Troilus in particular have varied. Windeatt gives an admirable account of his character, and a summary of varied reactions.[1] For centuries Troilus was seen, if commented on at all, as the noble if tragic lover, "true Troilus." Then he was derided, for example by D. W. Robertson, along with all medieval lovers, as the stereotype of foolish immorality, sexual love being so regarded by many medieval theologians and apparently by Robertson himself. A number of critics have found Troilus extravagantly self-indulgent in grief, or unduly timid. Lambert finds him boringly and exasperatingly faithful.[2] More recently political feminist critics have condemned him and his whole male-dominated culture as predatory, lustful, insecure, competitive, selfish, so emotional as to "invite psychoanalytical attention," little better than a rapist. His love is continually called in question by being placed within quotation marks, "love."[3] By contrast, most of my young women students used to regard him as a feeble creature, "a poor sap," "a wimp."

---

[1] Barry Windeatt, *Troilus and Criseyde*, Oxford Guides to Chaucer (Oxford: Oxford University Press, 1992), 275–79.
[2] D. W. Robertson, *A Preface to Chaucer* (Princeton: Princeton University Press, 1962). Mark Lambert, "*Troilus*, Books I–III: A Criseydan Reading," in *Essays on Troilus and Criseyde*, ed. Mary Salu (Cambridge: D. S. Brewer, 1979), 105–25.
[3] David Aers, "Masculine Identity in the Courtly Community: The Self Loving in *Troilus*

Not all recent critics have despised Troilus. Donaldson, for example, emphasizes Troilus's *trouthe*.[4] Mann notably expounds the growth of a trusting relationship between Troilus and Criseyde, and I myself have always maintained that he is a sympathetic and noble figure.[5] We have to remember that he lived in a small agrarian-based society, which was, like almost all such societies, hierarchical, aggressive, male-dominated, religious, with various other, to us, socially deplorable characteristics. Troilus fits the pattern of an idealized and idealistic young man in such a society.

Since critics nowadays often argue that individuals are "constructed" by their social circumstances, it seems pointless to condemn either a long-past society or the individuals it constructs. Rather, we should take seriously its often-mentioned "otherness" and study it for what it was, making a reasonable allowance, if not for free will, at least for good will. We should approach not as propagandists for a new social order which the past could not know, but in the spirit of sympathetic social anthropologists. We shall see more and learn more.[6] A study of *Troilus and Criseyde* in this spirit shows what Chaucer calls "manhood" and that Troilus accords with it. Troilus's manhood is a more delicate and complex condition than the word "masculinity" implies.

Youth, royalty and manhood in the fourteenth century

"Masculinity" as a word has become prominent only recently, as a product, appropriately enough, of feminism and gender-studies. Though first recorded in English in 1748 it has not been much used, and when used it has often had slightly derogatory, and French, connotations. Now it seems to be used as an apparently value-free scientific term, though it tends to retain its disagreeable – and French – associations, for example with violence.[7] It has also tended to be used, along with the adjective "masculine," with specifically sexual implications. Thus Aers writes of what he describes as Troilus's fantasies of rape and of his swoon at Criseyde's bedside, that they are "the product of 'drede' (III, 706–07), fear lest his masculine identity so heavily dependent on performance in the sexual domain, might not, as it were, stand up."[8] Leaving aside the gross allusion here, so inappropriate to the whole tone of Chaucer's poem, even to

and Criseyde," Chapter 3 in *Community, Gender and Individual Identity* (London: Routledge, 1988).

4 E. Talbot Donaldson, *Speaking of Chaucer* (London: Athlone Press, 1970), 96.

5 Jill Mann, *Geoffrey Chaucer* (Feminist Readings) (London: Harvester Press, 1991).

6 An illuminating introduction to this approach is by Aaron Gurevich, *Historical Anthropology of the Middle Ages*, ed. Jana Howlett (Cambridge: Polity Press, 1992).

7 See Thelma Fenster, "Preface: Why Men?" in *Medieval Masculinities: Regarding Men in the Middle Ages*, ed. Clare A. Lees (Minneapolis: University of Minnesota Press, 1994), xi–xii.

8 Aers, 129.

Pandarus, there is simply no evidence nor any reason to suppose that Troilus may fear sexual impotence. His love is naturally sexual, and Chaucer makes of it also a social and personal construct of great complexity, as Mann shows.[9] Troilus's "masculinity" is better described by Chaucer's word (and that of many later English writers) as "manhood."

To be in love is not essential to Troilus's identity, nor to the general concept of manhood. He is fully himself when he is seen at the beginning of the poem "guiding" his young knights, looking at ladies, and mocking lovers. It is typical of adolescent boys' behavior. Equally typical is his precipitate falling in love. The poem is remarkable for the way it constructs Troilus's love and manhood to give an individual cast to the ancient ideal of the brave man who is a "lion in the field and a lamb in the hall."[10] There are plenty of literary examples of young men's obsessive love, often leading to extravagant behavior – Romeo, Vronsky in *Anna Karenina*, and the heroes in Constant's *Adolphe*, Fromentin's *Dominique*, and Fitzgerald's *The Great Gatsby*, to mention only a few classic cases.

Some recent criticism so much emphasizes the degree to which character and action are socially determined that we are in danger of overlooking what is natural, or indeed "transhistorical." It now even seems worthwhile to emphasize what used to seem so obvious as to need no comment, that many young men naturally fall in love, are shy, and suffer the pangs of dispriz'd love in most if not all cultures, and certainly in ours. Sexual desire is strong. It is claimed that 72% of young people in the United States have had sexual intercourse by the age of seventeen.[11] This level of sexual experience must be comparable with aristocratic society in fourteenth-century England. As one example, John of Gaunt married the Duchess Blanche at the age of nineteen, apparently for love, but he had already had a mistress and an illegitimate child.[12] Even the extravagance of Troilus's grief for love can today be matched. Social factors are strong, but are sufficiently different in different centuries to enable us to recognize alongside or beneath these differences the existence of continuing transhistorical natural factors as well. A few hundred years within the same general culture are but an evening gone in the long course of human evolution and do not bring about fundamental change.

One important assumption that Chaucer relied upon in his presentation of

---

[9] Mann, *Chaucer*, passim.

[10] The lion/lamb stereotype is widely invoked. In English an early example is the praise of the hero at the end of *Beowulf*. The portrait of Chaucer's Knight in the General Prologue to the *Canterbury Tales* spells it out (I 43–78). At the other end of the time-scale we find the same sentiment in the threnody for Lancelot in Malory's *Morte Darthur*, *The Works of Sir Thomas Malory*, ed. E. Vinaver, rev. P. J. C. Field, 3rd ed. (Oxford: Oxford University Press, 1990), III, 1259.

[11] *The Daily Telegraph*, 17 May 1996, p. 26.

[12] C. Given Wilson and Alice Curteis, *Royal Bastards* (London: Routledge and Kegan Paul, 1984), 147.

Troilus is his extreme youth. There is some change in social expectation here. When I have asked students what age they assume Troilus to be they have tended to think of him as "about 25," and Criseyde "about 22." This assumption is deeply misleading. No wonder Troilus's emotions, hyperbolically expressed as we all agree they are, come to seem absurd. The tradition was that Troilus was very young. We should think of him as about 15 or 16. Even in World War II many fighting soldiers, sailors, and airmen were 19 or 20. We know well that men a good deal older and in grander positions than Troilus may be obsessed by love or sexual desire, and correspondingly lose respect and make fools of themselves. But it is more understandable at 16, and in a royal prince. Criseyde could well be about the same age, or a little older.[13]

English courtly society in the fourteenth century was dominated by what we might now think of as adolescent values in all their vigour, generosity, petulance, passionate egoism. These values are not limited to the period of adolescence, but that is their period of dominance, though modern, popular fiction is still dominated by them now. Adolescence is probably the most interesting and intense period of our lives. The actual concept of adolescence did not exist in medieval thought, though "youth" was recognized. Our modern notions of adolescence were then subsumed into young manhood.[14] Clerics might disapprove but had little notice taken of them then as now. Even older men and women subscribed to such values. Ideals of romantic love and extravagant bravery were shared by all, if not always practiced, as is the way with ideals now as then. Princes had their mistresses and took part personally in battles from an early age. In 1330 Edward III asserted his position as king by a coup against his mother's lover Mortimer in which he personally took part when he was 17. He had married Philippa of Hainault when he was 16 and she probably 14, in 1328, a political marriage but something of a love-match too. Their son Edward the Black Prince (so called from the sixteenth century) was born in 1330. In 1346 he at least nominally commanded the right wing and vanguard of the army in the great victory of the English at Crécy. Edward distinguished himself in the hand-to-hand fighting, and though he was at one time beaten to his knees and almost captured, he recovered and showed the great physical strength, bravery, and skill of the Plantagenet line. The poem *Wynnere and Wastoure* composed only a few years after describes him in splendid armour and says "he was ȝongest of ȝeris and ȝapest [liveliest] of wit" (119). All this at the age of 16.[15] He did not marry until he was 31, but by then had an

---

13 I have argued for this at greater length in Derek Brewer, "The Ages of Troilus, Criseyde and Pandarus," in *Tradition and Innovation in Chaucer* (London: Macmillan, 1982), 80–88.
14 James A. Schultz, "Medieval Adolescence: The Claims of History and the Silence of German Narrative," *Speculum* 66 (1991): 519–39.
15 *Wynnere and Wastoure in Middle English Debate Poetry*, ed. J. W. Conlee (East Lansing: Colleagues Press, 1991); R. W. Barber, *Edward Prince of Wales and Aquitane* (Woodbridge: The Boydell Press, 1978), 17, 64–66.

illegitimate son. His brother, John of Gaunt, born in 1340, took part in Edward III's campaign in 1359–60, as did Chaucer, born about the same date or a little later. Gaunt took a leading part in the fighting in December, aged 19, and even Chaucer, of about the same age, whom we may suspect was no fighting man, strayed sufficiently close to the enemy to be taken prisoner. Richard II, born January 1367, became king in 1377. In June 1381, aged 14, he gallantly confronted the rebellious peasants at Smithfield when his entourage seem to have been stricken with fear.[16] In 1385 Richard headed an army which invaded Scotland and devastated Edinburgh. In 1382, aged 15, he married Anne of Bohemia who was 16. At her death in 1394 he raged tempestuously and had their favourite palace at Sheen destroyed. Richard's behavior was as extravagantly emotional as Troilus's, and he was then 27.

Troilus fits well into this pattern of behavior of royal princes. Chaucer goes out of his way to emphasise his fighting prowess. True, he is second to Hector as "holder up of Troye" (II, 644), but no one could displace Hector from his supreme position in any version of the Troy story. To be second only to Hector is the highest praise. There is nothing realistically unlikely about Troilus's return from battle, looking as knightly a sight as Mars the god of battle, and

> So lik a man of armes and a knyght
> He was to seen, fulfilled of heigh prowess,
> For both he had a body and a myght
> To don that thing, as wel as hardynesse,
> And ek to seen hym in his gere hym dresse
> So fressh, so yong, so weldy semed he
> It was an heven upon hym for to see.   (II, 631–37)

The admiration expressed in the text here has no signs of irony. The admiration accords with the ideals of the time. His helm and shield are cut to pieces (and surely it is perverse to read the condition of his shield as symbolic of his psychic vulnerability, any more than of a young fighter-pilot returning to base with his plane full of bullet holes). The people cry out in his praise

> For which he wex a litel reed for shame
> When he the peple upon hym herde cryen
> That to byholde it was a noble game
> How sobrelich he caste down his yën.   (II, 645–48)

No one has so far suggested that all this is meant ironically as spoken by the stupid narrator in order to denigrate Troilus, though that critical method has been frequently employed in the adjacent lines in order to denigrate Criseyde.

---

[16] Derek Brewer, *Chaucer and His World* (London, 1978, re-issued Cambridge: D. S. Brewer, 1992), 133–51.

The description sums up Troilus's manly prowess in terms of unequivocal, and, naturally, "essentialist," praise – that being the only mode open to Chaucer. There is a genuine touch of non-ironical genial humor in observing Troilus's entirely proper embarrassment, youthful for all his manliness. There is an interesting real-life analogue to this princely embarrassment. After the victory at Crécy the king asked Prince Edward what he thought of going into battle and fighting, and whether he thought it good sport. The prince according to the chronicler "said nothing and was ashamed [*honteux*]."[17] This shame was modest embarrassment, not the humiliation of conscious wrongdoing. He had done extremely well, like Troilus. All the passage describing Troilus's return from battle is Chaucer's expansion. Boccaccio does not provide this glamorous spectacle of Troilus as a basis for Criseyde's musings on Pandarus's information about his love for her. After hearing his praise, then seeing him, she naturally rehearses to herself his good qualities, including his handsomeness and *gentilesse*, and most of all that "his distress was all for her" (II, 659–65). In other words, the sight of him is connected with all the praise given to him by Pandarus, and her own social knowledge of him. The poet in then looking forward to Criseyde's eventual love for him says that eventually it was "his manhood and his pyne" (II, 676) that made her love him. The two qualities are significantly joined here: neither one without the other would be enough. That he suffers for her is a guarantee of his love for her, but here we may first note the emphasis on "manhood." Alan Gaylord interprets this "manhood" as "what we would call sex-appeal," but this is quite the wrong meaning for "manhood" in Chaucer's works or generally.[18]

Troilus's manhood

The reference to "manhood" just quoted is the first ever made in Chaucer's work and has no counterpart in Boccaccio. A second follows at a most interesting stage in Book III, after Troilus, lying sick in bed, has had a satisfactory interview with Criseyde in the house of Deiphebus. It is not true that Troilus has feigned illness, "For I am sik in ernest, douteles" (II, 1529) as he says.

Muscatine long ago pointed out an interesting partial analogue for Troilus's taking to his bed and his interview with Criseyde. It is the story of Amnon's love for his half-sister Tamar (II Samuel 13), which according to D. W. Robertson was well known in the fourteenth century. The first point to note is that Amnon is reported to be genuinely "sick for his sister Tamar" and becomes noticeably lean (v.4). In this sickness Troilus resembles him. There is nothing

---

[17] Barber, *Edward*, 68.
[18] Alan T. Gaylord, "Gentilesse in Chaucer's *Troilus*," *SP* 61 (1964): 19–34, especially 26.

unmanly in being sick for love of a woman. The second point to note is the great
contrast between Troilus and Amnon. Amnon commits a rape. Troilus is so
overcome with love and shyness that he forgets all the fine words he has
prepared. Does this forgetfulness not seem natural, especially as referring to a
sixteen- or seventeen-year-old, perhaps even today? Criseyde sees well what
Troilus's difficulty is, and she likes him none the worse for it. She can read the
situation easily. She knows she has no grounds for fear, as the unfortunate Tamar
had. And surely Criseyde's perception is equally natural. In neither case is there
anything shameful.

The real point is that Troilus, though genuinely sick for love, is as far from
committing a rape as he could be. His sickness is the product both of his
naturally fine temperament and of his culturally produced *gentilesse*, the
combination which constitutes his manhood.[19]

The excuse for the meeting between Criseyde and Troilus is Pandarus's
account of the renewal of the lawsuit of Poliphete against Criseyde, in defense
against which he wishes in true medieval manner to gather the support of
powerful friends and their kin. The sickness of Troilus is real, though its cause
is love for Criseyde, as she is well aware, but she comes quite innocently to
Deiphebus' house, unaware that Troilus will be there lying sick (II, 1562). After
their meeting, during which Criseyde has confessed her love and kissed Troilus
(III, 176–82), Troilus asks to be left alone, except that Pandarus has a pallet-bed
set up for him in Troilus's room. They have a significant dialogue in which
Pandarus excuses his own role in bringing Troilus and Criseyde together – an
apology put in even stronger terms by Boccaccio, and slightly expanded and
softened by Chaucer. Chaucer adds to Boccaccio's account a substantial section
of Pandarus's speech recommending secrecy and loyalty in love. Troilus, in a
speech also much amplified from Boccaccio, excuses Pandarus on grounds of
his "gentilesse, / Compassioun, and felawship and trist" (III, 402–03) and in
return says he would do as much for Pandarus if he desires any of his sisters,
since Pandarus has saved his life and not acted for reward (III, 407–15).

The morality of Troilus's offer has been much debated. It illustrates masculine bonding, and it emphasizes that the male lover must be faithful to his lady.
Even if it is deplorably masculine it is highly masculine, though Troilus's
youthful enthusiasm may be thought to have rather carried him away. And now,
though cured of love-sickness, Troilus burns with sharp desire of hope and
plesaunce, but "He nought forgat his goode governaunce" (III, 427). (Windeatt
for "goode" reads "wise," a harder and preferable reading.) His self govern-
ment is his manhood, his manliness, "But in hymself with manhod gan
restreyne / Ech racle dede and ech unbridled cheere" (III, 428–29); that is, he
practiced restrained good manners and morality.

This self-controlled Troilus is a different side of his character, consequent

---

[19] Charles Muscatine, "The Feigned Illness in Chaucer's *Troilus and Criseyde*," *MLN* 63
(1948): 372–77.

on the certainty of being loved. He continues to do his full duty as a soldier though he suffers the pains of love. These lines are Chaucer's own, from III, 428 to III, 1295, and they take the place of stanzas 21 to 29, Parte Seconda in Boccaccio's *Filostrato*, in which Criseida makes arrangements to let Troilo secretly into the house and swiftly goes to bed with him. In Chaucer the actual arrangements are made by Pandarus, and Criseyde is entirely innocent of them. Boccaccio's stanzas 30 to 32 relate his Criseida's flirtatious coyness in abandoning her last garment, which Chaucer follows only at a great and discreet distance in III, 1296–1316.

This long, beautiful, complex account by Chaucer of "sweet, reluctant, amorous delay," including Troilus's swoon, has been much discussed, notably by Jill Mann[20] who illustrates most clearly the dilemma and conflicting feelings in Troilus, torn between desire and honorable refusal to coerce. This is manhood, the manliness which includes gentleness, generosity, and if necessary self-sacrifice. It is referred to by Mann as exemplifying "the feminised hero," whose role is passive, who forebears coercion, and whose surrender to love is the sign of a noble generosity. "Feminised" does not mean "effeminate."[21] Convincing as is Mann's exposition here, the word "feminised" has its dangers as well as its virtues. It is valuable in pointing out the possession by Troilus of those sterling virtues of constancy, patience, gentleness, goodness, and strength which Chaucer more frequently incarnates in women, but it may lead us to forget how seriously the traditional male stereotype for many centuries also incarnated these virtues in the chivalric ideal of manliness, which included being a "lamb in the hall" and in which dominating sexual prowess has no part. The example of the Knight in the General Prologue to the *Canterbury Tales*, so powerful a fighter, so "gentil" in ordinary life, is highly relevant. The ideal is reiterated in the poet's praise of Troilus as a "manly" knight. When Criseyde has her second glimpse of Troilus passing by – "God woot wher he was lik a manly knyght" (II, 1263) – he appeals to her the more in that he humbly salutes her and blushes. She is aware of his *gentilesse*. There is a combination of traditional chivalric virtues here, of the lion and the lamb. Later, with similar oxymoron, Troilus displays "manly sorwe" before Criseyde, which makes Pandarus weep as if he were turned to water, as the poet perhaps sarcastically remarks. Criseyde will accept him, "her honour safe," and in rather sprightly manner asserts her intention to govern him, which is far from detracting from his manliness. Pandarus next uses the word "manly" in a less favourable sense, to "sette the world on six and sevene" (IV, 622) but this sense is rejected by Troilus, and the last use of the word "manly" in the poem tells how Troilus, when he prepares to ride out with Criseyde when she is handed over to the Greeks, "gan his wo ful manly for to hide" (V, 30). He continues to conceal his sorrow as far as the public is concerned, though the poet gives

---

20 Jill Mann, "Troilus' Swoon," *ChauR* 14 (1980): 319–35.
21 Mann, *Chaucer*, 166.

us full access to his private sorrow in his letters to Criseyde and his talk with Pandarus, so that we have perhaps too strong a sense of self-indulgent grief. For a time he falls so sick that he can hardly walk with a staff, the poet anticipating modern psychoanalysis to remark, "And with his ire he thus hymselve shente" (V, 1223). Troilus punishes himself, suffering from jealousy, but still conceals the cause from his family – "He nolde his cause pleyne" (V, 1230). Eventually he realizes completely that he has lost Criseyde and though he does not commit suicide he seeks revenge and death in battle.

Troilus's end is manly enough but Chaucer uses the word no more in the poem. His other usages of the word "manly" are of the essentialist kind, historically inevitable, encapsulating the ideal of manly, that is, natural good male behavior. The Monk in the General Prologue is "A manly man, to been an abbot able" (I, 167), which excludes, like other usages, any specifically sexual implications.

Sexual prowess has never been of itself a marker of traditional manhood, though male sexuality itself is taken for granted. After his swoon at Criseyde's bedside Troilus is eventually thrust into her bed by Pandarus, and modern readers are often impatient with Troilus's slowness, his readiness to pray, and his deference to Criseyde. Nor are they alone: Pandarus breaks out, when Troilus faints, "O thef, is this a mannes herte?" (III, 1098), and even Criseyde, as Troilus begins to come to, says, "Is this a mannes game? / What, Troilus, wol ye do thus for shame?" (III, 1126–27). But she treats him very lovingly. All this is Chaucer's invention.

There is some gentle comedy here on Chaucer's part, though he leaves it to the reader to deduce how much. Even here "to be a man" is not, as it seems to me, simply sexual. It is rather "to keep one's nerve," "to behave sensibly." The sexual element may be stronger in the minds of Pandarus and Criseyde than in that of Troilus, and once again we may recall his youth. But at the last, with Criseyde's consent and joy, he is appropriately "manly."

Pandarus has a simpler notion of manhood than has Troilus. Chaucer's next use of the word "manhood" is placed in the mouth of Pandarus when Troilus has learnt that Criseyde must be sent to the Greeks. Troilus weeps. Pandarus says, since you are so distressed, and will not simply take another lady, of whom there are plenty (and anyway "it is but casuel plesaunce" [IV, 419]), why do you not act to help yourself, "And with thy manhod letten al this grame? / Go ravysshe here! Ne kanstow nat, for shame?" (IV, 529–30). Have you not the courage to take a woman who loves you "kith thow art a man," (IV, 538)? The encouragement to "ravish" Criseyde is in *Filostrato*, though instead of the reference to "being a man," Pandaro exhorts Troilo to show his "great spirit," *grande animo* (Parte Quarta, st. 65). In Pandarus's version we have the lower ranges of what it is to be a man – decisive, self-assertive, setting society at naught. The word "ravish" does not mean "rape," but to "carry off," and it has associations with delight, especially in the passive sense. Pandarus is recommending not rape but elopement. Nevertheless, it is a concept of "masculinity" rather than of "manhood" or "manliness." Troilus rejects it for a number of good moral and practical reasons, including his wish not to disturb Criseyde with violence. In Boccaccio Troilo does not wish to spoil her honor and repute, and is afraid he may displease Criseida. Chaucer separates out Criseyde's honor and amplifies its importance – Troilus would rather save Criseyde's honor than his own life (IV, 567).

Troilus's honor

Honor introduces yet another theme of great importance in the structure of the poem. It chiefly concerns Criseyde and I have considered this rather neglected topic at length elsewhere.[22] Troilus earns high honor by his bravery which Chaucer constantly emphasises though it is not his particular interest:

> And if I hadde ytaken for to write
> The armes of this ilke worthi man,
> Than wolde ich of his batailles endite;
> But for that I to writen first bigan
> Of his love, I have seyd as I kan.   (V, 1765–69)

His manhood is taken for granted and it is part of his manhood that he respects Criseyde's honor. Nor does Criseyde believe that she loved him or, as she says, took pity on his distress primarily for his valor, any more than for his royal rank, or "vain delight," i.e. sexual pleasure, or for pomp, array, nobility, or wealth:

> But moral vertu, grounded upon trouthe –
> That was the cause I first hadde on yow routhe!
> Eke gentil herte and manhod that ye hadde.   (IV, 1672–74).

She loves him because of his loyalty, nobility, manliness, "And that youre resoun bridlede youre delit" (IV, 1678).

"Delit" is certainly sexual appetite. Part of Troilus's manhood is that his reason controls his sexual desire. This control is a traditional virtue of manliness. Yet Troilus's moral virtue and his *gentilesse* have been seriously questioned.[23] The deceitfulness of Pandarus, the extremity of Troilus's behavior in private both before his acceptance by Criseyde and after her departure from Troy, have been held against him despite the constant witness of other characters in the poem and the authorial voice proclaiming his manly virtue. We may have here, I think, a certain distinction between what the character is, and what he

22 Derek Brewer, "Honour in Chaucer," in *Tradition and Innovation in Chaucer* (London: Macmillan, 1982), 89–109; Windeatt, 244–46.
23 Gaylord (see note 18 above) and Aers (see note 3 above).

or she does, that is sometimes found in traditional literature when the main outline of the story is received in an earlier version and the character is later remodelled.[24] Our sense of that distinction is enhanced when the actions derive from an historically different structure of society. Troilus's *character*, therefore, is presented as superior in quality to what he actually does, insofar as what he does is to seduce Criseyde, partly because he is presented as doing it with good will, as well as from unavoidable impulse. (The same is true for Criseyde – and may well be sometimes true of actual living people.)

A patriarchal society

It should go without saying that Troilus lives in a patriarchal society. Agrarian societies, whether fourteenth-century England or in this respect the not-so-different pagan society of ancient Troy as imagined by Chaucer, are hierarchical, male-dominated, aggressive, territorial, religious (though religious in a more integral yet more casual way than Western post-Reformation and post-Counter-Reformation societies conceive religion). Their nature is not a matter of individual choice, but how they are. Hierarchy affects gender-status. Women are relatively low and weak, though aristocratic women have a certain if limited power, especially if they are widows. Criseyde has, and apparently manages, her own estate and household. She relies, however, on Pandarus for advice and support "of hir estat and of hire governance" (II, 219) and even more so when a legal conflict with Poliphete concerning her affairs arises. She is clear that Pandarus ought to protect her, and is shocked that he advocates Troilus's cause. She takes the conventional moral view that she ought not to have a lover, and that Pandarus as her uncle and "best friend" should forbid her to love (II, 411–13). Criseyde's sense of her own vulnerability here, as in her earlier remark about her fear of the Greeks (II, 124), is acute, and all of Chaucer's invention. Yet as she also says,

> I am myn owene womman, wel at ese –
> I thank it God – as after myn estat,
> Right yong.   (II, 750–56)

She has no husband to check her or exert mastery. Part of Criseyde's problem here, as when she is sent to the Greeks, is that she is not only "slydynge of corage" but also over-confident of her own stability. In each case, however, Chaucer presents her as deserving of pity: "Iwis, I wolde excuse hire yet for routhe" (V, 1099). There are no signals here to tell us to take this as the comment of a stupid narrator, expressing the opposite of the poet's real meaning.

---

[24] Derek Brewer, "Retellings," in *Retelling Tales: Essays in Honor of Russell Peck*, ed. T. Hahn and A. Lupack (Cambridge, 1997), 9–34. Arthur Mizener, "Character and Action in the Case of Criseyde," *PMLA* 54 (1939): 65–81.

Pandarus, as we all know, exploits the lack of power that such a society enforces on women, Criseyde's timidity, and her confidence in him, all on behalf of Troilus. It is here that Troilus's passivity in love protects him from the accusation of cold-hearted seduction, and even Pandarus has the excuse of his devoted friendship to Troilus. What distinguishes Troilus is that under the guidance of love he himself will not seduce Criseyde. On the contrary he yields to her all power. The superiority, the "governance," of the beloved lady, and the humility of the lover are part of the convention of romantic love, part of Chaucer's "medievalising" the *Filostrato*, as C. S. Lewis remarked.[25] Conventional as these may be, it is important to recognize that Criseyde's status is genuinely superior and humility in love is genuine in Troilus. His surrender of all power to Criseyde is not feeble but is the product of choice and self-control. It prevents him from carrying her off rather than letting her be sent to the Greeks.

Nature and nurture

To call it "surrender" may inadvertently suggest unwilling capitulation. It is true that Troilus is said to be hit by the arrow of the god of love (I, 209), "For may no man fordon the lawe of kynde" (I, 238). His passion is entirely natural and to that extent involuntary. Love spared him in no way, "But held him as his thral lowe in destresse" (I, 439). Yet equally Troilus's own thought and intention develop his passion. Following his first sight of Criseyde there are a couple of hundred lines, partly suggested by Boccaccio and partly original with Chaucer, tracing most delicately the balance of involuntary and voluntary love. These lines illustrate the way that Troilus reorganizes his actions in service of love, as for example his increase of ferocity against the Greeks, not because he hates them, but in order to please Criseyde better with his renown (I, 477–83). All this is interlarded by the poet with half-humorous warnings about love, both its irresistibility and its danger. In the course of this almost Proustian passage about love it is said of Troilus, "Thus took he purpos loves craft to suwe" (I, 379).

In these matters nature and nurture, (or culture), interact. Troilus is represented as a more-than-willing victim of natural impulses, but he equally naturally *chooses* to follow the social construction. Too much has been written misleadingly about "the code of courtly love," but there is indeed a literary social construct, without being an external compulsion, that Troilus follows. It is best illustrated by Chaucer's interesting short poem now called the *Complaint of Venus*, translated with considerable alteration from a poem by Oton de

[25] C. S. Lewis, "What Chaucer Really Did to *Il Filostrato*," *Essays and Studies* 17 (1932): 65–75; repr. in Richard. J. Schoek and Jerome Taylor, eds., *Chaucer Criticism*, ii, *Troilus and Criseyde and the Minor Poems* (Notre Dame, IN: University of Notre Dame Press, 1961), 16–33.

Graunson. The "complaint" is to Love about jealousy. It is spoken by a lady expressing her own love and praising the knight she loves. It could be Criseyde speaking at the height of their love and Troilus whom she praises, in its applicability. The conventionality is here of value as establishing the norm. Every wight, says the lady, praises the knight's *gentilesse* (three times repeated). The lady takes pleasure in thinking

> Upon the manhod and the worthynesse
> Upon the trouthe and on the stidfastnesse . . .
> In him is bounte, wysdom, governaunce . . .
> That of knyghthod he is parfit richesse.
> Honour honoureth him for his noblesse . . .
> And notwithstondyng al his suffisaunce
> His gentil herte is of so gret humblesse . . .
> And me to serve is al his besynesse.   (4–20)

The first three stanzas selectively quoted here could be a character-sketch, or stereotype, of Troilus. The fourth, quoted below in full, describes his behavior:

> Now certis, Love, hit is right covenable
> That men ful dere bye thy nobil thing,
> As wake abedde and fasten at the table,
> Wepinge to laughe and singe in compleynyng,
> And doun to caste visage and lokyng,
> Often to chaunge hewe and contenaunce,
> Pleyne in slepynge and dremen at the daunce,
> Al the revers of any glad felyng.   (25–32).

All is there, from his manliness through his *gentilesse* and humility, to his dear purchase of noble suffering, sleeplessness, loss of appetite, down to changing his hue sixty times a day (I, 441).

The *Compleynt of Venus* has further interest in that Chaucer has changed the original male speaker in Graunson's poem to a lady, who describes both the manly *gentilesse* and the love-sickness of the lover as qualities both necessary and lovable in a knight. Criseyde, too, loves Troilus for the distress he suffers for her (II, 663–64). The greater the distress the greater the love. Love-sickness has been extensively studied[26] and Troilus demonstrates it fully in sincere if familiar form. Some illnesses are common and lack originality but may be no less painful. Nor should even familiar types of illness, especially of the psychosomatic type of love-sickness, be treated as culpable weakmindedness. They need not be hypocritical imitation of symptoms (though Diomede

[26] Mary F. Wack, "Lovesickness in *Troilus*," *Pacific Coast Philology* 19 (1984): 55–61.

practices this), nor in this case unmanly, though some early medieval authorities, especially medical ones, regarded love-sickness in men as indicating an undesirable femininity. The doctors' recommended cure, paradoxically, was the same as that sought by entirely manly lovers – sexual intercourse.[27] In Chaucer's poetry, as has been shown, love-sickness is regarded as a normal, even desirable, illness in the entirely manly knight.

The *Compleynt of Venus* exalts the honor of the beloved knight, and Troilus's honor, gained by his valor, has been sufficiently emphasised, though honor includes or is closely associated with other virtues. Criseyde loves Troilus for his honor and he loves her honor in her. (Criseyde's honor is a complex quality, of which the dominant element is reputation, but is too complicated to be summarized here.) The extent of Troilus's surrender of power to Criseyde is illustrated not only by his valuing her honor above his own life but also by his willingness to abandon his own honor, which includes his duty to his family and Troy, his valor in fighting to save them, in order to preserve his *trouthe* and his loyalty to Criseyde by offering to escape from Troy with her. "Trouthe is the hyeste thyng that man may kepe" according to Arveragus in the *Franklin's Tale* (V, 1479) and is superior to honor, though perhaps it depends on what quality *trouthe* is devoted to.

Troilus's surrender is further illustrated by his willingness to commit suicide, abandoning city and family when he thinks Criseyde dead (IV, 1198–1211). In this he resembles Troilo in the *Filostrato*, translated fairly closely here. For both Italian and English versions, the hero's readiness for death indicates both his bravery and his devotion. But it is Troilus, not Troilo, who says that if Criseyde does not return he will never have health, honor nor joy, and who warns Criseyde that she will not be able to outwit her father and return (IV, 1442–63).

Such devotion, and there are many more examples of it in the poem, has been called the "infantilisation of Troilus, a desire to be bound," "a desire for a metaphysical seigneur," while of Troilus's Boethian meditation in the temple it has been remarked that "Reading the Boethianizing attempt in Book IV it is hard not to conclude that no form of thumb-sucking, however sophisticatedly abstract, could defend the knight against the anxieties that flood over him."[28]

The imputation of anxiety to men has become a fashionable critical ploy by which the attribution of anxiety is made yet another cause for condemnation. Anxiety is a natural feeling and a biological necessity for survival. We need to be generally on our guard. The essence of anxiety as neurosis, however, is that it is excessive fear experienced without being able to assign a definite cause.[29] When there is a definite cause for fear the emotion felt is only in a general sense

---

[27] Vern L. Bullough, "On Being a Male in the Middle Ages," in Clare A. Lees, ed., *Medieval Masculinities*, 31–45 (also considers lovesickness).

[28] Aers, 147.

[29] *The Oxford Companion to the Mind*, ed. R. L. Gregory (Oxford: Oxford University Press, 1987), s. v. Anxiety, 30–31.

to be described as anxiety. A soldier going into battle may in the general sense feel anxious. Troilus lying in bed preparing to make his plea to Criseyde similarly feels anxious. It is quite reasonable, indeed, quite sensible, to feel this kind of anxiety about all sorts of real or potential difficulties and threats. The biological value of such anxiety is that it may prompt us to take some evasive or remedial action. Aers is correct in saying that Troilus is anxious when he forsees the loss of Criseyde. Troilus proposes various remedies, all of which she rejects. There is no justification in the text for attributing to him nameless and by implication childish, and by further implication reprehensible, fears. Quite the reverse: once Troilus is in love, "Alle other dredes weren from him fledde / Both of th'assege and his savacioun" (I, 463–64). The poem is quite explicit that love drives out even legitimate and appropriate fears.

Troilus's only desire is for Criseyde's

> compassioun
> And he to ben hire man while he may dure.
> Lo, here his lif, and from the deth his cure!   (I, 467–69)

Troilus may suffer from being in love but his love focusses his desire and relieves him, says the poet, of all other anxiety. When he wins Criseyde's love he has no anxiety at all. Of course, if you believe that the poem is told by a stupid narrator you can refuse to believe this statement. But in that case everything in the poem becomes open to uncontrollable interpretation, and no opinion is more tenable than any other; anything can be interpreted in any sense. But here we follow what the poem tells us in obvious good faith.

Aers argues that Troilus "has not the resources to assimilate the loss his colleagues forced him to confront."[30] It is true that Troilus's love is obsessive, and that not everyone suffers or has suffered from such an emotion. A more sympathetic way of describing Troilus's sorrow would be to say that Troilus's "moral vertu grounded upon trouthe" is so fully built into his character, such a combination of a noble nature and a consciously idealistic nurture "Following the art of love," that he has no choice but to be himself, and that this is the essence of both his misery and his manliness. The tragedy of Troilus is caused not by weakness but by the strength of his virtue, his *trouthe* and his "gentil manhode," his obsessive constancy. His grief comes from an intolerable deprivation of a kind by no means unknown even today. It may evoke some modern readers' impatience, but surely in the main body of the poem it is presented as deserving our sympathy, as with those other love-lorn heroes of the European tradition mentioned above (p. 239). Moreover, such love-tragedies are well-known in, for example, Eastern traditions. Childish or not, they are a transcultural, transhistorical phenomenon, even if there was sometimes a dangerously filial element in the medieval "art of love." They have traditionally

---

[30] Aers, 147.

been presented as arousing our sympathy, not contempt. Yet for Troilus that is not quite the whole story.

Despite my earlier argument it may well be that Aers, with his robust lack of sympathy for Troilus, correctly expresses the final judgment made in the poem itself. When at the end Troilus is carried to the eighth sphere he derides those who weep for his death and damns, as Aers does, all our "werk" (to be glossed as "suffering," "trouble") which follows blind pleasure (V, 1821–27). This ending, as we all know, is inconsistent with the general tenor of the poem. There is an even later twist, admittedly outside the poem itself, but revealing Chaucer's own personal final judgment. If we believe that the whole poem condemns Troilus and his love we disregard Chaucer's own last different condemnation of "the book of Troilus" as "enditynge of worldly vanitee" in his *Retraction* at the end of the *Canterbury Tales*. At the time of writing *Troilus and Criseyde* Chaucer was less rigorous. He no doubt intentionally leaves the ultimate destination to which Mercury leads the pagan Troilus unclear, though he has ascended "ful blisfully" (V, 1808). The vagueness shows that his final destination is unimportant. The ending is no condemnation of Troilus's *trouthe*, however misdirected his loyalty may have been. It is easy to think ill of those who in "real life" throughout the centuries have suffered death for a cause or a belief in which we cannot believe, or may strongly disapprove of. Yet we may admire their firmness. Troilus's misdirected loyalty, as some may think it, however misdirected, might still be, even for Chaucer, had he been asked, a virtue. Troilus seeks his death in battle, raging against and hoping to kill the successful seducer Diomede, whose "love" is truly hypocritical and insincere, and is frustrated even there, for Achilles slays him. We are surely meant to feel sympathetic pity for Troilus in the end; his behavior is natural and may be no less manly for being in this case sad. The pity does not blot out our memory of and admiration for the shining virtue of *trouthe*. Pity is aroused because the tragedy of Troilus is caused by his *trouthe*. Were he not utterly loyal and committed to Criseyde, however she behaves (he cannot stop loving her for a "quarter of a day" [V, 1698]), there would be no tragedy for him. The catastrophe is not solely in his separation from Criseyde but in the virtue, both natural and constructed, which makes her loss irredeemable. Aers, and at the end of the poem Chaucer himself, seem to condemn such earthly virtue as vanity. In a severely Christian sense they may be right though that could be a matter for argument. But earthly, manly, and virtuous Troilus does seem to be, as well as natural and deserving of sympathetic feeling.